The Abingdon
Introduction to the

BIBLE

Understanding Jewish and Christian Scriptures

Joel S. Kaminsky
Joel N. Lohr
Mark Reasoner

 Abingdon Press™

Nashville

THE ABINGDON INTRODUCTION TO THE BIBLE:
UNDERSTANDING JEWISH AND CHRISTIAN SCRIPTURES

Copyright © 2014 by Abingdon Press

Library of Congress Cataloging-in-Publication Data

Kaminsky, Joel S., 1960-
  The Abingdon introduction to the Bible : understanding Jewish and Christian scriptures / Joel S.
Kaminsky, Joel N. Lohr, Mark Reasoner.
    pages cm
  Includes bibliographical references.
  ISBN 978-1-4267-5107-3 (binding:soft back, perfect, adhesive, trade pbk. : alk. paper) 1. Bible—
Introductions. I. Lohr, Joel N. II. Reasoner, Mark. III. Title.
  BS475.3.K36 2014
  220.6'1—dc23

                                                                                                2013041822

Scripture quotations unless otherwise noted are taken from New Revised Standard Version of the Bible,
copyright 1989, Division of Christian Education of the National Council of the Churches of Christ in the
United States of America. Used by permission. All rights reserved.

Scripture quotations marked (CEB) are from the Common English Bible. Copyright © 2011 by the Common English Bible. All rights reserved. Used by permission. www.CommonEnglishBible.com.

Scripture quotations marked (NIV) are taken from the Holy Bible, New International Version®, NIV®.
Copyright © 1973, 1978, 1984, 2011 by Biblica, Inc.TM Used by permission of Zondervan. All rights
reserved worldwide. www.zondervan.com. The "NIV" and "New International Version" are trademarks
registered in the United States Patent and Trademark Office by Biblica, Inc.TM

Scripture quotations marked (KJV) are taken from The Authorized (King James) Version. Rights in the
Authorized Version in the United Kingdom are vested in the Crown. Reproduced by permission of the
Crown's patentee, Cambridge University Press.

Scripture quotations marked (NASB) are taken from the New American Standard Bible®, Copyright ©
1960, 1962, 1963, 1968, 1971, 1972, 1973, 1975, 1977, 1995 by The Lockman Foundation. Used by
permission. (www.Lockman.org)

Scripture quotations marked NJPS (New - Jewish Publication Society) are from TANAKH: A New Translation of The Holy Scriptures According to the Traditional Hebrew Text, copyright © 1985 by the Jewish
Publication Society of America.

Scripture quotations marked (AT) are the authors' own translations.

Scripture quotations marked (Knox) are from Ronald Knox. The Knox Bible. London: Baronius Press,
2012.

14 15 16 17 18 19 20 21 22 23—10 9 8 7 6 5 4 3 2 1

MANUFACTURED IN THE UNITED STATES OF AMERICA

THE ABINGDON
INTRODUCTION TO THE
BIBLE

I have learned much from my teachers, more from my colleagues,
and the most of all from my students.

—Rabbi Judah Hanasi

CONTENTS

LIST OF ILLUSTRATIONS

Figures

Tables

Acknowledgments

This book has benefited immensely from the input of a number of readers, even if at times we ignored elements of their sage advice. We want to thank especially Bradford Anderson, Garwood Anderson, Emily Branton, Richard Briggs, Anthony Le Donne, Rose Rotuno-Johnson, and Sarah Woodbury. We would also like to thank Smith College and University of the Pacific for providing various forms of funding and other resources that enabled us to collaborate in the writing process and obtain assistance with images (special thanks go to Martin Antonetti and Carmen Pullella). Lastly, we are indebted to the team at Abingdon Press, especially Kathy Armistead and Kelsey Spinnato, for their help and support in bringing this book to publication.

In this book we have striven to present an introduction to the Jewish and Christian Bibles in a clear and accessible manner. Our drive to do so is largely the result of our experiences in the classroom in which we have been challenged—and rightly so—to present complex matters in an accessible format. Further, our many excellent students have, at the same time, demonstrated that they are ready and willing to engage in complex and difficult questions if invited into the discussion without dumbing down the material. It is a delicate balance. So, we would like to dedicate this book to our students, those who have, past and present, taught us something of the importance of clear communication and have sharpened our arguments as well as presentations. We are delighted that some of you have gone on to become scholars yourselves and are now colleagues. We hope this book does justice to all that you have brought to our lives.

A NOTE TO THE READER

Throughout this work we refer to passages in the Bible according to a standardized convention, which first indicates the biblical book, then the chapter number, followed by a colon, and then the verse number (or numbers). The books of the Bible can be found in the tables of contents of most Bibles. In order not to overwhelm the beginner, we have kept biblical citations to a minimum; at times we use only one representative reference, and when possible we cite only the chapter without verse numbers.

There are a number of different expressions used to describe those books of the Bible that were originally written in Hebrew including: the Hebrew Bible (which *scholars* use to describe this collection); the Tanakh, Jewish Bible, or Jewish Scriptures (which refers to the same collection from a *Jewish* religious vantage point); and the Old Testament (a term used by *Christians* to describe the first part of the two-part Christian Bible, which contains a second major section called the New Testament). Because our discussion ranges through various contexts (Jewish, Christian, and secular), we use each of these terms when they are appropriate.

We have tried to bring our classroom voice into this book and thus we do our best to avoid technical jargon and to define terms that might be unfamiliar to readers when we first use them. In addition, the reader will find an approximate chronological timeline for the biblical period on pages 48–49. Most of our translations of the Bible are drawn from the New Revised Standard Version, even while we recognize that there are many excellent translations including the Common English Bible. However, in places we use our own translation in order to convey the flavor of the original Hebrew or Greek (marked AT). Finally, to put the reader in touch with the original biblical languages, on occasion we include important Hebrew and Greek words in a simple phonetic transliteration.

ABBREVIATIONS

AT	Authors' Translation
BCE	Before the Common Era (equivalent to BC, "Before Christ")
CE	Common Era (equivalent to AD, "Anno Domini")
D	Deuteronomistic Source
DH	Documentary Hypothesis
E	Elohist Source
J	Yahwist (or Jahwist) Source
CEB	Common English Bible
KJV	King James Version (of the Christian Bible)
NASB	New American Standard (version of the Christian) Bible
NIV	New International Version (of the Christian Bible)
NJPS	New Jewish Publication Society (version of the Jewish Bible)
NRSV	New Revised Standard Version (of the Christian Bible)
P	Priestly Source

WHAT DOES "BIBLE" MEAN? HOW MANY BIBLES ARE THERE?

The term *Bible* is an attempt to translate a Greek word *biblia*, a word that actually means *books*, not *book* in the singular. This small fact is an important one, highlighting one of the greatest impediments that one must overcome if a student hopes to understand what the Bible is. The Bible is not a book, but rather a *library* of books, which contains a wide array of different materials. In fact, many single biblical books are themselves also composite in nature—that is, they contain multiple stories or writings from different authors brought together into one—and thus Genesis, for example, contains creation and flood stories, ancestral tales, blessings, genealogical lists, laws, and so on.

But there is a further impediment in any attempt to understand exactly what the Bible is. The fact is that there is not a single, agreed upon set of scriptures shared by all Christians, let alone by all Christians and Jews. When westernized Jews speak of "the Bible," they mean the Jewish Bible, containing only the books found in the (Protestant) Christian Old Testament, and even then the Jewish order of books differs significantly from that found in Christian Bibles. Furthermore, even among Christians there is not full agreement on what books are considered part of the Bible. Catholic and Orthodox Christians treat the books in the Apocrypha section of many Bibles as Scripture, while Protestant Christians do not generally consider these books scriptural, even if they view them as useful in filling in perceived gaps in narratives (as in the Additions to Esther) or filling in an historical narrative for the intertestamental period (as in 1–2 Maccabees). Thus when someone claims that, "The Bible says . . ." we need to ask ourselves which Bible they are

1

referring to and which communities recognize the authority of the scriptural texts they are citing.

In this book we will, therefore, highlight how certain biblical texts function differently within Jewish and Christian contexts. In some ways this is one of the greatest strengths of this particular introduction, written by three scholars who stand in some way within Judaism, Catholicism, and Protestant Christianity, a point to which we'll return in a moment. For now, however, let us say that this is by no means to imply that all Jews, let alone all Catholics or Protestants, read every biblical book in a single way. But it is important for the reader to begin by first grasping the most fundamental distinctions between how Jews tend to read their scriptural books as opposed to how Christians read these same books. Christians believe the books Jews use as Jewish scripture make up only one half of a two-part Christian Bible. Thus the Christian Bible is composed of the Old Testament and another set of documents Christians call the New Testament, a collection of books that were produced at a later point in history. It is worth emphasizing that Jews do not refer to their scriptures as the "Old Testament."

As briefly mentioned above, although they contain all the same books with the same content, the names of these books are at times different and the books in the Jewish Bible are at times arranged in a different order than in the Christian Old Testament. The best way to grasp this distinction is by unpacking a common Jewish acronym for the Jewish Bible: The Tanakh, or TaNaK. The three consonants in the term TaNaK stand for *Torah*, a word meaning *instruction, teaching,* or *law* (Genesis–Deuteronomy); *Neviim*, the Hebrew word for Prophets (Joshua–2 Kings and Isaiah through Malachi); and *Ketuvim*, or the *Writings* (all the other books of the Jewish Bible). The most significant difference in the Christian order of the Old Testament is that the section containing the materials that run from Isaiah–Malachi occurs last in the Old Testament. To see just how different the Jewish Bible is from the Christian Bible, imagine the following. You go to a friend's house to watch a lengthy movie, which comes on a series of three DVDs. Before you begin watching, your friend says, "pay careful attention to the first DVD, it's the most important part of the movie." Then you watch the three DVDs in sequence. The following night, your brother goes to watch what he thinks is the same movie at his friend's house but he is told that the fourth DVD, one you did not even see, is the most important. He then watches all of DVD one, half of DVD two, then DVD three, then the last half of DVD two followed by the new fourth DVD. Did the two of you see the same movie? Not exactly.

Thus Jews and Christians often talk past each other because they each mean very different things by the term *the Bible*. For Jews, the first five books of the Bible, the Torah—which consists of Genesis, Exodus, Leviticus, Numbers, and Deuteronomy—sit at the very center of all Jewish tradition. These books influence Jewish perceptions of all the biblical books that follow the Torah, and all later authoritative Jewish traditions are viewed as a further unfolding of the meaning and the message of the Torah. For many Christians, the center of the Bible is the four gospels: Matthew, Mark, Luke, and John. Everything preceding them is read as foretelling the coming life, death, and resurrection of Jesus told in these gospels. The New Testament books that follow are seen as the unfolding of the gospel message in the early church. It is often said within Christianity that the "New" interprets the "Old"; that is, the Old Testament can only be understood in the light of the New Testament. Or, as the fourth-century church father St. Augustine once said, "The New Testament lies hidden in the Old, and the Old is unveiled in the New." This is something upon which Jews and Christians obviously disagree.

The fact that these very different biblically based communities share certain books in common creates difficulties when trying to describe that shared set of books. Thus in this introduction we will at differing times use each of the following terms, depending on the context, to describe those books of the Bible that were originally written in Hebrew. Sometimes we will speak of the Hebrew Bible, a somewhat neutral scholarly term used to describe this collection; at other times when we wish to communicate a Jewish view of the text we will speak of the Tanakh, Jewish Bible, or Jewish Scriptures; and when speaking of the first half of the Christian Bible, in reference to Christianity, we will use the term *Old Testament*.

This brings us to the question of why this introduction is unique. Most introductory textbooks to the Bible are written from a narrow vantage point, whether Jewish, a specific segment of Christianity, or an often artificially defined, academic, and supposedly "faith neutral" island. In this book, however, we present an introduction written by a Jew, a Protestant Christian, and a Catholic Christian. Scholars sometimes portray themselves as purely academic or neutral in issues of faith, and this may be appropriate in certain contexts. But when dealing with the Bible, a collection of books that various communities read as inspired by God and authoritative for faith and practice, it is inevitable that one's faith background—whether strong, minimal, previously important or even nonexistent—will affect one's interpretation. We've decided to be transparent about our religious backgrounds as we explore the Bible with you. We have learned a great deal about the Bible from our own teachers, who have had various perspectives, and by collaborating as authors from different backgrounds. In the same way, we hope that you too will benefit from this endeavor. However, although we have an interest in showing the continuing value of the Bible, this introduction is not an attempt to persuade readers to adopt a particular religious or academic approach toward the Bible. Our purpose is to describe and explain what the Bible is, how it has been interpreted in the past and might be productively read in the future, and why the Bible has been so influential religiously, socially, and historically.

This brings up a related issue, which we might call "the ethics of interpretation." As interpreters of the Bible we have attempted to strike a balance between reading the text sympathetically and at the same time critiquing aspects of the text that are indeed problematic from a contemporary viewpoint. At times reading this ancient literature is difficult. Although in places we provide strategies for approaching problematic sections in the Bible in thoughtful ways, we are also aware that certain aspects of the biblical text will (rightly) remain troubling to a contemporary audience.

What follows is an attempt to shed light on the Bible in a manner that is accessible and engaging to contemporary readers. The book assumes no previous knowledge of this literature, hence its title *The Abingdon Introduction to the Bible: Understanding Jewish and Christian Scriptures*. Our emphasis throughout is on *introducing* this literature. We invite you along for what should be a fascinating journey.

A FEW BASICS

Although it might be obvious to some, we should first note that the books of the Bible were not composed in English. Rather, the books of the Jewish Tanakh (or Christian Old Testament) were written in Hebrew, aside from approximately three hundred verses from Daniel and Ezra that are in Aramaic, or ancient Syrian. The books that form the New Testament were written exclusively in a popular, ancient form of Greek called *koinē* Greek. While it is possible that some of the materials found in these books were originally handed down in another language (in an oral or written form), there is no known record of this. However, it is generally accepted in historical-Jesus studies, for example, that Jesus spoke Aramaic and thus the words attributed to him in the Gospels have likely been translated from that language into their current—that is, Greek—form. Other parts of the Bible may have been translated as well.

Because language is so important to communication, and these languages differ from English in important ways, in this section we introduce some basics about the language, manuscripts, versions, and growth of various parts of the Hebrew Bible and the Apocrypha, before turning to these same issues in relation to the New Testament.

Hebrew

As we noted, aside from a few Aramaic passages in two later books, the Hebrew Bible was composed and preserved in the language of the Israelite people in antiquity: Hebrew. What difference does this make?

There are two important matters to keep in mind here, the first of which applies to any translation. First, what we read in an English translation of the Hebrew Bible will always be one step removed from the original. This does not mean that we cannot understand or make use of such a translation, but given that at times the Hebrew Bible contains highly stylized language and in places poetic material, it is difficult to appreciate many of its nuances in translation. We might say this compares to trying to read Shakespeare in German. Second, Hebrew presents some interesting challenges because in antiquity its written form included only consonants without vowels (the vowels were implied), making some words open to ambiguity. We will discuss both of these points, along with others, below.

Scrolls, Language, and Versions

Recently, archeologists discovered a silver amulet dating to the sixth century BCE, which contains an excerpt of Numbers 6:24-26, often called the "Priestly Blessing." This significant archeological find shows not only the importance of this passage but also just how early such texts were being used and circulated. In this case the text was worn by a person, and probably functioned like modern-day texts or proverbs that are framed and put on the walls of our homes, that is, as memory aids or charms. However, our oldest known *manuscripts* of the Hebrew Bible date to the second century BCE and are part

Figure 1. One of several caves in which the Dead Sea Scrolls were found. Courtesy James Elgin.

of an interesting story. In the late 1940s a collection of biblical, parabiblical, and sectarian documents was found in the Judean Desert near the Dead Sea. This cache of documents, dating between 200 BCE and 70 CE, came to be called the Dead Sea Scrolls. Found by two Bedouin shepherds, these scrolls eventually changed hands, appeared for sale in 1954 in the *Wall Street Journal,* and were purchased by a party interested in their publication (they are now housed in the Shrine of the Book Museum in Jerusalem). It took many years, however, along with much controversy, before they were published and made available for scholars and others to examine.

The Dead Sea Scrolls contain fragments from every book in the Hebrew Bible except Esther, and they are now the oldest existing biblical manuscripts. Like contemporary Torah scrolls, these ancient biblical books were composed using Hebrew consonants without vowels and were written in ink on parchment, that is, animal skins that have been cleaned, stretched, and dried. These biblical texts show some differences when compared with the Hebrew Bible manuscripts that Jews had preserved through the centuries (which are based on the Masoretic tradition; see below), though the variants are generally minor or provide clarification on well-known textual difficulties. The variations between manuscripts, however, suggest that one should think of biblical manuscripts as existing in families, families that share much in

Figure 2. Dead Sea Scrolls fragment of Genesis 39:11–40:1, which narrates Joseph's encounter with Potiphar's wife. Photo Shai Halevy. Courtesy Israel Antiquities Authority.

common with each other but may, at least in places, represent unique forms of various biblical books.

Let us reemphasize that these differences in manuscripts generally involve only minor variations, mostly the occasional word change or incorrect letter, not huge inconsistencies or changes in the Hebrew Bible's stories or commandments. However, it is often in the minor variants that scholars find interesting historical developments or theological slants. The science of determining the original wording of the text is called Textual Criticism, and this discipline uses a variety of biblical manuscripts in its task, Hebrew and non-Hebrew. For instance, in places in this book we will refer to the Septuagint, a Greek translation of the Hebrew Scriptures that dates before Jesus' time (between the third and first centuries BCE). There are Samaritan, Syriac, and Aramaic editions of the Torah and other parts of the Hebrew Bible as well.

The point to grasp here is that before one even begins to translate the books between Genesis and 2 Chronicles (the whole Tanakh), one needs to recognize that no matter how true one wants to be to the Hebrew, there are variations within the ancient manuscripts that contemporary scholars consider when making their translations. Some of this variance relates to the fact that all manuscripts are copies of copies of even more ancient copies. Further, even the Hebrew in any single manuscript is open to a certain level of interpretive difference because, as mentioned, ancient manuscripts like those found among the Dead Sea Scrolls contain no vowels, may lack a full space between words, or may not contain punctuation or periods at the end of sentences. The lack of vowels (small Hebrew markings under and above consonants) can be seen in comparing the following versions of Genesis 1:1:

בראשית ברא אלהים את השמים ואת הארץ

בְּרֵאשִׁית בָּרָא אֱלֹהִים אֵת הַשָּׁמַיִם וְאֵת הָאָרֶץ

Figure 3. Unpointed and pointed Hebrew text of Genesis 1:1.

This lack of vowels in early manuscripts sometimes allows for a single word to be vocalized in two or more different ways. One need only think of the letters *ctlg*, which can be vocalized in English as *catalog* or *cytology* or even *cat leg/cut log* if there was meant to be a space between letters. Of course, the act of translation itself always introduces additional elements of interpretation as one must decide whether to translate more literally or to translate more dynamically, aiming to capture the spirit of the Hebrew text. For this reason, the reader might wish to consult different translations, such as the New Revised Standard Version (NRSV), the Common English Bible (CEB), the New Jewish Publication Society version (NJPS), or, for those wishing to get a sense of the actual Hebrew of the Torah, we recommend the recent literary translations by Everett Fox and Robert Alter. If you are in doubt about which translation of the Bible to buy, it might be worth asking your professor about the strengths and weaknesses of various translations.

The Masoretes and the Masoretic Text

The manuscript tradition that has long been regarded as the most reliable, at least until the discovery of the Dead Sea Scrolls, is called the Masoretic Text. This title is derived from the group of scribes called the Masoretes who meticulously preserved this tradition in the sixth to tenth centuries CE. These scribes are regarded as having developed the now-common markings and vowel system around the consonantal text, seen in the pointed Hebrew excerpt above. However, it is believed that these markings attempted to preserve older, often oral traditions of vocalizations and cantillations (markings indicating how the text is to be sung liturgically), as well as alternate spellings or other details such as how the reader should divide each verse. Particularly interesting is the care these scribes used in maintaining the Hebrew text through the centuries. Because there were no printing presses and the transmission of texts was done entirely by hand through careful checking and rechecking, these scribes devised a counting system in which every word and even every letter of each book and each larger section of the Hebrew Bible was accounted for and tracked. For instance, according to their calculations, the Torah, the first five books of the Bible, contained 400,945 Hebrew letters and the letter at the middle of the Torah was a *vav*, in the middle of the word *gakhon* (meaning *belly*), found in Leviticus 11:42. Or, as we discuss later, the books we call Ezra and Nehemiah were considered in antiquity to be one book, something seen in the fact that the Masoretes determined that the middle of the book was at Nehemiah 3:32. Such a system allowed scribes to count forward or backward from the start or end of a book to its middle, thus ensuring that not one letter was missing. It is not surprising, therefore, that when the Dead Sea Scrolls were compared to these much later manuscripts, very few errors or changes were found.

The Growth of the Canon: The Hebrew Bible

One needs to keep in mind that ancient Israel was primarily an oral, not a writing, culture. This means that texts were likely somewhat fluid for hundreds of years before they achieved their final or canonical form. While written texts may well have existed even as early as the time of King Solomon, scribes thought it perfectly fine and even quite appropriate to add in clarifications, expansions of stories or laws, and even new traditions when writing out fresh copies of scrolls that inevitably aged and wore out over time. Most scholars believe that the Torah was the first collection of biblical books to achieve a fixed form and be granted the authority of Scripture, something that likely occurred by the fifth century BCE. The second century BCE prologue to the book of Sirach (found in the Apocrypha) suggests that much of the material in the Prophets, the second section of the Hebrew Bible, was read as Scripture by this period. The last part of the Hebrew Bible to achieve a fixed form was the Writings. It should be noted that some of the materials contained in this section are quite old, like particular psalms, and some are quite young, like portions of Daniel. Daniel 7–12, for example, though set as taking place in sixth century BCE Babylon during the rule of Nebuchadnezzar II, is now recognized to be written in the wake of events that happened in the 160s BCE. The evidence thus suggests that the Writings could not have achieved a fixed form until sometime after these events.

All of this, however, is rather oversimplified because scholars agree that certain materials in the later sections of the Hebrew Bible may well be older than the latest materials in the Torah. For example, parts of Amos and Hosea are recognized as predating much of the Torah and at times preserving alternate traditions. Thus Amos 5:25 implies that Israel did not offer any animal sacrifices to God during the forty years Israel wandered in the wilderness (between the exodus and the conquest of Canaan), while the Torah itself asserts that Israel offered sacrifices during this time.

For our purposes the reader need only grasp the following facts: (1) The process by which the books of the Hebrew Bible achieved their final, canonical form took hundreds of years, and (2) this involved an ongoing process in which new generations participated by contributing to the traditions of the past and making them speak to new historical contexts. Unlike the American Constitution in which official amendments can be added subsequently but are to be acknowledged as such, the ancient Israelite community simply incorporated these amendments as if they were part of the original texts. However, at times certain scribal practices or clear shifts in tone and language indicate that new materials have been grafted into an older text. Deciphering when and how this occurred has become an important part of scholarly study of the Bible. This information can tell us a lot about when the text was written, who might have written it, for what purpose, and so on. We will take up this last point at length later in this book.

The Apocrypha

The Apocrypha are the additional books (seven to thirteen, depending on how these are counted) found in Roman Catholic Bibles but not in Jewish or most Protestant Bibles. This collection includes narratives like Tobit and Judith, wisdom-oriented books like the Wisdom of Solomon and Ecclesiasticus (also known as the *Wisdom of Jesus the Son of Sirach* or *Ben Sira*), and books that narrate various historical periods from a religious or philosophical angle such as 1 and 2 Maccabees. The Apocrypha were produced by Jews and included in the Greek translation of the Hebrew Scriptures, the Septuagint, and then in subsequent Latin versions of the Christian Bible. Jerome (a fourth- to fifth-century church father who produced an important Latin translation of the Bible called the Vulgate) wrote that the extra books found in the Apocrypha were read by the church to provide examples and inspiration for Christian living, but were not used to form doctrine. In 1534, when Martin Luther, the figure who set off the Protestant Reformation, published a complete Bible for Christians, he decided to place these "extra books" between the Old Testament and the New Testament. This editorial decision made a statement saying: "These books are extra; they're not in either the Old or New Testament." Ultimately, the Council of Trent, a sixteenth-century Catholic council, responded to Luther and claimed that these books were definitely to be included in the Catholic Church's Scriptures.

The books in the Apocrypha at times fill in the gaps in certain narratives of the thirty-nine books of the Hebrew Bible. Thus the apocryphal material called the Additions to Esther adds the name of the God of Israel to the story of Esther (something otherwise absent) and provides narrative bridges and theological commentary to help readers understand all that is going on in the Hebrew version. The Apocrypha also provide readers with a great deal of useful social and theological information about ancient Jewish life both inside and outside the land of Israel. Those Christians who accept the Apocrypha as integral to their Old Testament tend to regard more of this testament as Wisdom literature in a way that those with the leaner Old Testament do not. This is because a significant section of the Apocrypha is fully rooted in the wisdom tradition—the books of Sirach, Wisdom of Solomon, and Tobit.

The New Testament

The twenty-seven books that appear as the second part of the Christian Scriptures are called the "New Testament," a term that indicates how early Christians understood and interpreted these writings in relation to others (particularly the "Old Testament") and one that is derived from a particular interpretation of Jeremiah 31:31 (see Luke 22:20 and 2 Corinthians 3:6). Christian tradition holds that Jesus' life, death, and resurrection activated a covenant arrangement between the God of Israel and the people of Israel that extended even to the Gentiles. This covenant arrangement, labeled with Jeremiah's phrase "the new covenant," is suggested, contested, and reconfigured in the narratives, letters, and apocalypse that make up the New Testament. In fact, the words "New Testament" are simply an attempt to render into English the Greek phrase for "new covenant" used in the Septuagint translation of Jeremiah 31.

From Scroll to Codex: Codices, Manuscripts, and Languages

Aside from a few philosophical works, most of the earliest, surviving examples of the codex—the collation of bound pages we would typically call a book—are parts of the New Testament. In the cultural moment of the first and second centuries, this new technology for recording words, the codex, was coming into its own. The "scroll" mentioned in the older book of Ezekiel at 2:9 thus becomes a "little book" when alluded to in the later book of Revelation at 10:9-10.

The use of the codex was not incidental. The technology of the codex facilitated Christians' formation of the New Testament canon, since it allowed them easily to add or rearrange pages when gospels or letters were copied and circulated, and it made copying itself more efficient because pages stayed open. It is possible also that this technology hastened the formation of the canon, since inclusion or exclusion of texts is a more pressing issue when texts are preserved in a codex format than when texts are preserved as scrolls stored in a basket. Also, the technological flaw of codices—the tendency for covers and back pages to become separated and lost after much handling—may account for the mysterious ending of one of the Gospels. The earliest manuscripts of the Gospel of Mark simply end with "And none of them said anything, for they were afraid" (16:8b). This seems to be an odd and unnerving ending. One of the most convincing explanations for this oddity is that, in the early transmission of this gospel, the last page of the codex that contained the original ending was lost.

The text of the New Testament was first copied in a script of all capital letters. Such manuscripts are called *uncials*. In the ninth and tenth centuries CE, a transition occurred in which New Testament manuscripts shifted to being copied in script that used all lowercase letters. These manuscripts are called *minuscules* (see images below). Few of those who copied New Testament manuscripts were as disciplined or conservative as the Masoretes (discussed above) who preserved the manuscripts of the Jewish Scriptures. That is, in New Testament scribal culture, it appears that strict adherence to the original manuscript when copying was not as important as it was for the Masoretes, especially if something needed to be explained or corrected to make sense. New Testament scholars thus pay close attention to manuscript variations, since such variations usually have a reason behind them. For example, why does one New Testament manuscript have 616 where most have 666 for the number of the beast (Revelation 13:18)? We will return to that question later in the book.

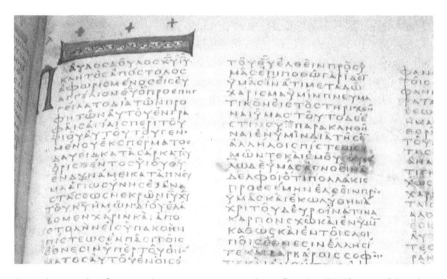

Figure 4. A sampling from uncial manuscript Vaticanus, dating from 400 CE. The tops of the columns, left to right, represent Romans 1:1, 1:10, and 1:19. Courtesy Mark Reasoner.

The earliest substantially complete manuscripts of the New Testament come to us in the form of codices, that is, in book form as opposed to in scrolls, and belong to three textual streams or traditions. There is the Alexandrian tradition, which seems to offer the earliest versions of the text of the New Testament. The second group of manuscripts is called the Western textual tradition. Interestingly, in this tradition the text is known for adding

Figure 5. A minuscule text of Matthew's Gospel. Courtesy The Walters Art Museum.

details such as the hours Paul taught each day in the school of Tyrannus (Acts 19:9-10). The final manuscript tradition is called the Byzantine textual tradition. This stream of manuscripts is massive, having the most manuscripts, though they are later than the above streams and thus often deemed less reliable. The translators of the New Testament in the King James Version relied heavily on the Byzantine tradition.

The New Testament was written in *koinē* Greek, a common form of Greek that arose out of the Hellenism that spread around the Mediterranean world as a result of Alexander the Great's conquest. For the authors of the New Testament, the Greek translation of the Hebrew Bible called the Septuagint was their "Scripture" or what they called "the writings" (Greek *hai graphai*). This Greek version of the Hebrew Bible has a wooden, word-for-word translation style in some places that follows the word order of the Hebrew text closely. Especially in the early chapters of Luke's Gospel, we see evidence that the author is trying to write his gospel in a style that matches these sections of the Septuagint. In other words, the author of Luke is seeking to write a gospel that reads like the Scripture he was reading. There are a number of places where a Hebrew or Aramaic term is simply transliterated in the Gospels and Acts. Usually these terms are explained, as occurs in texts like Matthew 1:23, Mark 5:41, or John 1:38. Sometimes they are not. For example, the final word of 1 Corinthians 16:22, "*maranatha*," is Aramaic for "our Lord, come," which Paul does not translate there. The phrase is expressed elsewhere in Greek (Revelation 22:20).

The world out of which the New Testament grew was clearly polylingual, a feature already seen above and that gets ample play in the New Testament (for examples, read passages like Acts 2; 1 Corinthians 14:22; Revelation 7:9). Here another specific example will help illustrate this point, this time with reference to Latin: In the Gospel of Mark, thought to have been written in

Rome, the word "executioner" used in 6:27 is a Latin word transliterated into Greek letters, *spekoulator*. Such words would have been readily recognized and understood by the early audience. Other common Latin words used in the New Testament include *praetorium, denarius, centurion, legion, caesar,* and so on.

The New Testament and early Christian literature give no indication that Hebrew, Aramaic, or Greek—the most valued languages of the New Testament and Hebrew Bible writers—are the only languages in which their stories can be written. The New Testament authors seem to be as linguistically utilitarian as the Roman officer who decided to put Jesus' title in three different languages above his cross (see John 19). No language is sacred for the New Testament's authors, even when they are describing divine encounters or other sacred events. This is quite different from the Jewish view of Hebrew, which is sometimes referred to as *lashon hakodesh,* "the sacred tongue."

The Growth of the Canon: The New Testament

The first New Testament writings appear to have been the letters of Paul, which were read aloud to churches, copied, shared, and collected, something that can be seen even from passages in the New Testament itself like Colossians 4:16 and 2 Peter 3:15-16. These letters seem to have been a sensation in some of the communities Paul founded, so much so that others tried to imitate them. This accounts for Paul's explicit concern in places about other letters forged in his name (see for example, 1 Corinthians 16:21 or 2 Thessalonians 2:1-2). There are thirteen letters associated with Paul—those extending from Romans through Philemon—though many scholars believe that only seven were actually written (or dictated) by him as we discuss in detail later in this book.

The Letter to the Hebrews was included in some collections of Paul's letters, but it makes no claim to Pauline authorship, and most scholars today do not regard it as coming from Paul. It is written by someone who indicates that he is living a generation after the apostles, and seems to provide a framework for understanding Paul's letters. Other letters, called the "general letters," were later added to the growing collection of Christian writings that came to be known as the New Testament. The Letter of James may have been written fairly early, since it does not seem to give evidence of an organized church structure. From a perspective of comparative religions, the New Testament Scriptures are unique in the number of letters they include (that is, many) and in the fact that they are so varied.

The Gospels, and Acts, would have been penned after Paul's seven authentic letters, probably between 70–90 CE, and at the same time as some of the general letters were written. Revelation may be among the later books composed, perhaps during the reign of Domitian (81–96 CE), but we have no real proof that it was composed last of all the New Testament books. The Gospels are a type of biography that spends considerable space on their hero's last days on earth. Acts presents itself as the second volume by the author of the gospel known as Luke. It is clearly written to serve as a bridge between the Gospels and the letters of Paul so that these letters will make sense. The only apocalyptic work of the New Testament, the Revelation of John (or Apocalypse), is a Scripture-based meditation on how Christians should respond to the Roman Empire.

Apocalypse and Apocalyptic

Apocalypse means "a revelation." *Apocalyptic* is thus a term used to refer to a genre of literature that purports to reveal, or be a special revelation of, how God will intervene on behalf of God's people who are oppressed by ungodly governments. The dream we find in Daniel 7 is a good example of apocalyptic literature. Although in popular Western culture these terms have become most commonly associated with the end of the world, or "end times," in the Bible the message of apocalyptic literature is one of coming events or divine judgment, whether ultimate or not.

In the first part of the second century CE, there was an influential Christian teacher named Marcion. He was virulently anti-Semitic (or, more accurately, anti-Judaic) and he developed a collection of books—something of a canon—to be used by Christians that showed his hatred of all things Jewish. He rejected the Jewish Scriptures and kept only one of the four gospels, the one credited to the Gentile, Luke, and attached it to a (modified) collection of Paul's letters. Early church leaders intuitively knew that it was wrong to jettison the Jewish heritage of Christianity as Marcion was attempting to do. They therefore condemned him as a heretic and began to reflect on the nature of their own scriptural collections in response to Marcion's proposal. It is interesting that Marcion appears to have coined the term "Old Testament" for the Hebrew Bible books that most Christians were reading in the Septuagint translation. This detail should prompt us to use the term cautiously and with respect for these books, in opposition to the slur that Marcion intended. A few recent theologians have argued that Christians should value the Old Testament more highly than the New Testament. These thinkers are trying to avoid Marcion's errors and respect the Jewish Scriptures as most early Christians did.

After Marcion was condemned, Christians continued to debate which books should be included in the collection of Scriptures we now call the New Testament. We have some evidence of Christians arguing over the authenticity and character of certain books, such as 2 Peter and Revelation, in the second and third centuries, but the four gospels now in the New Testament, Acts, the thirteen letters associated with Paul and most of the general epistles were already being circulated and used as Scripture by the end of the second century. The church seems to have "locked in" on the twenty-seven books we now call the New Testament at the following key moments: the Easter letter of Athanasius, bishop of Alexandria, Egypt, written in 367 CE, the council of Rome in 382 CE, and the council of Hippo in 393 CE. The councils mentioned are not major, ecumenical councils, but they provided decisive influence in recognizing what many churches already practiced, thus "fixing" the New Testament canon.

In subsequent church history, various books of the New Testament have been questioned. Martin Luther, in the sixteenth century, famously called the Letter of James "a letter of straw" and put it at the back of the Bible because he thought it contradicted the idea that one's righteousness comes by faith alone, a theme he found in Paul's letters. As mentioned, in more recent times, Paul's authentic letters have been reduced from thirteen to seven in the judgment of some scholars. For the Christian believer, however, the letters that are considered to be "deuteropauline" (associated with Paul but not written by him) are still Scripture and therefore can continue to be read and studied with profit.

Like family members who always tell certain stories at their reunions, Christians always seem to return to their Scriptures, at least thirty-nine books in the Old Testament and the twenty-seven books of the New Testament. We may wonder at the decision to include four gospels; wouldn't just one be enough? And Christians today may criticize the editor who redundantly included both Jude and its expanded form, the letter of 2 Peter, which contains the same material. But these are the stories, letters, and apocalypse that the ancestors of faith have left to the church to be read, heard, and studied in its gatherings.

This leads us to our next chapter, the Bible as a religious book, where we briefly explore how certain parts of the Bible have shaped Jewish and Christian religious practices and how the Bible is used and read by both traditions.

THE BIBLE
AS A RELIGIOUS BOOK

While historians and biblical scholars are naturally quite interested in the books of the Bible as artifact or literature, the truth is that the books found in the Bible were carefully preserved over the centuries because they are part of the Jewish and Christian bodies of sacred Scriptures. Because of their status as Scripture, various books in the Bible have received a great deal of interpretive attention from thinkers in both traditions and have deeply influenced each community's religious life. Of course each tradition reads their collection of sacred Scripture through unique interpretive lenses, and the material they share, the Hebrew Bible, is also read in a particular way—Jews through the vast array of rabbinic teachings, and Christianity through the New Testament and classical Christian tradition. In short, for Jews the larger "canon" of Judaism contains not only the Tanakh, but also the Mishnah, Talmud, and Midrash, collections of ancient rabbinic writings. For Christians, their canon includes the Old and New Testaments (the latter of which Jews do not recognize as Scripture) as well as the traditions and creeds of the church. Due to the fact that the Hebrew Bible is in some sense shared by both traditions but read quite differently by Jews and Christians, in this chapter, we will spend a bit of time showing how each tradition interprets and liturgically employs elements of this seminal text.

Traditional Jewish Interpretation of the Tanakh

Within Jewish tradition, the Torah occupies such a central space that the term has come to take on two meanings. The first simply refers to the opening five books of the larger Jewish Bible, the *Tanakh*. But in its more expansive meaning, the term *Torah* can refer to any part, or all, of the vast trove of

Jewish law and lore from antiquity to today. This dual usage is grounded in a larger rabbinic theory of the "Dual Torah." The ancient rabbis, teachers of Jewish law and lore who lived during the first few centuries of the Common Era, believed that Moses actually received two Torahs from God on Mount Sinai. One Torah was considered to be *written* (the Pentateuch and in some sense the whole Hebrew Bible) and the other was thought to be *oral* (or Oral Torah, the rabbinic traditions such as those found in the Mishnah and Talmud).

The centrality of the Torah can also be seen in how Jews understand the Torah's relationship to the larger Jewish Bible as well as in the disproportionate amount of commentary that later Jewish tradition produced on the first five books of the Bible. Within Judaism, the Torah is understood to contain God's direct revelation to his prophet Moses. The Torah itself asserts that Moses' place as one who speaks for God is preeminent. While the whole Hebrew Bible is viewed as sacred Scripture, Judaism sees the Prophets and Writings as containing stories, prophecies, wisdom, and prayers of post-Mosaic Jews who sought to live their life *according* to the Torah of Moses. In fact, it is interesting to note that these other two sections of the Tanakh (the Prophets and Writings) begin with strong injunctions to meditate on the Torah day and night (see Joshua 1:7-8 and Psalm 1:2).

The disproportionate attention that postbiblical Jewish tradition lavished upon the Torah further supports the central place of the Torah within the biblical canon. The fact is that Jewish tradition has come to see the Torah as the blueprint for Jewish life. Much of the Torah is filled with God's *mitzvot*, or commandments, concerning how one should live one's life, and in turn the rabbis spend a great deal of energy trying to apply these commands to ever-new life situations. The most important of these discussions are found in the Mishnah and Talmud (both are early collections of rabbinic legal debates; the Mishnah from around 200 CE, the Talmud building on the Mishnah composed between approximately 200–700 CE). The ancient rabbis in these collections thus understand their own activities of interpreting and applying the Torah to new situations as simply making manifest aspects of the Oral Torah that Moses received at Sinai.

The Oral Torah was also seen as containing much of the backstory that helps one understand the often cryptic narratives found throughout the Tanakh and enables one to unpack their meaning. This is done primarily through something called *midrash*, a verse-by-verse commentary that brings verses from across the Tanakh to illuminate a given passage, and which brings forth traditional rabbinic teachings about characters and events in the biblical text to expand upon and explain it. The ancient rabbis derived their interpretive insights from a very careful reading (some would say an *over*reading) of the Hebrew. Often rabbinic interpretation is based upon unusual word usage, or even the numerical value of words, allowing the rabbis to fill in certain narrative gaps or explain oddities of the text. Rabbinic interpretation also attributes significance to the juxtaposition of various passages, something echoed by recent narrative approaches to the Bible.

When one examines the ongoing Jewish tradition, which stretches over many centuries up to today, one quickly discovers that much of Jewish philosophical, mystical, legal, ethical, and theological thinking is preoccupied with attempting to understand and further elaborate upon the biblical text, especially the Torah, continually finding innovative and ingenious ways for Scripture to speak to a new generation living in a different historical context. Furthermore, the vast postbiblical Jewish interpretive tradition regularly preserves not only differing but also at times conflicting lines of interpretation. But this in fact carries on an ancient and venerable tradition that reaches back to the Bible itself, a point we will regularly highlight throughout this book.

The Liturgical Use of the Tanakh in Judaism

The word *liturgy* refers to the rituals practiced and the readings used in religious settings. There is evidence found within the Hebrew Bible as well as within the New Testament that portions of the Jewish Scriptures functioned liturgically in that they were read aloud in ancient communal religious gatherings, especially the Temple and synagogues. For instance, Deuteronomy 30:9-13 reports that every seven years "this Torah," likely referring to some form of the book of Deuteronomy, is to be read aloud to the whole community at the Festival of Booths (or Hebrew *Succot*). Luke 4:16-21 and Acts 15:21 imply that excerpts from the Torah and the Prophets were read on Sabbaths in synagogues. Further, it seems clear that psalms were recited by individuals or sung communally within the life of the temple in ancient times. However, the exact scope and regularity of the ancient liturgical use of the Torah and other parts of the Tanakh remain unclear.

Once Jewish liturgical readings and prayers became standardized several hundred years ago, various pieces of the biblical text came to be used in the prayer service on a regular basis. These fall into several different categories, including a cyclical pattern of communally reading through the whole Torah, a set of Prophetic extracts or lections paired with each Torah reading, the pairing of the five *Megillot* (Scrolls) with five specific Jewish holidays, and the incorporation of selections from the Torah, Psalms, and other biblical texts into the daily and weekly prayer service.

Certainly the most prominent use of the Jewish Scriptures is the tradition of reading through the entire five books of the Torah over the course of the Jewish ritual year. In this annual liturgical cycle, the Torah is divided into fifty-four portions, and each Torah portion, or *parashah*, is in turn paired with an excerpt from the prophetic books, called the *haftarah*. Because some of the standard weekly readings are displaced by Jewish holidays or the changing length of the Jewish lunar year, certain weeks may end up with double Torah portions. The reading cycle ends and begins each year at Simchat Torah ("rejoicing of the Torah") that occurs each fall.

Figure 6. An artistic representation of a Simchat Torah celebration. Courtesy of the artist, Aharon Yakobson, and the Alexander Gallery.

Each weekly excerpt is named after a Hebrew word or phrase that occurs in the opening verse of the lection. For example, the first is called *Bereshit*, the first word of Genesis meaning "in the beginning." In addition, the five short *megillot*, or scrolls, are read on the following holidays: Song of Songs on Passover; Ruth on Shavuot; Lamentations on the Ninth of Av; Qoheleth on Succot; and Esther on Purim.

As indicated above, a good deal of the daily and weekly prayers in Judaism are drawn from the Tanakh. Most noticeably, many psalms are included in the liturgy; references drawn from the Exodus account as well as famous passages like the *Shema*—"Hear, O Israel," drawn from Deuteronomy—occur regularly.

Further, the use of many ritual items like phylacteries—leather prayer boxes worn during weekday morning prayers—as well as *mezuzot*—miniature scrolls placed in metal or wood boxes that are mounted on doorframes in Jewish households and buildings—are derived from verses of the Tanakh (see image below).

Figure 7. A mezuzah. Courtesy Joel S. Kaminsky.

We would be remiss not to mention the vast array of Jewish ritual, ethical, and legal practices that are derived directly from the Tanakh or indirectly from practices exhibited by characters (including God) within the Jewish Bible. Thus rabbinic Judaism assumes that there are 613 commandments that totally pervade all aspects of Jewish life and it derives almost all of these from various biblical passages. And indirectly the rabbis probe the actions of characters in the Tanakh to derive moral norms. For example, notice how the rabbis derive a moral norm from the juxtaposition of the seemingly distinct stories found in Genesis 17 and 18. Male circumcision, a long-standing Jewish practice, is clearly authorized in Genesis 17, which describes how God commanded Abraham to have himself and all current and future males in his family circumcised. In the following story that appears to have occurred well after the events in Genesis 17, God visits Abraham to announce the future birth of Isaac once more, this time to Sarah. But the rabbis assume that because these stories are placed next to each other, Genesis 18 occurred a short time after Genesis 17. And they derive a moral lesson from this fact: Visiting the sick is so important that even God visited Abraham as he was recovering from his circumcision that just took place in Genesis 17, something never stated within the biblical text. Thus the Tanakh is not simply an ancient text that describes Jewish origins and ancient practices, but rather is the continuing focal point of contemporary Jewish practice as well as the touchstone of ongoing theological reflection.

Traditional Christian Interpretation of the Old Testament

Because Christian interpretation of the Old Testament has evolved over the past two millennia, it may be instructive to briefly survey how Christians have interpreted the Old Testament through the ages, beginning with the New Testament.

New Testament: Jesus

Within the Gospels, the books of the Jewish Scriptures—often called the "Law and the Prophets"—held a very high authority. At this point in time the main Scriptures the characters within these texts knew were the Hebrew Bible, which only came to be called the Old Testament after the New Testament came into being. We can see the importance of these writings in looking at the life of Jesus. When asked what one must do to inherit eternal life, Jesus immediately replies that one must keep the commandments of Moses, which he usually summarizes by quoting from the Ten Commandments, reciting the *Shema* (Hear, O Israel), or repeating the Golden Rule (for examples see Mark 10 and Luke 10). When challenged on certain Old Testament commandments, Jesus appears to have been aware of other schools of Jewish interpretation and uses similar rabbinic principles in his explanations. For instance, when asked about divorce in Matthew 19, Jesus views the matter quite stringently, relying on Genesis to argue that what God has brought together as "one flesh" humans are not to separate, except in instances of marital infidelity. Here Jesus appears to side with the stricter interpretation of his contemporary Jewish teacher Shammai over the more lenient teachings of Hillel, another ancient sage who permitted divorce in certain other circumstances.

Jesus also seems to be concerned to show that he did not come to abolish the Law and the Prophets. Thus within the Sermon on the Mount found in Matthew 5-7, Jesus does not make observance of the commandments in the Old Testament easier to follow, but instead he ups the ante by noting that one is guilty of certain sins even if one only thought about committing them but never acted upon the impulse. At other times, however, Jesus is criticized for his leniency in practicing certain laws. When confronted, Jesus often argues not that the Scriptures are unimportant but that the interpretation of the teachers questioning him is in error; that is, the teachers misinterpret the commandment.

In the postresurrection narratives of the New Testament Gospels, especially Luke, Jesus begins a long tradition of Christian scriptural interpretation. In these passages, Jesus makes use of the Law and the Prophets to explain to his disciples that he is the long-promised anointed one, or messiah. The story of the Road to Emmaus found in Luke 24 is probably our most important example. Although his two disciples do not initially recognize Jesus while with him on the road, Jesus, "beginning with Moses and all the prophets, . . . interpreted to them the things about himself in all the scriptures." Using the Old Testament to argue that Jesus is the Messiah came to be a pattern in the early church.

New Testament: Paul

It might be argued that prior to Paul, followers of Jesus were Jews who observed the teachings of the Law and the Prophets. It is really with Paul that we see the distinctive traits of the Christian religion (vis-à-vis Judaism) come to life: Non-Jews (or "Gentiles") are brought into the Christian community and ritual observance of the Old Testament's laws comes to an end (at least in large part). Paul's interpretation of the Old Testament is complex because of these developments and because he appears to have believed that Jesus' final return to establish his kingdom was close at hand and there was thus a limited time to bring Gentiles to God. In general, we can say that the Gospels interpret the Jewish Scriptures christologically—using them to prove that Jesus of Nazareth was the promised Messiah. By contrast, Paul interprets the Jewish Scriptures ecclesiologically—using them to prove that the Gentile church was the fulfillment of these Scriptures' portraits of Israel's relationship with the nations.

Paul's views regarding various Old Testament laws are radical, but his methods of interpretation share many similarities with those of the rabbinical schools in which he had likely been educated. Ultimately, Paul argues that reading the Jewish Scriptures rightly is a matter determined by metaphorical blindness or opening of eyes, the latter of which happens through faith in Jesus. Paul's statements that Israel's law was made complete in Jesus (and thus no longer applied in practice) certainly created its share of problems, as we discuss below and in greater detail later in this book.

The Church Fathers through the Reformation

Paul's approach raised a central issue for Christianity: How should the church make sense of the fact that certain laws and teachings of the Old Testament must still apply while others do not? Further, how exactly does the now "faded" Jewish law still speak to Christians and point to Jesus as the Messiah? Much of what propelled early Christian interpretation of the Jewish Scriptures was an implicit acknowledgment that finding such references or allusions to Jesus in the Old Testament was a complex and difficult process. Interestingly, questions even arose as to whether the Christian community should retain the Jewish Scriptures as their Scripture, and, if so, how these books were to be interpreted. As noted in the previous chapter, second-century debates with Marcion, an early Christian bishop who rejected the Jewish Scriptures and was later deemed a heretic, ultimately resulted in an agreement to retain all of the books in the Hebrew Bible as the first part of a two-fold canon within Christianity. The early church fathers were able to maintain Christianity's connection to the Law and Prophets by using an allegorical method of reading these texts and by understanding them in the light of Christian creeds. The allegorical method did not read these texts in a literal sense but rather understood them as cryptically pointing to the life, death, and resurrection of Jesus—the central Christian story. Beginning in the fourth century, a newer "Antiochean method" that focused on literal meanings of the Old Testament came to be used within Christian interpretation. This raised anew the need to explain how Christianity could both embrace the Old Testament yet not practice many of its laws.

The great medieval theologian-philosopher Thomas Aquinas is often credited with formulating a solution to the status of the Old Testament in Christianity. He proposed a three-fold schema in which all the Old Testament commandments could be categorized as moral, ceremonial, or judicial, of which only the moral commandments remained binding upon Christians.

With the Renaissance and the Reformation arose a host of changes in Christian interpretation, particularly because of these movements' emphasis on "returning to the sources" (that is, returning to the original texts in their own language, without the filter of tradition). This development eventually gave rise to modern historical criticism, which we will discuss in the following chapter. Although massive changes took place, Aquinas' tripartite division of Mosaic law largely remains in force in Christianity today. Hence few Christians today avoid pork (seen as a ritual commandment), but all believe stealing is a sin (a moral commandment). An emphasis on the moral law also shaped how the Old Testament came to be used in Christian worship and catechism, a topic to which we now turn.

The Bible in Christian Liturgy

It is difficult to separate the liturgical use of the Old Testament from traditional Christian interpretation. This is primarily because those who penned early Christian texts on the Jewish Scriptures were also churchmen—bishops or presbyters—those who taught and served in liturgical settings. The early church continued certain early Jewish synagogue practices such as delivering homilies or sermons based upon scriptural readings and the recitation of various prayers and psalms. Additionally, these meetings included early Christian hymns, collective confessing of creeds, baptism of new believers and, most important, partaking in the Eucharist (a communal meal of bread and wine, signifying Jesus' broken body and shed blood). Over time, Christian meeting places came to be adorned with visual art that celebrated the life and death of Jesus as well as the ancestors of the faith, including the major figures of the Old Testament. These important pieces of art served to point the illiterate masses to live by the examples of famous biblical characters.

Unsurprisingly, the early creeds of the church—those recognized by almost all Christian churches today (for example, the Apostles' and Nicene Creeds)—focus on the theological importance of Jesus and thus draw primarily on New Testament texts. These creeds make no direct reference to the Old Testament, its Patriarchs, the exodus, or Israel, though they reference God as the "Creator of Heaven and Earth." Further, the Nicene Creed confesses Jesus rising on the third day "in accordance with the Scriptures," and the Holy Spirit speaking through the prophets. Despite the sparse nature of these references, the importance of the Old Testament is seen more clearly in church fathers' acceptance, and regular use, of its content in their writings.

The situation is different with respect to Christian catechism, which often included teachings related to or derived directly from the Old Testament. Catechism itself arose out of a need to instruct new and young members of the church in things related to Christian faith. These summaries of Christian doctrine often took a simple question-and-answer format. The exact content of early Christian catechisms is difficult to ascertain but appears to have included basic teachings of the Old Testament such as monotheism and the repudiation of idolatry along with central Christian ideas and practices drawn from the New Testament.

When passages of the Bible are read in churches today, they often follow a common lectionary, a set of selected Bible passages that allow a church to read through large portions of the Christian Bible over the course of one or three years. These are structured so that each worship service includes a reading from the Old Testament, the Psalms, the New Testament epistles, and the four gospels. Despite the fact that passages of the Old Testament are read each week, it seems that often the contemporary church neglects or overlooks much of the Old Testament outside of certain psalms and the Prophets. This raises an issue to which we will return later in the book, namely, that the Prophets tend to gain special significance within Christianity because they are believed to have foretold the coming of the Messiah, understood to be Jesus Christ. Other content such as the Torah may occasionally be used to teach moral lessons based on the Patriarchs, or might be used to show God's faithfulness in delivering the Israelites from Egypt. Even when the lectionary ensures that the Old Testament is read, pastors and priests often struggle with its application to contemporary life. The complexities involved in reading the Old Testament as Christian literature make this understandable. However, it is hoped that some of the materials in the present book might provide an entry point for Christians hoping to understand how the whole Old Testament shaped historic Christianity and remains essential to the Christian faith.

Conclusion

The above summarizes some of the ways that Jews and Christians have and continue to use their Scriptures, especially the Hebrew Bible, religiously. When we examine the New Testament later in the book, we will highlight how various parts of the New Testament came to be used in religious settings by Christians. But there is another story yet to be traced out: how the Bible came to be studied in a critical academic fashion. Interestingly, much of the impetus behind the rise of modern biblical criticism arose among Protestant thinkers who sought to keep later religious ideas or agendas from being read back into the ancient biblical text. The key for this group was to use reason and critical distance to get back to the original meaning of the text, that is, the meaning intended by its authors. This required asking questions about the text in terms of who wrote it, what these authors meant by it, and where and when various passages and books were written. This type of enterprise brought about a renewed interest in reading the text in its original languages, the languages used by the author or authors. It also led to a drive to learn more about the context in which the Bible was produced, eventually leading to the rise of archeology and the study of allied cultures from the wider ancient Near East (or what we today call the Middle East). These research approaches brought great advancements in our understanding of the Bible, but they also raised many questions and introduced a host of problems still felt today. It is to this story that we now turn.

Modern Approaches to the Bible

Many books have been written on the various modern methods that scholars use when interpreting the Bible. Our purpose here is not to be comprehensive but to give the reader a basic overview of a few important approaches to the biblical text. In order to focus our discussion, here we will concentrate on showing how each of the modern critical approaches we discuss might be applied to particular texts drawn from the Torah, the first five books of the Bible. Then in later sections of this book, we will broaden the discussion to explore other books of the Bible, for example, how modern critics assess the historical reliability of books like Judges or the New Testament gospel accounts, or how one might try to read a book, like Job, holistically.

The Historical-Critical Approach

Historical Criticism lies at the heart of all modern approaches to the Bible. Broadly speaking, the historical-critical approach to reading the Bible seeks to determine what we can know about ancient texts in the light of their history, literary sources, and parallel ancient documents, as well as in the light of the communities that wrote, heard, and used these texts in the ancient world. Although at times this approach has become synonymous with the more narrow discipline of determining the authorship of various biblical books or passages, the approach in fact involves much more, especially regarding the historical background of the Bible. We will explore two important aspects of historical criticism as applied to the Torah: (1) the modern critical theory regarding who wrote these first five books of the Bible (the Documentary Hypothesis), as well as (2) how history and archaeology relate to the Torah and its stories.

The Documentary Hypothesis

One of the foundations of all modern critical study of the Bible is the Documentary Hypothesis, a theory that seeks to explain how the Torah came to be. This theory attempts to explain shifts in language, vocabulary, and literary style found in various sections of the Torah, many of which were noticed centuries ago by others, as well as seeking to make sense of certain references in the text that seemed to be later additions or appear anachronistic. By *anachronistic* we mean that a later historical viewpoint has been inserted into a story from an earlier period, usually in a way that, intended or not, reveals that later perspective. A good example is that archaeological evidence suggests that camels were not widely domesticated in the Near East until around 1200 BCE, but the Genesis narratives, which are set in an earlier period, mention domesticated camels at times.

The Documentary Hypothesis came to be most developed and popularized by Julius Wellhausen, a Protestant German biblical scholar of the late nineteenth century. Wellhausen focused not only on the differences in language and literary styles in the Torah but also he aimed to explain various tensions, contradictions, and differences of outlook that one finds in the Torah. For example, as noticed by others before him, Genesis 1–2:3 contains a seven-day creation story, which describes God as transcendently creating the world in an orderly and patterned manner, culminating in the creation of humankind followed by God's resting on the Sabbath. Yet, beginning in Genesis 2:4, one finds a second creation story that seems to happen in a day, and varies from the first, in that Adam is created early in the process and in turn the animals are created after (and for) him. In fact, Adam names all the creatures as each one is created and brought to him. Or, as another example, in the flood story of Genesis 6-9, some verses such as Genesis 6:19-20 describe Noah bringing two of each animal on the ark while others like Genesis 7:2-3 speak of seven pairs of clean animals and a pair of all other animals. Additionally, in Genesis 8:1-5, the duration of the flood is 150 days, while in Genesis 8:6 (and elsewhere) it lasts forty days and nights.

Wellhausen's Documentary Hypothesis (DH from this point forward) was an attempt to give a comprehensive explanation of this unevenness in a clear, logical, and scientific way. The DH posits that the Torah was not written by one person but was woven together from four major sources through a lengthy and complex process. Tensions in the text are attributed to the compilation process that drew these sources together and thus created various inconsistencies. Although Wellhausen did not invent the labels J, E, D, and P—letters which signify the four sources underlying the Pentateuch—he adopted these and linked each source to a particular historical context in ancient Israel. Much of the persuasive power of this hypothesis (and thus Wellhausen's fame) comes from the fact that it not only seeks to explain tensions in the Torah but also puts forward a theory about Israel's evolution as a people or nation. For example, the D source corresponds to the book of Deuteronomy (hence the letter D), a book that contains specialized vocabulary and appears to have been produced during the seventh century BCE by scribes who wanted to reform Israel's religion (as indicated by 2 Kings 22–23). So, although Deuteronomy reads as if it is the last will and testament of Moses, the DH contends that it was actually written well after the time of Moses by a group of Judean scribes and thus reveals more about seventh century Judean society than about the much earlier time of Moses in which it is literarily set.

According to the hypothesis, the other four books preceding Deuteronomy (Genesis–Numbers) contain materials belonging to the J, E, and P sources, designations we will explain in more detail below. Before proceeding further, however, the reader will need a short introduction to the names of God in the Torah because these are used in distinguishing the J and E sources. For an introduction to divine names in the Torah, see the accompanying textbox.

The Names of God

The Hebrew Bible refers to God by several different words and names. For example, God is regularly referred to as *Elohim*, the generic Hebrew term for "God." There are other names used of God as well. Thus God is sometimes referred to as "*El*," usually occurring with a second word such as *El Shaddai*, "God Almighty" or *El Elyon*, "God Most High," and so on. Most of these divine names are reasonably straightforward. However, one deserves special attention: God's personal name, YHWH.

God's personal name, YHWH, is used twice as often as *Elohim* and more than any other divine name, some 1,800 times in the Torah, and nearly 6,000 times in the Hebrew Bible. It is written using four Hebrew consonants: *yod*, *heh*, *vav*, and *heh* or in English transliteration Y–H–W–H. Scholars often call this the *Tetragrammaton*, a Greek word simply meaning "four-lettered word." In accordance with ancient practice, in English Bibles this name is most often substituted with a reverential title, written in small capital letters: LORD.

Historical evidence suggests that Jews more generally stopped pronouncing the Tetragrammaton at some point, though it is not easy to confirm the specific contours of this history. It is interesting to note that in early Christianity—itself a Jewish sect in the first century—Christians did not pronounce the name of God. Readers may be surprised to know that Jesus himself is nowhere recorded to have used the personal name of God, the one he usually called "Lord" or "Father" (as in the "Lord's Prayer" he taught to his disciples).

Wellhausen, along with others, noticed that a fairly unified set of materials, particularly found in Genesis, used the divine name YHWH. He called this set of materials J, standing for JHWH, since there is no consonant Y in German. Thus the J source is the only source in Genesis to use the four-letter name of God, YHWH. Wellhausen believed that the J source was the earliest of the Pentateuch's sources, dated to sometime around 850 BCE, and it originated in the southern area of Judah (rather than Israel, a name originally used to designate the northern ten tribes).

The letter E in the DH stands for the Elohist source, the source that used "Elohim" to refer to God within Genesis. E often provides alternative versions of J stories, and at times this source appears to be reacting to J. Here it was suggested that E often tried to "correct" J, in that it used less humanlike language and was more reverential in its descriptions of God. Wellhausen dated this material around a century later than J (sometime in the 700s BCE) and suggested that it was the product of the northern kingdom, Israel.

P stands for *Priestly*, and the remaining material in the Torah fell into this category. This P material is grouped together by the fact that the vocabulary and interests of this material are Priestly, likely penned by ancient Israelite priests. Thus the DH attributes the first, more orderly, creation story to P because it culminates in the Sabbath, a sacred occasion that involved specific rituals especially significant to priests. Leviticus, a book centered on questions of purity and sacrifice, is also attributed to P. In Wellhausen's theory, P is the latest source, dating to around 450 BCE, and he believed that this last source was added to J, E, and D to complete the Torah around 400 BCE, after Israel's exile in Babylon.

It is here that Wellhausen's particular evolutionary scheme becomes most intriguing but perhaps most troubling and biased. Wellhausen believed that P was the latest source because it is the most ritual oriented. He thought religions developed in a common pattern whereby a preferable, spontaneous religion (as in J) became rigid and ritualized at a later stage (as in P). It is likely no coincidence that Wellhausen's theory was developed within a Modern Lutheran Protestant setting where religious rituals were often criticized as additional, unnecessary elements introduced by the later church.

The DH was the subject of a long-running scholarly consensus that has all but completely broken down in the past few decades. While virtually every scholar would agree that the Torah is composed of different sources, many scholars disagree with Wellhausen's proposed dating. Further, recent scholarship has shown that the material of the Torah is much more unified than the DH acknowledged. Truthfully, it is not as easy to delineate these theoretical sources as was formerly thought. Yet, it is clear that various sources have been brought together in the Torah, and thus scholars continue to use the labels J, E, D, and P as we do at times in this book.

We have focused on the Torah here, yet one finds similar hypotheses about other sections of the Bible. For example, with the New Testament Gospels, there are heated debates over when each gospel was written and which gospel came first. As we discuss later, some scholars argue that Mark was written first and that this book deeply influenced Matthew and Luke, along with a source no longer available to us (which scholars call Q). Issues of authorship in many ways sit at the heart of all modern scholarly approaches to the Bible.

The Bible and History

Although matters of composition are complex, they pale in comparison to issues raised in trying to make sense of whether the stories we encounter in the books of the Bible are historical. These issues are especially acute in the first few books of the Bible. Did characters like Adam, Noah, Abraham, and Moses actually walk the earth? Did Israel's departure, or exodus, from Egypt really happen? Did all the people of Israel really hear God speak to them from Mount Sinai? These questions are not easily answered, and those who attempt to read the Bible's narrative as a linear, historically accurate report will quickly notice a number of problems. Where did Cain find his wife? Did someone named Noah really build an ark that could hold two of every land animal on earth? If Ishmael was already thirteen in Genesis 17, why does he appear to be a very young child in Genesis 21? Such examples could be greatly multiplied.

Rather than seeking to report events in a historically linear and accurate fashion, the books of the Bible appear to be more concerned to illuminate events from a religious perspective. This can be seen through a discussion of Hebrew names. Even a cursory survey of names in the Torah shows that they function as more than simple terms of reference. Adam, which in Hebrew means "man," "human," or "creature," comes from the Hebrew term *adamah*, which means "ground" or "earth," the very substance from which the first human was created according to Genesis 2. Genesis 3:20 relates Eve's name to the Hebrew verb *chayah*, "to live," and she is said to be the "mother of all living." Cain's name might mean "created" or "acquired one" (the first human "created" by Eve), while Abel's name is simply the Hebrew word for "vapor," "vanity," or "meaninglessness." The list goes on including Noah ("refuge" or "comfort"), Abraham ("father of a multitude"), Sarah ("princess"), Ishmael ("God heard"), Jacob ("supplanter"), and so on. The matter may seem trivial until one comes to ponder the fact that Adam, "earth creature," and Eve, "mother of all living," are said to have had a son named "meaninglessness," whose life is snuffed out quickly by his brother.

This is really just the tip of a very large historical iceberg. There are also problems related to archaeology and the Bible. Although we should respect the saying that "the absence of evidence is not evidence of absence," it is noteworthy that archaeology has little to show for people like Abraham, Joseph, or Moses, whom one would think were important people in the ancient Middle East given the length of their stories in the Bible and the roles they are said to have played in Egypt. While the archaeological record at times fits well with later biblical accounts of history, like that of later Israelite kings (for which some stone inscriptions do exist), there is widespread agreement among scholars that there is no direct archaeological evidence for the Patriarchs, for Moses, for the exodus, and some would even say for later figures such as King David. What do we make of this lack of evidence?

There are generally two camps in these debates, which scholars often call "minimalist" and "maximalist," with many biblical scholars falling somewhere in between. So-called minimalists are generally skeptical about anything that cannot be shown through external evidence, usually archaeological data outside of the Bible. Thus, because the only record we have of Abraham and Moses is from the Bible itself, their stories are labeled as ideologically driven fictions, perhaps the creation of fifth-century scribes hoping to convince Israelites living in Babylon to repopulate the land of Canaan, and to contribute to their new temple. Certainly, such thinking goes, there would be some record of a people leaving Egypt in such a magnificent way—given that Egyptians kept extensive histories—or, would there not be at least some archaeological evidence for Israel's large-scale entrance into Canaan through their alleged conquest? Maximalists, on the other hand, are often accused of taking the stories of the Bible at face value and at times employing arguments that others view as far-fetched or even intellectually dishonest. However, maximalists rightly note that many details in the Torah fit broadly into an ancient Near Eastern context, dating well before the exile of Judah in 587 BCE. Furthermore, some parts of the Torah comment upon and challenge other portions of it, likely suggesting a longer writing process than many minimalists allow.

Clearly, there are many complexities involved in relating the Bible to history, as well as in attempting to determine the Bible's authorship. Yet, one should recognize that historical study of the Bible has greatly advanced our understanding of this literature.

Feminist Interpretation

There are many different types of feminist approaches to the Bible, ranging from those interpreters who think the Bible's views of women are destructive and beyond redemption, to those who read the text suspiciously yet think the picture is mixed, to those who argue that certain biblical stories have a model view of women and in fact contain the rudiments of modern feminism. Although modern feminist interpretation began in the 1960s and became a major movement in the 1970s, it was the groundbreaking study of Phyllis Trible and her probing analysis of Genesis 2–3 in *God and the Rhetoric of Sexuality* (1978) that really propelled widespread interest in applying this type of reading to the Bible. In particular, Trible showed how a careful reading of Genesis 2 reveals much greater balance between Adam and Eve than was often granted. One might contest elements of Trible's argument, but her insight that subsequent, more patriarchal interpretive traditions have distorted our ability to read what the text actually says is of enduring value.

Hebrew Matters: Women as "Helpers"?

An example of feminist interpretation can be seen in Trible's discussion of the Hebrew term *ezer*, "helper," used in Genesis 2:18, 20 to describe Eve's relationship to Adam, which touches on a number of often overlooked facts. It had long been assumed by most interpreters that if Eve is described as Adam's helper, she must be inferior to Adam. But Trible notes that the context of this story and the word itself point to something different. Not only does the story make clear that the man, Adam, is incomplete and lacking something to be remedied by the woman, but the Hebrew term *ezer* is not necessarily a pejorative one, and is sometimes used of God's own role. That is, God is at times described as the great helper in his relationship to humans or the people of Israel, and clearly such usage is not intended to depict God as inferior to those he helps. Although it is evident that the text still reveals some gender imbalances, feminist interpretations like Trible's help us see how certain long-held interpretive assumptions and traditional views of women at times distort our ability to read what the Bible actually says about Eve's relationship to Adam.

It is impossible to deny the strongly patriarchal character of biblical religion, a feature shared by most ancient societies. However, it is equally unwise to deny that the Bible contains complex portraits of a number of female characters. Here we might name, among the many, Eve, Sarah, Hagar, Rebekah, Rachel, Leah, Dinah, Tamar, Potiphar's wife, Pharaoh's daughter, Moses' wife Zipporah, Hannah the mother of Samuel, Ruth and Naomi, Bathsheba, who came to marry David, and a striking number of women in the gospel stories including Jesus' mother Mary, Elizabeth, Anna, Martha, Mary Magdalene, the "woman at the well," and the Syrophoenician woman.

Furthermore, at least a few of these female characters are set in stories that one could reasonably call protofeminist in that such stories critique elements of the Bible's patriarchal culture. Focusing once more on Genesis, one thinks particularly of the story of Tamar in Genesis 38. This narrative interlude within the Joseph tale relates the strange manner in which Judah's lineage, the important lineage that will eventually lead to David, is continued. The story begins by indicating that Judah obtains a wife, Tamar, for his oldest son Er who dies prematurely and childless. Through an ancient form of surrogacy, Tamar is betrothed to Judah's second oldest son Onan, so that Onan might produce a child who would be legally Er's heir. But Onan engages in *coitus interruptus*, perhaps in self-interest to protect his own inheritance (producing offspring for his late, older brother likely meant forfeiting an inheritance), and thus he refuses to impregnate Tamar. God in turn kills Onan, once more leaving Tamar without a husband and Judah without a future heir. Judah decides to withhold his third son from Tamar because he assumes that Tamar must be responsible in some way for the deaths of his two older sons. The narrator, however, skillfully critiques Judah's patriarchal presumption of Tamar's guilt by attributing these two deaths to the sinful behavior of each man. Through a careful plan and audacious actions, the now disguised Tamar tricks Judah into impregnating her. Then Judah, the unknowing father, demands that Tamar be executed for committing adultery, inasmuch as she had sexual relations with a man other than Judah's third son to whom she was engaged. Immediately thereafter, Judah is indicted by his shrewd daughter-in-law. At the end of this clever story, Judah himself pronounces that Tamar "is more righteous than I" despite her actions, which might appear (to a modern audience at least) deceptive and even licentious.

One finds other protofeminist impulses elsewhere in the Hebrew Bible, as well as in the New Testament. So, for instance, feminist interpreters highlight the righteous and helpful actions of Rahab, a Canaanite prostitute whose story is told in Joshua 2. Similarly, Esther, an Israelite who became a Persian queen in the book named after her, is clearly a heroine in that she saves Israel from extinction, while Abigail, one of David's future wives, wisely negotiates for her life, in contrast to her dimwitted husband Nabal who dies (1 Samuel 25). In the New Testament Gospels, Jesus himself seems to be challenged and perhaps even outwitted by the Syrophoenician woman, and the women closest to Jesus are the first to whom he appears after his resurrection—women who show faith before certain male disciples. Critics will continue to argue over precisely how patriarchal the Bible is, or how one might assess the morality of certain specific women characters like Eve, Sarah, and Rebekah. But as the reader will see in our treatment of the individual books of the Bible, there is no doubt that theological reflection on the Bible has been greatly deepened by recent attention to gender issues raised by the text.

Ideological and Sociopolitical Criticism

Ideological and sociopolitical criticism developed in reaction to modern notions that one can objectively interpret texts without bias. These methods seek to expose the ideologies of the text by exploring the social and political biases within various books of the Bible. Their assumption is that these texts were written in order to establish or maintain the power of specific groups. However, these approaches not only recognize that ideology is a product of the past but also suggest that later interpreters who uphold these texts have ideologies as well. These groups or individuals *also* seek to establish or maintain power through their readings. Interpreting the text thus becomes concerned with how the author(s), original readers, and later interpreters all obtain, maintain, or take away power. As we shall see, and as others have suggested, an important problem can arise, however, in that these methods often lead to the conclusion that texts no longer have actual meaning, speak truth, or have continued relevance; rather, interpreting texts is reduced to questions about the struggle for—and maintenance of—power.

Despite this criticism, it is not difficult to demonstrate the usefulness of this method. For example, a number of critics have argued that the ancestral stories in Genesis 12–50 reflect concerns of a much later period in cryptic form. Thus several recent scholars have proposed that much of Genesis correlates with issues that would have been especially important to those exiles who were returning to Jerusalem after the Persians conquered Babylon in 538 BCE. Stories about Abraham, a character who begins his life in Babylon and journeys to Canaan, are viewed as mirroring the Persian context. In this case, such stories might reveal the wish of its writers to motivate those living in Babylon to return to their proper home, Judah, the land promised to Abraham in Genesis. Further, Abraham's various interactions with other groups living in Canaan are believed to set a paradigm for the Judean returnees, suggesting that they interact with those who currently occupy the land in ways similar to Abraham. Later in the book we will explore how our understanding of certain New Testament passages has been similarly deepened by our ability to grasp the social and political context in which they were produced.

We can see, therefore, that this method can illuminate the context behind the text. However, there are a number of ways that the method presents problems, one of which has been mentioned. First, even if one is able to determine the period in which something was written, it is not always clear that one can identify the exact ideological purpose for which a particular text was written. It is precisely this difficulty that is apparent in our example above that seeks to correlate a substantial block of Genesis to groups and events in the Persian period. Thus scholars argue over whether the stories in Genesis reflect an openness toward foreigners that challenged certain exclusionary ideas found in other Persian-era biblical texts such as Ezra and Nehemiah, or if on the contrary, the exclusion of Esau and Ishmael from Abraham's covenant are proof that these materials are ethnocentric and *supported* the exclusionary ideology found in books like Ezra and Nehemiah. These two viewpoints are actually in agreement on the historical context of Genesis' composition (the Persian period) but reach opposite conclusions about the ideologies that reside within the text.

A second difficulty is that a single passage can fit into a number of historical eras. This is especially true of the Hebrew Bible because much of Israel's history remains obscure and because over time a single passage may have been linked with a multiplicity of events. Further, as we already mentioned, this method tends to reduce the meaning of a text to the perceived ideologies of the text's authors. Nevertheless, despite these drawbacks, it remains a useful interpretive approach in that it forces us as readers to recognize the ideologies of the text as well as our own biases.

Holistic Approaches: Literary Criticism

Dissatisfied with biblical scholarship's tendency to privilege the historical-critical approach—which often focused on reconstructing the earliest sources that reside behind the text of the Bible—a number of scholars in recent decades have striven to read the biblical text in a holistic, literary fashion. Robert Alter, a literature professor from University of California Berkeley, helped propel this method forward with his widely influential book *The Art of Biblical Narrative*. In this work he, time and again, demonstrated that certain oddities in the text that historical critics regarded as evidence that the Bible had been haphazardly spliced together from multiple sources could just as well, or better, be explained on literary grounds. In many of his cases, Alter built upon the insights of traditional Jewish interpretation, interpretation that had long wrestled with the tensions in the text but saw these as contributing positively to a rich theological reading. Rather than attributing these textual tensions to conflicting accounts that stem from separate sources, both the ancient rabbis and contemporary critics like Alter assume that such variations produce a more complex narrative by creating ambiguities and representing the story from different angles.

Contemporary literary criticism, therefore, is concerned with the text itself rather than that which lies behind it (such as the world of the author and the circumstances that led to its composition). In short, literary criticism of the Bible is primarily concerned with things like literary artistry, plot, narrative development, the depiction of various characters, the implied reader, point of view, the effect and reliability of the narrator, use of key words or a *leitmotif* (a recurring theme), and so on.

Here we might return to the Tamar and Judah story in Genesis to provide an example of how one can glean significant insight into a textual tension that earlier source critics would have attributed to seemingly disparate sources (and thus separate stories) that have been spliced together in a clumsy fashion. Source critics view this story as out of place inasmuch as it interrupts the flow of the Joseph narrative, which begins in Genesis 37 and resumes in chapter 39. As we will see, literary critics agree that it interrupts the narrative but instead see this as integral to the larger story, its literary artistry, and message.

Alter, building on ancient rabbinic commentary on Genesis, astutely observes that several Hebrew expressions link Genesis 38 to both the preceding and following chapters in the Joseph story, and that these links additionally point to some significant thematic connections. In particular, he highlights that the Hebrew behind Tamar's expression "Take note, please" found in Genesis 38:25 is identical to the expression found in Genesis 37:32 on the lips of Joseph's brothers who ask Jacob to "take note, please" to see if he recognizes the torn garment as Joseph's. Unfortunately, translations like the NRSV obscure this connection by opting to render the two identical Hebrew expressions quite differently. An additional verbal connection is found in Genesis 38:1, in which we are told that "Judah went down," and Genesis 39:1, in which "Joseph was taken down." One quickly now begins to notice additional thematic links. While Judah allows himself to be drawn into an improper sexual relationship in chapter 38, Joseph adamantly rejects the sexual advances of Potiphar's wife in Genesis 39. In fact, Judah's behavior is uncovered when Tamar produces an item belonging to Judah, an act that resonates both with the garment produced by Joseph's brothers in Genesis

37 and with Joseph's tunic that Potiphar's wife retains and uses to impugn Joseph's integrity in Genesis 39. The close ties between Genesis 38 and the surrounding chapters not only allow one to compare Judah and Joseph, but also help one understand the way in which Judah's character begins to evolve and mature into the self-sacrificing Judah one finds later in Genesis 44. Additionally, by interrupting the flow of the Joseph story, Genesis 38 creates a time lapse, not unlike those used in modern movies, allowing the reader to feel that in the meantime Joseph has been journeying toward Egypt.

This type of close reading not only attends to connections between various passages, but also to unusual features within a single passage. For example, in Genesis 38:15, Judah assumes the woman he has met on the road to Timnah (who was Tamar, his daughter-in-law, in disguise) is a prostitute (in Hebrew a *zonah*). Yet in verse 21 when his friend Hirah asks around concerning the woman Judah had intercourse with, he uses a different Hebrew word, *qedeshah*, often rendered "sacred prostitute." It is difficult to know for sure exactly why this change in terminology has occurred, but many literary critics would see it as significant. One possible literary explanation is that Judah wished to obscure the fact that he slept with a regular prostitute by telling his friend Hirah he slept with a sacred or temple prostitute. Such an act may have been viewed socially as more positive. Of course one must entertain the possibility that these two differing words were simply used interchangeably in this instance. The larger point is that even though not every shift in Hebrew usage is significant, close attention to changes in vocabulary and style often yields insights into the passage under discussion.

Interestingly enough, very careful attention to the original language of the biblical text is a characteristic that undergirds the historical-critical approach as well, though to historical critics such variations are frequently seen as evidence of different sources or different editorial layers of the text. But in a literary reading this attention to the original language of the text is combined with a presumption that before fragmenting any story into its underlying components, one should first do one's best to read the actual text as a unity since presumably the Bible had meaning for those who put it in its final form.

There are definite limits to literary approaches, and in some way the method is only truly functional when used in conjunction with the insights gleaned from other methods that might illuminate the historical background of a particular passage, a word's potential meanings, or a phrase's grammatical structure. Literary readings that ignore the historical context in which the Hebrew Bible was written at times misrepresent the Bible because they misunderstand its vocabulary or grammar, often by reading contemporary usages into it. Words change meaning over time, so the more one knows of the context of a usage, the easier it will be to understand a specific text properly. A contemporary English usage example is that supposedly the King of England complimented the architect Christopher Wren upon his completing St. Paul's Cathedral in London by telling him he had "wrought an awful and artificial structure." If one did not know the seventeenth-century context, one might assume that these words were an insult as they would be today.

Literary criticism, like each of the approaches we examine in this book, should thus be seen as one of the many tools in the interpreter's toolbox, and one that often complements other approaches. In fact, one could argue that feminist approaches often combine a close literary reading with insights garnered from ideological and historical criticism and that historical critics frequently attend to the same details literary critics highlight. Truth be told, many biblical scholars today draw on all of these methods in an eclectic fashion depending on the specific passage under discussion. Different types of texts are illumined more by certain approaches and less by others.

Holistic Approaches: Canonical

Literary criticism's concern for the text as we have it is in congruence with what is called a canonical approach, which appreciates that individual passages sit within particular biblical books as well as within a larger body of literature (whether within the Torah, the Hebrew Bible, or the larger Christian Bible). However, canonical critics would find a purely literary approach to the Bible unsatisfying inasmuch as literary critics often read the Bible as simply another piece of literature. A canonical approach takes as its starting point the fact that many who interpret the Bible stand within religious communities that accept the Bible as a canon of Scripture. The term *canon* (from *kanon*, a Greek word meaning "rule," "standard," or "measuring stick"), used in biblical studies to refer to a set collection of writings deemed to be authoritative (in this case, the Bible), implies that texts within the canon carry religious authority. The canonical approach is thus interested in how this literature as a whole and its various parts speak to faith communities, both in church and synagogue.

This type of approach seeks to illuminate how certain books and passages in the Bible affect or are affected by one's understanding of other books and passages that share common content or ideas. Canonical scholars are also interested in why the canon contains the variety of books it does, how these books relate to each other, and whether there are unifying theological themes overall.

The canonical approach diverges from the historical-critical method in ways similar to the literary approach. While the historical-critical approach tends to focus on the historical backgrounds of a text, practitioners of the canonical approach have a theological concern with the text in its final form, the text "as we have it" in the canons of the Jewish, Catholic, or Protestant Bibles today. It places great significance on the final product and believes that the reasons for why it has been brought together in its current form are important *theologically*, even while it does not deny the prehistory of particular books or the extensive editorial activity that brought various sources together.

Taking the Torah as our example again, the results of the canonical approach can be noticed in a number of important ways. For instance, canonical interpreters might ask why Deuteronomy ends with Israel not having entered the promised land—something that takes place in the very next chapters of Joshua. In other words, this approach is interested in how the shape of the canon affects the reader and the story of the Bible more generally. Regarding the ending of Deuteronomy, one effect of the canonical shape of the Torah is that because Israel is left in the desert at the book's end, the listening audience is guided to focus more on Deuteronomy's instruction than on the immediate conquest of the land. Including the account of Israel's conquest might have distracted from or placed less emphasis on Deuteronomy's commandments. Such a proposal may be contested and debated, but such debate illustrates the interests and possible fruitfulness of the canonical approach.

Examples can be drawn from other places in the Bible as well. What is the effect of having four gospels, rather than just one that harmonizes the content of the others? Might the rest of the New Testament relate to the Gospels in a similar way to the manner in which the books of the Hebrew Bible that follow the Torah seem to build upon and interact with this primary material? A canonical reading refuses to let books of the Bible be read on their own, and seeks to understand their relation to each other, even if there is no question that they were produced by different authors with different perspectives. In short, a canonical approach seeks to respect those who shaped the canon as we have it today, arguing that the orientation of the canon itself has significance and affects our reading of each book.

One difficulty this approach encounters is that although Jews, Catholics, and Protestants view a number of the same books as scriptural, they do not share a common canon. In fact, even while the Jewish Tanakh and Christian Old Testament share the same books, as we noted earlier, these are in a significantly different canonical order, which affects how one interprets this literature. Additionally, the theological differences that separate various Christian denominations leave one wondering whether such an approach is capable of providing a meeting ground for these divergent traditions. Nevertheless, this approach remains valuable in that it recognizes that many who interpret the Bible do so within the context of a particular faith community.

Concluding Reflections

The purpose of this chapter was to give the reader a basic sense of a few important modern approaches to the biblical text and how they illuminate a specific section of the Bible. As we move through the larger Jewish and Christian Scriptures, we will at times explore historical-critical problems within a given text, ask questions about the sociological or ideological factors that may have given rise to certain passages, and we will regularly try to make literary and theological sense of whole books as well as explore how a particular biblical book resonates with other books in the Jewish and Christian Bibles.

THE BIBLE AS "STORY" AND "HISTORY"

The material in the Hebrew Bible, the Apocrypha, and the New Testament was written over more than a one thousand year span, likely between 950 BCE and 150 CE. From a narrative perspective, the Hebrew Bible begins at creation, thousands of years ago, and then tells the story of Abraham and his later descendants through Isaac and Jacob (that is, the people of Israel), focusing primarily on Israel's life in (and eventual exile from) what we today call the Holy Land. Later books in the Hebrew Bible, as well as most of the works in the Apocrypha, inform us about the Second Temple period. In this era some Israelite exiles from the tribe of Judah (or what we today call "Jews," meaning people from the land of Judah) repopulated parts of the Holy Land, while others who were exiled remained living in the wider Persian and Hellenistic diaspora (that is, scattered throughout a larger region). The New Testament is set in the Hellenistic period, with the Jewish people now both in the land of Israel and in the wider Greco-Roman world.

Contrary to the assumptions of many people today, the Bible is *not* strictly speaking a historical work. Even those passages that contain history-like narrations are not primarily intended to communicate history as we understand that term, and therefore readers must be cautious in how they read and interpret the Bible's stories. For example, stories meant to communicate theological lessons or teach something about human nature should not be read in the same way as a history book on World War II. Nevertheless, the Bible contains a treasure trove of historical information, although often the history revealed is of those who wrote and produced various parts of the Bible and not necessarily of the period actually being narrated in a specific story. For example, few scholars think that the stories in Genesis accurately reflect the history of Israel's oldest ancestors. However, many today would agree that these texts can tell us something, perhaps a great deal, about how later Israelites, those writing these texts, understood their origins. Many also acknowledge that these later Israelites on occasions may have preserved some snippets of material that actually do shed light on earlier periods in Israel's evolution. But one must critically evaluate the historical reliability of any given detail on a case-by-case basis.

Whether or not a particular biblical story contains accurate historical information, one can better understand the Bible by gaining a fuller knowledge of the historical setting of various biblical stories as well as understanding more about the period in which various biblical passages were produced. Further, our experience as teachers has taught us that students often come to a much deeper understanding of these texts if they have a general sense of the larger biblical "storyline," or "metanarrative," however historical or unhistorical that narrative actually is. We will treat both of these areas in turn.

Understanding the Bible's Historical Backgrounds

One can learn a great deal by examining the historical settings of the Bible, whether of the story being narrated or of the time period in which the author or compilers wrote. This can be done in a variety of ways, including the following:

• By gaining a basic sense of the Near Eastern and Mediterranean worlds in antiquity, and how ancient Israel as well as the Judaism of Jesus' day fit into and were affected by the wider world in which the stories of the Bible were written and set.

• By understanding how the many archaeological finds in Israel and the wider Near East help scholars critically evaluate the historical accuracy of various biblical accounts or how such knowledge can at times illuminate certain narrative or legal details previously not understood.

• By learning to read the Bible in a sympathetic but also critical fashion whereby one takes the text seriously but is also willing to, indeed committed to, question the text. It should be noted that the enigmatic quality of much of the content in the Bible regularly elicits questions from the attentive reader, something attested to in ancient religious commentary on the Bible as well as in the questions modern scholars ask. In truth, reading the Bible with a critical eye goes hand in hand with taking it seriously.

Although the book you hold in your hands is not a history book nor is it primarily focused on historical-critical issues, we will from time to time show how knowing the historical context can illuminate various biblical passages.

Understanding the Bible's Storyline

In order for the reader to grasp the basics, we give brief thumbnail sketches of both the history of Israel within the wider world in which it lived (as far as that can be known) as well as a general outline of how the Bible itself presents its storyline (also as far as that can be discerned).

While the Bible contains a wealth of material from the ancient Near Eastern world, it was produced by a rather small, backwater nation compared to the massive empires of Egypt, Assyria, Babylonia, Persia, Greece, and Rome—each of which at times imposed their will upon those living in the ancient land of Israel. One of the most difficult tasks the historian faces when mapping out ancient Israel's history is deciding where the mythic past ends and where something that might more properly be described as history begins. Scholars use the term *myth* to describe a type of story that communicates deep truths about the nature of human existence or about the human understanding of the divine. Myths contain profound truths even if they are open to question historically. Most critics today recognize that the description of creation in Genesis 1–2 or the flood story in Genesis 6–9 are more accurately described as myth than as history. But even setting aside these clearly mythic texts early in Genesis, scholars do not all agree where in the Bible we find the oldest historical remembrances. On the conservative end of the spectrum, some might begin to write a history of ancient Israel with the Patriarchs or perhaps with the events of the exodus, while more skeptical historians today might opt to begin their narration of Israel's history with the monarchic period beginning around 1000 BCE or even only with the people that emerged from Babylonian exile in 538 BCE. Whatever date one opts to begin a discussion of Israel's history with, one must always keep in mind that the Bible often aims to communicate religious insights about the past and its meaning rather than to narrate events as they actually happened. What this means is that even when the text is believed to contain trustworthy historical information, that information may be embedded in a narrative that, on the whole, is not historically accurate.

Having provided that preamble, we can now attempt to place the Bible's storyline within the general framework of ancient Near Eastern history. We will not place every biblical book in this framework but select a few examples particularly of works that contain some attempts to describe historical remembrances of each period (see timeline on pages 48–49).

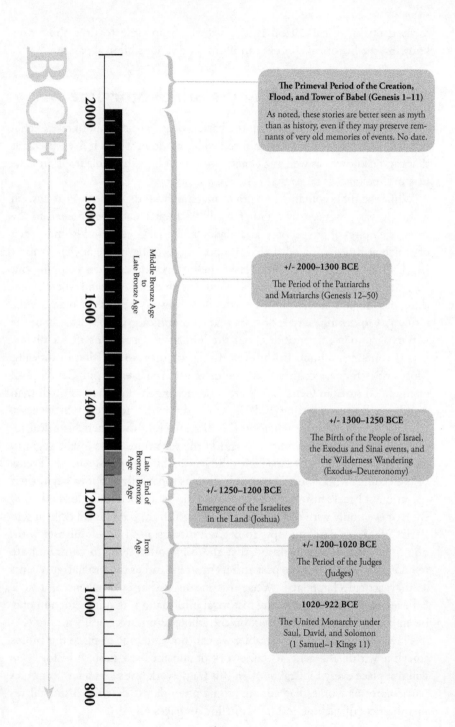

BCE

2000

1800

1600

1400

1200

1000

800

Middle Bronze Age
to
Late Bronze Age

Late End of
Bronze Bronze
Age Age

Iron
Age

The Primeval Period of the Creation, Flood, and Tower of Babel (Genesis 1–11)

As noted, these stories are better seen as myth than as history, even if they may preserve remnants of very old memories of events. No date.

+/- 2000–1300 BCE

The Period of the Patriarchs and Matriarchs (Genesis 12–50)

+/- 1300–1250 BCE

The Birth of the People of Israel, the Exodus and Sinai events, and the Wilderness Wandering (Exodus–Deuteronomy)

+/- 1250–1200 BCE

Emergence of the Israelites in the Land (Joshua)

+/- 1200–1020 BCE

The Period of the Judges (Judges)

1020–922 BCE

The United Monarchy under Saul, David, and Solomon (1 Samuel–1 Kings 11)

1000

922–722 BCE

The two kingdoms consisting of Ephraim (also called Israel) in the North and Judah in the South (1 Kings 12–2 Kings 17, Amos, Hosea, Isaiah 1–11). The later date is when the North was conquered and exiled by Assyria.

800

722–587 BCE

Judah remains an intact small state with a king on the throne until 587 BCE when the Babylonian empire destroys Jerusalem and exiles the population (2 Kings 18–Kings 25, Jeremiah, and Ezekiel)

600

The Exilic Period 587–538 BCE

The latter date is when Persia conquers Babylon and allows the exiles to return to Jerusalem (Isaiah 40–55, 2 Chronicles 36:22-23)

400

538–333 BCE (Persian rule); 333–63 BCE (Greek rule); 63 BCE–early first century CE (Roman rule)

The Post-Exilic or Second Temple period during which the territory of Judah is under foreign rule (Haggai, Zechariah, Ezra, Nehemiah, Ben Sirah, 1–2 Maccabees)

200

3 BCE–70 CE

The time of Jesus and the early church, Pharisees, Sadducees, Essenes, the Zealots movement, and the destruction of the Second Temple (Paul's letters including Romans, 1–2 Corinthians, and Galatians)

0

70 CE and beyond

Post-Second Temple Judaism and Christianity (the Gospels, Acts; later New Testament epistles, Revelation)

200

THE TANAKH—HEBREW BIBLE—OLD TESTAMENT

INTRODUCTION TO THE TORAH

Scholars refer to what Jews call the Torah—the collection of five books at the beginning of the Bible including Genesis, Exodus, Leviticus, Numbers, and Deuteronomy—as the *Pentateuch*. The term *Pentateuch* is a word derived from the Greek term *pentateuchos*, meaning "five scrolls" or "five vessels." Traditional Jews call the printed form of these five books the *Chumash*, a word derived from the Hebrew word for the number five. In popular parlance this collection is often called the Five Books of Moses. This latter designation likely arose both because Moses features prominently in these books and due to the traditional, long-standing belief that Moses authored them. Although other parts of the Hebrew Bible are considered to be divinely inspired, the Torah is often understood to be the most important section of the Jewish Bible or Old

Figure 8. A traditional handwritten Torah scroll on parchment. Scrolls like this are still widely used in synagogues today. Courtesy of Knox College, Toronto.

Testament, something of a "canon within the canon," that is, the most sacred subsection of the Hebrew Bible.

We should be clear that there is no title on this collection of books that names them "The Torah." The Hebrew word *torah* can sustain a range of meanings including: teaching, instruction, law, procedure, principle, and so on. It can even be used to describe a specific ritual procedure (as in Leviticus 6:2, 7, 18). The notion that the word *torah* might refer to this collection of five books likely arises from certain verses in Deuteronomy. Over time, various references in Deuteronomy to a Torah scroll, though initially referring to part or all of Deuteronomy, eventually came to be understood as references to the full text of Genesis through Deuteronomy.

As mentioned above, within modern Jewish culture, the word *Torah* is used to refer not only to the scroll containing the first five books of the Bible; but also to any and all aspects of Jewish wisdom, lore, or law produced at any time from the Bible until today. This can be grasped more clearly in imagining that you overhear the following conversation among two Jews, perhaps on a flight returning from Israel: "How long were you in Israel? What were you doing there?" "I was in Israel for six months studying Torah." What the person who replied likely means is not that they were literally studying material in the first five books of the Jewish Bible but that they were studying Jewish religious texts more generally, such as the Talmud.

In the Christian tradition, the Torah is often called "The Law," and sometimes this is contrasted with "The Gospel." The Christian tendency to think of law and gospel as opposing terms arose largely during the Reformation in Europe, when the Reformers argued that salvation was obtained not through practicing good deeds or doing good works (that is, obeying the law) but rather was received freely through grace. Many would suggest that this dichotomy is not reflective of the New Testament itself, a collection that needs to be read carefully in light of the debates Paul and others were having regarding Jewish-Gentile relations. Frequently in the New Testament the Torah is simply called "Moses" or the "Book of Moses"; and interestingly, when questioned, Jesus places high value on this collection, at times indicating that obeying its teachings will result in eternal life (see Matthew 19:16-19; Mark 10:17-19; Luke 10:25-28).

There is no question that the Torah has been deeply influential in Western civilization, and two of the world's major religions—Judaism and Christianity—consider the Torah to be sacred and to contain enduring truths about the creation of the world, the texture and meaning of human existence, and the nature and character of God. The story of the Torah covers some

2,700 years beginning with the creation of the world and ending with the death of Moses, with the Israelites poised to enter the land of Canaan under Joshua's leadership. While there is much that unifies the material in these books, the Torah contains a host of different kinds of material including mythic stories, genealogies, travel itineraries, census lists, many distinct types of narratives, poetic texts including prayers and prophecies to blessings and taunts, and legal texts dealing with criminal, civil, ritual, and ethical matters. With this in mind, we now turn to examine the content of the Torah in more depth.

GENESIS

Introduction and Overview

The name *Genesis*, meaning "beginnings," is derived from the Greek Septuagint's title for the book. In Jewish tradition, the book of Genesis is called *Bereshit*, a title derived from the first word of the book in Hebrew, which means "in the beginning" or "when it began." Both titles are especially apt for the first few chapters, but they also apply to the entire book. Not only is the creation of the world and humankind contained in these pages, but so too are the people of Israel brought into existence.

Scholars usually divide the book into two major sections, Genesis 1–11, called the *Primeval History*, perhaps better termed the *Primeval Story*, and Genesis 12–50, called the *Patriarchal Narratives* or *Ancestral Narratives*. The Primeval Story begins with the creation of the world and highlights God's formation—and thus ownership—of the earth and humankind. This story and those that follow contain a number of "what went wrong?" moments, events in the early history of the world that not only show an apparent downward spiral in human action but also a progressive change in God's dealings with humanity. Genesis 1–11 is rather more universal in scope, in the sense that it concerns all humanity and not only a specific people, something that shifts considerably in chapter 12.

Often referred to as the "Call of Abraham," the narrative that begins chapter 12 initiates a new era that will engage—and hopefully alleviate—the problems of the past through Abraham and certain of his descendants. However, this change in emphasis also brings about problems of its own, not least in how those who are not of Abraham's special lineage relate to God and those God favors. These narratives thus highlight the complex relationships between the chosen and those who stand outside the Abrahamic covenant.

The stories of Abraham, Sarah and Hagar, Isaac and Ishmael, Jacob and Esau, Rachel and Leah, and Joseph and his brothers dominate the Ancestral Narratives. The book eventually ends with Israel, now a small people, living in Egypt.

Controversies and Debates

A number of important scholarly debates grew out of and focus upon the book of Genesis. Some of these have been touched upon in our discussion of the historical-critical approach above, so here we briefly look at one issue that seems to receive abundant popular attention: Are the materials found in Genesis 1–11 historical, and if they are not, how are they best understood?

In reality, what some call the "creation and evolution" debate generates little scholarly interest outside of a small subset of those thinkers taking a very traditional or at times a fundamentalist approach to the text. The issues here are not as complex as some would have it, at least if one takes the genre of this literature seriously. Most scholars regard much of Genesis 1–11 to be mythic in nature. As we discussed earlier, in religious studies the term *myth* describes a type of story that communicates deep truths about the nature of human existence or about the human understanding of the divine (even if such stories are open to question historically). Inasmuch as these mythic texts from Genesis are primarily concerned with exploring what it means to be human, why life and work are difficult, why humans die, and so on, scholars generally view the popular tendency to focus on "creation science" or "evolution and the Bible" as a fundamental misreading of this type of material. It would be akin to trying to ask scientific and historical questions about the story of "Little Red Riding Hood" or asking literary questions about the list of ingredients on a cereal box.

Other closely related ancient Near Eastern texts provide further support for understanding these materials as mythic. Thus the two creation narratives as well as the garden of Eden and flood stories in Genesis share much in common with other ancient Near Eastern origin stories (for example, the *Enuma Elish*, the Epic of Atrahasis, and the Gilgamesh Epic). Yet, the Hebrew Bible generally portrays humans in a more dignified and exalted role. The God in whose image they are made is portrayed as remarkable in faithfulness and loving-kindness. In the *Enuma Elish*, for example, an ancient Mesopotamian creation epic, humans are created from the blood of the rebel deity Kingu to alleviate the workload of the lower gods. In contrast, Genesis 1 depicts the first ancestors of human beings, both male and female, as created in God's own image and given dominion over the world.

Creation: Genesis 1–2

Genesis begins with two distinct creation stories. The first account (Genesis 1.1-2.4a), which is more theocentric (or God-centered) in orientation, depicts Israel's God as a transcendent creator who stands apart from the created order. These characteristics, along with its poetic language and almost hymnlike structure, have led most modern scholars to attribute it to the P, or Priestly source. Unlike later Jewish and Christian readings of this story that assume creation out of nothing, here God neither creates the waters nor the dry land. Rather, God puts each in its proper place.

The subsequent creation story found in Genesis 2:4b-2:25 is notable for its earthy language and anthropocentric (or human-centered) viewpoint. God is here portrayed not only as much less transcendent but even as not entirely omniscient in that God at times engages in experimentation. Scholars attribute this seemingly more fallible image of God to the J source. In this account, the creation of animals appears to result from a trial-and-error attempt to find a suitable partner for the first human being. Discovering that none of the animals would serve as a helper to Adam, God removes a piece of Adam and builds a woman whom the earth creature recognizes as his partner. Here the Torah, in a brief aside, provides the reader with an etiological, or causal, explanation of the attraction to the opposite sex and the central role of the nuclear family.

Corruption: Genesis 3–11

For centuries, Christians have read Genesis 3 as the story of the "fall of man" (or "fall of humanity") in which God punishes all humans on account of Adam and Eve's disobedience by taking away the immortality he had initially bestowed upon them. This interpretation contributed to a doctrine of original sin, held by many Christians, the idea that all humans are sinful at birth as a result of the first humans' actions. However, there is little evidence to suggest that Genesis 3 marks a complete change in the human-divine relationship. Furthermore, it is not clear that Genesis 3 describes a loss of human immortality, but rather the loss of the potential to obtain it. We would suggest, along with others, that Genesis 3–11 contains many interconnected stories that describe a "falling out" between God and humans through the deepening corruption of human beings.

Genesis 4 furthers the Torah's probing of human corruption by narrating the first murder, a fratricide inspired by jealousy over God's preference for Abel and his sacrifice over Cain and his. This short episode is the first of a host of stories in Genesis in which God's favor toward a specific person sets off the jealousy of those not chosen (a theme we return to below). After this incident the chapter goes on to describe a number of technological innovations, which it places between Cain's murder of Abel and Lamech's vengeful taunt. The growing ability of humans to manipulate the natural world is presented as a mixed blessing in that this evolving technical mastery is tainted by a lack of human moral development.

Monotheism or Monolatry?

The Israelites are often credited with inventing the idea of monotheism, that is, the belief that there is only one God. Further, it is often presumed that the Hebrew Bible is monotheistic throughout. However, while certain later texts such as Isaiah 40–66 contain something approaching what we today might call monotheism, much of the rest of the Hebrew Bible can better be described as endorsing monolatry. The term *monolatry* recognizes that although multiple divine forces may exist, Israel is permitted to worship only one specific deity. The plural usages found in Genesis 1:26 ("Let *us* make humankind") and 11:7 ("Come, let *us* go down," emphasis added) seem to indicate that God was speaking to other divine beings who function as part of his courtly retinue, but generally are subordinate to God. It is these divine beings, literally called "the sons of God," who mate with human women in Genesis 6:2. These beings often function as agents who work for God, and thus are sometimes called divine messengers or what we call angels. This is exactly the English term used to describe the two divine beings who are sent to rescue Lot and punish the residents of Sodom in Genesis 19:1.

When one examines the flood narrative, one once again discovers the juxtaposition of differing theologies. One strand of the narrative (P) views the flood as God's righteous judgment on a wicked humanity as seen in Genesis 6:11. In contrast, the other version of the story (J) shows a more reluctant and ambivalent deity. This deity initially exhibits regret at having created humankind and at the end of the flood regrets having destroyed the world by the flood. Although the larger story can lend itself to the idea of an unmerciful God who destroys all at will, one can also read the text as suggesting that an evil and corrupt world exists only due to God's continuing mercy toward humanity, despite its continued corruption and rebellion (compare Genesis 6:5-7 with 8:21).

This story concludes with the Bible's first covenant in which God promises all humanity and all animals that he will never again flood the world. From this, and the accompanying commandments given by God to Noah and his family, traditional Judaism derives what it calls the Noahide laws, a short list of basic commandments such as not murdering, not stealing, and not committing adultery that apply to all humans, since in the biblical view everyone is a descendant of Noah. Despite God's attempt to set the human-divine relationship on a new footing here, the subsequent stories of Noah's sons and the Tower of Babel indicate that God is still failing to obtain the response for which he had hoped.

God and Abraham: Genesis 12–25

As already mentioned, in some ways Genesis 1–11 represents not only human failure but also God's failed attempt to create a proper set of relationships between humans, nature, and himself. In the wake of these failures, God moves from a plan in which he demands equal obedience from all humans to a two-tiered plan in which most people are held to a minimal religio-moral standard (the few basic Noahide laws) while one man's family is given a special place in the divine economy requiring that they maintain a higher religio-moral standard (the full teachings of the Torah). As Genesis 12:3 makes clear, God's special favor toward Abraham, as well as Israel, Abraham's descendants, is closely bound up with God's larger plan to bring blessing to the whole world, as God assures Abraham:

> I will bless those who bless you, and the one who curses you I will curse; and in you all the families of the earth shall be blessed.

There is a great deal of debate regarding whether the conclusion of Genesis 12:3 should be translated as, "In you all the families of the earth shall be blessed" or as, "In you all the families of the earth shall bless themselves." Will Abraham and his later descendants, the Israelites, mediate God's blessings to the other nations of the world through their actions? Or will the nations bless themselves through Abraham in some way, perhaps by blessing him or by saying, "May you be blessed like God blessed Abraham"? How one translates this ambiguous verse can significantly affect one's understanding of Israel's purpose and mission in the world (see "Genesis in Christianity" below).

The call of Abraham also includes God's gift of land to Abraham and his descendants (identified as the land of Canaan), a theme that plays a central role in the Hebrew Bible and the New Testament, as well as within postbiblical Jewish thought. This initial mention of land in Genesis 12:7 becomes a promise that reverberates throughout Genesis and indeed the Bible. The Bible understands the land of Israel as a holy place where God is especially present and thus as the one place where the people of Israel can fully realize their potential to live as God's chosen people.

59

Genesis includes two main covenants, one between God and Noah, discussed above, and one between God and Abraham, found in Genesis 15 and 17. A covenant is a way to formalize an agreement between two parties, and it sometimes involves a ritual element or a type of sacrifice. There are two broad categories of divine-human covenants in the Hebrew Bible: conditional (or treaty) covenants in which the bulk of the burden falls on the humans involved, and unconditional covenants (or covenants of grant) in which most of the obligations fall upon God. Both God's covenant with Noah and his one with Abraham are unconditional in that the obligations fall primarily, if not exclusively, upon the Deity. In the case of the Abrahamic covenant, God promises to give Abraham numerous descendants as well as the land of Canaan as an everlasting possession.

Chosenness, Strife, and Reconciliation in Genesis

The remainder of Genesis is largely a saga involving three generations of one family. The first generational story rotates around two major themes, that of Abraham and Sarah's inability to have children and (later) who, of Abraham's two sons, will carry on God's covenantal relationship with Abraham. Here one finds that major tensions erupt between Sarah and Hagar (the maidservant who gives birth to Ishmael), tensions that in the end lead to Hagar and Ishmael's expulsion from Abraham's household.

The second set of stories takes place in two households between two rival sets of siblings whose destinies become intertwined. It begins in the household of Isaac and Rebekah, the matriarch who bears the twins Esau and Jacob. After obtaining Esau's birthright and blessing by questionable means, Jacob, for fear of death, is forced to flee to his uncle's home in Mesopotamia. It is in Laban's household that Jacob becomes entangled in the rivalry between two sis-

Figure 9. Marc Antonio Francheshini, *Hagar [and Ishmael] and the Angel in the Desert,* **undated. Done with pen, light brown ink and wash, and accented with pencil on cream paper. Courtesy Smith College Museum of Art, Northampton, Massachusetts (SC 1947:6-1).**

ters, Leah and Rachel, both of whom he ends up marrying. Both women (and their maidservants Bilhah and Zilpah) bear a total of twelve sons to Jacob, who become the forefathers of the twelve tribes of Israel. After tensions arise between Jacob and his father-in-law, Laban, Jacob, along with his now large family, returns home to face Esau. A moving story of partial reconciliation occurs and then the third family saga begins in Genesis 37, which runs through the end of Genesis.

This final story concerning Jacob's sons—called the Joseph story—is driven by the theme of both Jacob and God's favor toward Joseph and the deep jealousy it evokes in Jacob's ten older sons. The ten brothers conspire against Joseph, and he is ultimately taken to Egypt as a slave as a result. Through a series of dramatic and wondrous events, Joseph becomes vizier (the highest official in Egypt under the Pharaoh) and he has the chance to test his brothers when they come to buy grain in Egypt. In some sense, Benjamin, Jacob's youngest son and Joseph's only full-blooded brother, serves as the means by which the reconciliation takes place between Joseph and his ten estranged brothers. By the end of this engaging story, Jacob and his whole family are living as well-treated guests in Egypt.

As one can see, the themes of chosenness and the strife it engenders play a central role in the Ancestral Narratives. The same themes keep recurring in ever more developed and complex forms in Genesis, with reconciliation serving as an important motif (something precluded from occurring in Genesis 4 in that Cain murders Abel). In the story of Isaac and Ishmael, there is a single verse, Genesis 25:9, that hints at a possible late-life reconciliation between these two brothers in that they both are present to bury their father, Abraham. In the Jacob and Esau narrative, almost all of Genesis 32–33 is taken up with the question of whether and to what extent Jacob and Esau can reconcile. In the Joseph story, the theme of reconciliation comes to occupy all of Genesis 42–45 as well as Genesis 50 and thus stands at the center of this whole narrative section.

In all of these stories a divine preference for the younger sibling seems to suggest that God favors individuals not favored by human convention (in antiquity, typically the eldest son was favored and given a double inheritance). One likely factor contributing to this motif's prominence is the people Israel's self-perception. While we today think of the Israelites as an archaic culture, Israel saw herself as a younger upstart who arrived on the scene long after cultures like those found in Mesopotamia and Egypt.

It is important to point out that within these narratives of sibling rivalry and divine favor, the nonfavored are not necessarily hated by God or excluded

61

from God's blessing. In Genesis 17 and 21, Ishmael receives a special divine blessing. Much the same can be said of Esau, who prospers in life and fathers a host of progeny (Genesis 36). Nonchosenness is not a sign of damnation and, for that matter, chosenness is not to be equated with a guarantee of salvation or a good life. In fact, chosenness often brings mortal danger in its wake, something seen in Abel's death, Abraham's encounter with famine, Isaac's near sacrifice, Jacob's fleeing for fear of death, and Joseph's near death at the hands of his brothers. This pattern of the endangerment of the chosen, which usually precedes the eventual triumph or exaltation of the divinely favored one, is central to both the Hebrew Bible and the New Testament. Thus both the master story of Israel, which is the account of the Egyptian enslavement and eventual freeing of Israel from this bondage found in Exodus 1–15, and the gospel Passion Narratives, which describe the death and resurrection of Jesus, are intensifications of this major theme. In short, both Jews and Christians see themselves as God's favored child who experiences a tribulation that may result in death, but who ultimately triumphs and is symbolically or actually resurrected into a new life provided by the grace of God.

Genesis in Judaism

The Jewish legal and moral tradition has often probed the characters in Genesis and their actions to derive legal and behavioral norms. Thus the rabbis condemn Noah for failing to object to God's plan to flood the world, while they praise Abraham for engaging in a lengthy argument to prevent God from destroying the cities of Sodom and Gomorrah too hastily. One of the largest imprints left upon Jewish tradition by Genesis is found in the way that the story of Abraham's near sacrifice of Isaac, what Jewish tradition calls the *akedah* (or *binding*) of Isaac, has affected the daily and yearly liturgical cycle. This story is recited during the preliminary prayers of the daily morning service. Furthermore, the *akedah* is the Torah portion read on the second day of Rosh Hashanah, the Jewish New Year festival that occurs each fall. In Jewish tradition, Rosh Hashanah is the time when God takes stock of all human lives and determines one's destiny for the next year. The reading of this Torah text on Rosh Hashanah suggests that Jews recognize that God has a claim on their lives that he could choose to exercise at any time. If one is given another year to live, this is an act of pure divine grace, like God's provision of the ram caught in the thicket that provided a substitute for the life of Isaac in Genesis 22. Thus the community as a whole as well as its individuals see themselves as only continuing to exist by an ongoing act of divine grace.

Genesis in Christianity

The importance of Genesis to the New Testament and Christianity is indeed great. However, probably more than any other passage in Genesis—indeed in the Torah or even Hebrew Bible—the Call of Abraham in Genesis 12:1-3 stands at the center of Christian theological reflection. Christian theology has built much upon Genesis 12:1-3 in that many Christians see here the foundations of mission and God's bringing of salvation to the larger world (for both Jew and Gentile). There is little debate that the Jewishness of Jesus is important to Christian theology, and it is important precisely because he is a descendant of Abraham, and eventually David (to see this, read the genealogy that begins Matthew's Gospel). The thinking in Christianity is that God will bless the entire world through Abraham as stated in Genesis 12:3. Jesus is seen to be the seed of Abraham who mediates God's blessing to the larger world. The Apostle Paul underlines this point and takes it further in Galatians 3:1-14 where he highlights Abraham's belief in God's promises, citing Genesis 15:6. What is interesting here is that Paul argues that, through his belief in the promise (and *not* through keeping the law), Abraham is said to attain righteousness, or salvation. Paul then goes on to explain that Genesis 12:3 *is itself the very gospel*, or good news, by drawing an analogy between Abraham's belief and the belief of those who recognize that Jesus is the Christ (a Greek word meaning "the anointed one" or "messiah").

Concluding Reflections

Studying Genesis is far from an exercise relevant only to historians interested in ancient Israelite culture or to theologians seeking to ground various doctrines in the biblical text. Genesis is not only the first biblical book in literary sequence but also the book that contains the foundation for biblical teachings on the character of God, the root causes of human sin, and ultimately what it means to be human—created in God's own image yet dwelling on earth. Equally important, it sets the stage for the rest of the Bible's story by explaining Israel's origins—a people, like their ancestors, specially favored by God.

EXODUS

Introduction and Overview

The second book in the Torah is called Exodus in English, a reference to the book's central narrative about God's redemption of the Israelites from Egyptian enslavement. Jews refer to this book as *Shemoth*, meaning "Names" (short for "And these are the names"), from the opening Hebrew words of Exodus 1:1 that introduce the names of the sons of Jacob who journeyed down to Egypt.

Exodus is relatively easy to outline. Exodus 1–15 contains the story of the Egyptian oppression of the Israelites, which leads into the Ten Plagues and culminates in Israel's crossing of the Sea of Reeds (traditionally but likely incorrectly rendered as the Red Sea), and the drowning of the pursuing Egyptian army. Exodus 16–18 contains several narratives dealing with Israel's journey to Mount Sinai. Chapters 19–24 relate the story of the encounter between God and the Israelites at Mount Sinai, which includes the giving of the Ten Commandments and other legislation. Chapters 25–31 and 35–40 contain detailed instructions on building and consecrating the portable tent-shrine (or tabernacle) that the Israelites travel with on their wanderings toward the Holy Land. In the middle of this material one finds the Golden Calf episode and a reaffirmation of God's covenantal relationship to Israel in the wake of this breach.

Controversies and Debates

Scholars have long argued over the extent to which Exodus grew out of memories of actual historical events. The current consensus is that the general portrayal of a united Israelite people going down to Egypt, multiplying, being enslaved and being freed *en masse*, is based on a national legend popular during the monarchic period that articulates Israel's understanding of her peoplehood and national origins. However, many scholars do believe that at least some ancestors of the ancient Israelites may have escaped Egyptian bondage and that the book contains a number of details that illuminate aspects of the origins of Israel's religion. Thus the role played by Jethro, Moses' Midianite father-in-law, is often understood to provide an important clue about ancient Israel's attachment to a God who appeared at a mountain in the Sinai Peninsula near Midian. Further, Israel's monotheistic impulses are sometimes traced back to a specific period in Egypt's history in which monotheism was prevalent, with Moses having learned about this while being raised in Pharaoh's palace. Perhaps the most useful way to think of the narratives in Exodus is as a blend of myth and history by which Israel expressed her historical origins in mythic terms, a point that will be discussed in greater detail below.

Two related issues tend to animate a good deal of historical scholarship on the book of Exodus. The first is the *date* of the migration from Egypt (and the eventual "conquest" of Canaan) and the second is the *route* that the people took in travelling to Canaan. Depending on one's stance toward the historical

---

Does the Bible Ever Permit Lying?

Exodus 1:15-22 narrates a brief attempt at ethnic genocide when Pharaoh commands the midwives who attend to the Israelites to kill every male Israelite immediately upon delivery. The midwives, fearing God, ignore Pharaoh's orders and lie to his face. In turn, God rewards them. This midwives' lying to Pharaoh has been assessed very differently by Jewish versus Christian tradition. Classical Jewish interpreters have not been troubled by the fact that the midwives lied, because in rabbinic Judaism one may not only suspend certain religious behaviors to save a life, but in special circumstances one may be commanded to invert certain rules. Thus, among traditional Jews, one may not drive a car on the Sabbath, but if a life is in danger and driving is necessary, one *must* drive on Sabbath. Since the midwives were saving lives, Jewish interpreters see no problem with the behavior of the midwives. One finds a substantially different view in the work of St. Augustine called *Against Lying* in which he argues that although the midwives are to be praised for sparing Israelite babies, they are to be criticized for lying to Pharaoh. Augustine acknowledges that if the midwives told the truth they may well have been killed, but he asserts that having been killed, and in some sense martyred, they would have received a heavenly reward greater than the earthly reward the text describes God giving them in verse 21. Our point here is not to endorse one view as correct, but to demonstrate how small details in Scripture are often used to bolster the larger theological claims of each faith community.

reliability of the book (that is, how much "actually happened" and how much is better characterized as mythic in nature), scholars will spend extensive, little, or no time discussing such questions. The issues are complicated for a number of reasons, not least because the book itself is generally uninterested in these questions and it gives little by way of detail to assist the scholar in the task (for example, the names of the Pharaohs in Egypt are not given and neither is the precise location at which Israel crosses the ambiguously named "Sea of Reeds").

The Hardening of Pharaoh's Heart and the Meaning of the Plagues

The bulk of chapters 7–15 is taken up with the sequence of escalating plagues. It is worth noting that because of certain peculiarities and repetitions in the plagues, almost all critics believe that the current plague narrative combines several sources, each of which had fewer plagues in them. This can be easily seen by the fact that the fifth plague describes the total destruction of Egyptian livestock, but one finds livestock alive and well in subsequent plagues, ready to be destroyed again (see Exodus 9:6, 10, 25; and 11:5). It is possible that the variant portrayals of exactly how Pharaoh's heart (or will) is hardened with each plague also ultimately stems from the fact that Exodus is a composite narrative:

Plague 1. "Pharaoh's heart stiffened" (Exodus 7:22)
Plague 2. "He [Pharaoh] hardened his heart" (Exodus 8:15)
Plague 3. "Pharaoh's heart stiffened" (Exodus 8:19)
Plague 4. "Pharaoh hardened his heart" (Exodus 8:32)
Plague 5. "the heart of Pharaoh hardened" (Exodus 9:7)
Plague 6. "the LORD stiffened Pharaoh's heart" (Exodus 9:12)
Plague 7. "he sinned once more and hardened his heart" (Exodus 9:34) followed by "Pharaoh's heart stiffened" (Exodus 9:35)
Plague 8. "the LORD stiffened Pharaoh's heart" (Exodus 10:20)
Plague 9. "the LORD stiffened Pharaoh's heart" (Exodus 10:27)
Plague 10. (before crossing the Sea of Reeds) "the LORD stiffened Pharaoh's heart" (Exodus 14:8 AT)

There are two different Hebrew words being used here (translated "hardened" and "stiffened") with two different subjects, thus creating four distinct descriptions of Pharaoh's implacability. It may be that variant sources spoke of God's control of events using different language because each source had a unique view regarding the balance between God's providential control of events and the ability of humans to affect a particular situation.

However, it is possible to give a holistic literary reading to the current form of the text. In fact, some scholars challenge the suggestion of a composite text (at least with regard to the hardening of Pharaoh's heart) in that there does seem to be a balanced symmetry in the verbs used to describe the hardening of Pharaoh's will; of the twenty occurrences of the verbs used, ten have God as subject, and ten have Pharaoh (or his heart) as subject. In such a holistic reading one might emphasize that early on Pharaoh had more control over events but, as is common with, say, addictive personalities, at a certain point one loses control over one's ability to resist certain patterns of action. The text could be read as signaling a growing loss in Pharaoh's ability to act freely as God's control grows ever greater over the course of the unfolding narrative.

Similarly, while the multiplication of plagues may stem from the text's composite character, one can see progressions in the narrative as a whole. Thus the series of plagues arises out of God's wish to demonstrate to Pharaoh that God's claim on the Israelites supersedes Pharaoh's. Here one must remember that the Egyptian Pharaoh was considered to be a divine being, and it is precisely this claim that the exodus story tests. In fact, one might usefully understand the plague sequence as a contest, perhaps a showdown of sorts, between two personalities, each of whom claims to be God. The God of the Hebrew Bible triumphs in this story by demonstrating that he, *not* Pharaoh, is the God who created and controls the universe, and is the rightful owner of the Israelites.

The Bible's Ability to Meld the Past and Present

Chapters 12 and 13 contain detailed rules for the celebration of Passover. What is odd is that one would expect the first ritual reenactment of Passover, the holiday that celebrates the exodus from Egypt, to occur after the event. But in Exodus, the very Israelites about to leave Egypt are also the first participants to celebrate the *remembrance* of leaving Egypt by following a prescribed ritual. (Exodus 12:48 even specifies who may partake in the Passover as if already in the land of Canaan.) Interestingly enough, later Jews who celebrate Passover read from a set liturgy (called the Haggadah) that includes a command that individuals are to celebrate as if they themselves came out of Egypt *this very night*. Thus time is collapsed in both directions in this ritual, in that those Israelites leaving Egypt act like later Jews celebrating Passover and later Jews celebrating Passover act as if they are ancient Israelites leaving slavery in Egypt. Furthermore, a very close analogue to this situation can be found in the origins of the Eucharist (or Holy Communion), in which Jesus self-consciously creates a ritual that he sees future Christians following. It should be noted that this ritual created by Jesus occurs at the Last Supper, a meal that several gospel writers place at Passover and which has traditionally been linked to its observance, even regarded by many Christians to replace it—Jesus himself becoming the sacrificial lamb (see 1 Corinthians 5:6-8).

Counting the Ten Commandments

Exodus 19–24 stand at the beginning of the very long central portion of the Torah that runs all the way from Exodus 19:1 to Numbers 10:10 dealing with Israel's time encamped at Mount Sinai. While the vast majority of the material from Genesis 1–Exodus 18 is narrative, the fact is that the Torah is in many ways primarily a law book. Therefore one should not be surprised that the story of God's revelation of his divine law to Israel features so prominently.

Exodus 20 contains the first recounting of the so-called Ten Commandments, words repeated a second time in Deuteronomy 5 in a slightly modified form. Although the term "Ten Commandments" is not incorrect conceptually, the Hebrew text (and Jewish tradition) refers to these as the "Ten Words" or "Ten Principles" or "Ten Utterances." There are at least three ways different religious groups count the Ten Commandments. According to Jewish tradition, the first "commandment" is really a statement, found in Exodus 20:2: "I am the Lord your God, who took you out of the land of Egypt, out of the house of slavery." The Protestant tradition, on the other hand, understands Exodus 20:2 to be a preface to the Ten Commandments, and the first command begins with Exodus 20:3. Other variations can be seen below.

While the Ten Commandments are specially marked out by the narrative framework of Exodus 20 and they contain several laws fundamental to human society, one must not lose sight of the fact that for ancient Israel all of the laws within Exodus 20–23, and even more broadly within the larger Pentateuch, are understood to be divinely revealed at Sinai and of utmost importance.

Comparison of the Ten Commandments in Judaism, Catholicism, and Protestantism			
Commandment	*Jewish*	*Catholic*	*Protestant*
I am the Lord your God	1		Preface
You shall have no other gods before me	2	1	1
You shall not make for yourself an idol			2
You shall not make wrongful use of the name of God	3	2	3
Remember the sabbath day, and keep it holy	4	3	4
Honor your father and your mother	5	4	5
You shall not murder	6	5	6
You shall not commit adultery	7	6	7
You shall not steal	8	7	8
You shall not bear false witness	9	8	9
You shall not covet your neighbor's wife	10	9	10
You shall not covet anything else of your neighbor		10	

Table 1.

Law, Community, and "Freedom" in Exodus

When one examines the array of laws in Exodus 21–23, a collection schol-ars call the Covenant Code, one finds many differing categories of law. There are of course criminal laws like the law against kidnapping found in Exodus 21:16, laws concerning civil matters such as the law about damages caused by leaving a pit open in Exodus 21:33-34, ritual laws like those concerning certain festivals discussed in Exodus 23:14-17, and even moral laws such as the com-mand in Exodus 23:4 to return the stray ox or donkey of one's enemy. From an Israelite perspective, all human behaviors, whether primarily involving God or primarily involving one's neighbor, are behaviors God has an interest in seeing performed properly. Furthermore, God issues these commandments to the community as a whole, and the whole community is held responsible for their observance. Therefore, when one wrongs one's neighbor, one also wrongs God and the larger community. Similarly, an offense against God is also an offense against one's neighbor that implicates the larger community.

The close link between the exodus story and God's giving of the commandments at Sinai affects one's understanding of the narrative as a whole. Many contemporary interpreters read the exodus event as a story about being brought from slavery into freedom. According to the story itself, however, the real issues relate to who Israel is, to whom they belong, and whom they will serve. The story describes a *change of ownership* in that it narrates Israel's movement from degrading bondage to Pharaoh, who claims to be a god but is simply an arrogant human being, to the humane serving of God, who in fact has a right to claim human beings as his slaves. That the Israelites are considered "God's slaves" is evident from passages like Leviticus 25:55, though this is often obscured because many translations render the Hebrew word for "slaves" as "servants." But unlike Israel's harsh enslavement by Pharaoh, Israel's service to God is an affirmation of life's highest possibilities, often characterized by the image of Israel peacefully resting in the Holy Land, the land that God shares with his chosen people, and God's blessing flowing outward and resulting in material and spiritual fulfillment for God's people and the larger world.

Jewish Use of Exodus

The story of God's redemption of the Israelites and his giving of the laws at Sinai remain at the center of postbiblical Judaism. As mentioned briefly above, the exodus events are retold at length in Jewish households on Passover Eve. But this is far from the only time they are mentioned. Jews recite the story of their redemption from Egypt multiple times a day in the daily prayer liturgy, and the liturgy of almost all Jewish holidays includes a reference to the exodus experience. In fact, the manual used on Passover, the Haggadah, at one point assimilates the many tribulations experienced by Jews over thousands of years to the exodus pattern of tribulation, which is followed by eventual divine redemption. This should not be surprising because already within the Jewish Bible itself the exodus is regularly invoked as the prime example of God's redemptive abilities and it is seen as a harbinger of God's future redemptive activities (Psalm 106; Isaiah 43). Furthermore, the very structure of the book of Exodus, which closely ties God's redemption of Israel from Egypt to her subsequent acceptance of God's laws at Sinai is key to Judaism's self-understanding and usefully illuminates the meaning of a number of important biblical commandments. Postbiblical Jewish tradition regularly emphasizes that freedom is not found in moving from slavery to personal autonomy, but, counterintuitively, in being placed under the yoke of God's commandments.

Christian Use of Exodus

There are many ways in which the Christian tradition has appropriated the book of Exodus and its story. We have mentioned above that Jesus came to be seen as the sacrificial lamb of the Passover, and we should also mention that Matthew 2 connects Jesus to Israel's history when it describes Jesus as God's son taken out of Egypt. Perhaps more important, as we discuss later in the book, in the New Testament Jesus is linked to Moses and in a sense he becomes a "Second Moses." This is seen especially in his giving of the "Sermon on the Mount" in Matthew 5–7, which might more appropriately be titled "The Torah on the Mount." What is interesting for our purposes is the story Christians call the "Transfiguration of Jesus," found in Matthew, Mark, and

Figure 10. Rafaello Morghen, after Rafaello Sanzio, *The Transfiguration*, 1811. Etching and engraving on paper. Jesus is depicted as elevated above Moses, left, who holds the tablets of the Law, and Elijah, right, who is holding the books of the Prophets. Courtesy Smith College Museum of Art, Northampton, Massachusetts (SC 1944:12-12).

Luke's gospels. Here Jesus ascends a mountain and is said to change form (or be "transfigured"); further, Jesus' face shines like Moses' did after he received the Torah in Exodus 34. What happens next is remarkable. Moses and Elijah, two figures seen to represent the full teachings of Judaism at the time through the Law and the Prophets, appear and are told—by God himself from clouds on the mountain—to "listen to him." In effect, the gospel writers are attempting to make clear that the teachings of Moses and Elijah (the Torah and the Prophets) are all subservient to Jesus and his teaching. Unfortunately, one negative side effect of this idea is the tendency to neglect or ignore the teachings of Moses rather than to read the Torah in the light of what Jesus taught.

Concluding Reflections

It is often assumed that ancient religious texts are inherently conservative and thus by nature they underwrite the status quo. But Exodus describes the story of a group of oppressed slaves who at God's call successfully challenge a very powerful socio-political system in the name of a higher divine order. Having been redeemed from Egypt and received the divine law at Sinai, Israel set about building the portable tent-shrine, which in some way created a movable Mount Sinai, allowing Israel to live in close proximity to God's presence perpetually. But, as we will see, living so close to God required that Israel maintain a very high level of ritual, ethical, and moral purity. It is these issues that are taken up in the next book, Leviticus, to which we now turn.

LEVITICUS

Introduction and Overview

Leviticus is the third book of the Pentateuch and thus sits at the very center of the Torah. Its English name is derived from *Liber Leviticus*, a Latinized version of the Septuagint's Greek name for the book, *leuitikon biblion*. Both mean "book of the Levites." In time the book came to be known simply as *Leviticus*, meaning, "pertaining to the Levites." Jews traditionally call the book *Vayikrah*, "And he spoke" or possibly "And he called," after the first Hebrew word of Leviticus, which tells us that God spoke to Moses from the Tent of Meeting. It is more aptly titled in early rabbinic texts as *Torat Kohanim*, "the Priestly Torah."

Leviticus can be divided into two main blocks, chapters 1–16, (which scholars call the Priestly Code), and chapters 17–26, (referred to as the Holiness Code). There is also an appendix of additional laws found in chapter 27. Chapters 1–7 give detailed information on various sacrificial procedures. Chapters 8–10 describe the inauguration of the sanctuary and the opening sacrificial service. Despite its legal nature, the book does contain occasional narrative asides, such as that found in Leviticus 10:1-11, which relates a story about how a breach in the sacrificial procedures resulted in the death of two of Aaron's sons. Leviticus 11–16 deals with many different types of ritual impurities and touches on a host of topics including: food laws that describe pure and impure animals (chapter 11), rules surrounding the ritual impurity that accompanies childbirth (chapter 12), ritual treatment of skin diseases (chapters 13–14), and regulations for normal and abnormal genital discharges (chapter 15). This section concludes with instruction on the yearly Yom Kippur (Day of Atonement) procedures that occupy all of chapter 16. This most sacred day in Israel's calendar is dedicated to ritually cleansing the sanctuary and removing any sins of the Israelites that were not properly atoned for previously.

The Holiness Code begins in chapter 17 with rules surrounding the consumption of meat. Leviticus 18 and 20 focus mainly upon illicit sexual unions. Leviticus 19, the heart of the Holiness Code, contains a rich array of ritual and ethical commandments designed to help Israel maintain a holy state. Leviticus 21–22 discusses who may conduct priestly duties and some general rules surrounding these duties. Chapter 23 contains the yearly liturgical calendar and gives a brief description of each sacred occasion. Of note is that the weekly Sabbath is given pride of place as the first holiday in the yearly cycle. Chapter 24 is a hodgepodge of various laws, including the rules surrounding the Menorah (or oil lamp) and the showbread (loaves of bread set out once a week in the sanctuary), as well as a short narrative that leads to a new law on blasphemy. It concludes with some general reflections that stress the principle of equality before the law.

Leviticus 25 explains rules surrounding the sabbatical and Jubilee years, which call for the land to rest every seventh year and the return of all lands to their original familial owners every fiftieth year, respectively. Chapter 26, in a manner similar to Deuteronomy 27–28, lists the blessings and penalties Israel will experience based on the people's response to God's instruction. Finally, chapter 27 is an appendix of laws providing guidance on how one might buy back sacred gifts that were previously donated to the sanctuary.

Controversies and Debates

The study of Leviticus has been significantly affected by the work of a prominent twentieth century British anthropologist, Mary Douglas (1921–2007). Her work on purity, danger, ritual, and taboo was groundbreaking. Her theories developed over time (and were modified) but, among other things, she argued that distinctions in Leviticus regarding purity and pollution are not simply primitive superstitions but rather reveal a complex, ordered system reflecting larger ethical and societal norms. For example, Douglas rejected the widespread idea that the distinctions between clean and unclean animals in Leviticus were arbitrary. These distinctions, according to Douglas, reinforce the created order as reflected in Genesis 1, a text which scholars believe comes from the same Priestly authors who produced Leviticus 1–16 (P). In P's view, only animals that fully conform to one of the three realms of creation—sky, land, and sea—are fit for Israelite consumption. As Douglas makes clear, this is because there is a direct correlation between P's conception of holiness and the idea of wholeness. To maintain holiness not only must one avoid unethical behaviors but also one must not consume things that are viewed as unwholesome. Thus one avoids eating animals like a pig because pigs do not exhibit all the characteristics of exemplary four-footed domestic land animals, in that unlike cows and sheep they do not chew their cud. As Douglas notes in her book *Purity and Danger*, "The dietary laws would have been like signs which at every turn inspired meditation on the oneness, purity and completeness of God. By rules of avoidance holiness was given a physical expression in every encounter with the animal kingdom and at every meal" ([New York: Routledge, 2005], 71).

Another issue related to the study of Leviticus is that of composition. Contemporary scholars attribute the two large blocks of Leviticus to distinct sources, both of which belong to a larger Priestly school of writers. Because of the strong holiness language and ethos of chapters 17–26, scholars now speak of this material as a unified block that they call the "Holiness Code" (or "H" for short). The other main section, the Priestly Code (Leviticus 1–16), is generally considered to be penned by the same writer (or writers) of the other P material in the Pentateuch.

The Inseparability of Ethics and Ritual

Almost everyone has heard the injunction, "You shall love your neighbor as yourself." However, many people seem unaware that Jesus, who uses this saying in the Gospels, is in fact quoting from Leviticus 19:18. Fewer still are aware of the larger context of Leviticus 19 in which this passage sits. Leviticus 19 opens with a miniature version of the Ten Commandments: respecting one's parents, keeping the Sabbath, and not worshiping idols (verses 1-4). After some general sacrificial rules (verses 5-8), the passage turns to a number of social issues such as: feeding the poor (verses 9-10), not stealing or lying, not swearing falsely (verse 12), the strong not oppressing the weak and vulnerable (verses 13-14), rendering even-handed justice to all (verse 15), and not slandering one's fellow Israelites (verse 16). Most interesting is that the immediate context of verses 17-18 on loving one's neighbor speaks of the necessity of reproving a neighbor who is acting wrongly even while not taking revenge against him. Clearly the word "love" in this passage is communicating something more akin to proper treatment of one's fellow citizens than some type of emotion. The emphasis on tactfully reproving a wayward fellow citizen is a far cry from the now widespread idea that loving one's neighbors means not judging them but rather accepting them as they are. It should be noted that the same concern for reproving one's neighbor occurs in the New Testament (Matthew 18:15-20).

The unusual mixture of ritual, moral, and criminal laws found here—unusual at least to our contemporary sensibilities—continues throughout the rest of Leviticus 19, fleshing out the complexity of the concept of holiness in the Hebrew Bible stressed in the chapter's opening verses. Westerners tend to highlight ethics over ritual and view religion as a matter of personal preference. However, Leviticus conceptualizes holiness as a unity of proper ethical *and* ritual conduct, and it does not see religion as a private matter (that is, between each individual and God). Much the same can be said about the New Testament, in which the communal dimensions of religious life are stressed (see, for example, 1 Corinthians 11–14). The priestly authors of Leviticus 19 as well as other major streams of biblical theology envision life as an ongoing encounter between the sacred community and the divine, and an individual who sins against God also offends and harms his or her community. In Leviticus, religion pervades all domains of life rather than being confined to the private sphere as it frequently is in the modern West.

Oppressive Hierarchies or Orders of Holiness?

Levitical texts are sometimes seen as hegemonic because they presume certain hierarchies between differing groups of Israelites, between various geographical places, as well as between Israel and other nations. However, viewing the carefully ordered holiness structure of Leviticus as hegemonic is too simplistic. Many would suggest that P, and even more so H, did a great deal to ensure that various theological ideas were understood and applied broadly, and without distinction. The fact that Leviticus 19 begins with a call for *all the congregation of the people of Israel* to be holy as God is holy suggests a bold attempt to make Israel a nation of priests. Now every Israelite must maintain not only a higher level of ritual purity but also higher standards of behavior toward each other because they live in close proximity to the divine presence. In some sense each member of Israel helps mediate the divine to the larger world, a world composed of the other peoples and nations who are held to a lower standard. However, if certain resident aliens wished to participate in living near and helping to mediate the divine, the Priestly writers make space for such individuals if they are willing to abide by Israel's ritual rules (Exodus 12:48-49 and Leviticus 19:33-34).

Hebrew Matters: The Meaning of Purity in Leviticus

Throughout much of Leviticus and in particular in chapters 11–16, the discussion centers on questions of purity and impurity. The terms *purity* and *impurity* carry connotations in English that at times interfere with understanding how these terms function in certain biblical passages. In English, when one hears someone or something labeled as impure, it often implies that they are of less worth or even sinful or immoral. Thus when we as contemporary readers learn that Leviticus 15 considers a menstruating woman impure, we often bristle and reply that this is a perfectly natural process. Why should something that occurs naturally make one impure?

There is now a growing consensus that within Leviticus 11–16 the terms pure (*tahor*) and impure (*tamay*) are used in a strictly ritual sense to describe passing bodily states. In this view all humans at times experience life events that make them temporarily impure ritually (not ethically) and ritual procedures are put into place to bring them back to a state of purity. One sees this more clearly when one examines the context surrounding the menstrual laws in Leviticus 15:19-24, a passage discussed below.

The laws in Leviticus concerning what is clean and unclean range from the general to the more specific. To give a taste of some of these laws, we will examine Leviticus 15. This chapter presents five pieces of legislation dealing with various bodily emissions arranged in an orderly fashion. Leviticus 15:1-15 begins with the case of a man who has an abnormal genital discharge and then verses 16-17 regulate what is to occur if a man has a nocturnal emission, an event the text seems to view as quite natural. Leviticus 15:18 discusses the impurity that arises from sexual intercourse between a man and a woman. It should be noted that not only is such sexual contact viewed as normal, but it is divinely ordained, especially when we consider that according to P, God's first command to humans in Genesis 1 is to be fruitful and multiply. Leviticus 15:19-24 discusses the ritual rules surrounding menstruation, also a completely natural event; although one that women in antiquity experienced with less frequency than women in the modern West due to the larger numbers of pregnancies, the longer length of nursing time, and the less-protein-rich diets such women experienced in their lives. Leviticus 15:25-30 then turns to irregular female genital flows and the chapter finishes with a summary statement. The fact that one becomes impure through normal intercourse or menstruation demonstrates that, for this literature, becoming impure is not to be equated with committing a sin or being an inferior person. According to Leviticus 15, becoming impure is not a problem but rather something that occurs periodically throughout one's life. What is considered a sin is failing to observe the rules of impurity and the rituals that move one back to purity.

A Matter of Life and Death

One might still ask, however: If these laws are not aimed at identifying sinners, then what are they about? States of impurity symbolize a fracture in the fabric of an ideal, ordered life. The most likely explanation for many of the laws found in Leviticus 12–15 is that they are attempting to rectify various symbolic encounters with death. In ancient Israel death and life were seen as existing on a continuum and in a certain sense death represented a significantly diminished form of life. In turn, certain types of sicknesses that diminished one's quality of life were seen as a form of death. This explains why according to Leviticus 13–14 one who experiences a severe skin disease becomes impure, and it also explains why a male or a female who has an abnormal genital discharge is impure. Those who suffer from these conditions are living a diminished life.

Now one might ask: Well, why do a normal seminal emission, normal menstruation, and normal sexual intercourse make one impure? The answer appears to be that although these are natural bodily functions, they still symbolize an encounter with death. This is most obvious in the case of menstruation, which, when it occurs, indicates a lost chance at a potential pregnancy and thus a new life. The logic is likely the same for a nocturnal emission in that it too is a lost chance to procreate. Concerning intercourse, it is possible that ejaculation was perceived to bring about a waning in the male life force, bringing the male participant closer to death.

Concluding Reflections: Leviticus in Judaism and Christianity

Leviticus is much more than an obscure manual for ancient Israelite priests. This short book that sits at the center of the Torah has had immense influence on later Jewish and Christian religious practice. Thus, for example, observant Jews today still keep the food laws found in Leviticus 11 and observant Jewish women still maintain the rules surrounding menstrual impurity. And even though sacrifices cannot be offered in the absence of the Jerusalem temple, the traditional Jewish daily and Sabbath prayers include excerpts of the biblical rules of sacrifice that function as a symbolic form of sacrifice. While Christians no longer mark the yearly "Day of Atonement," they preserve its logic in affirming that such a day is thought to have taken place in an intensified and final manner in Jesus' sacrificial death, which functions to remove the sins of the human family forever (for more, see Hebrews 9). One can see the deep imprint that Leviticus has left on both Judaism and Christianity in the distinct ways adherents of both religious groups seek to imbue everyday life with holiness and to create a holy community in which God can dwell.

NUMBERS

Introduction and Overview

Numbers, the fourth book in the Pentateuch, derives its name from the Greek Septuagint, where it is called *Arithmoi*. This term was picked up by Jerome in his Latin Vulgate, where he calls it *Numeri*. The title likely came about due to the fact that Numbers contains two detailed census lists of the twelve tribes of Israel, one in chapter 1 and another in chapter 26. The title for the book in Jewish tradition, *Bemidbar*, or "In the Wilderness," is derived from the fifth word in Numbers 1:1. This title may capture the content of this book more adequately, inasmuch as the events of the book take place during Israel's forty-year desert sojourn.

Numbers continues the story of Israel after the people receive the detailed legal instruction found in Leviticus. By the end of Numbers, the leader, Moses, is prepared to be replaced by Joshua, and a new generation is ready to enter the promised land. The stage is thus set for Deuteronomy, Moses' parting words to Israel before they cross the Jordan River into Canaan.

Controversies and Debates

On a surface reading, it could indeed seem that Numbers is not terribly coherent. Unlike the narrative material of Genesis and much of Exodus, and the legal material in Leviticus, Numbers contains a variety of genres and materials all brought together into one whole. We find two detailed census lists; narrative materials regarding Israel's journey; details on priestly duties; a peculiar test for adultery; discussion on who speaks for God and the nature of prophecy; a story of sibling rivalry and unhealthy in-law relations; instructions for Passover; a lengthy, seemingly out-of-place story regarding a foreign seer; laws for life in Canaan, and so on. One might be tempted to call it the "junk-drawer" of the Bible, that is, a book like that one drawer in many people's houses where they put things they otherwise don't know where to store.

However, various intriguing proposals suggest this book is more unified than once imagined. One recent proposal argues that the book can be divided according to the locations where the action takes place. In this geographically oriented scheme, Numbers 1:1–10:10 occurs at Mount Sinai, thus linking the first section of the book with the material in Leviticus and the second half of Exodus. The second section, Numbers 10:11–20:13 chronicles Israel's journey from Sinai to Kadesh (an area believed to be north of Sinai, at which Israel spent much of her time in the wilderness). Finally, Numbers 20:14 to the conclusion of the book covers the movement from Kadesh to the plains of Moab (an area immediately north of the Dead Sea, east of the Jordan River), and describes the first stages of Israel's conquest of Canaan, which involves taking certain lands east of the Jordan.

Another way to divide the book is into two halves, based on the placement of the two census lists. In this model, the first census and what follows (chapters 1–25) contain the actions of the rebellious generation of Israelites, who all, apart from Caleb and Joshua, end up dying in the wilderness. The second census list in Numbers 26 follows, and it begins something of a new section (26–36) that deals with the next generation of Israelites, who are generally portrayed as obedient and faithful as they initiate the process of conquering the land of Canaan. These proposals need not be mutually exclusive, and each suggests that the book was woven together with some care.

A completely different sort of problem raised by the book of Numbers concerns the very large numbers of Israelites that the text reports left Egypt. The difficulty is that Numbers indicates some 2 million Israelites leaving Egypt. Archaeological records indicate that Egypt's army around this time would likely have only had approximately 20,000 men, a force that the 600,000 Israelite soldiers that Numbers 1:46 counts could have easily overpowered. To put matters in perspective, even conservative scholars admit that 2 million people leaving Egypt would entail, based on the land's geography, a line of people that would extend over one hundred miles long.

Some scholars suggest that the numbers are hyperbolic or superlative in order to stress Israel's divine blessing. Alternatively, according to other scholars, the Hebrew word *eleph*, used to indicate 1,000, could instead represent military or family units, thus bringing the number down to approximately 6,000 soldiers or 20,000 Israelites total. Such numbers would be more in line with population estimates for the ancient Near East at the time.

Narratives at the Heart of Numbers: Complaints, Strife, and Who Speaks for God

At the core of this book stand a number of compelling but less widely known stories. In Numbers 11 one finds a retelling of the manna and quails stories, which were first reported in Exodus 16 when Israel had just come out of Egypt. However, in Exodus 16 the manna story is lengthy and the quails are mentioned in passing; further, generally speaking the tale has a happy ending. Here in Numbers, however, the quail story is told in much greater detail and it now concludes with a punishment. These paired stories are part of a larger cycle of complaint that animates some of Exodus and much of Numbers. Within this story in Numbers, a separate narrative strand relates how the overburdened Moses, after complaining to God, is permitted to distribute his charismatic authority to a wider group of seventy tribal elders.

The theme of Moses' authority is taken up once again in Numbers 12, which recounts how Miriam and Aaron spoke against their brother Moses, and were reprimanded with Miriam receiving a severe, near deadly punishment. This chapter contains one of the clearest statements in the Torah of Moses' unique prophetic status in that Moses hears God through direct divine-human speech; however, the text also specifies that God extends lesser gifts of prophecy to others via dreams and visions. The theme of "who speaks for God" is revisited again in Number 16–17 as well as in the so-called book of Balaam, Numbers 22–24.

Numbers 13–14 is certainly one of the most memorable narratives in the book. This passage recounts how God commanded the Israelites to send spies (or scouts) into Canaan and how these spies, apart from Caleb and Joshua, brought back a negative report that led the Israelites to reject God's command to take possession of what would become the land of Israel. In turn, God once more considered destroying the Israelites and starting over by building a new nation from Moses and his future descendants. Moses, in a heroic act of intercession similar to Exodus 32–34, is able to convince God to relent and refrain from wiping Israel out completely. However, in this case, unlike in Exodus, the rebellious generation is condemned to die in the wilderness and would therefore not see the land they refused to go up and conquer. This, according to Numbers, is the reason for the Israelites' extended stay in the desert, lasting for forty years. However, alternative explanations for Israel's forty years in the wilderness are offered elsewhere in the Bible.

Chapters 16–17 contain yet another pair of intertwined stories of distrust and rebellion. One storyline involves Dathan and Abiram who challenge

Moses' authority once more, and the other strand tells the story of Korah and two hundred and fifty Levites who question the special status of Aaron. The theme of a distrustful and rebellious people steadily grows in these chapters.

Numbers 20 and 21 narrate several loosely related stories mainly about the transition between generations and the beginnings of the conquest of the land of Canaan. Chapter 20 begins with Miriam's death and then tells another story of rebellion, in which an explanation is given as to why God did not permit Moses to enter the promised land. Moses himself, like his generation, seems to rebel and usurp God's power in an episode in which he strikes a rock with his staff to find water, though the specifics of his offence are unclear. This story eventually ends with Aaron's death.

Numbers 22–24 recounts the story of Balak, the King of Moab, who hires a professional diviner named Balaam to put a hex on the people of Israel. This highly entertaining story, which includes a talking donkey, relates how Balak's attempt to curse Israel is unsuccessful. And, as mentioned, it picks up the theme of prophecy and divine speech through its continual references to only speaking that which Israel's God permits. In the end, Balaam delivers some of the most profound blessings and prophecies concerning the Israelites found anywhere in Scripture. It is remarkable not only that such words come from a non-Israelite, but that this non-Israelite later becomes one of the most reviled characters in later Jewish and Christian texts (see for example 2 Peter 2:15-16 and Revelation 2:14).

A New Generation: Numbers 26–36

Chapter 26 contains the second census list in this book, which, after cataloguing its precise numbers, makes clear that apart from Caleb and Joshua (the faithful spies): "among these there was not one of those enrolled by Moses and Aaron the priest, who had enrolled the Israelites in the wilderness of Sinai" (Numbers 26:64). The reason? That generation "shall die in the wilderness" as decreed by God (Numbers 26:65). From a logistical point of view such an idea is unlikely, in that generations do not start and stop every forty years. It is remarkable that unlike the former generation—which was marked by punishment and death—there is not one Israelite death reported in the rest of Numbers. And, contrary to the former generation that murmured and rebelled continually, this new generation is one that does not complain but rather negotiates with Moses and God to find solutions that suit all parties involved. Clearly there is a transition from a sinful to an obedient generation.

Women's Voices in the Bible

There have been many recent attempts to present fuller and more complex treatments of women in the Bible through reexamining texts that have been underemphasized or unnoticed in the past. In the story of the daughters of Zelophehad found in Numbers 27, it is noteworthy that although ancient convention would have resisted women speaking out publicly against their leaders, the daughters of Zelophehad here do exactly that and demand that their father's property be given to them. Moses presents their case to God and God takes their side. While it is sometimes asserted that the Torah is a document produced by men for men, the actions of these women testify to the fact that women's voices are not only present in the Torah, but at times were instrumental in shaping the biblical legal tradition.

Jewish Use of Numbers

There are many places where Numbers has left an imprint on Jewish life and liturgy. One thinks, for example, of the priestly blessing found in Numbers 6:22-27, a prayer whose significance is readily apparent from the fact that, as mentioned earlier, our oldest known fragment of a biblical text is of this passage, in the form of an amulet. This prayer is invoked by parents when blessing their children each week at the Sabbath eve meal. And in Orthodox settings it is still chanted by those of priestly lineage on certain religious occasions. In fact, when priests say this blessing formally, they split their fingers apart to form the Hebrew letter *shin*, the first letter of one of God's names, *Shaddai*, often translated as *God Almighty*. This particular hand motion (see image below) is now widely recognized because Mr. Spock on *Star Trek* used it in slightly modified form as the Vulcan greeting gesture.

Figure 11. The traditional hand-gesture made by Jewish priests upon blessing the people, as seen on the doors of the Alte Synagogue in Essen, Germany. Courtesy Aaron Olaf Batty.

Numbers 15:37-41 has also left a deep imprint on Jewish life and liturgy. This text, recited as the third paragraph in the *Shema* (the central Jewish prayer that begins "Hear, O' Israel" discussed in detail in the following chapter on Deuteronomy), contains the commandment to make fringes on one's garment. Jews today continue to wear a tasseled prayer shawl or *Tallit* during morning prayer services, and observant Jewish men wear an undergarment called a *tallit katan*, or *tzitzit*, that has fringes on its four corners.

Figure 12. Example of a tallit, worn here in prayer at the Western Wall in Jerusalem. The partially visible object on the man's forehead is a phylactery (or *tefillin*), a small box containing verses from the Torah traditionally worn by men during weekday morning services. Courtesy Dan Blumenthal.

Christian Use of Numbers

One very interesting use of Numbers in the New Testament stands out—that of Jesus and the bronze seraph, a model of a snakelike, winged angelic being, which Moses crafted at God's instruction in Numbers 21. John 3:16, perhaps the most famous passage of the New Testament, is prefaced by words that use an analogy to depict Jesus as the snake that was lifted up:

And just as Moses lifted up the serpent in the wilderness, so must the Son of Man be lifted up, that whoever believes in him may have eternal life. (John 3:14-15)

85

It is worth noting that although serpents generally are viewed negatively in the Jewish and Christian traditions, it is not the case here. Of course, here Jesus is seen not so much as a normal snake but as the angelic *seraph*, which was raised and healed those Israelites that looked up to it. Early church fathers interpret the Numbers passage in light of John's Gospel reading. Justin Martyr (100–165 CE), for example, asks why God would instruct Moses to violate the Torah's commandment not to make a graven image of anything in the heavens above or on the earth below. Justin suggests that Moses was to do so because he is announcing the great mystery of the one (Jesus) who would come to break the power of the serpent, and thus the sin that came through Adam.

Concluding Reflections

Despite looking like a mishmash of stories, laws, prophecies, instructions, and other tidbits of information, the recurring themes of the deterioration of trust and rebellion in the first twenty-five chapters and trust and negotiation in the final chapters (27–36) unify the book. Each section begins with a census, and both generations, wicked and good, are the ancestors of Israel, and thus the foreparents of contemporary Jews and Christians. The message of Numbers is to avoid the pitfalls of the past and walk in the ways of those who have learned to trust and obey.

DEUTERONOMY

Introduction and Overview

Deuteronomy is the fifth and final book of the Torah. Its English name comes from the Vulgate, the Latin translation made by Jerome, and literally means the "second law" (*deuteros nomos*). While this is somewhat accurate in that Deuteronomy contains a second telling of many laws given earlier in the Torah, the exact phrase is drawn from Jerome's rather wooden rendering of an expression found in Deuteronomy 17:18, *mishneh hatorah*, which might be better translated "copy of the law." Jews traditionally call the book *Devarim*, "words," after the second Hebrew word of Deuteronomy 1:1.

Deuteronomy can be divided into four main sections: (1) an extended recital of the events that Israel experienced during Moses' lifetime that runs from chapters 1–11; (2) a large block of legal materials that occupies chapters 12–26; (3) a set of blessings and curses found in chapters 27–28, which are pronounced upon those who will observe or disobey the commandments; and (4) some final instructions and poems from Moses that foretell the future and report Moses' death (chapters 29–34). From a narrative perspective, Deuteronomy might best be viewed as Moses' last will and testament to his people Israel. In a way unlike the rest of the Torah, Deuteronomy reads as if it is one long speech, or sermon, from the mouth of Moses prior to his death and Israel's entering Canaan. Some have called it Moses' farewell speech.

Controversies and Debates

Almost all modern biblical scholars believe that Deuteronomy contains a unique vocabulary that can be traced to a school of thinkers responsible for the religious reform of Judah in the late seventh century BCE. It is believed that the book supposedly discovered in the Jerusalem temple during Josiah's reign (640–609 BCE) contained some form of Deuteronomy (see 2 Kings 22–23 for the fuller story). So, although the book is framed as the last will and testament of Moses, much of its content actually addresses Israelite life in seventh century BCE Judah.

Another important scholarly debate surrounding Deuteronomy centers on the discovery and translation of various ancient Near Eastern treaties in which certain emperors laid out the terms of their relationship to smaller powers. Scholars refer to these as suzerainty-vassal treaties. There is general agreement that the overarching structure of Deuteronomy resembles patterns found in these Near Eastern treaties. It seems that when Israel looked for language to express her relationship to God, her sovereign, she borrowed models from the wider Near Eastern diplomatic realm.

Deuteronomy and Ancient Near Eastern Treaties

In the middle of the twentieth century, a number of scholars began to argue that Deuteronomy shares much in common with treaty documents of the ancient Near East, particularly Hittite (an empire located in Asia Minor, or today's Turkey) suzerainty-vassal treaties of the fourteenth century BCE. These treaties follow a relatively fixed format and read like ancient legal documents. They typically (1) introduce the parties involved, (2) give the historical background of their relationship, (3) list the conditions of the treaty, (4) explain the terms for the public reading and storing of the document, (5) include a call for witnesses (often divinities), and (6) conclude with blessings and curses, based on each party's compliance or failure to comply with the conditions.

Some assert that Deuteronomy followed the Hittite conventions so closely that the book should be viewed as contemporary to the Hittite documents. This would place the authorship of Deuteronomy firmly in the mid-second millennium BCE, or generally in the time when Moses would have walked the earth. Deuteronomy can thus be divided in a manner that correlates the book's format to that found in these ancient treaties:

Hittite Suzerainty-Vassal Treaties	Deuteronomy
1. Introduction / Preamble	Deuteronomy 1:1-5
2. Historical Background	Deuteronomy 1:6–3:29
3. Conditions / Stipulations	Deuteronomy 4-26

4. Publication / Public reading	Deuteronomy 27:1-10; 31:9-13
5. Divine / Other Witnesses	Deuteronomy 30:15-20; 31:19-22
6. Blessing and Curse Formula	Deuteronomy 28

Table 2.

However, the analogies drawn between Deuteronomy and these Hittite treaties are sometimes forced or inexact, and it is of no real surprise that the strongest arguments along these lines came from those with religious motivation to "prove" that Moses authored the Pentateuch. Many today find the parallels to be less convincing than originally proposed. Some have argued that the language, phrasing, and treaty format of Deuteronomy resembles other, later documents such as the seventh-century BCE Assyrian state treaties of Esarhaddon. Still, there is broad agreement that in Deuteronomy, Israel expressed her formal relationship to God in terms drawn from the wider Near Eastern political realm. While today many politicians invoke religious language in their speeches, here we see the appropriation of ideas drawn from the political realm to express a religious concept.

Hebrew Matters: What Does the Most Important Passage in the Bible Mean?

No other passage in the Bible, whether Jewish Tanakh or the two-Testament Christian Bible, can rightly claim to have the significance and influence that Deuteronomy 6:4-9 does. Not only have these words been repeated each morning and evening by observant Jews for millennia, but when Jesus was asked what the most important commandment is, he immediately quoted from this passage (see Matthew 22:34-40; Mark 12:28-31). Our concern here, however, involves the Hebrew of the *Shema*, and it is remarkable that a centerpiece of Jewish and Christian theology is not straightforward, but ambiguous, in meaning.

Leaving aside debates as to where the *Shema* ends, there is little question that its central teaching is contained in the first statement: "Hear, O Israel, The LORD is our God, the LORD alone." The problem is that although the first two words are clear (*shema yisrael*; "Hear, O Israel"), the following four words are not: *YHWH eloheinu, YHWH echad* (pronounced in Jewish prayer as *adonai eloheinu, adonai echad*). Quite literally, the words translate: "YHWH our-God, YHWH one [or alone]." The ambiguity arises here because in Hebrew, as in other ancient languages, the relationship between subject and predicate is often implied rather than stated. It is unclear, therefore, where the reader or translator should insert the word "is." There are four main options, as listed in the footnotes of many Bibles:

1. The LORD our God, the LORD is one. (NIV)

2. The LORD is our God, the LORD alone. (NRSV, NJPS) [or similarly,] Our God is the LORD! Only the LORD! (CEB)

3. The LORD our God is one LORD. (KJV)

4. The LORD is our God, the LORD is one! (NASB)

We will not resolve this translational difficulty here; rather, our aim is to highlight just how different each of these grammatically acceptable translations is. In option one, the nature of God is stressed, in that it teaches us that Israel's God, YHWH, is "one" (or perhaps "unique" or of "one essence"). The second option stresses a relationship, one that is exclusive: *YHWH* is Israel's God and no one else. The third option may seem strained, though in antiquity it was common for a deity to be associated with various locales, thus making it possible for there to be many YHWHs. This translation clears away any debate; there is only one YHWH, not many. The fourth translation provides a combination of options one and two, stressing both the nature of God (YHWH is one) and the idea that *he* (not another) is Israel's God.

This important passage has had a tremendous influence on Judaism and Christianity, and it has contributed to each tradition's understanding of God and the issue of whether monolatry or monotheism best describes Israel's religious outlook. Perhaps part of the attraction and intrigue of this passage is its potential multiple meanings. It is not out of character for Judaism and Christianity to have a central teaching with a meaning that can be debated.

Retelling Israel's Law: Deuteronomy 12–26

There is a vast array of legislation in this block of material, some of it reinforcing or slightly modifying legal materials found elsewhere in the Torah, some of it strongly challenging or even overturning certain legal precedents, and some of it found only here and nowhere else. There are a number of important legislative innovations that we will touch on in our discussion, including what one might call early environmental legislation and changes in the law, making Israelite worship and society more egalitarian.

Why Retell the Torah?

An obvious question comes to mind, especially when we read texts like the Ten Commandments in Deuteronomy 5—virtually a verbatim retelling of Exodus 20—and the laws of Deuteronomy 12–26, many of which overlap with laws found in Exodus 21–23 and in Leviticus. Why retell these laws? Why a "*deuteros-nomos*" (second-law)? One suggestion is that the Torah must be renegotiated with each new generation. As argued in our chapter on Numbers, there is an emphasis on a new generation of Israelites, those who will enter the land, and they need to commit to the covenant as their parents did at Sinai back in Exodus 19–24. Deuteronomy 5:3 drives this point home in an interesting way when it refuses to allow time to advance; it states that God gave the Torah *to this very people*, even though it is clear that the people hearing these words are a new generation that was not present at Horeb. In learning to negotiate its teachings, each new generation must commit to it actively. The long stream of rabbinic teaching on the Torah testifies to this principle as well.

In terms of unique materials, one of the most unusual types of laws found in Deuteronomy 12–26 is what might be termed early environmental legislation. Deuteronomy 20:19-20 prohibits the unnecessary destruction of the natural environment during warfare, and 22:6-7 prohibits the taking of a mother bird along with her young or eggs. The latter was likely put in place to prevent the total decimation of an animal population.

An example of reinforcing a preexisting law with slight modifications can be found in the prohibitions surrounding the planting of mixed grains in one field, plowing with two different animals, and wearing of mixed garments. These are all mentioned in Leviticus 19:19 in very terse form. Deuteronomy 22:9-11 appears to fill out these rules by applying them not only to grain fields but to vineyards as well, by further noting that plowing with two differing animals applies specifically to yoking an ox and donkey together, and by specifying that wearing mixed garments is limited to a wool and linen combination. It is difficult to know if Deuteronomy is changing the legislation found in Leviticus or is simply repeating the laws found in this part of Leviticus in fuller form but in full agreement with the original intent of Leviticus.

There are indeed examples in which Deuteronomy rather radically changes certain laws found elsewhere in the Torah. Thus Deuteronomy 14:21 permits an Israelite to sell meat to a resident alien from an animal that died of natural causes rather than from being purposefully slaughtered. This law conflicts with Leviticus 17:15 which requires resident aliens (just like Israelites) to avoid ingesting meat from animals that died on their own or, if they do eat such meat, to engage in a purification ritual normally reserved for Israelites alone.

Is Deuteronomy More Egalitarian?

In looking at Deuteronomy's various retellings of laws also found in Exodus, some have noticed a pattern toward, among other things, more egalitarian modes of life and worship. Two examples stand out. The first involves the release of Hebrew slaves. In antiquity, a person who owed a debt to another but could not repay it might sell himself or herself (or a son or daughter) into "debt slavery." This was often regulated so that it was not abused, but it is interesting that the once preferential treatment of male slaves is adjusted in Deuteronomy to include women. Deuteronomy 15:12-17, for instance, rewrites Exodus 21:2-7 to include the release of female Hebrew slaves after six years, which was formerly only possible for males. The second example involves male and female participation in religious feasts. Deuteronomy 16:13-15 appears to rewrite Exodus 23:17 by mentioning women and female slaves, therefore permitting female participation in three important festivals, the Feast of Unleavened Bread, The Feast of Weeks, and the Feast of Booths. Perhaps the most obvious move toward greater egalitarianism is that of Deuteronomy 14–15, which, unlike the Priestly text of Numbers 18, sees tithes and the offering of firstborn animals as something to be enjoyed by all Israelites rather than items that go exclusively to priests and Levites.

The Theme of Oneness in Deuteronomy

A recurring theme within the book of Deuteronomy is that of oneness. We have already discussed the *Shema*, the central teaching of Deuteronomy that YHWH, Israel's God, is one, and we noted its importance within Jewish life and prayer as well as the fact that it was not infrequently on the lips of Jews who were martyred. However, there is more to the theme of oneness in Deuteronomy than is communicated in this single passage. Yes, God is one, God is unique, but oneness in Deuteronomy may be seen in at least three other important ways.

The first theme of oneness relates to Israel. According to Deuteronomy 7:6, this people is like no other on the face of the earth, because Israel is chosen by God to be God's treasured possession. The theme of election, the idea that God chose Israel, is developed in Deuteronomy in important ways through its novel and regular use of the Hebrew word *bachar*, meaning "he chose." Deuteronomy is careful to specify, however, that Israel's status is *not* due to an inherent moral quality Israel possesses but rather rests purely upon God's love for the Patriarchs and their descendants through Jacob, that is, the people of Israel.

There is also the theme of oneness with regard to the land that Israel will possess; it is considered to be an abundantly good land, a unique land, *the* land that has been promised to Israel as an eternal possession. As a subset of this specific theme, Deuteronomy also places great emphasis on the one "place the LORD your God shall choose," a place designated in the land in which God will "put his name" and Israel will worship. It seems clear that this refers to the Jerusalem temple, but the authors do not indicate the exact location, possibly in order to guard against obvious anachronism or perhaps to ease tensions between the rival territories of Judah and Israel over which city, Jerusalem or Samaria, was the specified place.

Finally, there is also a strong sense in Deuteronomy that the teachings given by Moses, this Torah itself, constitute a unique law code that, when enacted, will provide for a good and abundant life, perhaps even leading other nations to recognize the power of Israel's God as suggested in Deuteronomy 4:5-8. It is implied that there are no teachings or law code like it. It is truly the one Torah and when followed, the people will live and worship in the one true way.

The result is remarkable: One God, One People, One Land, One Place, One Torah, One Way. This overarching sense of oneness is attested to on every page of Deuteronomy. This multifaceted theme established in Deuteronomy comes to animate the rest of the Bible.

Concluding Reflections

Deuteronomy ends the Torah, but it is really also a book of beginnings. In the next section we will discuss what scholars call the Deuteronomistic History, and there is debate about whether Deuteronomy should belong to the Torah or the books that follow. In some ways this points to the fact that the authors of Deuteronomy, and those who shaped the rest of the Hebrew Bible, were skillful in their work. They wove together a collection of writings that became closely linked and cannot be separated. Deuteronomy stands together with the rest of the Bible in important ways.

INTRODUCTION TO THE PROPHETS

The Prophets section of the Hebrew Bible is normally divided into two large subsections called the Former and Latter Prophets. There is a difference in the way the Jewish and Christian traditions organize this material (and which books are included), a point we have already mentioned and will discuss in more detail below.

The Former Prophets are the six books that immediately follow the book of Deuteronomy in the Tanakh. These include Joshua, Judges, 1–2 Samuel, and 1–2 Kings. These books narrate the history of the people of Israel from the conquest of the land under Joshua, through the period of loose tribal confederation found in Judges, to the rise of the united monarchy under Saul, David, and Solomon reported in 1–2 Samuel, through the divided monarchy and the eventual exile of first the Northern Kingdom of Israel and then the Southern Kingdom of Judah, events that occupy most of 1–2 Kings. One important point to highlight here is that although Samuel is considered to be a prophet, the books named after him do not contain a collection of prophetic writings by Samuel. Rather they contain a type of religious history. On the other hand, embedded in the middle of Kings one finds a collection of legends about Elijah and Elisha, two miracle-working prophetic figures (1 Kings 17–2 Kings 9). The Latter Prophets are the fifteen books running from Isaiah–Malachi in the Tanakh, containing oracles and biographical stories about each of these named prophets as well as material from various other anonymous prophets.

The Nature of Prophecy

The fact that the materials in Joshua–2 Kings may not appear to be "prophetic" in nature to modern readers brings up two important issues. The first is the nature of prophecy in the Hebrew Bible, and the second is the issue of what constitutes "The Prophets" for both Jews and Christians. Jews and Christians organize the same material in different ways, and much of this relates to how each group understands prophecy within the Tanakh and Old Testament respectively. In many ways the differences point to a much larger question about the function of this literature. For the sake of simplicity, we might put it this way: Do the prophets point forward, to a messiah, or backward, to the Torah, interpreting this instruction for the ongoing life of Israel?

First, as mentioned above, within the Hebrew ordering, the Prophets contain two large subsections called the Former and Latter Prophets. However, modern Christian Bibles tend to divide the Prophets into the categories of "Major" and "Minor" Prophets. The books that are included within each of these categories are significantly different than those found in the traditional Hebrew ordering, as seen in the following table:

The Prophetic Literature				
Hebrew Canon		*Christian (Protestant) Canon*		
Prophets come after the Torah: they interpret the Torah for the on-going life of God's people		Prophets come before the New Testament: they point forward to Jesus and the coming of the Spirit		
Prophets in 2 parts:	Former Prophets Latter Prophets	Prophets in 2 parts:	Major Prophets Minor Prophets	
Former Prophets	*Latter Prophets*	*Major Prophets*	*Minor Prophets*	
Joshua Judges Samuel Kings	Isaiah Jeremiah Ezekiel The Twelve	Isaiah Jeremiah Lamentations Ezekiel Daniel	Hosea Joel Amos Obadiah Jonah Micah	Nahum Habakkuk Zephaniah Haggai Zechariah Malachi

Table 3. Adapted from Richard S. Briggs, *Reading the Bible Wisely: An Introduction to Taking Scripture Seriously* **(Eugene, Org.: Cascade, 2012), 81.**

The reader will immediately notice that Joshua, Judges, Samuel, and Kings are included among the Prophets in Judaism, while in Christianity they are not (they are called the "Historical Books"). Also, Daniel and Lamentations are included under the category of Prophets in the Christian canon, while for Jews these books fall under the category of the Writings (or Ketuvim).

As we have already touched upon earlier, what stands at the heart of this issue is the differing ways that Jews and Christians understand the books of the Hebrew Bible they both regard as Scripture. For Christians, the coming of Jesus as Israel's Messiah is the defining moment in God's history, and thus the Old Testament prophets are understood as pointing forward to this event. The very arrangement of the Old Testament, ending with Malachi's final verse that looks forward to "the day of the Lord" (4:4-6), speaks to this focus. For Jews, however, the *Torah* is the heart of Jewish life, and *it* is the determining factor in how everything else is read and understood. Thus the Prophets and the Writings point back to, and in some sense are commentary on, these first five seminal books.

For the purposes of this book, we have opted to follow the Jewish canonical order of the books, not only out of respect for Judaism but also because the language of "the Law and the Prophets" is important not only to Judaism but was foundational to the early church's self-understanding in the first century. What the early church called the "the Prophets" would likely have included those books Jews consider to be the Prophets today.

What Is the Deuteronomistic History?

From a secular viewpoint, one discovers that scholars now regularly call the books of the Former Prophets the Deuteronomistic History. This stems from the widely accepted thesis of Martin Noth (1902–1968), who argued that regular editorial asides found throughout this collection echo the language and concerns of the authors of Deuteronomy. This does not mean that these editors penned all these materials, because clearly there are large blocks of stories and annalistic reports that these editors incorporated into this greater work. But these editors (or what scholars call *redactors*) gave the larger work an overarching point of view. They did this through their vision of the unfolding of Israel's history in terms of times of blessing, which they correlated to Israel's obedience to God's prophetic word, and times of national defeat, which were linked to Israel's disobedience to God and God's messengers, the prophets. Or, to put it simply, this material is called the Deuteronomistic History because it shares with Deuteronomy a distinct emphasis on retributive justice: That is, if Israel does rightly, the people will be blessed; if not, the people will be cursed. Many argue that this material has been shaped in such a way to address why Israel went into exile. Thus, just as our own perceptions of the past continually evolve as new events reshape our understandings of history, so too ancient Israel's past is narrated from a particular context that helped her make sense of her turbulent and at times traumatic history.

Overcoming the Confusion:
The "Former" and "Latter" Prophets

The second major category of the Prophets is the Latter Prophets. The Latter Prophets are divided into two major blocks of material often called the Major and the Minor Prophets. These titles have to do with the size of the specific books in each collection, not their importance. Thus the Major Prophets include three large books, Isaiah, Jeremiah, and Ezekiel, which total some one hundred and sixty-six chapters. On the other hand, the twelve prophetic books called the Minor Prophets, or "The Book of the Twelve," contain fewer than seventy chapters. Taken together, these fifteen books are similar in that they contain oracles delivered by various prophets and biographical stories about some of these personalities.

It is worth noting that the term "prophet" in Hebrew (*navi*) may mean "called one" (or possibly "one who calls/proclaims"); and thus prophecy was not so much a profession one trained for as one the person was called to, perhaps reluctantly and often at one's peril due to the unpopular messages he or she was sent to proclaim. Speaking hard words of judgment and calling for national repentance was dangerous. The Bible contains reports of certain prophets being threatened, jailed, or even killed for delivering their unpopular messages.

One of the most confusing things for readers of the Bible is that each of the three collections just described contain materials that occur during the same historical period. Thus 1–2 Kings, Isaiah, Jeremiah, and Ezekiel, and several of the prophets in the Book of the Twelve (or the twelve Minor Prophets) all describe events that occur between 750 and 550 BCE, during the Assyrian and Babylonian periods. One can see this most clearly by comparing 2 Kings 18–20 to Isaiah 36–39 where the same events are described from differing angles and in substantially different ways. What this means is that often when reading through parts of the Latter Prophets one will want to flip back to relevant parts of 1–2 Kings to understand the fuller historical and political context. It also means that people like Isaiah or Jeremiah may have been contemporaries with other prophetic figures found in the Book of the Twelve. And here we should mention that although Isaiah, Jeremiah, and Ezekiel are placed in chronological order within the Bible, the books in the Minor Prophets are not in a historical order. In fact, Amos lived before Hosea, whose book is placed first. And both Amos and Hosea lived before Jeremiah or Ezekiel, whose are placed earlier in the canon.

Another difficulty for many readers is that not all the materials in books named after certain prophets come from the prophet named in the title of the book. Thus almost all scholars believe that most of Isaiah 40–66 stems not from the eighth-century prophet, but from a writer or group of writers who lived in the sixth century BCE and who believed that Isaiah's words and visions were now coming to fruition. Even a short book like Amos likely contains materials that over the centuries were added to the book in order to make it speak to new historical contexts. Thus Amos delivered his oracles to a Northern Israelite audience, but passages like Amos 2:4-5 and 9:11-15 appear to address a later Judean setting. Since the larger Hebrew Bible was ultimately edited by Judean editors, it is not surprising to find such expansions.

Concluding Reflections: The Prophets in Contemporary Religious and Popular Usage

The books found in the Prophets have come to occupy an important place within both the Jewish and Christian traditions. As noted earlier in this book, every weekly Torah portion is paired with a prophetic lection called the *haftarah* chanted during the Sabbath morning service. In the church, sections of the Prophets are read throughout the year in most Eastern and Western lectionaries, and specific passages from the Prophets (for example, Isaiah 9) often play a central role in the Advent readings that prepare the church for Christmas. In popular usage, "biblical prophecy" has come to be associated with predictions about the end of the world. Given that biblical prophets at times speak of coming judgment or even a "world to come," perhaps this is understandable. However, as we point out above and explain in more detail in the chapters that follow, the biblical prophets seem most preoccupied with matters related to the present and near future—the here and now—and a desire to see Israel return to their God and to construct a more just society.

JOSHUA

Introduction and Overview

The book of Joshua narrates Israel's divinely ordained entry into and military conquest of the land of Canaan through a particular narrative and theological lens. The major focus is on Joshua's leadership of Israel from Moses' death, evoked in the book's opening verses, until Joshua's death, mentioned near the very end of the book's concluding chapter. The theology of the book highlights how the obedience of this new generation of Israelites to God's commandments results in a fulfillment of God's promises. There is also a subtheme of how possible missteps can quickly derail these very promises. The book can be rather neatly divided into two large blocks: Chapters 1–12 narrate Israel's preparations and then actual conquest of Canaan, and 13–24 describe the allotment of the land and Israel's settlement of it. This latter section concludes with farewell addresses by Joshua that recount Israel's history and stress that the people must serve the Lord faithfully.

Controversies and Debates

Scholars have long argued about how much, if any, of the details reported in Joshua are historically accurate. Some substantial problems arise here both in looking at the material from within the Bible itself as well as in seeking to correlate the stories in Joshua with physical evidence found by archaeologists. Within the biblical text, there are internal inconsistencies between the overall viewpoint of Joshua—which can be summed up as a total and complete conquest of all of Canaan (Joshua 10–11)—and the viewpoint found in the opening chapters of Judges as well as in a few passages in Joshua that report Israel was not entirely successful in its conquest. To understand the contrast in presentations, compare Joshua 10–11 with Joshua 13:1-13 or 23:1–24:33 or Judges 1. These internal inconsistencies suggest that the authors of Joshua were not attempting to write history in the way we think of it. Rather, they were producing a theological reflection on Israel's first entry into Canaan in order to articulate the meaning of God's gift of the land to Israel and the responsibilities this gift entails for those living at a later time. Perhaps one way to think about this is that often there is a time to report victory as a sign of God's faithfulness, and another time to acknowledge the realities of life, in that not everything has yet been accomplished. This is akin to when modern-day nations claim success in war even though the ongoing challenges of stabilizing the area may continue for years to come.

The archaeological record is no less problematic. While at one time it was proclaimed that the walls of Jericho that tumbled down in Joshua's time had indeed been found, now scholars recognize that those layers of material date around 1,000 years before Joshua lived. In fact, Jericho seems to have been an unwalled and barely inhabited location at the close of the Late Bronze Age (which ended around 1200 BCE), the period when most scholars would place the conquest traditions (if they are taken to be historical). The city of Ai, whose conquest is reported in Joshua 7–8, also appears to have been uninhabited at this time. While there are sites such as Hazor that do show major destruction levels from this period, potentially substantiating the reports given in the Bible, most scholars today believe that the processes by which Israel grew into a distinct people living in Canaan took longer than, and involved a more complex set of factors than, the portrait drawn by the book of Joshua suggests.

Four Theories of Conquest or Occupation

There are at least four competing theories that attempt to explain Israel's arrival in the land. One view, which we will call the *Blitzkrieg* theory, takes the narratives of Joshua at face value. We have already noted the difficulties inherent in this view. Other scholars believe Judges to be more or less historically accurate and subscribe to what might best be named the "slow conquest" theory. Some have even attempted to combine these two theories in hopes of maintaining at least the partial truth of both Joshua and Judges by arguing Israel made a quick initial invasion of Canaan and then settled in the hill country. Over time Israel would have slowly driven the Canaanites out, as suggested by texts like the first chapter in Judges.

A third hypothesis, sometimes dubbed the "no conquest" theory, suggests that the earliest Israelites arrived in the land by peaceful means. This proposal imagines that the

Israelites moved their flocks to differing locations in various seasons and that eventually they took up more permanent residence in the central hill country of Canaan, an area that they, at one time, used only part of the year. One of the most serious difficulties with these three theories is that archaeologists debate how early one can speak of a distinct Israelite culture or ethnicity. In fact, many archaeologists argue that one cannot yet detect distinct Israelite cultural forms in the Late Bronze or even in the Early Iron Age (1200–1000 BCE), which one would expect to find if the Israelites had arrived from an external location as a unique cultural group. The archaeological data suggest that this period was still heavily if not completely dominated by Canaanite, not Israelite, culture.

A bold and more complex theory sometimes called the "peasant revolt" hypothesis attempts to explain why we have so little evidence of a distinct Israelite culture in the Late Bronze Age. This fourth model imagines that most of the people who in the monarchic period came to identify themselves as Israelites were in fact descended from Canaanite stock. The theory suggests that only a small band of people experienced the exodus events and that this group eventually infiltrated Canaan and helped instigate a widespread rebellion of the Canaanite populace against various petty tyrants and the oppressive aristocracy that supported them. In the process, the rebelling Canaanites came to adopt Israel's identity and story as their own.

While this latter theory is intriguing and might help explain why it is difficult to detect a new distinctive Israelite culture in the Late Bronze Age, it is important to note that we have no evidence of any other peasant revolt from this early historical period. Also, and more troubling, it seems hard to believe that the vast bulk of Israelites were once Canaanites, who now no longer remember this fact, even when it would be rather useful. Thus, instead of Israel having to rationalize its entitlement to the land of Canaan by suggesting it was a gift from God, emphasizing the sinfulness of the Canaanites, they could have simply claimed that they had always lived in the land and it belonged to them from the beginning. It is hard to overlook the fact that there is a very strong and persistent memory that the people of Israel were not and had never been native inhabitants of the land—an idea that would have been convenient to discard.

Reckoning with the Violent Images in Joshua

There is little doubt that one of the most difficult problems raised by the material in Joshua is that a just and loving God, the God of the Bible, here instructs Israel to wipe out the Canaanites and destroy any trace of their culture. Can a good God really command what appears to be genocide? As discussed elsewhere in this book, one must correctly determine the genre of material one is reading if one has any hope of understanding what it is attempting to communicate. Here it is important to recognize that both internal inconsistencies in Joshua as well as external evidence all indicate that the book is not intending to report a strict factual history of how Israel came to possess the land of Canaan. It seems fairly certain that some form of the book of Joshua was addressed to a seventh-century BCE audience living in Judah at a time when few if any actual Canaanites existed. This means the book's violent images are likely functioning as metaphors employed to explore what being a true Israelite who is devoted to God means. Such a reading is reinforced by the fact that the only individual Canaanite we meet in any detail is Rahab. Yet even though Rahab is a prostitute who runs a brothel, she acts like a true Israelite, who is single-mindedly devoted to Israel's God and God's plans for the people of Israel (see her words in Joshua 2:8-13). In fact, she becomes a type of honorary Israelite. In an ironic contrast, one of the few Israelites we meet as an individual is Achan, who has a genealogy that goes back to Judah's own son. But this Israelite of high Judahite stock acts as a "Canaanite" by illicitly appropriating various Canaanite items that were to be destroyed. These two stories, neatly juxtaposed as they are, suggest that in the narrative world of Joshua being a Canaanite or an Israelite may be at least as contingent on how one acted as on one's ethnicity.

Establishing the metaphoric nature of these narratives does not mean that they are entirely unproblematic. This is because metaphors can shape the ways we think and act and thus one needs to recognize that some metaphors can still be dangerous. While one might argue that we use similar warlike metaphors in sports contests quite regularly (e.g., we "annihilated the competition," we "slaughtered them"), the biblical images are linked to war reports, not a sportscast. These war reports may be exaggerations or a type of fiction, but they can easily be read as suggesting that if one did encounter some person or group like the actual Canaanites, that one should indeed act like Joshua and annihilate them. In fact, not infrequently in Western history various religious groups, who believed that the book of Joshua is the inspired word of God, have indeed invoked images drawn from Joshua to justify the conquest and annihilation of certain enemies.

Joshua, Land, and Blessing

To read the story "with the grain" is to celebrate Israel's long-awaited gift of the land, something promised to Abraham, their forefather, generations earlier. God's grace, goodness, and mercy are prominently displayed throughout the book, seen especially in the fact that the narrator recounts that God himself does much of Israel's "fighting," alongside of and at times for Israel:

"The LORD God of Israel fought for Israel" (Joshua 10:14, 42; 23:3, 10). In fact, certain battles in Joshua resemble more an act of worship—a ceremony of sorts—than warfare, as demonstrated by the elaborate processional scenes leading up to the conquest of Jericho. In this first, and thus paradigmatic, conquest story, the ark, an ornate chest which at one time held the Ten Commandments, is processed around the city six times over the course of six days, followed by seven times on the seventh day when trumpets are blown, people shout, and walls miraculously fall down. These powerful images, usually associated with worship in Israel, remind the reader that the land of Israel is in every sense to be understood as a sacred gift from God, not something won by a superior human military force.

Joshua in Jewish Tradition

It is important to keep in mind that Jews read Scripture through the lens of Jewish tradition. Thus, many problems inherent in Scripture are addressed and at times mitigated in later Jewish interpretation. Building on scriptural antecedents like Genesis 15:16 and Joshua 11:20 that suggest that Canaanites were destroyed due to their sinful actions and their obstinate nature, later Jewish tradition argued that the Canaanite nations were given warning and time to repent in that they could read the writing on the stones that Joshua erected in the Jordan River. Furthermore, classical rabbinic tradition argued that because Sennacherib, the Assyrian king, moved various populations around and intermingled differing ethnic groups together back in the eighth century BCE, the laws calling for the killing of the Canaanite nations were from that point forward no longer in effect.

Joshua in Christian Tradition

If we understand these things spiritually and manage wars of this type spiritually, and if we drive out all those spiritual iniquities from heaven, then we shall be able at last to receive from Jesus as a share of the inheritance even those places and kingdoms that are the kingdoms of heaven.

—Origen (184–253 CE)

Thus states Origen in response to those who teach "a certain cruelty through these things that are written [in Joshua]" (see Douglas S. Earl, *The Joshua Delusion* [Eugene: Cascade, 2010], 9–10). Origen's words give clear indication that

103

early in the life of the church the text of Joshua was read metaphorically. This way of reading, he suggests, is in line with the teaching of the Holy Spirit.

The Christian Reformation, with its emphasis on *ad fontes* ("back to the sources"), brought with it a desire to get at "what really happened" in a new way, to read the text at face value. John Calvin, for instance, was more interested to let the story stand and not ask questions about why God was so severe or took pleasure in ordering the deaths of the Canaanites. Unfortunately, this way of reading, despite its seeming humility, is out of line with long-standing church tradition and fed into regretful ways of reading the text that fostered violence. In short, it was out of line with Irenaeus' foundational Christian idea that parts of Scripture were to be read in light of the whole. To read Joshua in a nonviolent manner, seeking love of neighbor and the death of hate and iniquity, is to tap into a long tradition of Christian (and Jewish) reading. Despite its stained past, the church also provides many examples of this type of interpretation, some of which surface in hymns used in worship. One such example, which will conclude our chapter, can be found in the popular eighteenth-century hymn "Guide Me, O Thou Great Jehovah," especially the third verse:

When I tread the verge of Jordan,
Bid my anxious fears subside;
Death of deaths, and hell's destruction,
Land me safe on Canaan's side.
Songs of praises, songs of praises,
I will ever give to Thee.

JUDGES

Introduction and Overview

Judges is the seventh book of the Hebrew Bible. It tells the story of Israel between the death of Joshua and the rise of the monarchy that begins in the following book, 1 Samuel. Judges receives its name from Israel's leaders in this era who are said to have *judged* (Hebrew *shaphat*) Israel for a period of time. However, "judging" in this book more often involves being a military leader than deciding legal matters.

The shape of Judges as a whole, as well as its use of certain recurring themes and specific terminology, shows why scholars think it was edited by the school that produced the book of Deuteronomy. These include: (1) the tendency to correlate Israel's suffering directly with her disobedience of God—most especially Israel's worship of idols like the Canaanite fertility deity Baal and his consort Asherah; (2) the periodic use of prophets, divine messengers, or even God to deliver oracles of judgment against an idolatrous Israel who abandoned YHWH, the God who brought Israel out of Egypt and into the Holy Land; and (3) a strong ambivalence toward rule by dynastic kings.

Controversies and Debates

The current consensus is that the narratives in Judges were written down and shaped during the monarchic era, long after their implied setting. Furthermore, some argue that individual tribal stories, which may have occurred during the same timeframe, are narrated as if they pertained to a united confederation of all twelve tribes and occurred one right after the other. Because of these factors, it is unclear how much one can use the details in Judges to reconstruct Israel's history in the period before the rise of the monarchy.

Having said that, however, many would suggest that the Song of Deborah in Judges 5 is one of the oldest texts in the Hebrew Bible and that it contains information that can shed light on Israel's earliest tribal history. Furthermore, even scholars who believe that the stories were brought into final form in a much later period still recognize that Judges as whole sheds light on the social and political concerns of later Judeans. In fact, many scholars detect a pro-Judean or pro-Davidic editorial shaping within Judges as seen for example in the fact that the first—and many would say the model—judge, Othniel, has a Judahite background. Thus, while one cannot use Judges as if it were an accurate reporting of premonarchic history, one can still use Judges in a careful and critical manner to shed light on aspects of ancient Israel's history and culture.

Incomplete Conquest and the "Judges Pattern"

Judges begins with a double introduction, the first describing the attempts by individual tribes to gain a foothold in the land (Judges 1). This is executed in a geographical pattern that generally runs from south to north and from somewhat more successful to less successful in outcome. The second introduction occurs in Judges 2:6–3:6 and begins at an earlier time than 1:1, which opens with a notice of Joshua's death. In contrast, 2:6 describes Joshua sending the tribes home after the conquest was completed and thus focuses on all Israel's failure to obey God once Joshua and his generation are no longer present. This second introduction lays out the general pattern found in Judges 3–16. This "Judges pattern" might be summarized as follows. Israel does evil in God's sight by worshiping Canaanite deities. In turn, God becomes angry with the people and sells them into the hands of their enemies. Eventually God has mercy on them due to their cries and raises up judges who save them from their oppressors. Unfortunately, as soon as the judge who saved them dies, the people revert to their evil ways. While there are variations on this formula throughout Judges, a number of these elements recur time and again throughout the book.

Early Successes: Judges 3–5

The center of Judges runs from 3:7–16:31 and contains the stories of the various judges who emerge from individual tribes of Israel in times of trouble as military and political leaders. The named judges are categorized under two rubrics: major and minor Judges. The minor judges are a group of figures who receive only short notices, while the major judges are given greater narrative space. The first major judge is Othniel, who is associated with Judah and whose judgeship leads to forty years of quiet in the land, forty years signifying an ideal period in the Bible (3:11). It is reported not only that God raised him up as a savior (3:9) but also that the spirit of God was upon him and that he judged Israel (3:10). He is followed by Ehud, a Benjaminite from the territory of Benjamin just north of Judah. While Ehud is also said to be raised up by God as a savior (3:15), he never is called a judge. In this narrative, which contains humorous touches, Ehud kills an enemy king by telling him he has a secret message for him, to be delivered in private, after which he delivers a dagger into the belly of the overweight oppressor and escapes undetected. The narrative ends by reporting that the land was peaceful for eighty years, the longest quiet period listed in Judges, perhaps implying he was the greatest of the Israelite judges.

Judges 4–5 tell the Deborah and Jael story, first in prose and then in poetry. While generally positive, it could be read as criticizing certain Israelites. In this engaging story, some see Barak's answer to Deborah's call as exhibiting a hesitance that results in God allowing Jael, a foreign woman, to kill the enemy general (4:8-9). In the poetic account a number of tribes appear to be castigated for their failure to show up to battle (5:15-17). Still, here too the land rests for forty years, a round number that, again, almost surely symbolizes Israel's success. Thus the initial Judges through the end of chapter 5 are portrayed in a mainly if not a wholly positive light.

When Leaders Make Mistakes: Judges 6–16

However, with Gideon, the judge that follows, one begins to see a marked deterioration in the standing of Israel and its leaders. Thus, while Israel calls out for help, when they receive a prophetic rebuke over their idolatrous ways they never repent (6:7-10). More telling is that Gideon's father appears to possess a Baal shrine. In fact, when Gideon destroys this idolatrous site, the populace seeks to kill Gideon. Some scholars also detect weaknesses in Gideon's character, including his constant need for reassurances (6:36-40; 7:9-14), his tendency to gain glory for himself along the way (7:18, 20), his rough treatment of certain Israelite cities (8:4-17), and finally his making of an idolatrous object, an act closely paired with his taking many wives (8:24-31). Still, the land once more has peace for forty years. And, aside from the single verse that mentions his making of an idolatrous object, Gideon received no other explicit criticism. He is even mentioned in the New Testament as an example of "faith" (Hebrews 11:32).

Shady Characters of the Bible

With the possible exceptions of Abraham, Isaac, and Moses, many of Israel's ancestors, judges, and kings are not exactly the model Israelites that modern readers might expect. Even Abraham and Moses have their moral shortcomings, seen in Abraham's passing off Sarah as his sister (Genesis 12 and 20) and Moses' apparent disobedience in striking the rock at Meribah, an act that bars him from entering the promised land (Numbers 20:12). Jacob is a deceiver and David is clearly a man of bloody hands, too bloody, God says, to build the temple (1 Chronicles 22:8). The stories of the Judges only further highlight the moral ambivalence of these characters. These judges make questionable oaths (Judges 11:30-31), construct idolatrous shrines or objects to foreign gods (8:24-27), and take wives from among non-Israelites (14–16; something expressly forbidden in the Torah).

At times the Jewish and Christian traditions have downplayed or sought to cover up these negative traits. One thing is clear, however: These characters are particularly compelling and believable because of these traits, and God works with them despite their flaws, at times even moving the divine plan forward by means of these character flaws. Within the Hebrew Bible, God works with human beings as they are, as people with moral and physical strengths and weaknesses. In fact, much of Judges 3–11 might be seen as a study in the many differing types of leaders and the various positive and negative traits that leaders have.

Judges 9 seems like an object lesson about the consequences of choosing the wrong leaders. Abimelech, who first convinces the men of Shechem to choose him as king over Gideon's other sons because he is a native, begins his reign by killing his seventy half brothers, except for Jotham, who escapes. After three years, relations between the people of Shechem and Abimelech sour, leading to escalating warfare between the residents of Shechem and Abimelech, finally resulting in Abimelech's ignoble death at the hands of a woman. Both Jotham's speech and Gideon's earlier explicit rejection of kingship (see 8:23) suggest that much of the material in the first half of Judges is antimonarchic.

Brief reports about two minor Judges, Tola, who judges for twenty-three years, and Jair, who judges for twenty-two years, come next, followed by an extended meditation on Israel's disloyalty to God. While Israel does repent in this instance, the ambiguous language leaves one unclear if God accepts their repentance (10:16). If God did not fully forgive Israel, this might explain why Jephthah, the next judge, was not raised up by God but rather was selected by the elders of Gilead. Jephthah's character is also suspect due to a rash (and possibly unnecessary) vow he makes that results in the sacrifice of his only daughter. Furthermore, his judgeship lasts only a mere six years and it ends with a disturbing tale about how Jephthah and his troops massacred 42,000 members of the northern tribe of Ephraim.

After information about three other minor judges, the final four chapters of the large middle section of the book relate the highly entertaining set of narratives surrounding Samson the Danite's birth, life, and death (Judges 13–16). While Samson is said to judge Israel for twenty years (15:20; 16:31), it is far from clear that he ever intends to act on behalf of Israel. Rather, God appears to use Samson's lust for Philistine women and competition with various Philistine men as a way to begin to free the Israelites from Philistine hegemony. Samson is undone by his love for Delilah, who betrays him to the Philistines, who in turn capture and blind him. His story closes with his heroic but suicidal act of revenge against his captors when he single-handedly brings down a Philistine building, killing more of the enemy with this one act than he had during his lifetime.

Violence and Civil War: Judges 17–21

Judges 17–21 tells a number of troubling stories, most of which involve inner-Israelite tensions. Much of the violence in these chapters seems to be linked to acts of idolatry. The most disturbing story is probably the last, which narrates a horrific incident in which a Levite from Ephraim goes to Bethlehem in order to woo his concubine, a type of wife, back home after she fled to her father's home. On his return to Ephraim with his concubine, he stops to spend the night in Gibeah of Benjamin. In an incident resembling Lot's final night in Sodom narrated in Genesis 19, the residents in Gibeah want to rape him, but instead he surrenders his concubine to the crowd. After being abused and raped all night by the crowd of men, she collapses at the entrance of the house where her husband spent the night (whether dead or close to death is not clear). Finding her as he exits the house that morning, he takes her home, cuts her in twelve pieces, and sends one piece of her body to each of the tribes in hopes of obtaining justice. When the Benjaminites refuse to surrender the culprits to the other tribes of Israel, a civil war ensues, which almost results in the elimination of the entire tribe of Benjamin. These five chapters, filled with stories of Israelite idolatry, theft, rape, murder, and intertribal warfare, indicate that Israel's lack of good leadership results in violence, chaos, and possible extinction, showing that infidelity toward God is mirrored in the infidelity and treachery various

Israelites display toward each other, resulting in an almost complete breakdown of Israelite society.

Judges in Later Biblical and Jewish and Christian Tradition

The compelling, albeit at times disturbing, stories in Judges have had a rather large impact on later Jewish, Christian, and Western culture. Already in the later biblical period, one finds the Apocryphal book of Judith, whose central character is modeled after Jael in Judges 4–5. One of the most interesting recent developments has been the way in which modern Zionism has reclaimed the heroic and at times militant figures found in Judges. Not only has Judges influenced some streams of Zionist literature and political thinking, but one of Israel's generals who recently served as Prime Minister was named Ehud Barak (originally Brog), a combination of the names of two heroic figures within Judges.

As mentioned above, in the Christian tradition, many judges, despite their moral failings, are cited in the New Testament as models of faith (particularly "Gideon, Barak, Samson, [and] Jephthah" of Hebrews 11:32). It also seems quite likely that the story of the Annunciation—when an angel visits Mary to tell her that she is miraculously pregnant—has been influenced by the story of Samson's conception, which occurs when an angel visits his mother. While some might question a connection between Samson and Jesus, or ask how such shady characters could earn the status of "the faithful," classical Christianity saw these characters as persons of faith and read their stories as pointing to the coming life, death, and resurrection of Jesus.

1 SAMUEL

Introduction and Overview

The books of the Bible we call 1 and 2 Samuel are considered to be one book in the Hebrew tradition. They were first separated in the Greek Septuagint. Because of their extensive content and variation, we treat each book separately here. 1 Samuel narrates the events that led up to Israel's transition from what we might call a theocracy to a monarchy under Saul, Israel's first king. It then narrates the sinking fortunes of Saul and the corresponding rise of David, the person who eventually becomes Israel's second, and most celebrated, king. While named after the prophet Samuel, Samuel himself is only featured in 1 Samuel, most prominently in the first half of the book.

The book opens with the story that explains how a barren woman named Hannah eventually, after prayerfully petitioning God, gives birth to Samuel, a child she in turn gives back to God by bringing him to live out his life at the sanctuary in Shiloh. At a tender age Samuel receives his first prophecy, when God informs him that he must tell Eli the high priest at Shiloh that God will severely punish Eli's household because Eli's two sons are acting corruptly. Samuel's disturbing oracle comes true in chapter 4 when Eli's two sons, Hophni and Phineas, are killed and the ark of God is captured by the Philistines. When Eli learns of what happened to his sons and the ark, he falls out of his chair, breaks his neck, and dies. The following chapters record how God's ark plagues the Philistines, eventually forcing them to return it to Israel. Then in chapters 8–15 we hear several differing explanations regarding how Saul became Israel's first king, but soon thereafter falls from God's favor. David is introduced in chapter 16, when God commands Samuel to anoint David in place of Saul as Israel's king. The rest of the book recounts David's rising fortunes, which are correlated with Saul's tragic fall from power. First

Samuel ends with the death of Saul and his three sons in a battle with the Philistines.

Controversies and Debates

It is widely acknowledged that 1 Samuel includes a diverse set of opinions on how the monarchy arose. Biblical scholars usually note two major voices in the text, one often labeled antimonarchic, and the other promonarchic. For example, 1 Samuel 8 describes how the people demand a king from Samuel in a manner that suggests they are rejecting God's kingship and seeking to become like all other nations who have kings, rather than acting like God's specially chosen people. Yet, in contrast, chapter 9 begins with an almost fairytale-like story about how a young man named Saul sets out to find some lost donkeys and along the way becomes king over Israel. In this rather promonarchical story, God initiates the kingship by ordering Samuel to anoint Saul as king so he can defend the Israelites against the Philistines. First Samuel 11 narrates yet another, but different promonarchic story that attributes Saul's rise to kingship to his heroic military action that saves the besieged town of Jabesh-gilead from the Ammonites. In chapter 12, however, the earlier antimonarchic voice returns, with Samuel pronouncing that the people have committed evil in their requesting a king.

Here a number of features are worth highlighting. First, these differing voices likely reflect differing Israelite constituencies. The rise of the monarchy ultimately took power away from various tribal leaders, and thus much of the antimonarchic rhetoric may stem from these groups along with other parties who disliked the monarchy. The promonarchic texts, on the other hand, were likely produced in David's court in an attempt to justify the attendant shift in power from tribal leaders to the king's court or to provide divine justification for the kings' various policies. Second, the Bible's inclusion of these varying voices preserves them for posterity, thus allowing later communities to construct their politics along several different lines but still informed by the Bible's vision. This is somewhat similar to the way that American debates about the proper balance between the states' power and the federal government draw from discussions between various founding fathers who either articulated a federalist or a more states' rights viewpoint. Finally, the reader should note that the preservation of differing juxtaposed viewpoints creates a final text that is neither pro- nor antimonarchic, but rather is cognizant of the benefits and problems inherent in a monarchy.

Figure 13. Medieval Bible manuscript leaf depicting Samuel anointing Saul, Michael Wolgemut, 1483. Woodcut printed in black with hand coloring on paper. Courtesy Smith College Museum of Art, Northampton, Massachusetts (SC 1950:25).

The Many Roles of Samuel

Samuel is quite akin to the figure of Moses. Like Moses, he functions as a prophetic mediator between God and the Israelites. In this capacity he often delivers criticism and sometimes foretells the future or works miracles. Samuel also shares other traits with Moses. Like Moses, who sets up law courts in Exodus 18, Samuel appears to settle complex legal cases in 1 Samuel 7:15-17. Earlier in chapter 7, Samuel helps muster troops in a defensive battle against the Philistines like Moses had done in Exodus 17 against the Amalekites, a group Samuel also fights in chapter 15. Further, Samuel is a priestly figure who regularly conducts sacrifices, a role Moses occupied until the sanctuary was fully set up (see Exodus 24 and Leviticus 8). Scholars sometimes speak of a distinction between Israel's "founding" prophets (Moses, Samuel, Elijah), who had multiple roles, and Israel's "classical" or "canonical" prophets (Isaiah, Jeremiah, Ezekiel, the Twelve). From the death of Samuel forward, the various roles occupied by a Moses or a Samuel typically come to be divided up among three differing groups: kings, prophets, and priests.

What Does Samuel Tell Us about Early Prophets in Israel?

This brings up the important question of the role of the prophet during Israel's earliest days. First Samuel tells us quite a bit about the many different roles of some of Israel's earliest prophetic figures. To begin, 1 Samuel 9:9 informs us that people who in later Israelite history were called prophets were at one time called seers. In this passage, Samuel is depicted as something of a fortuneteller, predicting future events or people's fates. Yet, later in this passage Samuel is the person who gives God's imprimatur to Israel's kings when he anoints Saul with oil (as he does in chapter 16 with David). Samuel also plays another role seen in certain prophetic figures, that of miracle worker. Thus in chapter 12 he makes it rain in the summer season (a very uncommon occurrence in the climate of Israel). Finally, in 1 Samuel 19:18-24 we see that Samuel is not a lone prophet but rather the leader of a larger band of prophets, and that such figures could be swept up in a prophetic frenzy, an ecstatic state that at times caused those in it to break social conventions such as when they stripped off their clothes.

Are God's Plans Affected by Humans?

Traditional Western models of theism tend to think of God as unchanging and unaffected by emotions. Yet the Bible regularly portrays a personal God who is highly emotional. Interestingly enough, even within the Bible there is some debate about whether God changes his mind, as seen quite clearly within 1 Samuel 15. This chapter discusses Saul's failure to obey God's commands

Saul: A Good King or a Bad One?

As noted, there seem to be two streams within 1 Samuel, one promonarchic and one antimonarchic. So too do there seem to be pro- and anti-Saulide streams within these stories, those that present Israel's first king positively and those that focus on his downfall and shortcomings. For example, despite God's explicit rejection of Saul in chapter 15, this passage shows something of a sympathetic picture, portraying a repentant Saul who made a regrettable error in judgment in listening to the people. Further, some readers have found themselves sympathetic to Saul's unwillingness to destroy all the captives and the booty as Samuel commanded. Other passages like 1 Samuel 14:47-48, 52, and 11:11-13 show that Saul was successful (and strategic) in numerous battles. We might also note that he, unlike the kings who followed him, lived a relatively modest life, having only one concubine (as opposed to the many of David and Solomon), probably lived in a modest palace at Gibeah—at times still tending to his fields—and he, unlike David and Solomon, was not guilty of the royal excesses about which Samuel had warned the people. Whatever the case, the text ultimately finds Saul deficient in comparison to David or even Solomon. For a discussion of why this is so, consult the discussion in the textbox titled "Contrasting David and Saul" in the next chapter.

fully, which in turn leads God to regret having made Saul king. Interestingly enough, Samuel tells Saul that God's rejection of him is final since God, unlike mortals, does not change his mind or show regret. Yet, in verse 11, God, using the exact same Hebrew root, says he indeed has "regretted" making Saul king. Clearly, the authors of the Bible are highlighting both the fact that God is unlike humans and thus reliable and constant, and the fact that the God of Israel is a personal God, deeply affected by human behavior.

Samuel and Hannah in Jewish Tradition

The character of Samuel is very positively regarded within postbiblical Jewish tradition. The opening story of Samuel is particularly influential in that Samuel's birth and dedication story is read as the *haftarah* (the accompanying prophetic lection to the Torah) on the first day of Rosh Hashanah, the Jewish New Year. Inasmuch as the community seeks to sway God through prayer to annul any possible evils and to grant them a new lease on life during Rosh Hashanah, the barren Hannah's ability to convince God to supply her with a miracle baby through her sincere and heartfelt prayer is a fitting reading. Yet, there is likely more at stake. Hannah dedicates the son she receives from God to serve God his whole lifetime. Similarly, the Jewish community is thus recognizing that if God grants them renewed life for another year that life is to be lived in service to God.

Samuel and Hannah in Christian Tradition

When we come to 2 Samuel we will explore the significant attention David has received within the Christian tradition. For now, it is interesting to note parallels between Hannah, Samuel's mother, and Mary, the mother of Jesus, in the New Testament. That their stories share a similar theme of a faithful, obedient woman obtaining a son through miraculous circumstances is readily apparent. It is also interesting that Mary's song in Luke 1:46-55—traditionally called the *Magnificat*—contains clear allusions to and shares the themes of the Song of Hannah (1 Samuel 2:1-10). This much-celebrated song, regularly sung or recited in traditional Christian worship services, shows that both Mary and Hannah consider themselves to be "handmaidens of God," further connecting these two important figures who, through divine intervention, each bore a special son whose life was totally dedicated to serving God and was understood to bring about renewal for the people of Israel (compare 1 Samuel 1:11 and Luke 1:38).

115

2 SAMUEL

Introduction and Overview

Considering they were originally one book, it should come as no surprise that 2 Samuel continues where 1 Samuel left off. The first ten chapters of 2 Samuel thus focus first upon David's personal and political reactions to the deaths of Saul and Jonathan, events that concluded 1 Samuel. Through a combination of intrigues, personal vendettas, some fortunate coincidences, as well as some tactful political and strategic military moves, David comes to secure control first over Judah and eventually over the Northern tribes. He also conquers Jerusalem and makes it his capital city, the place where he built his palace and to where he moved the ark of God. After defeating various external and internal enemies, David's kingdom appears to achieve political stability. Then, beginning in chapter 11 and running through chapter 20, one finds an extended and detailed narrative that depicts the unraveling of the very stability that David had spent a lifetime achieving. This rich narrative describes how David's act of adultery with Bathsheba sets off—as prophesied by the prophet Nathan—internal strife within David's household that ultimately results in a civil war.

By the end of this brilliant but disturbing story, David is somewhat a broken man in that he indirectly played a role in the rape of his daughter Tamar, which in turn led David's son Absalom to murder Amnon, his half-brother, the rapist. To make matters worse, David restores Absalom to the palace, a move that eventually results in Absalom's attempt to kill David and replace him on Israel's throne. Before the book finishes, Absalom himself is killed at the hands of David's army, a tragic and moving story that readers may recognize from the famous, heartfelt cry of David: "O my son Absalom, my son, my son Absalom! Would I had died instead of you, O Absalom, my son, my son!" The book concludes with some poems and other assorted stories that are placed in an appendix occupying chapters 21–24.

Controversies and Debates

For much of the twentieth century, scholars had come to see 2 Samuel 9–20 and 1 Kings 1–2 as a unified block of material that they called the Succession Narrative. This title was used to underline that these materials primarily explore the question "Who will succeed David?" These chapters show how the much younger son, Solomon, ultimately came to succeed King David despite David having several older sons. Furthermore, it was widely believed that this section contained a finely crafted historical account of the events it narrates, likely penned soon after they happened, early in the reign of Solomon.

Both of these assertions have more recently come under serious fire. Today critics tend to highlight that this block of material is clearly composed of several, likely once-discrete stories. Many of these stories seem less preoccupied with the question of who will succeed David than with exploring and criticizing David's monarchy and perhaps monarchical rule more generally. In addition, there is growing skepticism that the narrative was written shortly after the events it narrates, as exhibited by the following quotation from 2 Samuel 13:18: "Now she was wearing a long robe with sleeves; *for this is how the virgin daughters of the king were clothed in earlier times*" (emphasis added). Clearly, the phrase in italics was added to explain a detail that the author's audience who lived in a much later time would find confusing. It is evident that at least portions of David's story were penned long after the events.

The Davidic Covenant and the Idea of Messianism

Second Samuel 7 articulates the theological view that undergirded the kingship and dynasty of David. In this text, God makes an eternal promise to maintain a descendant of David on the throne of Judah forever. However, the text also indicates that, if a Davidic descendant sins, God reserves the right to punish him. Yet, God promises that David's dynasty would indeed endure. When the Babylonians destroyed Jerusalem and deposed the reigning Davidic monarch in 587 BCE, these promises seemed to have been proven false. Yet, the belief that God does not make false promises eventually gave rise to the idea that at some future point a descendant of King David would arise and be anointed and crowned as king, in turn restoring Israel to its former glory. In fact, the word *messiah* is itself a transliteration of the Hebrew word *moshiach*, a word that means "the one anointed with oil." Israelite kings were anointed with oil upon accession to their kingship. Thus messianism is a belief that such a Davidic royal figure will arise and inaugurate a new age of world peace and prosperity and the people of Israel will experience a rebirth. Such ideas came to animate early Christianity and its belief that Jesus, a descendant of David, fulfilled this role. Traditional Judaism likewise holds to the idea that a Davidic messiah will eventually rule over a restored people of Israel, living in the land.

Contrasting David and Saul

When one compares Saul's acts of disobedience to David's sins, it appears that David's sins are much more serious. Saul failed to wait for Samuel to conduct a sacrifice, and then in 1 Samuel 15, Saul took some of the booty of the Amalekites, which he was commanded to destroy entirely. Further, he failed to kill King Agag as ordered. In contrast, David committed adultery by sleeping with Bathsheba—the wife of Uriah, one of David's soldiers—and then David directed that Uriah be exposed to mortal danger in combat, resulting in Uriah's death. Saul loses the kingship over his sinful disobedience while David, the adulterer and in effect murderer, is forgiven. How can this be?

Here we will offer one modern historical explanation and one theological interpretation. Contemporary scholars are fond of saying that "the winners write history." Since David's dynasty was ultimately established and flourished for hundreds of years, indeed, in the end gave way to "Judaism" (that is, Judah-ism), people employed by this dynasty, members of the "winning team" we might say, produced texts more sympathetic to David than to Saul. While both figures suffer punishments for their poor behavior, Saul's punishment may be more severe because those writing 1–2 Samuel felt pressure to justify why David was anointed in place of Saul and his family.

A theological approach, on the other hand, might provide a different explanation. It would likely note that the differing outcomes can be explained best by attending to the details not of the differing sins of Saul and David, but rather to their differing reactions when they are confronted about their wrongful behavior. In 1 Samuel 15, when Samuel reprimands Saul for failing to obey God's orders concerning the Amalekites, Saul twice denies that he was disobedient. Instead, Saul initially maintains that he did follow the orders he was given, even while explaining and giving excuses for why certain goods were not utterly destroyed as commanded. In contrast, in 2 Samuel 12:13, after Nathan confronts David about his despicable actions, David makes no excuses and he replies simply and firmly, "I have sinned against the LORD." One could argue that David's full willingness to own up to his failures immediately creates more of a window for God to forgive David and maintain his promises to David and his posterity. Perhaps there is a lesson here for modern politicians as well. Quite frequently politicians are destroyed not by a scandal, but rather by their failure to confess their wrongful behavior when first questioned. Perhaps God and people alike are more willing to forgive others when a full confession is made promptly, followed by a willingness to accept the consequences that flow from one's actions.

Connections to Genesis

As a number of literary critics have noticed, a host of motifs and phrases are shared by both the Succession Narrative and the Joseph story. Thus, both stories have a Tamar who is involved in an inappropriate sexual act, both mention or involve a friend who is around the protagonist immediately before he sleeps with the Tamar character (Hirah in Genesis 38:12 and Jonadab in 2 Samuel 13:3), both use the words, *ketonet passim*, only found in these two passages, to describe a special garment (one Joseph received from his father in Genesis 37 and one worn by Tamar in 2 Samuel 13), and both revolve around rivalries between various brothers, in which the eldest living son of the most recent wife ends up ruling over his siblings (Joseph, son of Rachel and Solomon, son of Bathsheba). There are also occasional references to other Genesis sibling stories such as the link between the woman of Tekoa in 2 Samuel 14, who mentions two sons who had a mortal encounter in the field, and the story of Cain murdering Abel in the field. Finally, there is the fact that a rape occurs in Genesis 34, leading to the fall of the two brothers Simeon and Levi; in 2 Samuel, a rape leads to the eventual fall of Amnon and Absalom.

What is one to make of all these interconnections? From a historical perspective we are left to choose between the following options: Either one set of stories was dependent on the other (although which way such dependence might run is disputed) or perhaps both were produced at a similar time or possibly by a similar writer or school. Alternatively, maybe both stories are drawing on a common set of stock motifs out of which they are weaving their tales. From a theological vantage point, whatever the exact compositional history of these stories, these close thematic and verbal connections demonstrate that the later tendency of both Jews and Christians to link different parts of Scripture associatively in new and illuminating ways is a practice that goes back to the formation of the biblical text itself. The tendency of later Judaism and Christianity to view the whole of Scripture as a unity in which each passage of Scripture is interlinked with the whole appears to be a guiding principle employed by the Bible's authors, editors, and those who shaped the larger biblical canons.

David in Later Biblical and Jewish Tradition

One of the most interesting features of the Bible's portrayal of David is that even while David remains Israel's ideal king, indeed the model of the future messianic king, he is presented as a flawed human being. One should note that later streams of biblical tradition, such as the retelling of the history of Israel found in Chronicles, seem less comfortable presenting David in the critical light we find in 1–2 Samuel. Thus 1 Chronicles 20, which covers the same time period as the Succession Narrative, leaves out all the troubling material about David and his family, even the momentous Bathsheba affair, creating a much more idealized portrait of him. Later rabbinic interpretations also at times seek to explain away some of the more unsavory actions committed by David. However, it is important to underline that one of the most compelling features of the biblical narrative is that it does not shy away from describing Israel's ancestors, whether David, Moses, Jacob, Sarah, or Abraham, in critical terms when they engage in questionable or immoral actions.

Davidic Themes in Christian Tradition

Similar to Jewish Tradition, David is something of a sacred character in Christianity, one in whom many Christians have difficulty finding fault. Perhaps most interesting, however, and closely related, is the role David plays in the New Testament. As will be discussed in our chapter on Matthew, the book of Matthew places great emphasis on and traces in detail the lineage of Jesus back to David. This relates to the prophecy, discussed above, that a descendant of David would always reign over Judah. Jesus' title "son of David," used throughout the Synoptic Gospels, seems to function as convenient shorthand to indicate this relationship. Further, the question asked of Jesus at his execution trial, "Are you the King of the Jews?" and the sign "King of the Jews" said to be fixed above him on the cross speak loudly to the early church's belief that Jesus was in fact the long promised "messiah," or "anointed one"— the royal descendant of David who would restore Israel to her rightful place in the world.

1–2 KINGS

Introduction and Overview

Like the books of Samuel, the "two" books of Kings should be thought of as one book. These forty-seven chapters of the Bible open with the account of Solomon's rise to power, explain how upon Solomon's death the united monarchy split into the Northern Kingdom (often called Ephraim or Israel) and the Southern Kingdom (Judah), and then narrate historical and religious events. These include: the chronological sequence of Northern and Southern kings, the many miraculous stories involving Elijah and Elisha, the fall of the Northern Kingdom, the reforms of Hezekiah and Josiah, and finally the destruction of Jerusalem resulting in the Babylonian exile. As will be discussed in more detail below, Israel and Judah's kings are evaluated by how closely they adhered to the theological viewpoint associated with the scribes who produced Deuteronomy. One finds these assessments in the concluding summaries given for each king, and in many ways they read like the short biographies one finds in obituary notices today. The authors of these books and the Deuteronomistic History more generally believed that the only legitimate place of sacrifice was the temple in Jerusalem and the only God to be worshiped was YHWH. Because all Northern (Israelite) kings sponsored their own temples, and many Southern (Judahite) kings were lenient on this rule, every Northern king and almost every Southern king—Hezekiah and Josiah being the major exceptions—are given negative assessments.

It is also important to point out that while these two books cover approximately four hundred years of time, they do so selectively, that is, they devote much attention to certain characters and periods and very little to others. Thus eleven chapters, nearly one quarter of these two books, detail Solomon's reign, including several chapters devoted to the building of the

Jerusalem temple. Another long block running from 1 Kings 17 to 2 Kings 9 seems to be a distinct collection that narrates a number of striking prophetic legends and miracle stories connected to the prophets Elijah, Elisha, and Micaiah ben Imlah. While one finds three whole chapters (2 Kings 18–20) dedicated to events in Hezekiah's approximately thirty-year reign, nearly two hundred years of Northern history are covered in less than four chapters spanning 2 Kings 13–16, some of which also covers events in Judah. To get a sense of just how variable the attention to different kings and events can be, one can turn to 2 Kings 15:1-7 where the editor, in extremely terse fashion, narrates the fifty-two-year reign of the Judean king Uzziah (also called Azariah).

The Lost "Book of the Annals of the Kings of Israel/Judah"?

In reading through the books of Kings, the reader will become familiar with a recurring phrase that references another book or books that apparently chronicled the life of Judean and Israelite Kings. Often the authors of Kings summarize the history of a king and then conclude by indicating that more details can be found elsewhere:

As for the rest of the acts of [king x], and all that he did, are they not written in the Book of the Annals of the Kings of Judah[/Israel]?

Many scholars believe that the authors of Kings made use of court annals of the two kingdoms, which we no longer possess, as a primary source. Most agree that the title used here is not so much an exact title as a descriptor, likely referring to a common collection that included the histories of both Israel and Judah.

Controversies and Debates

Perhaps the biggest single controversy surrounding Kings concerns the issue we discussed when we introduced the Prophets more generally, namely, when, by whom, and for what purpose the larger history running from Joshua–2 Kings (the Deuteronomistic History) was first brought into a unity. Thus we will dedicate discussion here to another issue deserving attention, how some of the stories found in the Bible overlap with texts from contemporaneous ancient Near Eastern cultures and how such evidence informs the critical study of the Bible. A prime example of this can be seen in comparing the account of Judah's King Hezekiah, found in 2 Kings 18–19, with Sennacherib's prism, a clay monument with an inscription commemorating the Assyrian King Sennacherib's achievements.

What is particularly interesting in the case of Sennacherib's prism is the remarkable agreement between it and the biblical text of 2 Kings 18–19 (as well as another version of this story found in Isaiah 36–37), and also the clear slant each source puts on the details of the same event. In the Bible's version of the encounter, God acts on Hezekiah's behalf to preserve Jerusalem. Thousands of Sennacherib's soldiers are miraculously killed, even while it is mentioned that Hezekiah lost control of his outlying cities to Sennacherib. In Sennacherib's account, an excerpt of which we include below, there is no mention of his army's defeat, but we are told that Sennacherib took these outlying cities by force and that Hezekiah remained locked up in Jerusalem "like a bird in a cage." Sennacherib's prism goes on to indicate that the siege was lifted because Hezekiah capitulated, the size of his kingdom was reduced, and that he paid a tidy sum as a form of punishment for rebelling against the Assyrian emperor (the latter fact is acknowledged in passing in 2 Kings 18:13-16 but is missing

Sennacherib's prism reads:

As for Hezekiah, the Judean, I besieged forty-six of his fortified walled cities and surrounding smaller towns, which were without number. Using packed-down ramps and applying battering rams, infantry attacks by mines, breeches, and siege machines, I conquered (them). . . . He himself, I locked up within Jerusalem, his royal city, like a bird in a cage. I surrounded him with earthworks, and made it unthinkable for him to exit by the city gate. His cities which I had despoiled I cut off from his land and gave them to Mitinti, king of Ashdod, Padi, king of Ekron and Silli-bel, king of Gaza, and thus diminished his land. (Translation taken from *The Context of Scripture*, ed. William W. Hallo and K. Lawson Younger Jr. [Leiden: Brill, 2000], 2:303.)

Figure 14. The Taylor Prism, Sennacherib versus Hezekiah, 700 B.C.E. Courtesy Todd Bolen/BiblePlaces.com

from the version in Isaiah). The biblical text also implies that Sennacherib was assassinated sometime shortly after this, but in reality this occurred a full twenty years later. In short, 2 Kings celebrates the lifting of Sennacherib's siege as a sign of miraculous divine intervention, but it seems quite likely that Hezekiah made a huge political blunder in rebelling against Sennacherib, a blunder that was rectified at a tremendous cost of land and money. Thus, this case is a good example of how external textual evidence can substantiate the accuracy of the *general* historical sequence of events described in the Bible while calling into question many of its more detailed claims.

Solomon's Reign

Solomon's rise to power occurs through an act of political intrigue. First Kings 1 indicates that one group of David's palace officials was supporting David's son Adonijah to be king while another, ultimately more successful, group promoted Solomon's cause. Solomon still needed to consolidate his power, which he did by eliminating a number of his father's and his own enemies and rivals. In some ways, David's deathbed instructions to his son Solomon to take out his enemies (see 1 Kings 2) read like those of a Mafia crime boss to his successor. Solomon is then depicted as engaging in many large-scale building projects, most especially the Jerusalem temple and his own very ornate palace. While clearly impressive, the early chapters in Kings note that he accomplished these tasks by conscripting forced laborers, even from among his own people, suggesting that he at times acted like the harsh Pharaoh who had once enslaved the people of Israel. More than any other king of Israel, Solomon is portrayed as very wealthy and highly cosmopolitan, a fact that seems to earn him both praise and criticism. While 1 Kings 10 reports on the monies Solomon generated by importing horses from Egypt, and 1 Kings 11 talks about his many foreign wives, Deuteronomy 17 specifically condemns any future kings who engage in exactly these two behaviors. It is hard to escape the conclusion that this is an implicit criticism of Solomon's kingship, even if archaeologists believe that the account of Solomon's wealth is greatly exaggerated in these pages.

The Split of the North and the South

Chapters 11 and 12 in 1 Kings give two distinct accounts of why the united kingdom that had been ruled by Saul, David, and Solomon split apart. The first, in chapter 11, offers a Deuteronomic theological explanation of why the united monarchy dissolved upon Solomon's death. Here we are told that God became angry with Solomon because Solomon accommodated the non-Israelite religious practices of his many foreign-born wives. Chapter 11 proceeds to explain that God sent the prophet Ahijah of Shiloh to inform Jeroboam son of Nebat, who was by lineage a Northerner and by vocation one of Solomon's high officials, that he was being made king over the Northern ten tribes because Solomon had angered God with his religious infidelity. In chapter 12, however, we get a sociopolitical explanation of why the kingdom split. Upon Solomon's death, representatives from the North, including

Figure 15. Map of the Divided Kingdom. Copyright Common English Bible.

a leader named Jeroboam, indicated that if Solomon's son named Rehoboam was willing to place a lighter tax and service burden on the Northern tribes, and treat the North as Solomon had treated his own Judean counterparts, then they would willingly serve Rehoboam. But Rehoboam, foolishly taking the advice of his cadre of childhood friends over the advice of his father Solomon's more seasoned counselors, told the Northerners that he would actually increase their tax burden. Only at this point did the North break off from David's dynasty and proclaim Jeroboam king. It is quite common for the biblical authors to include both a theological and a humanistic explanation for a particular event. This suggests that they saw both explanations as providing insight into why history unfolded as it did.

The Early History of Prophecy in Israel

Many of our earliest accounts of ancient Israelite prophecy are found in 1–2 Kings. The view we gain of prophets between the time of Solomon, who lived in the mid-tenth century BCE, and Amos (the earliest classical prophetic book in the Bible), who lived in the mid-eighth century BCE, indicates that prophets were often involved in royal politics, at times anointing kings and at others challenging or destabilizing various monarchs. Thus already in the first chapter of 1 Kings, Nathan the prophet helps orchestrate Solomon's rise to power. As noted above, 1 Kings 11 gives divine sanction to the revolt of the Northern Kingdom through Ahijah the prophet. First Kings 17–2 Kings 9 contains a series of wondrous acts performed by Elijah and his disciple, Elisha, in close relation to the lives of Israel's kings. While some of these narratives portray the true prophet as a lonely man set against the king and various false prophets who live in the palace, a careful reading of these materials reveals that characters like Elisha lived with a band of prophetic disciples (2 Kings 6:1-7) and that these groups had a distinct look that marked them as prophets (2 Kings 1:8).

While few would see these vivid prophetic tales as containing accurate historical reporting, a number of stories have details that suggest they are quite archaic and contain important historical insights. For example, at the end of 1 Kings 21, one finds a brief paragraph attempting to explain why Elijah's prophecy against Ahab did not happen in his lifetime, indicating that Elijah had actually spoken a prophecy against Ahab that did not come true. In fact, a later author appears to have added Ahab's name at the very the end of the following story in 1 Kings 22 that describes the violent death of an unnamed

Figure 16. The Dothan Valley, a battle site where Elisha has a vision of "Chariots of Fire" in 2 Kings 6. Courtesy Miriam Ben-Haim.

Northern king, so that Elijah's prophecy is now made to ring true! More important, Elijah and Elisha are some of the earliest representatives of those who believed Israel should worship YHWH exclusively, a belief that eventually resulted in Western monotheism. Thus in 1 Kings 18, Elijah engages in a contest with the prophets of the Canaanite god Baal on Mount Carmel that shows YHWH to be the one true God and concludes with the violent slaughter of several hundred prophets of Baal. In 2 Kings 9, Elisha sends one of his prophetic disciples to anoint Jehu as the new Northern king and to charge him to kill the current king, thereby overthrowing Ahab's dynasty. One chapter later, Jehu engages in a massacre of a large number of devotees to Baal, furthering the cause that YHWH, not Baal, is God.

True Prophecy? The Case of Micaiah ben Imlah

Apart perhaps from that of Job, there are few stories in the Bible that give as clear a view into how the heavenly realm functions and how its activities affect life on the earth as that of Micaiah ben Imlah (1 Kings 22). This story relates how God seeks the advice of other divine beings in his heavenly coterie of helpers concerning how to lure the current king of Northern Israel into a battle where he will be killed by the enemy. Ultimately, one particular divine being suggests he will be a "lying spirit" in the mouth of the kingdom's state sponsored prophets (v. 22).

128

This passage raises difficult theological issues in that in it God seems to be involved in deception in order to further his plans. Of course one could counter that God sent Micaiah to inform this king that he had sent a lying spirit to deceive him, information that the king chose to ignore. Thus in certain ways this episode resembles the plague narrative in Exodus in which God hardens Pharaoh's heart, and both passages suggest that at certain times God's providential control may severely circumscribe the freewill of particular humans.

1–2 Kings in Jewish Tradition

There are many places in which the rich array of materials found in these books have come to influence later Jewish tradition. Already within the biblical period, Solomon is seen as the author of Proverbs or at least the patron of proverbial tradition. This likely stems from the narrative in 1 Kings 3 about the great wisdom he employed in discerning which prostitute was the mother of a particular infant, as well as from 1 Kings 4, which tells us of Solomon's great wisdom and the fact that he composed three thousand proverbs. From a Jewish perspective, Solomon's greatest act was the building of the temple in Jerusalem. While actual sacrifice is not to be performed in the absence of the temple, the traditional Jewish liturgy expresses hope for the restoration of the Jerusalem temple, and for millennia Jews have prayed facing toward Jerusalem. Interestingly enough, the prayer that Solomon offers in 1 Kings 8 at the consecration of the temple recognizes the legitimacy of offering prayer directed toward Jerusalem by those who might be exiled from God's presence, because they had sinned and thus were not in a position to offer sacrifices in Jerusalem.

Another very important figure in postbiblical Jewish tradition is Elijah. Inasmuch as 2 Kings 2 reports that Elijah was taken up alive into heaven, Jews have come to see him both as an intercessor who can answer prayers and perform miracles, and on the basis of the end of Malachi as the one who will herald the arrival of the messianic age. Finally, one might highlight the importance of the theological attempt by the editors of these books to understand why even after Josiah's great reforms God allowed Jerusalem to be destroyed. While various biblical authors propose a variety of related but distinct explanations for why this huge tragedy occurred, the quest to give theological meaning to consequential historical events sits at the heart of biblical and all subsequent Jewish theology.

1–2 Kings in Christian Tradition

Naturally the temple, associated with Solomon, was no less important to the early followers of Jesus, this group being a Jewish sect. When the rebuilt, or second, temple was eventually destroyed in 70 CE, the life of Judaism and Christianity would never be the same. The gospel writers regularly refer to the Second Temple, the most sacred site in Judaism, a place of sacrifice and pilgrimage during Jesus' life. Jesus teaches in the temple precincts, sends those he heals to be inspected by the temple priests, at times questions its leaders, and in one instance turns over the tables of those selling goods there, complaining that Solomon's original desire for a "place of prayer for the nations" has instead been turned into a "den of thieves." Many scholars believe that Jesus' bold action in this latter story put in motion the events that led to his execution.

Although figures like Moses and David are foundational within the gospel stories, a central character of Kings, Elijah, also features prominently. As mentioned above, the Jewish people have long understood Elijah to be one who will herald the arrival of the messianic age. What is interesting is that John the Baptist is portrayed to be Elijah within the Gospels, thus fulfilling this important role. In the words of Jesus himself:

> He [Jesus] replied, "Elijah is indeed coming and will restore all things; but I tell you that Elijah has already come, and they did not recognize him, but they did to him whatever they pleased. So also the Son of Man is about to suffer at their hands." Then the disciples understood that he was speaking to them about John the Baptist. (Matthew 17:11-13)

This example clearly portrays Jesus as taking up a messianic position.

In the same way that modern-day Jews await the rebuilding of the temple, so too does the Christian tradition testify to the return of God's temple on earth, seen especially in the book of Revelation. This book depicts a time in which a new temple descends from heaven onto the earth, once and for all establishing God's kingdom (see Revelation 21). Perhaps most striking within Christian thinking, however, is the idea that Jesus himself is the temple, the locus of God's powerful presence. This is seen clearly in the Gospel of John where Jesus speaks of the temple being destroyed and rebuilt in three days, to which John adds that Jesus was speaking about his body (see John 2:20-22; Revelation 21:22).

ISAIAH

Introduction and Overview

The book of Isaiah is the longest, probably the most complex, and possibly the most influential prophetic book in the Hebrew Bible. It contains sixty-six chapters, and more words than the Twelve Minor Prophets combined. The prophet Isaiah began prophesying sometime in the 730s BCE and was active at least through Sennacherib's invasion of Jerusalem in 701 BCE. The book can be divided as follows: Chapters 1–12 contain many of Isaiah's earliest prophecies that appear to have been delivered in reaction to the events surrounding the Syro-Ephraimite war when Syrian and Northern Israelite armies attempted to force Ahaz, the King of Judah, to join their fight against the Assyrian state. Chapters 13–23 are mainly what scholars have come to call Oracles against the Nations. Thus differing chapters are addressed to various surrounding peoples. Chapters 24–27 are seen as containing a distinct set of late apocalyptic prophecies about God's coming cosmic judgment of the whole world. Chapters 28–33 also have material that may stem from the historical Isaiah, composed of various "woes" or words of judgment to different groups, some of which appear to have been spoken during the Assyrian crisis in 701 BCE. Chapters 34–35 are likely part of a bridge linking the materials in the first part of Isaiah to chapters 40–66. Isaiah 36–39 narrates the events surrounding Sennacherib's invasion of Judah under King Hezekiah in 701 BCE and closely parallels materials found in 2 Kings 18–20. As we will discuss in more detail under the heading "Controversies and Debates," scholars have long suggested that all of chapters 40–66, which largely outline God's redemption of Israel, were penned by one or more authors who lived after Judah was exiled from Jerusalem. This large block can be broken into two further sections (40–55 and 56–66), thought to come from different authors.

It is important to point out that even scholars who emphasize that the book grew over a very long span of time have come to recognize that it is not simply a loose collection of prophecies. Rather, the larger book was tightly knit together so that earlier passages point forward to later concerns and later parts of the book pick up upon and develop earlier themes.

Controversies and Debates

Perhaps the most debated issue in Isaiah studies concerns the book's authorship and dating. That the book might not all have been written by the prophet Isaiah has long presented problems for conservative scholars, especially given the first verse of the book that introduces what follows as a vision of Isaiah, son of Amoz. However, as we discuss elsewhere in this textbook, such information given at the beginning of a book need not be taken as a claim of authorship or understood as a claim that everything that follows stems from that one person. While there are great disagreements about how much of chapters 1–39 belong to the historical Isaiah, the largest issue relates to the materials in 40–66. The modern scholarly view until quite recently was that chapters 40–55 were authored by an anonymous prophet (referred to as Second Isaiah) who lived in Babylon close to the time when Cyrus conquered the greater Near East including Babylon in 538 BCE. Chapters 56–66 are often attributed to another even later prophet (referred to as Third Isaiah) who lived and wrote among those exiles who had returned from Babylon to Judah. But there are those who believe that 40–66 is more unified than previously acknowledged and others who argue that there is more diversity within 40–55 and 56–66 than the labels Second and Third Isaiah imply. Whatever the case, it seems clear that 40–66 contains materials different in language and style from most of the material in 1–39, and the prophet Isaiah does recede from the scene in this latter part of the book. For example, although he is mentioned some sixteen times in 1–39, his name is entirely absent in 40–66. Further, the events spoken of in 40–66 clearly move well beyond the time of the prophet Isaiah's life. Although these need not be taken as surefire proofs of multiple authors, such factors do suggest that the book is likely a composite penned over a long period of time by more than one author. Still, some recent voices have rightly begun to ask what we can learn from the book as a whole, in its final form, regardless of how many authors contributed to its composition.

132

The Inaugural Vision

Isaiah 6 recounts how Isaiah received his prophetic commission directly from God. It appears that Isaiah is sitting in the temple in Jerusalem when the religious imagery in the shrine comes alive and he suddenly finds himself present in the heavenly retinue. The narrative conveys that Isaiah's reaction upon finding himself before God's throne was a strong sense of his own sinfulness. In fact, an angelic being purifies his lips with a hot coal taken from the heavenly altar, cleansing his sins. He is then given a rather disturbing message that he is to preach to the people with the hope that they will not listen or comprehend and then repent. The result will be a great devastation, but one that will preserve a purified remnant of survivors. Interestingly, the angelic beings referenced in this passage, called seraphs, are a type of six-winged heavenly being that resembled a snake. Given the stories of Numbers 21:4-9 and 2 Kings 18, it seems likely that the bronze snakelike statue that was housed in the Jerusalem temple until the late 700s BCE "came to life" in Isaiah's vision.

Isaiah 7 in Context and Its Reuse in the New Testament

Isaiah is one of the most cited books of the Hebrew Bible within the New Testament. One of the most well-known New Testament uses of Isaiah is when Matthew links the reference in Isaiah 7 to a child being born to a young woman to the virgin birth story of Jesus. Many Jews think that Isaiah 7 never mentions any virgin birth and thus Christianity is mistaken in claiming the Bible endorses such a notion. Many Christians, on the other hand, believe it does indeed say such a thing, and thus Christianity is correct when it argues that the virgin birth story is prophesied in Isaiah. However, we would suggest that framing the debate in this way is wrongheaded. The fact is that those who belong to communities that read these texts as sacred Scripture have long recognized that a text might have had a particular meaning in its earliest context but that they also recognize that over time a text can speak to new generations living in new historical circumstances. To put it simply, sometimes prophecies can be fulfilled in more than one way. To be sure, it strains credulity when certain Christians attempt to argue that the plain sense or intent of the prophet Isaiah living in the 700s BCE was that everything would be fine 700 years later when a virgin would bear a son. Isaiah is clearly attempting to communicate to King Ahaz and the other people of Judah that the current threat will pass in the near future. Furthermore, the Hebrew speaks of a young woman giving birth, not necessarily a virgin, and the emphasis is on the threat passing before the child is fully grown up, not on a miraculous birth. In fact, some argue that the woman is actually Isaiah's wife inasmuch as Isaiah, like Hosea, has children with symbolic names like this child who is to be named Immanuel, meaning "God is with us."

That said, both Jews and Christians affirm that the words contained in Scripture can transcend their original historical context and have deep, unforeseen meanings that speak to later faith communities in profound ways. Both traditions engage in theologically creative interpretations, often bending the plain sense or contextual meaning of a passage to help free the text from its original context and allow it to speak anew to later generations living in different times. In this case, the author of Matthew built upon the pervasive biblical theme of God intervening to help women like Sarah and Rachel and Hannah give birth to important children, and was able to intensify this theme by linking it to the reading found in the Greek translation of the Hebrew Bible that does refer to the woman in Isaiah 7 as a virgin (Greek *parthenos*). The readers of this book will hopefully come to see that this is a type of theological reuse of Isaiah 7 and that one can appreciate the creativity of such an interpretation even while recognizing that the original prophecy of Isaiah is directed to an audience and a situation far different than the context to which Matthew speaks.

The Heart of Isaiah's Message

The expression "Lord of hosts" features prominently in Isaiah's prophecies and signals the great emphasis Isaiah places on God's transcendence. In fact, Isaiah regularly points out how human pretensions will be punctured in God's coming judgment. These themes point to the book's emphasis on the creaturely status of human beings and the superiority of YHWH, Israel's God. Part of the prophet's message therefore is a call to humility before the Lord to act with righteousness and justice, lest the "day of the LORD" be one of great judgment. Isaiah makes clear that God will use whatever means necessary to chastise Israel and Judah for their lack of justice and self-reliance, even foreign nations like Assyria and Babylon. In fact, Isaiah goes so far as to state that Assyria is a tool in the hand of God used for his punishment: "Assyria, the rod of my anger—the club in their hands is my fury!" (10:5). In all cases, the message to the people is clear: Trust not in self or the powers of this world but in God. Doing so can avert the coming judgment.

A key term used throughout the book is the Hebrew word *amn*, to trust or be faithful. An example can be seen in the following words of the prophet:

Therefore thus says the Lord GOD,
> See, I am laying in Zion a foundation stone, a tested stone,
> a precious cornerstone, a sure foundation: "One who trusts [*ma'amin*]
> will not panic." (Isaiah 28:16)

This passage conveniently brings up another important theme within the book of Isaiah: Zion. The importance of Jerusalem and the temple mount, together taken as Zion (the holy place where God is present), is probably clearer in Isaiah than any other book of the Hebrew Bible. Isaiah overall has a special concern for this place in terms of providing a vision in which all things will be made right—restoring this place as the focal point of God's interaction with Israel and all people through them. Thus Isaiah 2 describes all the nations of the world making pilgrimage to the Jerusalem temple and God's peace reigning on earth (see the U.N. building inscription toward the end of this chapter). In the later chapters of Isaiah, written during the Second Temple period, the author presents a vision in which Zion is restored from chaos (or ruins) into a center of religious and human activity, becoming a beacon of light and a place of joy, one where God is worshiped and people live righteously. This notion of the Jewish people ensconced safely in their homeland and the accompanying notion of the pilgrimage of the nations to Zion recurs throughout the book and helps unify it.

Isaiah 40–66: The Tradition Continues

As noted above, there is a wide consensus that these chapters were written by a writer or writers who lived substantially after Isaiah's time. Chapters 40–55 are addressed to the exiles living in Babylonia announcing the end of Babylonian hegemony and attempting to motivate these exiles to return to Judah and rebuild Jerusalem. Chapters 56–66 seem to stem from a slightly later period, and this section hints at various communal tensions that arose during the initial very difficult years when this group began the rebuilding process. Isaiah 40–66 contains some of the most moving images of God's concern for Israel found anywhere in Scripture. Chapter 40 opens with God comforting his beloved people Israel and announcing their imminent restoration. Several of the following chapters use creation and exodus imagery to describe the new thing that God is about to do with Israel, and along the way they develop the idea of Israel as God's chosen people in strikingly profound ways. For example, in Isaiah 49, God assures those returning to Zion that he cannot forget them because he has tattooed them and the walls of Jerusalem on the palms of his own hands. Furthermore, several distinct passages within 40–55 that some have labeled the "Servant Songs" probe what it means to be God's chosen servant. The images in these poetic passages are ambiguous, and thus Christians see them as referring to one special servant of God, Jesus, while Jews tend to understand them as referring to the whole people of Israel or a specially loyal vanguard of Israelites (sometimes called a "remnant" [Hebrew *she'ar*]). The book concludes with a vision of a renewed heaven and earth with everyone coming up to worship in Jerusalem. It is no small wonder that both Jews and Christians have found solace in these chapters for so many generations.

Isaiah in Judaism

Two very prominent examples of the influence of Isaiah on Jewish liturgical practice stand out. The chorus, "Holy, Holy, Holy is the LORD of hosts; the whole earth is full of his glory," that the angelic beings sing before God in Isaiah 6 features prominently in the Jewish liturgy. The central prayer in the Jewish prayer service is the *amidah*. After reciting it silently the prayer leader recites it aloud and adds a section called the *kedushah* or sanctification. The centerpiece of the *kedushah* is this verse from Isaiah 6; and the congregants, who are standing during its recitation, actually lift their heels off the ground each time they say the word "holy," symbolizing one's spiritual elevation during this prayer, mirroring the actions of the angels in heaven.

More weekly prophetic lections are drawn from Isaiah than from any other single prophetic book. This is especially evident in the weeks between the Ninth of Av (a fast day marking the destruction of both temples in Jerusalem) and Rosh Hashanah (the Jewish New Year). During the late summer and early fall, the prophetic lections, week upon week, are drawn from Isaiah 40–66. These prophetic selections, which were addressed to the Babylonian exiles, now serve to comfort the wider Jewish community as they move from marking the destruction of the temple to celebrating God's renewal of the world that the Jewish New Year marks.

Isaiah in Later Christianity

The importance of Isaiah to the life of the church can probably not be overstated. Perhaps because Isaiah presents a vision of a time when the world will be at peace under God's sovereignty and rule, this has been linked to the kingdom of God proclaimed in the New Testament, a time ushered in by the Messiah. It is interesting to note the extent to which the imagery of "the lion lying down with the lamb," symbolizing a time of peace, has captured the imagination of Christian thought. This image has been portrayed in numerous pieces of Christian art as well as put to a beautiful score in Handel's *Messiah*. Although this imagery is derived from both Isaiah 11:6 and 65:25, the specific wording in both places is more accurately that of a lion with a calf while the lamb is spoken of with reference to a wolf. The powerful influence of Isaiah's peace imagery is attested to by the fact that a quote from Isaiah 2:4 was engraved into a monumental wall near the United Nations building in New York City, seen below.

Figure 17. The Isaiah Wall in New York City. Courtesy Wikimedia Commons.

Christianity, like Judaism, has also incorporated the chorus of Isaiah 6 "Holy, Holy, Holy is the Lord of hosts; the whole earth is full of his glory" into its liturgical life in significant ways. This may point to a common worship heritage in the first century—that is, both groups inherited the use of this passage in worship—or it could simply point to the importance of this passage's vision of God's holiness in worship more generally. In most Western church liturgies, this cry has become part of what is called the *Sanctus*, words said or sung following the preface to the Eucharistic Prayer in which the bread and wine are consecrated and then received by communicants. It comes as no surprise that the thrice repetition of God's holiness in this passage has been seen by many Christians to anticipate Christianity's worship of the triune God.

JEREMIAH

Introduction and Overview

The book of Jeremiah contains messages of both judgment and hope. It is set in the period leading up to and during the Babylonian destruction of Jerusalem, which resulted in the forcible exile of much of the Judean population to Babylon. According to the book's first few verses, it records the message of the prophet Jeremiah, who lived during the reigns of Josiah, Jehoiakim, and Zedekiah (approximately the 620s to the 580s BCE). As we discuss below, however, the textual history of Jeremiah is particularly interesting in that portions of the traditional Jeremiah text, some 10 percent of the book, are not found in the Septuagint or some of the Dead Sea Scrolls. Given that the missing sections are largely positive in nature or contain passages of hope, scholars have suggested that they were added at a later time to round out the prophet's originally more gloomy message, a point to which we will return.

The book itself can be broadly divided as follows. Chapter 1 serves as a prologue and relates God's commission of the prophet Jeremiah. Chapters 2–25 mainly contain words of judgment that Jeremiah delivered to the people of Judah. Chapters 26–29 and 34–45 are stories about the prophet and those with whom he interacted. In chapters 30–33, set in between these stories and often called the book of consolation, one finds a series of hopeful oracles of restoration. Chapters 46–51 are filled with prophecies that Jeremiah delivered against various nations. Chapter 52 serves as an epilogue, essentially an appendix that provides a description of the fall of Jerusalem. It is similar in content to 2 Kings 24–25.

The reader might be curious to know that Jeremiah's notoriously long-winded sermons railing against the corruption of the times gave rise to the

English word *jeremiad*. This term, indicating a long, mournful complaint often containing woes, is still in use today.

Controversies and Debates

Perhaps no single issue regarding Jeremiah has been more hotly debated than the question of how much reliable information one can glean from the book about the actual prophet and the times in which he lived. Thus while some biblical scholars argue that we have more information about the historical Jeremiah, the details of his life, and his personal psychology than any other figure in the Hebrew Bible, others would contend that all we have is a literary construct of Jeremiah created by those who edited his book and that we should not confuse this construct with the actual prophet Jeremiah.

But the issue becomes even more complicated when we consider that the biblical text itself is under some dispute, and it is difficult to know how much of the material in Jeremiah stems from the prophet and how much editing the book has undergone. Here we return to the issue mentioned above of different manuscript versions having missing or added verses, and the order of certain passages differing from version to version as well. Further, even if we leave this particular question aside and start from the traditional (longer) text, it is important to point out that scholars often speak of three broad types of material in Jeremiah, which they label A, B, and C. The A materials are actual prophetic sayings (often called oracles) that Jeremiah spoke. Usually within the English translation of Jeremiah this type of material is formatted as poetry. Scholars use the letter B to refer to the many biographical stories about Jeremiah and the times in which he lived. Generally these materials are formatted as prose in the English text. The C material in Jeremiah contains distinct features that have led many to conclude that it stems from the same scribes who edited Deuteronomy and Joshua–2 Kings (commonly called the Deuteronomistic History).

Comparing Jeremiah "C" to Deuteronomy

In order to understand something of the work biblical scholars do and to explain why they claim that the authors of the Deuteronomy may have influenced the so-called C material in Jeremiah, we here provide a comparison of a portion of this C material with an excerpt from Deuteronomy. The bold type below reflects an exact correspondence of Hebrew words or the same words in different order.

> *Deuteronomy 29:24-27: All the nations will wonder, "Why has the* Lord *done thus to this land? What caused this great display of anger?"* **They will conclude, "It is because they abandoned the covenant of the** Lord**,** *the God of their ancestors, which he made with them when he brought them out of the land of Egypt. They turned* **and served other gods, worshiping them,** *gods whom they had not known and whom he had not allotted to them."*
>
> *Jeremiah 22:8-9: And many nations will pass by this city, and all of them will say one to another,* **"Why has the** Lord **dealt in this way** *with that great city?"* **And they will answer, "Because they abandoned the covenant of the** Lord *their God,* **and worshiped other gods and served them."**

Jeremiah's Commission

There are a number of unique features in the first chapter of Jeremiah, a chapter that describes God's commissioning of Jeremiah to be a prophet. To begin, we learn that Jeremiah receives a prophecy telling him that God appointed him to be a prophet even before he had been born. We are also told that God touched his mouth and placed the prophecies he was to speak within Jeremiah. The idea that prophets were in some sense not only speakers of God's word but actually "containers" of God's word is important for understanding the role of the prophet in ancient Israel. Many of Israel's prophets were not only people who deliver God's words but also figures whose very lives in some sense incarnate and communicate God's word to his people. Thus, as we discuss later, Hosea's very life is part and parcel of his prophecy. Jeremiah too engages in many actions that carry a prophetic resonance. For instance, in chapter 16, God prohibits Jeremiah from marrying, an activity associated with joy and gladness, in order to communicate that dire times are quickly approaching. Or, in chapter 32, in the midst of the siege of Jerusalem, God commands Jeremiah to purchase some land as a sign that even though Jerusalem will be destroyed God will, in the future, restore the people of Israel to their land. The idea that not only what a prophet says but that his actions and his life are prophetic communications is found in more intensified form in the New Testament notion that Jesus is God's word incarnate.

The Temple Sermon

Two separate passages in Jeremiah, Jeremiah 7 and 26, discuss the same incident from distinct angles. Chapter 7 reports Jeremiah delivering an important and rather stunning oracle of potential judgment on the people of Judah. In this passage, Jeremiah comes to the temple in Jerusalem to tell his contemporaries that God's willingness to dwell in the temple and to protect the people of Judah is contingent on their proper ethical and ritual behavior. Jeremiah proclaims that even though Israel is God's special people, it is a mistake to believe that this, in turn, means that God will protect them no matter how they act. Chapter 26 reports what happened to Jeremiah when he engaged in this action. Here we are told that Jeremiah's life is threatened because his proclamation was viewed as a form of treason, a capital crime. While Jeremiah was spared in this instance, we know from other parts of this book that his life was often severely endangered, as seen in chapters 37 and 38 that report that Jeremiah was under arrest and for a time was thrown into confinement in a cistern. Furthermore, according to Jeremiah 26, another prophet named Uriah delivered a similar oracle of doom against Jerusalem and Judah and, even though he fled to Egypt, he was captured by a squad of soldiers, brought back to Jerusalem, and then killed by the king. These passages make clear that being an Israelite prophet is an inherently dangerous job because prophets tend to criticize the status quo, often in ways that are designed to attract the attention of those in power.

The Confessions of Jeremiah

Jeremiah 11–20 includes eight "confessions" or "laments" of Jeremiah found at 11:18-23; 12:1-6; 15:10-12, 15-21; 17:14-18; 18:19-23; 20:7-12; and 20:14-18. Some scholars wonder whether these words are more general laments that have been placed in Jeremiah as a literary device, rather than Jeremiah's own speech. In any case, within the book these speeches articulate the types of deep spiritual and psychological battles faced by those who speak words of judgment upon the society in which they live. Themes emphasized in these passages include: feeling anger at God because he fails to punish the wicked, feeling persecuted by those who plot to silence the prophet because he is delivering a social critique, and feeling abandoned by both God and by former friends and neighbors.

The Difficulty of Discerning
True from False Prophets

One of the most gripping sections of the book of Jeremiah is found in chapters 27 and 28, a scene that occurs after 597 BCE but before Jerusalem is destroyed. For the reader to fully appreciate and understand this section, one needs to have a little background information and know that, due to a previous revolt against Babylon a few years earlier, the Babylonian army invaded Jerusalem in 597 BCE and took various valuable objects from the temple and palace. But most important, the Babylonians took away many nobles including the king, named Jehoiachin, as hostages back to Babylon and then set up another king named Zedekiah as a puppet king in the hopes that he would be less prone to rebel.

Chapter 27 opens with God telling Jeremiah to put on an oxen yoke and then present himself at a meeting between the current king of Judah and dignitaries from some nearby nations. It is clear that the attendees at the meeting are plotting their rebellion against the Babylonian emperor Nebuchadnezzar. The yoke is meant to symbolize God's intention to place all the nations in this vicinity under the rule of Babylon and that rebellion against Nebuchadnezzar is in effect rebellion against God and God's plan. In chapter 28, a prophet named Hananiah comes into the picture, and he delivers an oracle proclaiming that within two years Judah will be freed of Babylonian domination and Jehoiachin and the other nobles taken hostage will return with the temple implements that were taken to Babylon. But now both the reader and the ancient audience are faced with a crucial question: Who is telling the truth? That is, who is a true prophet and who is a false one?

Jeremiah contends that the threshold is higher for believing a prophet who proclaims that peace or good news is on the way than it is for a prophet who brings words of judgment and doom, inasmuch as Israel's true prophets have historically prophesied judgment and humans tend to experience misery more often in history than quiet lives filled with peace. However, the reader should also know that Deuteronomy 18, another passage that addresses this issue, informs us that one can ultimately only be sure that someone is a true prophet after events have unfolded in the manner he or she prophesied. From our vantage point we can clearly see that Jeremiah was a true prophet and Hananiah was a false one. But, if one had been in Judah in the early sixth century BCE, it may have been quite difficult to discern the true from the false prophet, especially since most people prefer to listen to optimistic predictions over predictions of doom.

Baruch the Scribe

While Jeremiah was obviously a very articulate person, like most people in ancient Israel or the broader ancient Near East, he did not possess writing skills and likely did not use pen and parchment on a regular basis. The professionals who wrote and kept books were called *scribes*. In the case of Jeremiah we know from passages like Jeremiah 36 that he had a scribe named Baruch, who wrote out the prophecies that Jeremiah dictated to him on a scroll. At this time in history, most of the people lived in an oral culture, and writing did not function as it is does today where books, newspapers, and other written media are widespread. Even when books were read, they were generally read aloud to others, not silently to oneself. In fact, the biblical Hebrew word for *read* really means "to call aloud."

Jeremiah and Moses

Jeremiah is in many ways a prophet like Moses and in other ways a kind of anti-Moses. Like Moses, who initially refuses God's commission, Jeremiah at first attempts to turn down his divine commission. And like Moses, Jeremiah's life is often threatened by the very Israelites he is trying to help. Further, both prophets are deeply concerned with the issues of Israel's idolatry and the people's tendency to be unfaithful to God. Jeremiah is an anti-Moses figure inasmuch as instead of bringing Israel to the Holy Land like Moses had done, he announces the coming exile of Judah and Jerusalem from the land. And, although Jeremiah only went along unwillingly, he ultimately ends up back in Egypt with a group who fled the land of Israel, reversing the course of Moses' life.

Jeremiah in the Jewish Tradition

Jeremiah's prophecies had immense impact on later biblical and Jewish tradition. Within later biblical tradition, texts like Haggai and Zechariah suggest that there were internal arguments among those who returned from Babylon to Jerusalem over whether the seventy-year exile Jeremiah predicted (see Jeremiah 29:10) had indeed ended, and thus whether it was time to rebuild the temple. As we discuss in our chapter on Daniel, some Jews who lived under the oppressive Syrian–Greek rule in the 160s BCE speculated that the seventy-year figure given by Jeremiah really referred to a longer period of seven times seventy years since the Judean monarch had yet to be restored at this late juncture.

One can also witness the immense sway of Jeremiah's oracles of restoration by the fact that the *haftarah*, or prophetic lection, on the second day of Rosh

Hashanah (the Jewish New Year) is drawn from Jeremiah 31. This text describes God's passionate and enduring love for his special people Israel and includes the powerful image of God responding to the weeping of the matriarch Rachel by assuring her that he will restore her children to the land of Israel.

Jeremiah in the Christian Tradition

As mentioned above, Jesus seems to function like a Jeremiah figure in that he, like Jeremiah, suffers on behalf of his people, is rejected by them, and is considered in some way or another to be the word of God incarnate. In fact, in the Gospel of Matthew (at 16:14) Jesus is compared directly to the prophet. Perhaps more significant, however, is the role that Jeremiah 31:31-34 came to play in Christian self-understanding. This passage, speaking of a coming time of hope in which a new covenant would govern God's relationship with his people, came to animate the Christian imagination in profound ways. In fact, the words "New Covenant" can be translated as "New Testament," and thus this passage came to provide the commonly used title for the second part of the Christian Scriptures.

EZEKIEL

Introduction and Overview

Ezekiel is in many ways a dark book. Not only is it set during the period of Israel's exile, when Israel was forcibly removed from her homeland, but also the book and the visions it contains—especially those at the beginning—focus with particular gloom on Israel's sin. Further, it highlights Israel's unworthiness to receive God's favor and redemption and spends a great deal of time announcing God's coming judgment of Israel and its capital city, Jerusalem. However, it must also be said that this is not the whole picture. The book progresses and also speaks clearly to the hope Israel can have in a gracious God and that, despite their current circumstances, they will not only survive the exile but will also be reunited as one people in a rebuilt Jerusalem with God's presence returning to a new temple where he will dwell among his people forever.

The book itself can be subdivided as follows: 1–24 are prophecies of judgment against Israel; 25–32 and 35 are prophecies against various nations; 33–34 and 36–39 speak about Israel's ultimate restoration; and 40–48 is a vision of the ideal temple of the future and the community surrounding and maintaining the temple. If one trusts the thirteen dates found at regular junctures but not in chronological sequence (see 1:1; 8:1; 20:1; 24:1; 26:1; 29:1; 29:17; 30:20; 31:1; 32:1, 17; 33:21; 40:1), then one can place all the contents of the book between 593–571 BCE.

Controversies and Debates

Various scholars, particularly those interested in gender studies and feminist interpretation, have raised concerns about the way in which certain prophets use negative images of women in their attempt to describe Israel's unfaithfulness to God. This problem is particularly apparent in chapters 16 and 23 of Ezekiel, which employ graphic, some would argue pornographic, descriptions likening Israel and Judah's idolatry to explicit sexual acts committed by unfaithful women in order to demonstrate how offended God is by Israel's unfaithfulness.

The problems here are readily apparent, and most scholars would acknowledge the disturbing content of these chapters. However, others, while acknowledging the problem, highlight that the crux of the issue centers on whether Ezekiel's use of such troubling language is employed in a one-sided and gratuitous fashion, and thus should be criticized, or whether such language is included precisely to shock those Ezekiel addressed in hopes that they might understand how offensive their behavior was to God. Though it does not altogether lessen the problem or answer all the questions raised, such an approach reminds us that ancients may also have had similar reactions, finding these images equally disturbing.

A second, perhaps somewhat related, question concerns whether Ezekiel's oftentimes extreme behaviors, a topic we will discuss further below, indicate that he had what we today would label as a mental illness, or whether these irregular behaviors are better understood as a type of performance designed to engage and at times shock his listeners. Another possibility is that certain types of people we today may well label as mentally ill might in other cultures be treated as having the unusual ability to hear messages from the divine realm. It is worth pointing out that prophets in ancient Israel at times engage in unusual behavior due to God's spirit coming upon them (see 1 Samuel 19:23-24) and such people could be viewed as being mentally unhinged. In fact, prophets are at times called madmen (2 Kings 9:11 and Jeremiah 29:26). However, a mentally unstable person could still deliver true prophecies.

Ezekiel's Extreme Sign-Acts

As noted earlier in this book, many prophets engage in symbolic acts. Thus in 1 Kings 11 the prophet Ahijah tears a garment into twelve pieces and gives ten of them to Jeroboam to symbolize that Jeroboam will soon rule over the northern ten tribes. Earlier prophets certainly engaged in odd or even socially unacceptable behavior. One need only think of how Isaiah walks around barefoot and partially naked for three years to depict what will soon be happening to the Egyptians and Ethiopians (see Isaiah 20). But Ezekiel is a figure who seems to engage in a great number of these kinds of symbolic actions, several of which are quite extreme. Thus chapter 4 describes how Ezekiel spent over a full year laying down on one side with a mock model of Jerusalem under siege in front of him. Furthermore, during this time he ate a type of retrograde bread composed of various grains and legumes that he cooked over dung in order to teach his audience in Babylon that those still living in Jerusalem would soon be suffering the depredations of a siege mounted by the Babylonian army and would only be able to make bread by mixing together whatever supplies of different grains they had left. Do these behaviors reveal that Ezekiel was mentally imbalanced, or is it simply that he had a keen sense of showmanship as suggested by Ezekiel 33:30-33? Even if we could prove Ezekiel was afflicted with some diagnosable condition, one must still decide in what way, if any, would this fact affect his ability to be a prophet. The truth is (according to the story at least) that Ezekiel's message of judgment proved right on all counts. Further, it is important to remember that the difficult yet ultimately hopeful messages of prophets like Ezekiel may well have helped the people to survive through dark periods of history.

Figure 18. Interestingly, bread made from the ingredients specified in Ezekiel 4:9-17, a *defiled* bread meant to symbolize Israel's coming destruction and famine, has come to gain popularity as a commercial product in modern America.

The Prophet as Watchman

An important recurring motif in Ezekiel centers on the role the prophet plays in relation to his/her community. This role is not one performed in order to gain recognition or popularity but instead is done in duty to God; delivering the prophetic message is not optional. In chapter 3, for example, as part of Ezekiel's commission, he is told that regardless of the response he receives from those to whom he communicates, he will be held innocent if he delivers God's warnings and guilty if he fails to fulfill his prophetic task. This idea is reiterated in Ezekiel 33. An additional nuance of the prophet's task is found at the end of Ezekiel 22, where the reader learns that God seeks a prophetic figure who can "repair the city wall" so to speak, as well as "stand in the breach" to turn back God's anger, a point that calls to mind the greatest Israelite prophetic intercessor, Moses (Ezekiel 13:5 and 22:30; compare Exodus 32:1-14 and Psalm 106:23). Furthermore, Ezekiel 13 highlights that the many false prophets who proclaim that "all will be fine" are like those who place whitewash over a crumbling wall, and thus are failing in their duty to turn back God's anger and protect the people of Israel from imminent destruction. Being a prophet not only involved criticizing one's fellow citizens when they acted corruptly but also cajoling God into forgiving those sinful behaviors.

Ezekiel's Visit to the Temple

Ezekiel 8–11 reports a vision that Ezekiel experienced in 592 BCE in which he was transported in spirit to the Jerusalem temple while his body was physically located in Babylon. In this vision Ezekiel is shown various troubling unorthodox religious practices that explain God's ongoing wrath against the people of Judah. It should be noted that there is disagreement about whether the practices Ezekiel witnesses taking place are historically accurate, or if they are a figment of Ezekiel's imagination, or possibly even based on earlier things he had witnessed while still living in Jerusalem before he was forcibly taken to Babylon in 597 BCE. In any case, in reaction to these practices, we are told that God ordered various angelic beings to kill the population and destroy the city, except those who had avoided these detestable practices. The vision then narrates the movement of God's presence out of the temple by way of his mobile throne-chariot, an image that, along with others elsewhere in Ezekiel, gave rise to a tradition of "chariot mysticism" within Judaism (to be discussed below). Here the reader needs to keep in mind that the book of Ezekiel offers a religious explanation of events that historians would explain in more mundane terms. A historian would likely conjecture that the Babylonians conquered Judah and burned the temple because the Judeans who remained in Jerusalem became so factionalized and financially distressed that they mistakenly thought resisting Babylon was the wisest course of action. Ezekiel, on the other hand, believes that God permitted the Babylonians to invade Jerusalem in 597 BCE because he was angry with the people of Judah. In Ezekiel's view, the eventual destruction of Jerusalem (which would occur five years after this vision) happens because God finally abandons his abode in the temple. And in his view God is driven to abandon the temple due to the sinful actions of the populace. While those in Jerusalem will come to witness the Babylonians killing their people and destroying the city, Ezekiel sees the destruction taking place in the heavenly realm and being executed by various angels.

Individual Versus Collective Responsibility

A surface reading of Ezekiel 18 suggests that Ezekiel rejects the view of earlier biblical texts such as the Ten Commandments passage found in Exodus 20 in which the guilt of the parents can negatively affect the fate of their children and grandchildren. In fact, Ezekiel 18 could suggest that even one's earlier righteous or wicked actions are irrelevant. Rather, one will be judged by how they act in this very moment. However, a careful reading of this passage and of Ezekiel's larger theology suggests that it is unlikely that Ezekiel, or any other ancient Israelite thinker, rejected all notions of collective responsibility, let alone affirmed that one's earlier actions had no bearing on one's current and future situation. One can glean that Ezekiel still affirms collective responsibility by the very fact that he addresses chapter 18 to the house of Israel, that is, the whole people of Israel. And, while upon an initial reading Ezekiel 18 does appear to suggest that God does not punish children for the sins of their parents and that one's previous actions are irrelevant, it is important to see that these statements are made as part of an imaginative sermon. In this sermon, Ezekiel is addressing the people of Judah who are currently experiencing a terrible tribulation. Many of the elite, including Ezekiel—likely at one time a priest in the Jerusalem temple—were among a first group of deportees taken to Babylon as hostages after a revolt that the Babylonians put down in 597 BCE. Yet, a good deal of Judah's population remained in Israel. Ezekiel notes the fact that those who experienced these events attributed Judah's misfortune to the sins of the previous generation. In response, Ezekiel countered this notion by arguing that God only punishes those who warrant punishment and thus this generation was suffering for its own sins. However, Ezekiel also suggests that any time before the full punishment has arrived God remains open to complete repentance. In this act of imagination he wants the audience to realize that neither their previous behavior nor their current distress is definitive. That Ezekiel does not completely reject the idea of corporate responsibility is evident from the fact that the punishment described in Ezekiel 20 and the later restoration of Israel discussed in 36–48 are all described in communal terms.

150

God's Transcendence and Ezekiel's Dimming Vision of Israel's Prospects

While the text of Ezekiel 18 held out hope for Israel's repentance, readers of Ezekiel will notice that Ezekiel quite quickly came to believe that Israel would not, or perhaps could not, repent. In fact, even in the wake of the punishment of the people, Ezekiel, unlike other biblical prophets, saw little evidence that Israel would turn and be obedient to God. Thus Ezekiel 36 describes how God begins the process of Israel's eventual restoration with the image of God conducting a heart (or perhaps better a "will") transplant. God removes Israel's old heart of stone and gives them an obedient heart of flesh. Furthermore, Ezekiel asserts that God restores the people of Israel not out of love or compassion, as one finds in Isaiah 40–66 or Jeremiah 30–33, but because Israel's sinfulness has marred the holiness of God. Ezekiel's belief that humans were unable to act correctly and that God would be gracious despite Israel's disobedience provide some of the earliest scriptural roots of certain Calvinist and Lutheran ideas that flourished during the Reformation in the sixteenth and seventeenth centuries, ideas still very much alive among certain Protestant groups. Such groups stress that humans cannot take any steps toward their own salvation, but rather it is an act of grace bestowed by God on completely undeserving humans.

Jewish Use of Ezekiel

Ezekiel left a major mark on the Jewish mystical tradition, eventually giving rise to what came to be called *merkavah* or "chariot" mysticism—a reference to the elaborate vision of God's chariot that occurs in the opening of Ezekiel. Merkavah mysticism teaches those who study it how to ascend to various levels of heaven and how to conduct oneself during such spiritual journeys. It grew in popularity to such an extent that rabbinic authorities warned that one should not study such traditions before the age of forty and even then these esoteric ideas were to be transmitted only directly from the teacher to a single student rather than be taught publicly. Interestingly, some have suggested that the Apostle Paul was influenced by an early form of this tradition, on the basis of his statement that he was taken up to the third heaven in 2 Corinthians 12.

Ezekiel has also been influential in other areas of Jewish thought and identity. For example, the national anthem of the modern state of Israel, entitled "Hatikvah" ("the hope"), draws on language found in Ezekiel 37's vision of

151

the dry bones, which describes the people of Israel being resurrected. This vision obviously spoke powerfully to those reclaiming the Jewish homeland after a two thousand year hiatus, and in the wake of Hitler's destruction of European Jewry.

Figure 19. Artistic depiction of Ezekiel 1–3, which includes Ezekiel's chariot vision, God handing Ezekiel the scroll he is to swallow, and Jerusalem burning in the background. *Ezechiel* from *Icones Biblicae*. Amsterdam: Dankertz, 1648. Courtesy Smith College Libraries.

Christian Use of Ezekiel

In addition to the influence Ezekiel had on Paul, Ezekiel seems to have had made an impact upon the writer of the book of Revelation. This book ends, like Ezekiel, with its main character—in this case, John—being given a vision from a mountain of a new Jerusalem and temple, which is then measured. In another place, Revelation picks up a motif in Ezekiel when it reports that John is instructed to eat a prophetic book, which then becomes bitter in his stomach similar to the story found in Ezekiel 3 (see above image).

The book of Ezekiel did not capture the post-first-century Christian imagination quite like the other two big prophetic books of Isaiah and Jeremiah, perhaps due to its esoteric and at times complex nature. However, a number of early church fathers comment on it, including Origen, Jerome, and Gregory the Great. A particular oddity of modern Christian interest in the book re-volves around Ezekiel 38–39, chapters that describe an end-time battle that will precede the final and permanent restoration of the people of Israel in their land. Some Christian interpreters attempt to correlate the events described in this passage, and others found in Daniel and the book of Revelation, with contemporary events. In fact, during the Cold War years, it was not uncommon for certain interpreters to assert that the Hebrew words found in Ezekiel 38:2, *rosh meshech* (usually translated as "the chief prince of meshech"), as well as the names *Gog* and *Magog* (possible place names or areas, found also in Revelation 20:8), were references to Russia/Moscow, and that these verses were predicting an end-time battle involving the Soviets.

THE BOOK OF THE
TWELVE

Introduction and Overview

The twelve books that follow Ezekiel in the Hebrew Bible are often called the Minor Prophets or the Book of the Twelve. The title "minor" refers not to their lack of importance but to each book's diminutive length (when combined, the books contain fewer than seventy chapters total). Amos and Hosea are among two of the oldest collections of oracles attributed to single figures in the Bible. As a result, these books likely exerted a considerable influence on the content and style of later prophetic figures and books. Yet, at the same time, this collection includes some of the latest prophetic oracles preserved in the Bible, found in texts like Haggai, Zechariah, and Malachi. Some have speculated that the order of this collection in the traditional Hebrew sequence that we follow here (and the slightly differing ordering found in the Septuagint) reflects an attempt to place these books in roughly chronological sequence. However, we know, for example, that the events of Amos predated Hosea, and thus by today's historical standards they appear to be out of order chronologically. It seems equally likely that theological concerns played an important role in the shaping and ordering of this collection. By way of illustration, notice that the Book of the Twelve begins with Hosea, a book that speaks of Israel being an unfaithful spouse to God, and ends with Malachi, which speaks of God's hatred of divorce and God's desire that Israel return to him.

Like the larger prophetic books, most scholars believe that not all of the content in each book within this collection was actually spoken by the prophetic figure named in that book. Some materials may have been added by disciples of a particular prophet or by editors of the larger collection. Thus one will find many different proposals about each book's editorial history. In fact, it is possible that some of the books may be named after figures who never existed, or who never engaged in the activities attributed to them. For example, Malachi means "my messenger" and many believe that this short, concluding book of oracles was composed to complete the collection by adding a twelfth book, a number that signifies completeness in the Bible, a fact illustrated by Israel's twelve tribes or Jesus' twelve disciples. Similarly, while a prophetic figure named Jonah the son of Amittai is mentioned in 2 Kings 14:25, almost all modern commentators believe that the book of Jonah relates a fictional story.

Hosea

Hosea lived and prophesied during the final years of the Northern Kingdom. He is an unusual and compelling prophetic figure in that his prophecies and his life are utterly intertwined. This is because God commands Hosea to marry a prostitute as a sign-act to his audience to explain how God viewed his relationship to the people of Israel. Further, each child his wife bears (it is not clear all three are his children) is given a symbolic and highly disturbing name at God's instruction. The first is named *Jezreel* to announce the coming end of Jehu's dynasty, a dynasty that began with a bloody and violent coup d'etat. It is difficult to draw an exact contemporary analogy but naming a child Jezreel might be akin to naming one "Gettysburg" or "Hiroshima" today. Hosea's next child is a daughter he names *Lo-ruhamah*, which means "not pitied," or "lacking compassion," or even, in a sense, "not to be loved." If parents were to name their child with an equally offensive name today, they might be deemed sick or cruel and even expect a visit from child welfare services. Finally, God instructs Hosea to name his third child *Lo-ammi*, which means "not my people." Hosea is not the first prophet to engage in such sign-acts, a topic we discussed in some detail when we examined Ezekiel's life. But he seems to be the earliest example of someone whose sign-acts are fully embedded in his personal life.

One of the most distinctive features of Hosea is that he is unafraid to link Israel's God to deep emotions, most particularly to love and pity. God is not a distant creator but Israel's husband, and Israel's sins directly pain God and do harm to this very intimate relationship. For Hosea, Israel's primary violation is idolatry, most particularly the worship of the Canaanite fertility deity Baal. The message is therefore one of repentance or turning back to God—Israel's true and faithful marriage partner. The use of the metaphor of adultery to criticize Israel's unfaithfulness to God is highlighted regularly in later biblical books like Jeremiah, Ezekiel, and the Deuteronomistic History. However, this is not the only familial metaphor Hosea exploits. In chapter 11, God speaks movingly as a father to his wayward child, Ephraim. In searing imagery the book records how difficult it is for God, the loving father, to punish his beloved child. Hosea's prophecies helped lay the foundation for the Western idea that God is indeed a personal God.

Jewish and Christian Use of Hosea

Perhaps the most prominent use of Hosea in the Jewish tradition is that Hosea 2:19-20 (Hebrew verses 21-22) is recited on weekday mornings as observant Jewish adult men wind one of the phylactery straps around their finger. These verses speak of Israel's relationship to God as that of a bride to a groom and thus one prepares for the daily morning service by reaffirming one's covenantal commitment to God. In Christianity, the Apostle Paul creatively combines verses from Hosea (1:10 and 2:23) and Isaiah to suggest that the "not my people" who become "my people" in Hosea in fact includes the Gentiles. Though it is difficult to find this idea in the book of Hosea itself, Paul's reading represents only one of his many creative reworkings of the Jewish Scriptures.

Joel

Unlike Hosea and Amos, the beginning of Joel does not provide any chronological information about when this prophet lived. Scholars have had wide disagreements over dating this book, and much turns on whether one sees the book as a composite containing some older pieces or as a unity so that its reference to Greeks means it comes from a later time (Joel 3:6). Also, some of Joel's eschatological images of the coming future, such as 2:28-31, a passage quoted in Acts 2, seem more closely aligned with later apocalyptic imagery. Of course certain verses might suggest an early date. For instance, some scholars suggest that Joel 3:10, "Beat your plowshares into swords, and your pruning hooks into spears," is the original saying that Micah 4:3 and Isaiah 2:4 invert.

The most prominent imagery in the book describes a plague of locusts—which some think is a metaphor for soldiers—and the community's response to this affliction. Of particular note is the ritual nature of this response. Thus one finds fasting and communal lamentation in the temple mentioned in 1:14 and 2:15-17. Many mistakenly assume that prophets rejected ritual behaviors in favor of ethics, but here we can clearly see that some prophets actually call for ritual action and understand it to be effective. Amos 9:13b and Joel 3:18a are strikingly similar, perhaps explaining how these two books came to sit near each other in the canon.

A major theme of the book of Joel is "the day of the LORD," a phrase used in a variety of ways—at times signaling a strong judgment of the nations. In Joel 2:28-32, however, we also have imagery suggesting that the Day of the Lord will include God pouring out his spirit upon all humanity and new revelation coming to the people of Israel. Unsurprisingly, the early church understood the event of Gentiles joining Israel as God's people, and the Holy Spirit as being sent by God, as a direct fulfillment of this passage (see Acts 2).

Amos

A surface reading of these twelve prophetic books might leave one with the mistaken impression that the biblical prophets all said the same thing. But Amos and Hosea present a number of stark contrasts when read carefully. While Hosea's critique is most deeply focused on Israel's religious or cultic infidelities, Amos' criticism is primarily directed toward societal inequities and abuses, things today we might call areas of "social justice." Most particularly, Amos delivers a number of jarring critiques of the wealthy who engage in a host of wicked behaviors in their quest to maintain and enhance their wealth and status. Of course some of the differences between the prophets can be attributed to their distinct contexts. Amos prophesies a bit earlier in time when social and economic conditions were stable enough to allow for the rich to accumulate large holdings (see 3:15). Hosea speaks his message during a period of social and political turmoil.

But the differences between Amos and Hosea go deeper yet. While Hosea expresses God's difficulty in punishing Israel and envisions God's eventual restoration of Israel's fortunes, Amos is more of a "fire and brimstone" prophet announcing God's severe coming judgment. The very end of Amos does include a restoration oracle, but there is a widespread consensus that this is a late addition to the book that ill fits the general tenor of Amos. Although Hosea's actions are at times shocking, Amos' rhetoric is downright abrasive. In chapter 4 he describes the wealthy women of Samaria as fat cows, and in chapter 7 we are given a short biographical episode in which Amos not only announces the fall of the Northern Kingdom but tells the high priest at Bethel that when the kingdom falls his own wife will become a prostitute. Contemporary readers who think of the Bible as prim and proper are often taken aback when they learn that prophets will at times employ offensive and even crude language to communicate their message. But delivering such shocks is exactly the job of the prophet, who must wake up those who mistakenly believe that all is fine when it is not. In fact, some speculate that the beginning of Amos, which opens with a number of oracles against various other nations and turns to Israel last, may demonstrate that Amos began his career as a state prophet, a job that involved delivering negative oracles against state enemies (see Numbers 22-24 and 1 Kings 22). If so, Amos' sudden turn to deliver an oracle against his own employer's kingdom would itself have been a slap in the face.

Contemporary Use of Amos

It is worth pointing out that Martin Luther King, Jr.'s famous "I Have a Dream" speech draws on the language of Amos 5:24: "let justice roll down like waters, / and righteousness like an ever-flowing stream." And, like Amos' own context, it is delivered in the equivalent to a state sanctuary, that is, at the Lincoln Memorial in Washington, D.C. Like Amos, King too critiques societal inequities and injustices in the name of God. Like the exodus story, also at the heart of the rhetoric of the civil rights movement, Amos' words clearly are capable of transcending their ancient context and transforming our own world today.

Obadiah

As the shortest book in the Hebrew Bible, Obadiah is a mere twenty-one verses. Several parts of Obadiah have close parallels in Jeremiah 49:7-22, which may suggest that Obadiah was split off from that passage into a separate book to attain the round number of twelve shorter prophetic books. Though Obadiah opens with the words "the vision of Obadiah," no further information about this prophet's lineage or when he may have lived is given.

The book itself is an anti-Edomite oracle, a kind of extended curse directed at the descendants of Esau who lived southeast of Judah. It is generally believed that the harsh sentiments are a reaction to the behavior of the Edomites when Judah fell to the Babylonians. The book informs us that the Edomites stand accused of helping pillage Jerusalem and handing over fleeing Judean refugees to the Babylonian overlords (verses 10-14). There is some evidence that over time Edom came to symbolize those evil forces opposed to God's rule on earth. Thus it is hard to know how much of this language should be read as speaking about a historical event and how much is to be taken as a metaphor for God's coming justice for those wrongly oppressed by the various powerful nations more generally.

Jonah

Many people today seem to know that a person named Jonah was swallowed by a whale, but few know the larger outline and details of this profound and moving short prophetic story. In it, God commands Jonah to prophesy against Nineveh, the capital city of Israel's oppressor at the time, the Assyrian Empire. Jonah flees in the opposite direction and proceeds to get on a boat headed west, climbing down into the interior of the boat, soon falling asleep. God sends a severe storm against the boat to prevent Jonah from fleeing his prophetic duty. Eventually, the pious sailors learn that Jonah is the cause of their travails and they, at Jonah's instruction, throw him overboard to save their ship and their own lives. Once in the sea, the storm calms and Jonah is swallowed by a large fish (biblical Hebrew has no exact word for *whale*). After three days in the fish's belly, Jonah is spit out on dry ground and is commanded a second time to prophesy against Assyria. Oddly enough, in an almost humorous fashion, the whole city—everyone, including the cattle—heeds Jonah's message of divine judgment and repents, leading God to annul his decree against Nineveh. Jonah in turn becomes quite unhappy that God is merciful, something not entirely inexplicable given Assyria's status as Israel's enemy. The book ends with God first providing a fast-growing plant to shelter Jonah from the sun and then God appointing a worm to kill the plant, leaving Jonah even more disconsolate. But God uses Jonah's attachment to the plant to justify God's own attachment to humans and his willingness to forgive them, even at the last moment.

Because God shows concern for a foreign nation and corrects a prophet who does not want to see that nation repent, some have read Jonah as a criticism of Jewish ethnocentrism, in particular the idea that God only cares about the Jewish people. Though perhaps understandable, the thrust of the story is more concerned with exploring how difficult it is to be a prophet, perhaps even explaining why biblical prophecy eventually died out. After all, if a prophet is right about God's coming judgment, his audience will suffer greatly and many will die, leading to the destruction of the prophet's own society. And if he does his job and actually convinces his audience to repent, then he appears to be a false prophet because the judgment he announced never comes to pass. This difficulty arises because within biblical (as well as later Jewish and Christian) thinking, God's mercy consistently trumps God's impulse to be just. And this is exactly why this book is read as the prophetic lection on the afternoon of Yom Kippur. This holiest day of the year is when Jews fast and pray, begging God to accept their belated repentance and not treat them as they deserve, but rather according to his mercy.

Micah

The structure of the book is quite easy to outline in that it has a regular rotation between oracles of judgment followed by ones of restoration. Chapters 1–3 (minus 2:12-13) are judgment oriented, followed by 4:1–5:9, which contain a series of hopeful oracles of promise. Then the pattern repeats itself with judgment texts found in 5:10–7:6, and the book concludes with the hopeful words found in 7:7-20. The idea of movement between the two poles of judgment and promise is a literary pattern commonly found in the Near East. It is not clear that the promised golden future that the earlier prophets like Micah evoke was thought to last forever. Here, as in other prophetic books, many wonder whether the same prophet delivered oracles of both woe and weal or whether the more hopeful oracles were added by a later editorial hand.

While it seems plausible that Micah did indeed speak of a hopeful future for those small landowners living in the Judean countryside, he is remembered more as a prophet of judgment. Thus Micah is quoted in Jeremiah 26:18, where we learn that he had preached of Jerusalem's coming destruction, a fate avoided when Hezekiah's repentant response caused God to annul his negative decree against Jerusalem and Judah. Many wonder whether this story is a literary invention, since we do not hear of any direct encounter between Micah and Hezekiah in either Kings or in the book of Micah. Interestingly, the author of 1 Kings 22 sought to link Micah to a similarly named earlier prophet, Micaiah ben Imlah. Thus the exact and quite rare opening words spoken by Micah in 1:2 are used by Micaiah ben Imlah in 1 Kings 22:28b to close Micaiah's speech. Both of these references to Micah likely reflect the deep esteem in which this short prophetic book was held.

One important passage from Micah is 6:6-8, worth quoting in full:

With what shall I come before the Lord, and bow myself before God on high? Shall I come before him with burnt offerings, with calves a year old? Will the Lord be pleased with thousands of rams, with ten thousands of rivers of oil? Shall I give my firstborn for my transgression, the fruit of my body for the sin of my soul?" He has told you, O mortal, what is good; and what does the LORD require of you but to do justice, and to love kindness, and to walk humbly with your God?

This passage has captured the imaginations of Judaism and Christianity for its powerful words, and not infrequently has been taken as evidence that the prophets rejected sacrifices and rituals more broadly in favor of ethical living. Now it may be that Micah actually rejected all sacrifices, perhaps because he saw the sacrificial cult as an expense that was paid for by taxation on rural farmers. But before assuming this, it is probably worth noting that the inhabitants of ancient Israel were part of a wider world that believed that one communed with God through the act of sacrifice and through communally sharing in meals provided by these sacrificed animals. If so, such words may well be directed against those who see sacrifice as having the ability to automatically influence God, regardless of their ethical behavior. A strikingly similar critique can be found in Psalm 50 where we are told that since God created and owns all the animals in the world he does not need humans to offer them as sacrifices. Yet this same psalm still envisions sacrifice as normative (Psalm 50:14, 23).

Jewish Use of Micah

On Rosh Hashanah in the afternoon, Jewish communities around the world observe a longstanding ritual called *Tashlikh.* Typically this ritual involves taking pieces of bread to a nearby body of water and casting the bread into the water while reciting Micah 7:18-20. In fact the name of the ritual itself is drawn from Micah 7:19, which describes how God, in an act of compassion and forgiveness, throws or casts off the people of Israel's former sins into the depths of the ocean.

Nahum

Little is known about the prophet Nahum. Even the location of his home city Elkosh (derived from his title "Elkoshite") is disputed. All the oracles attributed to him that are preserved in this book are concerned with the imminent destruction of Nineveh. Assuming the book is a unity and was not edited multiple times, it seems unlikely that it was composed before 663 BCE because the fall of Thebes, which occurred in that year, is mentioned in 3:8. The latest date for the book's composition would be 612, the year Nineveh fell. But of course one could argue that the book or parts of it are later and give a retrospective view on the fall of the great Assyrian empire.

The book contains a number of distinct genres. It begins with an alphabetical or acrostic hymn in which the first verse begins with a word using the first Hebrew letter *aleph* and the second verse begins with a *bet* word and so on, through half the Hebrew alphabet. The use of such acrostic poems is common in certain psalms (Psalms 37; 111; 112) and the book of Lamentations, and such arrangements likely helped those living in an oral culture remember these poems. This is followed by a few short prophetic oracles. Nahum 2:1-13 and 3:1-19 contain extended woe oracles directed against Nineveh. One interesting feature is that both Jonah and Nahum deal with the fate of Nineveh and in doing so both cite a listing of God's attributes first found in Exodus 34. Jonah, on the one hand, which deals with God's last minute sparing of the sinful residents of Nineveh, stresses the more merciful attributes in this list (see Jonah 4:2). On the other hand, Nahum, a prophet who announces a seemingly unalterable judgment against Nineveh that does come to pass, stresses God's attributes of judgment more strongly (Nahum 1:2-3).

Many today might be disturbed by the graphic, violent images and the call for God's vengeance on the Assyrians. This is understandable, especially given our distance from the events and our lack of personal investment and understanding of what Israel experienced at the hands of their oppressors. However, within the Bible, God's punishment of the wicked is an essential part of God's duty to execute justice. And, while we might hold reservations regarding vengeance as problematic, many modern readers would agree that justice does require that the wicked be punished for their oppression of others.

Habakkuk

Habakkuk was likely produced in the late preexilic period after Babylon rose to prominence in the last years of the seventh century BCE. Habakkuk is the only preexilic prophet called a *navi* ("prophet") in the title of the book. The use of this title may indicate that he held an official position of prophet, possibly connected to the temple cult. However, apart from this title, we know very little about the prophet. Although a "watchpost" is mentioned in Habakkuk 2:1, this may function as a metaphor, though some think it implies that Habakkuk was some type of official watchman.

While the various parts of the book may have originally been spoken in distinct contexts, the current book can be read in unified fashion. In such a holistic reading, the book opens with a prophetic lament in 1:2-4 that highlights the rampant injustice in Judean society. Already here the prophet raises a central theme of this book, the failure of God to punish wrongdoing quickly. In 1:5-11 an answer comes, namely, that the Babylonians, here called Chaldeans, will be sent as a punisher. Yet, the rise of this nation, one also deemed to be wicked, leads the prophet to respond that this is more of an injustice than the original problem (1:12-17). The formula here of complaint and answer is somewhat common in the Bible and the wider ancient Near East (see for example 1 Samuel 1 or Psalm 6). Habakkuk 2:1 and 3:16 may even suggest an incubation ritual whereby one awaits an answer from God to a difficult life issue, something also seen in the story of Solomon in 1 Kings 3.

It is not clear whether chapter 3 was the original answer to the prophet's question, but it now functions as such within the book. That this final section may have been added to the book is supported by the fact that the commentary on this book found at Qumran (*Pesher Habakkuk*, part of the Dead Sea Scrolls) ends after the second chapter. This magnificent poem, occupying the entire final chapter of the book, is analogous to the end of Job and its theophany, or self-revelation of God, in relation to Job's questioning of God's justice. The poem here describes the ritual march of the divine warrior who goes out to conquer the forces of chaos and restore justice to the world. It invokes ancient Near Eastern imagery of the high storm deity accompanied by lower deities in his pantheon (see 3:5) who battle and defeat opponents associated with watery chaos before creating the world.

"The Just Shall Live by His Faith"

Habakkuk 2:4 is quoted three times in the New Testament, twice by Paul and once in the book of Hebrews. In particular, Paul's use is interesting in that he quotes only a portion of the text, "the just shall live by faith," also omitting the accompanying pronoun found in the Hebrew ("*his* faith") or Greek ("*my* faith") texts (compare, for example, Galatians 3:11). This omission of the pronoun gives the passage a slightly new meaning, generalizing faith to be an abstract principle, minimally removing it from its immediate context in Habakkuk. It is interesting to note that Martin Luther was said to be deeply inspired by Paul's more generalized understanding of this text, even adding the word "alone" to it ("the just shall live by faith alone"), a reading that many argue set the Protestant Reformation in motion.

Zephaniah

Zephaniah means "the Lord has hidden" or "protected." It appears to be a somewhat common name inasmuch as there are four individuals by this name in the Hebrew Bible. A somewhat lengthy genealogy is given for Zephaniah, and one of his ancestors is a certain Hezekiah. It is possible that this is actually the Judean King Hezekiah who lived at the end of the eighth century BCE and, if so, Zephaniah would be a prophet with a royal lineage.

Zephaniah can be subdivided as follows: 1:2–2:3 tells of God's judgment against Judah and Jerusalem; 2:4-15 contains oracles against foreign nations; and 3:1-20 reports the judgment and deliverance of Jerusalem. This exact pattern occurs in other books like Ezekiel. Regarding date, the superscription at the head of the book places this prophet as living within Josiah's reign (640–609 BCE) but it seems likely that at least parts of the book, like the oracle of restoration in 3:14-20, were added in the postexilic period. If the majority of the book is indeed from Josiah's time, the syncretistic practices (that is, the blending of acceptable and foreign religious activities) mentioned in 1:4-9 suggest a time early in Josiah's reign before he introduced various reforms that purged such practices from the temple cult (see 2 Kings 22–23). In many ways Zephaniah is similar to Isaiah in that both prophets see judgment serving a positive, purifying function, one that leads to a new state of affairs for the surviving humble remnant as described in Zephaniah 3:11-13.

There are two passages that likely play off images in Genesis. In Zephaniah 1:2-3, the prophet seems to abrogate the promise God made to Noah never to destroy the whole world due to human evil. In fact, the destruction mentioned here is even more severe in that even the fish will be destroyed. While a bit more obscure, Zephaniah 3:9 speaks of all nations being given a pure speech (or language), something that seems to signal a reversal of the separation of nations that occurred through the imposition of multiple languages in the wake of the Tower of Babel incident in Genesis 11. The New Testament book of Acts reports that tongues (or languages) were given to certain Jews, enabling them to speak with those from "every nation under heaven" (Acts 2:5), something that appears to draw on and point to the fulfillment of this passage.

Haggai and Zechariah 1–8

The opening verses of Haggai give no genealogical information about this prophet. His name is related to the Hebrew root that means "to make a pilgrimage." He, along with Zechariah, is mentioned in Ezra 5:1 and 6:14 as being connected with the efforts to rebuild the temple after the Persians defeated Babylon in 538 BCE and allowed those exiled Judeans who so desired to return to Jerusalem. In some ways, Haggai and Zechariah are the most chronologically precise prophetic books. Haggai contains material from the sixth to ninth month of 520, and Zechariah 1–8 runs from the eighth month of 520 to the ninth month of 518. Interestingly enough, neither Haggai nor Zechariah 1–8 speak about the actual completion of the Second Temple, which occurred in 515 BCE.

In order to understand these books more fully, a little background information might be useful. We have evidence that Cyrus, King of Persia, upon conquering the Babylonians, issued a general amnesty that would have released captive populations and allowed suppressed religious groups to restore their sacred sites. We know from accounts outside of the Bible that new emperors often did such things to gain the favor of their citizens, perhaps like politicians today who give large tax breaks upon being elected.

Haggai and Zechariah address those who returned from Babylon under the amnesty with the hope of rebuilding the temple. Both books indicate that the efforts to rebuild the temple had stalled. The reasons for this are not that difficult to locate. To begin, the returnees would have arrived home to an impoverished state with an economy in shambles and a social situation that was radically different from what existed before the exile. There was no longer a monarchy or a fully functioning government, and we know from Ezra and Nehemiah that conflicts arose between those returning from Babylon and those who never left the land of Judah. Furthermore, there was some debate over who was a legitimate priest or Levite since at least some of the records were lost during the exile, as indicated in Ezra 2:59-63. Finally, while a functioning temple cult provided a ritual procedure to overcome impurities, it was undoubtedly difficult to reinitiate the temple service from a state of impurity, a problem addressed in Zechariah 3.

Both Haggai and Zechariah also take up one other issue: How can one be sure that the exile, which Jeremiah has indicated would last for seventy years, had come to an end and thus that God now permitted the temple to be rebuilt (compare Haggai 1:2 and Zechariah 1:1-17 to Jeremiah 29)? Both prophets are engaged in convincing the Judeans who had returned to Jerusalem that the exile Jeremiah announced had indeed come to an end and that God had authorized the rebuilding of the temple. Both also interact with two important figures: Zerubbabel, who seems to be in line to be the next Davidic king, and Joshua, the son of Jehozadak, who would come to be the high priest in the reconstructed temple.

If Zechariah is the same person listed in Nehemiah 12:16, then he is a priest. His name means "the Lord remembers." Within Zechariah 1–8, the prophet uses his visionary experiences to explain how a new social order is to be created in the difficult and chaotic situation that those who returned to Jerusalem experienced. Zechariah lets the community know that work on the temple here on earth can proceed because up above God has initiated the healing and purification process. Also of significance is that Zechariah has an angel help explain the meaning of each vision. Scholars tend to see this as a marker of late biblical prophecy, in that, rather than having God speak directly to the prophet, we now have the more distant angelic intermediary addressing prophets.

Chapters 7–8 of Zechariah contain material similar to Haggai in that they are oracles based on inquiries. Both Haggai and Zechariah in some sense echo the modern refrain "build it, and they will come," because their message is an attempt to rally the demoralized and economically depressed returnees to realize that if they trust in God and move forward with reconstructing the temple, even though it will take precious resources, the investment will yield spiritual and earthly dividends. Unfortunately, these very prophecies are sometimes cited by unscrupulous clergy to line their own pockets with monies gained from much poorer, devout believers. But such misuses of Scripture should not obscure the point that communities are often deeply dependent upon and owe their survival to visionaries as well as communal rituals that help them see and build that brighter future that seems unobtainable in their current downtrodden state.

Deutero-Zechariah and Malachi

Here we treat Zechariah 9–14 together with Malachi based on the interconnected nature of their content. Zechariah 9–14 contains two collections of materials, chapters 9–11 and 12–14, and each collection begins with the words "An oracle, the word of the LORD," the exact same words found in Malachi 1:1. As a result, scholars tend to view all these materials as a series of late anonymous prophecies that were appended to the end of the Book of the Twelve. It should be noted that the tendency to append materials at the end of a collection occurs elsewhere in the Hebrew Bible, such as the poems one finds at the end of Deuteronomy or the poem followed by the list of David's officials in 2 Samuel 22-23.

Zechariah 9–14 contains many images of God battling the enemies of his chosen people and portraits of the dawning new era that will arrive once these forces are defeated. These texts contain a great deal of mythological content, and the writers of the New Testament often drew from them. Thus the image of the restoration of the Davidic king found in Zechariah 9:9 is cited in Matthew 21. In fact, Matthew 21 reads this prophecy a bit woodenly, and unlike the other gospel writers he has Jesus enter Jerusalem riding on two animals because he mistakenly thought the poetic repetition in this verse referred to two differing animals rather than one animal described by two differing terms. It also seems likely that the imagery in 12:10 that speaks of the house of David and all Jerusalem mourning one who was pierced helped the gospel writers make sense of Jesus' violent death. On a different note, Zechariah 13:2-6 seems to imply that prophecy is so problematic that it should be suppressed, perhaps signaling why, at least in part, prophecy eventually ceased in ancient Israel.

The name *Malachi* means "my messenger," and as noted earlier some have suggested that this group of anonymous exilic oracles was added to round out the number of books in the minor prophets to an even (and symbolic) twelve. The idea of God sending a messenger occurs in Exodus 23:20. Deuteronomy 18:15 mentions something similar when it speaks of a future coming prophet like Moses. Malachi 4:4 likely reflects an attempt to integrate the Prophets and the Torah into a larger canonical whole by suggesting that even though certain prophetic texts at times critique ritual norms and laws found in the Torah, ultimately the Torah itself flows from the same source as the later words of the prophets. From this canonical viewpoint, the words of the prophets are to be read as a further extension of the Torah, not its abrogation.

Malachi in the Jewish and Christian Traditions

The ending of Malachi contributed to the widespread Jewish belief that Elijah will return to announce the dawning of the messianic age. To this day, Jews place a cup of wine for Elijah at every Passover Seder meal ("Elijah's cup"). Elijah's cup symbolizes that the redemption experienced in the exodus is in some sense a "down payment" on the coming, fuller redemption that Jews look forward to in the messianic era. It also functions as a compromise to answer the question of whether four or five cups of wine should be consumed at the Passover meal. Hence Jews drink four cups of wine over the course of the Passover Seder meal, but fill the fifth cup, waiting for Elijah to return, announcing the arrival of the messianic era as well as resolving this and other longstanding legal disputes. The belief that Elijah would return to usher in the messianic age also shaped the gospel accounts that depict John the Baptist as an Elijah-like figure who announces the impending arrival of the messiah, in this case, Jesus. This linkage is further underlined by the ordering of Christian Bibles where the Latter Prophets come last in the Old Testament, thus placing this passage immediately before the opening of Matthew's Gospel, which describes the birth of the Christian Messiah, Jesus.

INTRODUCTION TO THE KETUVIM, OR THE WRITINGS

The third and final section of the Tanakh is called the Ketuvim, which means "Writings" in Hebrew. The Ketuvim contains some of the latest books found in the Hebrew Bible, and evidence suggests that the Torah and the Prophets had become recognized collections earlier than this section of the Tanakh. Some have suggested that this collection was not entirely set by the time of Jesus and the New Testament inasmuch as the Dead Sea Scrolls do not contain the book of Esther (although this could be due to the fragmentary nature of these finds).

There is a wide array of differing types of books in the Writings including: Wisdom books like Proverbs and Job, many genres of psalms ("praises," most of which are musical in nature), the love poetry found in Song of Songs, sophisticated narratives like Esther and Ruth, a biblical history found in Chronicles, and even apocalyptic literature found in Daniel 7–12. While we generally follow the order found in important Hebrew manuscripts, there are other ancient alternative lists about how these books should be ordered. Even among parts of the Ketuvim that are commonly grouped together such as the five *megillot* (Hebrew for *scrolls*) that are read over the course of the Jewish liturgical year, one finds differing ordering schemes. In the standard Masoretic Text, these books appear to be ordered according to a historical schema with Ruth, whose story is set in the period of the Judges, first, Song of Songs and Qoheleth, both associated with Solomon, next, then Lamentations, which is associated with Jeremiah, and finally the Persian-era story of Esther. However, today there are printed versions of the five megillot that order them liturgically (that is, according to the Jewish liturgical calendar), an order we follow in this book: We begin with Song of Songs (which is read on Passover, a holiday set in Nissan the first month of the biblical calendar), followed by Ruth (read on Shavuot), then Lamentations (read during late summer when the destruction of the temple is marked), Qoheleth (read on Succot in the fall) and Esther (read during Adar, the twelveth biblical month).

The truth is that the historic Jewish community adopted the book (or "codex") format much later than the Christian community, and many of these texts would have been preserved on scrolls kept on shelves or in baskets in no particular order. Thus the concern about the exact order of a diverse collection of scrolls would have only become an issue after the early book, often called the codex, became more widespread among Jews. Historically, it is important to note that although the Jewish community reads through the entire Torah in synagogues over the course of the year (or three years in some synagogues), it does not read through the whole Tanakh in the same way as if it were a single book that one reads from cover to cover.

In comparing Jewish and Christian Bibles, the reader will quickly see that the books that the Jewish Bible places in the third and final section of the canon, Christians Bibles place in the central section of the Old Testament called the "Historical Books." This placement thus signals something about how these books came to be understood within Christianity. Furthermore, the Christian order of these books is quite different. Ruth is placed next to Judges; Chronicles along with Ezra–Nehemiah and Esther are viewed as historical works and thus placed after 1–2 Kings; and then follows the rest of the books found in the Ketuvim except for Lamentations and Daniel, which Christian Bibles tend to place among the Prophets following Jeremiah and Ezekiel respectively. This Christian ordering reflects the arrangement found in Septuagint manuscripts dating from the third and fourth century CE, though the truth is that many Christian interpreters today now use the Jewish divisions and ordering, which may in fact correspond to New Testament assumptions about these books (see further above, "Introduction to the Prophets").

PSALMS

Introduction and Overview

The word *psalms* comes from the Greek word *psalmoi*, which means "songs" or perhaps "songs accompanied by music." Although this is the book's name in English and Greek, in Hebrew the book is called *tehillim*, which means "praises." Both the Greek and Hebrew titles remind us that this is not a book to be read so much as songs to be sung or performed. The practice of singing the psalms is still very much alive in both Judaism and parts of Christianity, and it was almost certainly the practice of the ancient world, where literacy was low and the psalms were likely sung from memory. In some respects these songs may have functioned similar to what we today call liturgy, with portions sung by temple singers and other parts, perhaps responsively, by the people of Israel. Whatever the case, that all of the psalms in the Psalter can be called "praises" teaches us something about the nature of praise according to the Hebrew Bible. Many psalms, indeed the majority, fall under the genre of lament, showing us that ancient Israel understood complaint to be an important form of praise to God, something that often challenges modern readers.

The book of Psalms contains 150 compositions that fall into five books, or sections, perhaps structured this way in an attempt to mirror the five books of the Torah: Psalms 1–41; 42–72; 73–89; 90–106; 107–150. Each of these sections ends with a doxology; that is, a line or two praising God in emphatic terms. These can be easily recognized in English Bibles (see 41:13; 72:18-19; 89:52; 106:48; and all of 150, which also functions as a doxology for the entire Psalm book). Most English Bibles also note the start of each of these five books with a heading (Book I, Book II, and so on.). While the book of Psalms overall is often attributed to David, this is more of a recognition that David is the patron or forefather of psalmody in ancient Israel than a claim that

David penned every song and prayer in Psalms, or even all of the seventy-three psalms that mention his name in their headings. This should not be taken to mean that David did not compose some psalms or commission others such as Psalms 73–83, which are all attributed to Asaph, one of David's musicians (see further the textbox on "Superscriptions, David, and the Psalms" below).

While much of the material in the Torah and the Prophets is recorded in God's voice addressing the people of Israel, a number of books in the Writings, especially books like Psalms and Lamentations, record humans expressing their deepest emotions to God. This small but important fact reminds us that Scripture in Judaism and Christianity takes many forms, not all of which are necessarily top-down pronouncements from a deity to various people.

Superscriptions, David, and the Psalms

When reading individual psalms in an English Bible, the reader will notice that most (116 of 150) begin with a small fine print description indicating details about the psalm, perhaps its setting, musical arrangements, or what appear to be authorship notes. These "superscriptions" were likely added to the Psalms, perhaps when the Psalter was compiled after the exile. Most scholars agree that these short markers are of limited value in assessing the historical composition of the Psalms they describe, though they are still important in that they reveal conceptions about particular psalms during the time the book was being compiled. One of the most common superscriptions reads "A Psalm of David." It is important to note that the Hebrew letter behind the word "of" (*le*) can also be translated as "for," "belonging to," "for the use of," or "concerning/about." Although in places it may mean "by" (as in "David wrote this"), it does not always or necessarily mean that.

Controversies and Debates

Perhaps the most central critical insight concerning Psalms in the past hundred years was that one can detect a number of distinct types or genres of psalms, including: songs of praise, enthronement psalms, royal psalms, complaint psalms, psalms offering thanks, historically oriented psalms, and wisdom psalms (a number of these psalm types will be discussed in more detail below). At one time scholars sought to link each specific psalm type to a particular sociological or religious situation. For example, one major controversy involved the question of whether the enthronement psalms discussed below were composed for an Israelite festival at which God was once a year enthroned in the same manner that Marduk (the chief god in the Babylonian pantheon) was enthroned at an annual New Year festival. Such a suggestion is possible but remains highly speculative, since the Bible never mentions a holiday or a ritual in which God is enthroned. More secure is the probability that Psalms 15 and 24 were engraved on the outer temple gates and recited by pilgrims who would declare that they had acted with integrity before they could be admitted to the sacred precincts.

Recent discussion has concentrated on both the poetic dimensions of various psalms as well as on the many metaphors that one finds in these compositions. For example, the complaint psalms regularly speak of sickness and social alienation with metaphors of death and dying. When the psalmist in 88:6 speaking to God calls out in despair: "You have put me in the depths of the Pit" he seems to be saying that his situation is so bad that even though he may be alive, it is as if he is dead. Recognizing these metaphors and understanding how the ancient audience heard them is essential if one hopes to grasp the meaning of these strikingly beautiful and often quite disturbing compositions.

Songs of Praise

As mentioned above, in Hebrew the book of Psalms is called *Tehillim*, a noun that is derived from the verbal root *hll*, which one can recognize in the word Hallelujah. Hallelujah is an attempt to transliterate and thus borrow a Hebrew word and employ it in English. The word means "praise the LORD." Thus one should not be surprised that an important genre of psalms are those that engage in extended praise. A prime example is Psalm 150, which we include here. Note that each time the word "praise" is used in the text (except once in the last verse) it is translating the Hebrew word *hallelu*:

Praise the LORD!

Praise God in his sanctuary!
    Praise God in his fortress, the sky!
Praise God in his mighty acts!
    Praise God as suits his incredible greatness!
Praise God with the blast of the ram's horn.
    Praise God with lute and lyre!
Praise God with drum and dance!
    Praise God with strings and pipe!
Praise God with loud cymbals!
    Praise God with clashing cymbals!
Let every living thing praise the LORD!

Praise the LORD! (CEB)

173

Enthronement Psalms

Several psalms numbered in the nineties fall under this category. Psalm 93 is a short psalm that conveniently demonstrates what we mean by an enthronement psalm:

> The LORD is king, he is robed in majesty;
>   the LORD is robed, he is girded with strength.
> He has established the world; it shall never be moved;
>   your throne is established from of old;
>   you are from everlasting.
>
> The floods have lifted up, O LORD,
>   the floods have lifted up their voice;
>   the floods lift up their roaring.
> More majestic than the thunders of mighty waters,
>   more majestic than the waves of the sea,
>   majestic on high is the LORD!
>
> Your decrees are very sure;
>   holiness befits your house,
>   O LORD, forevermore.

The psalm opens with a proclamation that God is king and he is royally robed. It then digresses to tell the story of how God came to be established as king of the universe. We are told that God's kingship is linked to his act of creating and stabilizing the world. The psalm fills in this story by noting an alternate creation story than one finds in Genesis, where the matter God deals with is totally passive. Psalm 93 likely draws from the Babylonian creation myth of Marduk's conquest over his watery opponent, Tiamat the sea dragon, and portrays God as having subdued the primordial waters. And just as the Babylonian creation story reports that after creating the world a temple was built for Marduk, so Psalm 93 reports that God is securely ensconced in his house, which is simply another word for his temple. One finds very similar imagery in other psalms, such as Psalm 29, where in verse 10 we are told that: "The LORD sits enthroned over the flood; / the LORD sits enthroned as king forever."

Royal Psalms

A number of psalms, including Psalms 2, 45, 72, and 101, appear to have been written with the king in mind. Sometimes they are linked to an event in the king's life such as his wedding (the focus of Psalm 45), and at other times they touch more directly on the duties of the king (the focus of Psalms 72 and 101). One should remember that in ancient Israel, as in much of the rest of the world until quite recently, religion and state were intertwined ("religion" as we know it—something potentially separate from one's identity as a citizen or tribe member—is really a modern idea). Thus the king helped support the temple and its many personnel, and in turn the religious establishment prayed for the stability and prosperity of the royal household. It seems clear that in doing so the religious establishment could also ensure that it held the king to a high moral standard.

Complaint Psalms

The book of Psalms has a striking number of both individual and communal complaints that contain very strong indictments of God. Many readers assume that the Bible is a pious book and as such it should not have passages that question God's behavior. But ancient Israel believed that God had a personal side to which the worshiper and the larger nation could appeal in very personal language. Much of the continuing power of this wonderful book is that it compellingly communicates the pain and suffering that are too frequently a part of our human experience. It might be said that the theme that pervades these psalms is *distress*. Some have estimated that lament psalms constitute over half of the psalms in the Psalter. Many of these psalms contain insights concerning the articulation of pain and how one learns to work through life's difficulties and still embrace God.

There is some evidence that individual complaints, like the following one found in Psalm 13, below, reveal a two-step process in which the person first approached God to articulate his or her complaint, and after receiving an assurance either from a priestly official, or perhaps just from the experience of worshiping in the temple, they are bolstered and reassured.

How long, O Lord? Will you forget me forever?
　　How long will you hide your face from me?
How long must I bear pain in my soul,

175

and have sorrow in my heart all day long?
How long shall my enemy be exalted over me?

Consider and answer me, O LORD my God!
    Give light to my eyes, or I will sleep the sleep of death,
and my enemy will say, "I have prevailed";
    my foes will rejoice because I am shaken.

But I trusted in your steadfast love;
    my heart shall rejoice in your salvation.
I will sing to the LORD,
    because he has dealt bountifully with me.

This is not to say that all such psalms end on an upbeat note. Thus the concluding line in Psalm 88, one of the darkest psalms in the Bible, is a thought that seems to trail off and whose final word is not one of hope, but actually the word "darkness" or a "dark place."

One of the clearest examples of a communal complaint is Psalm 44, as one can see from the excerpt below. The psalm begins by recounting how Israel had always acknowledged that God, not Israel's own armies, had conquered other nations and planted Israel in its homeland. Yet it then goes on to note that things have gone completely awry and that after examining their own deeds the evidence suggests that God is not maintaining his part of the covenantal relationship with Israel:

Yet you have rejected us and abased us,
    and have not gone out with our armies.
You made us turn back from the foe,
    and our enemies have gotten spoil.
You have made us like sheep for slaughter,
    and have scattered us among the nations.
....
All this has come upon us,
    yet we have not forgotten you,
    or been false to your covenant.
....
Rouse yourself! Why do you sleep, O Lord?
    Awake, do not cast us off forever!
Why do you hide your face?
    Why do you forget our affliction and oppression? (verses 9-11, 17,
    23-24)

One can see here quite clearly the forceful language the community uses to ask pointed questions of God when the evidence suggests that God, not the community, has fallen short. In fact, nowhere does Israel acknowledge sin as part of this psalm, something largely out of character for communal lament psalms in the Psalter. One also finds here the idea that God needs at times to be awakened through the calls of the oppressed and downtrodden, just as God only begins to redeem Israel from Egypt when the cries of the slaves cause him to remember his covenantal obligations (see Exodus 2:23-25).

Wisdom and Torah Psalms

While scholars agree that there are indeed psalms that were strongly influenced or even produced by the same scribes who produced books like Proverbs, there is less agreement about what exactly counts as a wisdom psalm. An expansive list might include Psalms 1, 8, 19, 34, 37, 39, 49, 73, 78, 92, 94, 104, 105, 106, 112, 119, 127, 128:1-4, and 139. It might be said that certain psalms like 1, 37, 49, and 112 are widely acknowledged as wisdom psalms, while others, like Psalm 94, though evoking certain ideas associated with the schools that produced Israel's wisdom texts, do so in a non-specific way. Arriving at a firm consensus of a particular psalm's genre is complicated for several reasons. First, many psalms are complex and some appear to contain several genres. Second, certain ideas that are central to much of Wisdom literature are central to other genres of Israelite literature as well. For example, that the wicked may prosper briefly before they are undone by their wickedness, or that the righteous may experience adversity for a time before God rewards them, is indeed affirmed within Wisdom literature, but also affirmed by the text of the Torah and by many prophetic thinkers. These same ideas pervade many of the Bible's greatest narratives as well. Thus it is not simply the use of such themes that make something a wisdom text, but also that such texts contain a critical mass of markers that strongly suggest they were produced in Israel's wisdom circles.

One can see such wisdom markers quite clearly in the following excerpt from Psalm 37 (verses 12-16):

The wicked plot against the righteous,
    and gnash their teeth at them;
but the LORD laughs at the wicked,
    for he sees that their day is coming.

The wicked draw the sword and bend their bows
    to bring down the poor and needy,
    to kill those who walk uprightly;
their sword shall enter their own heart,
    and their bows shall be broken.

Better is a little that the righteous person has
    than the abundance of many wicked.

Not only does this passage stress that the wicked will soon receive punishment, but in a classic expression found in Wisdom literature, the very weapons that the wicked use to oppress others are turned back upon them. Finally, the passage ends with a short proverb advising the righteous person to be happy with his lot and to see that the wealth of the wicked is not really valuable.

As mentioned above, it is not always clear when a genre starts or stops, and this is indeed true when it comes to classifying Torah Psalms. Part of the problem is related to the fact that the word for the books we call Pentateuch or Torah is the Hebrew word *torah*, meaning "instruction" (or "teaching"). God's loving instruction, or *torah*, is a theme in many of the psalms. This body of teaching clearly comprises the greatest wisdom known to Israel. Psalm 1, which opens the Psalter, and Psalm 119, the longest psalm in the Bible, are well known and generally classified as Torah Psalms inasmuch as they speak about the virtues of living a life guided by God's instruction or *torah*:

Happy are those
    who do not follow the advice of the wicked,
or take the path that sinners tread,
    or sit in the seat of scoffers;
but their delight is in the law [torah] of the LORD,
    and on his law [torah] they meditate day and night.
They are like trees
    planted by streams of water,
which yield their fruit in its season,
    and their leaves do not wither.
In all that they do, they prosper. (Psalm 1:1-3)

Happy are those whose way is blameless,
    who walk in the law [torah] of the LORD.

Happy are those who keep his decrees,
    who seek him with their whole heart,
who also do no wrong,
    but walk in his ways (Psalm 119:1-3)

Historical Recitals and Psalms Related to Specific Times in History

While it is unclear if one can accurately speak of a genre of historical recital psalms, or whether differing types of genres evoke recitals of Israel's history, it is useful to know that a number of psalms contain historical recitals. Israel's history is evoked for a variety of reasons including: to offer praise and thanks to God as is the focus of Psalm 136, to confess Israel's misdeeds and call upon God's forgiveness as in Psalm 106, and to explain why David and the tribe of Judah became preeminent as occurs in Psalm 78.

It is also clear that a number of psalms relate to specific, often traumatic, events in Israel's history. Thus Psalm 89 describes a Davidic king being humiliated, indicating a major defeat in battle that called into question God's oath to David. And Psalm 137, a psalm whose final graphic images might rightly disturb contemporary readers, gives voice to the calls of the Judean exiles for divine vengeance against their Babylonian oppressors, those who destroyed Jerusalem and killed many of its inhabitants in a violent manner.

Why Are Some Psalms Nearly Identical?

It is interesting that a few psalms are almost identical. Thus if one compares Psalm 14 and 53, for example, the reader will notice that the two psalms are almost identical except for some minor variation near the end and the fact that one uses the term *Elohim* ("God"; Psalm 53) while the other uses YHWH ("Lord"; Psalm 14). It seems likely that entire sections (or collections) of psalms came from different areas and some scholars suggest that Psalms 3–41 came from Judah, the southern kingdom (using the special divine name YHWH), while 51–72 came from Israel, the northern kingdom (using the more generic name Elohim). When the Psalm book was put together in the postexilic period, those compiling it may have wished to preserve both versions to be inclusive.

Psalms in Jewish Tradition

It is often said that the Psalms were ancient Israel's prayerbook, and it is certainly true that they remain central to Jewish prayer life. The traditional

Jewish liturgy includes many psalms. Even among more liberal groups that liturgically innovate, there is a tendency to retain these psalms that have been part of the Jewish liturgy for centuries, if not millennia. For example, on the evening of the start of every Sabbath (called *erev Shabbat*), Jewish congregants recite (usually sung in celebratory tones) a number of the enthronement psalms such as Psalms 93, 96, and 97. These are quite appropriate because Jewish tradition sees the Sabbath, the day that Jews are required to cease from their daily work, as a public acknowledgment of God's creation of and lordship over the universe. While not an enthronement psalm, the heading in nearby Psalm 92 notes that it is indeed a song for the Sabbath day.

Psalms 113–118, called the *Hallel*, are recited to praise God during the annual Passover ritual meal (the *seder*) as well as being recited on the other two pilgrimage festivals of Succot (Booths) and Shavuot (Weeks). Many psalms also feature prominently in the regular liturgy. Thus the alphabetic or acrostic Psalm 145, a poem in which the first word of each verse begins with a letter of the Hebrew alphabet in order, is sung responsively in the daily prayer liturgy. And many other psalms are recited during the preliminary morning daily prayer service. Psalms are also recited in an ad hoc fashion during times of personal and communal emergency. Thus traditional Jews can probably recall a time in life when a psalm like 130 was recited for a direly ill person, or when it was used during the Yom Kippur War in 1973 to invoke God's help in protecting the Jewish people and the state of Israel from a grave threat.

Psalms in Christian Tradition

The earliest Christians were part of a Jewish sectarian movement and thus it is not surprising that Psalms played an important role in the New Testament and remain a central part of Christian prayer life. Within the New Testament there are a number of important uses of Psalms. It seems likely that the "hymn" the disciples and Jesus sang at the end of the Last Supper (see Matthew 26:30) was drawn from the Jewish recitation of the Hallel (Psalms 113–118), traditionally sung at Passover. Even more evident is that two psalms in particular directly shaped the way the Passion Narratives describe Jesus' betrayal, torture, and gruesome death. Psalm 22:18 reports that the person in this psalm experienced such alienation that those around him have taken possession of his clothing, and 69:21 has the singer of this complaint say he was given vinegar to drink. Each of these elements is evoked in

Matthew 27:34-35. Most prominent is that Jesus' last words, "*Eli, Eli, lema sabachthani,*" Aramaic for "my God, my God, why have you forsaken me?" are the opening words of Psalm 22. It is often suggested that reciting the first words of this psalm was a way to draw attention to it in its entirety; the rest of Psalm 22 clearly speaks of a person abandoned, mocked, and "poured out like water" with "bones out of joint" (22:14).

The Psalms are still used by many contemporary Christian groups. Churches that follow the common lectionary (a cyclical set of select biblical readings, used by many traditional Christian groups like Catholics and Anglicans) will read or sing psalms each week, or even twice each day if daily services are observed. Other Christian groups may use psalms only in private reflection or occasionally in formal worship, perhaps reading portions of a psalm for special occasions or as prayers. Some groups within the Reformed Christian tradition will sing entire psalms that have been put to music, usually accompanied by an organ. At certain times in the Christian calendar, portions of Psalms are used, sung, or recited within the liturgy to emphasize the event being observed. Thus during Lent, a time traditionally associated with repentance, Psalms 6, 32, 38, 51, 102, 130, and 143 are used to express sorrow for sin, forming what the historic church has called the Seven Penitential Psalms. Conversely, psalms of praise are used during the Easter season, and so on. Furthermore, the practice of adding the following saying, called the *Gloria Patri*, to the end of the psalm being recited has become common in many modern liturgical settings:

Glory be to the Father, and to the Son, and to the Holy Ghost;
As it was in the beginning, is now, and ever shall be, world without end. Amen.

Lastly, there is evidence that collections of psalms (called the Psalter) were produced with elaborate art in ways similar to that of the illuminated gospels (see section on "Introduction to the Gospels" below), especially during the last millennium. These highly ornate and lavishly decorated books were especially popular during the Middle Ages, and became part of a church's prized possessions. Some Psalters even contained pages or portions of the Gospels, demonstrating just how valued the Psalms have been to generations of Christians.

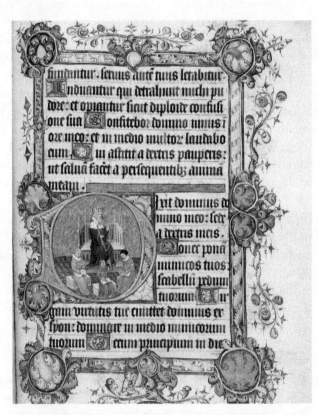

Figure 20. Page of an illuminated psalter, known as the *Bedford Psalter and Hours*, which depicts David enthroned, playing a harp, with three scribes preparing to write (at Psalm 109 [110 in English]). 1414–1422. © British Library Board. All Rights Reserved 10/10/2013, Add. 42131, f.183.

Introduction to Wisdom Literature

One could argue that the central theme of most books found in the Hebrew Bible is the story of God's unique and ongoing relationship with his chosen people, Israel. One thinks particularly of the importance of the exodus event, or God's sustaining of Israel for forty years in the wilderness, or God's help in Israel's conquest of Canaan, themes that are echoed in many books of the Tanakh. Yet, biblical critics have long recognized that a number of books in the Hebrew Bible have a theological orientation distinct from much of the rest of the Hebrew canon in that they never explicitly mention God's special relationship to Israel. Four books come quickly to mind: Proverbs, Job, Ecclesiastes (also called Qoheleth), and the Song of Songs. The Song of Songs will be discussed separately later in this book, as it contains a series of love poems that make it unique in the Bible. On the other hand, Proverbs, Job, and Qoheleth all belong to a genre of literature that scholars refer to as Wisdom literature, a genre that contains an outlook one could call a type of natural theology. This means that the way God operates in these books reflects a more universal, or less Israel-focused, picture, with a message that any intelligent human can attempt to discern by carefully observing the natural world in which we live. This does not mean that humans can therefore fully understand God's workings in the world, or that all humans have an equal understanding of God. Further, it does not mean that all one needs to know can be found by simply looking at nature or observing the world around us. Rather, it means that through a disciplined life of learning how to be wise and how to avoid folly, humans can, over time, gain greater insight into the way the world God created and controls works.

While there is broad agreement that Proverbs, Job, and Qoheleth are best viewed as wisdom texts, there is a good deal of debate about what other books in the Hebrew Bible and the Apocrypha might also fall into this rubric. Thus many recognize that the apocryphal book Sirach is a wisdom text, but a rather late and somewhat unique book, in that it has a number of chapters that speak about the details of Israel's history with God (Sirach 44–50). As noted in the previous chapter, there are also certain psalms like Psalm 37 that are widely viewed as wisdom texts in that they are composed of short proverbial sayings strung together and espouse a viewpoint, found widely in wisdom texts, that God has set up the world so that the wicked eventually receive their comeuppance while the virtuous are in the end rewarded. Additionally, some passages in the Prophets have at times been categorized as wisdom texts. For example, Isaiah 28:23-29 gives a detailed description on how an intelligent farmer plants and harvests, highlighting that God is ultimately the source of such knowledge. There are also narrative texts elsewhere in the Hebrew Bible that certain scholars believe show wisdom influences indicating they may have been authored by the same scribes who produced texts like Proverbs. Thus the Joseph story in Genesis 37–50 or the book of Esther are sometimes labeled as narrative wisdom tales in that God is very much in the background in such stories and they focus on how wise human behavior is richly rewarded and the wicked are punished. Finally, some have even speculated that Deuteronomy's tendencies toward rationalizing the commandments, as well as its heavy emphasis on teaching one's children how to love and fear God, could suggest that wisdom teachers helped shape the book's orientation.

Again, as we mentioned when we looked at wisdom psalms, it is important to remember that while certain scholars have indeed sought to construe Wisdom literature rather broadly, others have argued that only texts that have many if not all of the characteristics found in books like Proverbs and Job should be labeled Wisdom literature. Doing otherwise, such thinking goes, dilutes the usefulness of the label and fails to take into account that other genres of literature can also touch upon universal themes—like the punishment of the wicked and the reward of the righteous—without necessarily earning the title "Wisdom." Of course part of the problem here stems from our fragmentary understanding of Israelite society. Frequently one hears talk of the distinct social roles of monarchs, priests and Levites, prophets, and sages who are each depicted as controlling certain domains of society and thus in competition with each other for control over society. Yet such strict categorization reflects more our current society—with its job descriptions, official titles, degrees, and employment protections—than ancient society. We know from the Bible that certain figures occupy multiple roles. Ezekiel was both a priest and a prophet. Ben Sirah is clearly a sage but one who has very deep respect for the priesthood. David was a king but also considered to be a prophet. Current sociological models of ancient Israel may portray the division between various societal roles in a much too static form. Might the scribal sages who produced wisdom texts that have a more naturalistic understanding of God's presence in the world have done so because they were writing in a particular key, a key similar to the one in which contemporary academics write? Yet a contemporary academic might at other times in his or her life engage in less rationalistic thinking, perhaps when playing an imagination-based game with a child or participating in a religious ritual. If so, it could be that ancient wisdom teachers were the same scribes who also helped produce the Torah and edit the Prophets.

PROVERBS

Introduction and Overview

The book of Proverbs is distinct, even within the collection of books we call Wisdom literature. The book as a whole contains, well, proverbs, whereas Job and Qoheleth, though certainly not without examples of proverbs or similar material, are more linear in their presentations in that there is a progression in a story or a development of a larger theme. However, as we discuss below, although Proverbs at times seems to contain a string of loosely connected proverbs, there is also a larger theme and progression to the book as well.

The book can be divided as follows: Chapters 1–9 contain a collection of introductory sermons or poems that both attempt to persuade the reader of the value of studying Wisdom and lay out a theology of Israel's wisdom tradition; Proverbs 10–29 consists of several collections of proverbial sayings that cover a very wide range of topics and situations; in chapters 30 and 31, one finds collections of proverbs attributed to two otherwise unknown figures (Agur and Lemuel) followed by a final acrostic poem that praises the "good wife," or "wife/woman of noble character," using letters of the Hebrew alphabet in succession to begin each new verse.

Controversies and Debates

It seems clear that the different sections of Proverbs come from different time periods. It is also likely that these sections themselves contain collected materials, and they were not necessarily written by the same scribe at one time, if they indeed began as writings at all (as opposed to orally transmitted "sayings"). Furthermore, although there are places in which a few related sayings are grouped together, such as in 16:10-15, where one finds several sayings concerning the proper behavior of young courtiers around the king, no one yet has been able to find a systematic explanation for the current order of the bulk of Proverbs 10–29. Scholars have also long argued over the context in which the proverbial literature in chapters 10–29 was produced and transmitted. Little is known about ancient Israelite educational practices and while places in Proverbs such as 10:1 and 25:1 indicate that the collecting and copying of proverbial literature was done under royal auspices, this does not tell us who coined these sayings.

Many of the sayings in Proverbs belong to the wider ancient Near Eastern cultural context in which Israel developed. To state this another way, wisdom sayings found in Proverbs are similar in many respects to the sayings found in other cultures contemporaneous to Israel. The fact that Proverbs 22:17–24:22 has striking similarities to the Egyptian *Instruction of Amenemope* has led some to speculate that Israelite scribes borrowed this Egyptian text and incorporated much of it into Proverbs.

One of the most important scholarly arguments about Proverbs concerns how best to describe the figure of Lady Wisdom found in the introductory sermons, in especially vivid form in chapter 8. Is Lady Wisdom simply a literary trope or what might be called a personification, like we today refer to "old man winter"? Or is Wisdom here something more concrete and substantial, perhaps in a way similar to when we speak of something or someone being a force of nature? Some scholars speak of Wisdom as a hypostasis, by which they mean she seems to function as an attribute or extension of God. Or, one could go further yet and argue that within texts like Proverbs 8 we are dealing with a goddess named Wisdom. We will return to the idea of wisdom (and folly) personified below.

Some Examples of Proverbial Literature

The book of Proverbs of course shares much in common with any collection of folk wisdom sayings. Thus the modern English saying, "Spare the rod, spoil the child" is simply another form of Proverbs 13:24, 22:15, or 23:13. Like this English language proverb, the proverbs of the Bible aim to articulate much in very few words. In fact, Hebrew proverbs can at times be much terser than various English translations imply because the Hebrew often omits the connective particles between words. At times the Hebrew simply projects various images next to each other, allowing the reader to draw out the implications. Thus the English of 13:12 reads, "Hope deferred makes the heart sick, but a desire fulfilled is a tree of life" (using 15 words). The Hebrew in a mere eight words actually reads as follows: "Hope deferred, sick heart, tree [of] life, desire fulfilled." The reader or hearer naturally grasps that A=B like C=D and that AB and CD are opposites.

Many of these proverbs are quite profound and even disturbing. Notice, for example, 14:10, "The heart alone knows its own bitterness, and no stranger shares its joy." In our culture we often feel the need to tell others that we understand their feelings. Yet, is this really true? Can anyone truly grasp the exact import of a particular event in another individual's life? Proverbs 14:10 communicates something deep and disturbs us by articulating something that we may well fear, that ultimately each of us is utterly alone with our own feelings, even when we are in close communion with other human beings.

One topic touched upon several times in Proverbs is poverty and wealth. Proverbs is very clear that one must treat the poor with dignity. Thus Proverbs 14:31 declares that "Those who oppress the poor insult their Maker, but those who are kind to the needy honor Him." This short wisdom saying is built upon the biblical insight articulated in Genesis 1 that each human being is created in God's image and likeness, and to insult God's image (that is, another human) is to insult God, who created this image. One should note that Jesus' parable of the Sheep and the Goats in Matthew 25 is essentially an elaboration of this seemingly simple but profound observation. Of course having knowledge of this proverb and actually acting upon it are two different matters. How many of us have looked with disgust upon a fellow human being, especially someone in poor circumstances? One can see the difficult daily discipline involved in actually internalizing what may appear as self-evident truisms.

Continuing our examination of poverty, Proverbs recognizes that at times poverty should be chosen over dishonest gain or a life filled with stress (Proverbs 15:15-17; 22:1). But generally speaking, Proverbs endorses the view that wealth comes from hard work and poverty is often due to laziness. This is articulated rather pointedly in Proverbs 6:6-11 and 24:30-34, both of which draw this conclusion on the basis of carefully observing nature and human nature. While some might find this assessment harsh and possibly inaccurate from a sociological perspective, it is, whether correct or not, quite similar to the widespread (albeit often unvoiced) sentiment in Western culture that poverty is oftentimes at least partially attributable to laziness or a moral defect on the part of those who are poor.

Another central theme articulated in Proverbs 10–29, as noted earlier, is the notion that the universe is constructed in such a way that the righteous ultimately receive their just reward and the wicked are done in by their own evil behavior. There are times in this literature where this is articulated like an iron law of nature such as in 26:27, "Whoever digs a pit will fall into it, and a stone will come back on the one who starts it rolling." Similarly, note how 11.17 describes proper behavior as inherently producing reward and wicked behavior inherently leading to punishment: "Those who are kind reward themselves, but the cruel do themselves harm." Two points are worth raising here. First, it is important to note that statements like the above are not necessarily intended to be inverted, as if the converse of such statements is automatically true. Thus, for example, one should not deduce from 26:27 that "whoever finds oneself in a pit, dug it." Second, it is also clear that no one in wisdom circles thought the balances of reward and punishment were instantly set aright. Rather, it was recognized that the righteous might sometimes suffer at the hands of the wicked and that for a time the wicked might prosper. Thus 24:16 tells us not to mistreat the righteous "for though they fall seven times, they will rise." Similarly, in 13:22b we are told that "the sinner's wealth is laid up for the righteous."

Yet another theme worth drawing out is that while Proverbs believes humans can obtain insight into God's universe and the way it functions, there are limits on human knowledge while God's freedom to upset expectations is preserved. Thus we find "The human mind may devise many plans, but it is the purpose of the Lord that will be established" (Proverbs 19:21), a saying quite close to the contemporary proverb, "man proposes but God disposes." Or, as the book states elsewhere, "no wisdom, no understanding, no counsel, can avail against the Lord" (Proverbs 21:30).

Finally, let us turn to a well-known problem raised by Proverbs 26:4-5. Verse 4 reads, "Do not answer fools according to their folly, or you will be a fool yourself." Immediately thereafter, verse 5 counsels, "Answer fools according to their folly, or they will be wise in their own eyes." The most likely explanation for this seeming contradiction is that in truth there is no contradiction at all. Various truths are appropriate for different circumstances. Thus today we have many wise sayings that give opposing advice. For example, we hear "A penny saved is a penny earned" and at other times "Spend it while you can; you can't take it with you when you go." One might argue that Proverbs' placing of the two sayings side by side reveals a sophisticated framework as well as a clever way to communicate a message effectively, and in a way that permits ease of retention. In addition to the actual content of the two proverbs, the juxtaposition of these two sayings teaches that what makes a person wise is having the ability to discern which situation one is in and thus which piece of advice is proper.

189

Proverbs 1–9

Much of the material found in the collections of the terse proverbs that occupy most of the book likely arose earlier than the long, somewhat preachy speeches found in the opening nine chapters. This introductory material articulates an explicit wisdom theology by drawing out the implications that undergird the larger outlook of Wisdom literature and in turn frames the book. A number of these speeches are presented as fatherly or motherly advice to one's young son in an attempt to guide the child along the path to a righteous and blessed life. One of the most striking innovations is found in the tropes of Lady Wisdom (or in Hebrew *Hokhma*) and her opposite, Lady Folly, who each seek to lure the child down the respective paths of righteousness and life, or wickedness and death. Many believe that the heavy sexual overtones of some of these passages suggest that they are directed toward young male courtiers-in-training who need to be cautioned about controlling their sexual urges. However, it should be noted that the choice of the feminine figures "Lady Wisdom" and "Lady Folly" may well speak to something greater, and thus represent a larger theme of the book, something especially relevant when we keep in mind that "Lady Wisdom" comes to be associated with God's special revelation of the Torah to Israel (more on this below). Chapters 1–9 set up the theme of a man choosing one lady or the other (wisdom and folly, respectively) as a type of ultimate choice, as if choosing God or a non-god, so much so that, when the book concludes with its description of an ideal woman in chapter 31, it seems strategic—that is, the conclusion is doing more than simply listing qualities of a woman that a man might look for in a wife. Rather, though containing culturally conditioned descriptions of an ideal woman in the ancient world, this concluding and perhaps climatic text may well be speaking more fundamentally to the joy of finally finding wisdom in all its glory and living a happy life having found it—which, according to later Jewish writing like the apocryphal book of Ben Sirah, is a life lived in communion with God and his Torah. Indeed, by bookending Proverbs 10–29 between an opening that highlights Lady Wisdom as a woman to pursue, and chapter 31, that speaks of finding the ideal wife, the quest for true wisdom takes on an erotic dimension.

Jewish Use of Proverbs

At least since the time of the apocryphal book of Ben Sirah, Jewish thinkers have equated *Hokhma*, "Wisdom"—which the book of Proverbs speaks of as bestowing long life upon those who seek it—with Torah. This is seen quite clearly in the prayers surrounding the reading of the Torah in the synagogue liturgy. Thus as the congregation returns the Torah scroll to the ark after the Torah reading has been concluded, words from Proverbs 3:17-18 are recited, which speak of Wisdom as "a tree of life for those that grasp her" (Wisdom and Torah are both spoken of with feminine gender terminology). In short, Judaism asserts that God's most profound wisdom has been transmitted to the Jewish people when God revealed the Torah to Moses on Mount Sinai. One cannot overstate the seminal importance of the Jewish insight that the Torah is *Hokhma*, that is, wisdom incarnate.

One other interesting use of Proverbs is that in a traditional Jewish home, the husband commonly sings the acrostic poem in Proverbs 31:10-31, which speaks of a good wife, to honor his own wife at the dinner table on the eve of Sabbath (Friday night).

Christian Use of Proverbs

Given that Solomon was regarded to be the wisest of all people in the ancient world, and was considered to be the primary author of the book of Proverbs (see 1:1 and 10:1), it is no small matter when the gospel writers report that Jesus claimed to be greater than him (Matthew 12:42; Luke 11:31). Perhaps equally interesting is the Apostle Paul's idea in 1 Corinthians 1:30 that Jesus "became for us wisdom from God," essentially equating Jesus with wisdom itself. But it seems no passage has gathered more interest in relation to Jesus and Wisdom than the opening of John's Gospel. The attentive reader of Proverbs 8, which speaks of Wisdom being present at the beginning when God created the world, will likely hear echoes in John when it identifies Jesus as the word (Greek *logos*) who was "with God in the beginning. Through him all things were made" (John 1:2-3). This idea came to animate a great deal of discussion in the early church, and thus second-century church fathers like Justin Martyr and Athenagoras argued that Jesus was the Wisdom of Proverbs 8. However, given that Proverbs 8:22 speaks of Wisdom being created, such an association gave way to the debates of the fourth century about whether Jesus was created, one of the ideas the Council of Nicaea discussed (and ultimately rejected) in 325 CE.

JOB

Introduction and Overview

The book of Job narrates the story of a wealthy and righteous man named Job, who is put through a severe set of tribulations to explore whether even a very righteous person will fear God without reward. The book begins by reporting on Job's extremely pious life up to this point and then turns to a dialogue between God and "the Satan." The Hebrew in Job refers to this latter character as *hasatan*; the "ha" indicates the definite article "the," which is followed by the Hebrew word *satan*, which means "adversary," "opponent," or "accuser." This angelic being here functions as God's attorney general, "the Accuser" who brings charges against human sinners, and like the FBI, he also engages in running sting operations to see who might be tempted to act wrongly. When God praises Job to the prosecutor Satan, the Satan responds by suggesting that Job fears God only because God has blessed him so greatly. But, the Satan maintains, if God removes Job's wealth and standing, Job will curse God.

God authorizes the Satan to begin the challenge, and Job loses all his possessions and his whole family, apart from his wife, in one day. Yet, Job accepts this tragic set of events with total equanimity. The Satan then suggests that God should enhance the test by taking away Job's physical health. Even after this, Job still remains steadfast to God. At the end of chapter 2, three of Job's friends arrive to comfort him and they mourn with him for a full week. Following this, beginning in chapter 3, Job's disposition noticeably shifts and he begins to unburden himself and wonder why he is suffering the way that he is. Between chapters 3–31 Job engages in an extensive set of dialogues with his three friends, which include his many laments. Generally speaking, Job questions God's justice while his friends defend God and indicate that Job is

192

likely suffering because he offended God in some manner. Chapters 32–37 introduce yet a fourth character, who, being dissatisfied with the defense of God mounted by Job's three friends, engages in a monologue that somewhat anticipates God's own response found in Job 38–41. In this penultimate section of Job (38–41), God speaks to Job out of a whirling storm and questions what standing Job has to question the creator of the universe. The book finishes with a short epilogue in which God tells Job's friends that they, unlike Job, spoke wrongly about God and need to make sacrifices for their folly while Job is to pray for them. At the end of the book, God restores Job's fortune and eventually grants Job a new set of children, allowing him to return to his once blessed life.

Controversies and Debates

One question that has animated much critical reflection on this powerful biblical book is how to make sense of its composite nature. There is a strong consensus that disparate materials have been brought together and sit somewhat uneasily within this book. The most obvious division is between materials that depict what might be described as Job the pious defender of God found in Job 1–2, 27, and 42:7-17 versus the vast bulk of 3–31, which portrays Job as a critic of God. There is little doubt that all of the speeches of Elihu found in 32–37 have been added to the book rather late inasmuch as he is missing from the party of three friends both at the outset in Job 2:11 and at the end in Job 42:7. The striking and beautiful hymn to wisdom found in Job 28 is also believed by many to be borrowed from elsewhere and inserted here. All of these facts point to the probability that the book passed through more than one edition and thus evolved over time, although reconstructions of the book's development are speculative. Further, some have argued that the various fractures and seams in the book add to its literary richness and that in spite of any fractures it is possible to read the book holistically.

One other pressing problem is the actual language of the text of Job. Translating any language is easiest when one can see a single word in a variety of contexts. This provides a range of possible meanings for a given word. In the Hebrew Bible, certain words only occur once and when this happens their meaning is inevitably somewhat obscure. Job contains more instances of singly occurring words than any other book in the Hebrew Bible. One possible explanation for the obscurity of the vocabulary is that the book might originally have been an Edomite text. Although difficult to prove, this theory makes some sense in that Edom was a country that bordered ancient Israel and whose inhabitants are linked in the Bible to Jacob's brother, Esau. A number of names in the Edomite genealogy found in Genesis 36 sound like people or places in Job. Thus Genesis 36:10 mentions a person named Eliphaz, a name of the first friend of Job to speak in Job 4. Job's town Uz is also the name of an Edomite ancestor in Genesis 36:28.

Theodicy

Job is the most widely known and probably the most sophisticated ancient text to engage in what philosophers, since Leibniz, who coined the term in the 1700s, call theodicy. The word *theodicy* literally means "to defend or justify God." The problem that theodicy wrestles with is the existence of certain evils, most particularly innocent suffering and the lack of punishment of those who deserve to be punished.

It seems quite likely that the book of Job was written by theologically imaginative scribes and sages as a thought experiment that would probe issues of God's justice. This helps explain why the text tells us up front that Job is a perfectly pious person who assiduously avoids all sin or even the appearance of sin. He even repents for his children and makes sacrifices on their behalf. The way Job is portrayed early in the book, along with the fact that he suffers a terrible set of blows in a somewhat implausible fashion, suggests that Job is a fictional construct intended to teach profound truths about life, suffering, and God.

Some Important Observations on Job

Too often today Job is read solely through a contemporary lens that assumes that Job's friends are shallow in their belief that Job is suffering because of his sin and God is therefore just, that God is a blowhard who ultimately ignores Job's damning critique, and that Job's words contain the true viewpoint of the book's authors. In fact, it is much more likely that the ancient audience would have read the book with more sympathy and nuance. Here, a few examples are in order.

It is not exactly correct that Job's friends think Job is being punished because he is a sinner. Throughout at least the first twenty chapters, the argument is not that Job is getting what he deserved but that Job, like every other human being alive, is flawed. Being flawed does not make one evil. It does require that one take spiritual inventory regularly and pray that God forgive human lapses. Thus the friends regularly point out that God even finds flaws in the heavenly host (Job 4:18 and 15:15), and they urge Job to act like others and pray for God's mercy and forgiveness which God will surely grant to someone as righteous as him (Job 8:5-7; 11:13-20). Furthermore, the comforters' belief is not that the righteous will never suffer or that the wicked never prosper. It is rather that eventually, over the long arc of time, God's justice prevails (Job 8:11-22; 20). The belief in the eventual triumph of justice over evil is not some naive belief we have now outgrown but rather a widespread idea that many intelligent people still affirm today, or at the very least an ideal toward which society should strive. If such a belief was dead, it would be hard to explain why people flock to blockbuster movies like *Star Wars*, *Spiderman*, and *Batman*.

While it is true that God does not directly answer Job's critique, God's long speech on the wonders of nature is not simply an attempt to tell Job that he is out of order. Rather, part of Job's worldview is that Job sits at the center of the world, and thus he is under the delusion that he is in a position to evaluate God's justice. God's speech so widens Job's view of the universe that he comes to see that he is not only *not* at the center of the universe but also that his life is just one very small part of a grander world. Most people will agree that humans, especially humans who experience a devastating blow, at times come to think that the universe is conspiring against them. Inevitably, they also ask how they could possibly deserve the fate they are suffering. It is likely that God's speech is suggesting that the wondrous complexity found in God's creation means we must exercise extreme caution when we seek to explain the life tragedies we experience.

Finally, we might suggest that there is growth in Job's character, which likely indicates that the book thinks he had things to learn. Thus, at the very end of the book in Job 42:11, Job is able to accept the fellowship and help of his larger community. This contrasts with Job earlier in the book, someone who could help others but seemed unable to receive help from anyone else.

Job and Other Near Eastern Literature

There are a number of significant parallels to Job in other ancient Near Eastern literature including (to name two) the *Babylonian Theodicy*, a poetic dialogue between one man who laments his suffering and his friend who argues that his experience is divinely just (the sufferer appears to win the debate), and an Akkadian poem titled *Ludlul Bel Nemeqi* (meaning "I Will Praise the Lord of Wisdom"), which tells of a man who is tormented despite his proper treatment of the gods, later restored by Marduk. Like Job, these texts, in the end, agree that the ways of the gods or God are not entirely clear, and thus difficult to discern completely by humans.

Why Is Job in the Bible?

The biblical character of Job often challenges viewpoints taken for granted elsewhere in the Hebrew Bible. This leaves one wondering why those who shaped the canon of the Bible included this controversial book. Here it might be useful to point out that this question presumes a certain view about the function of religion that is worth examining more closely. One frequently encounters students and other lay readers who assume that the Bible and religion in general is primarily intended to provide easy answers to life's most difficult questions. It often comes as a shock to many people therefore to learn that the Bible contains books like Job and Qoheleth, which not only question God's justice, but do so with great force and clarity. In reality, neither the Jewish nor the Christian Bible contains easy answers that explain away human suffering. Rather, both canons are filled with texts that force one to contemplate life in all its fullness, and thus both canons contain a wide array of viewpoints that attempt to make sense of life with all its wonders and difficulties. In fact, the Bible often unflinchingly explores such difficulties and thus it actually raises tough questions for those who thought there were easy answers to life. In short, those who canonized the Jewish and Christian Bibles recognized that there are times when it is fully legitimate to question God's justice.

Job in Jewish Tradition

Unsurprisingly, Job has influenced a number of later Jewish practices surrounding death and mourning. Job 1:21 states, "the LORD gave, and the LORD has taken away; blessed be the name of the LORD" and this is used in the funeral service as an acknowledgment by the mourners of God's righteousness. In the days following a Jewish funeral, friends and family come to the house of the mourning family to comfort them. Here too Job has influenced practice, in that comforters are supposed to imitate the practice of Job's three friends who show up to be with Job in his time of difficulty, but who refrain from speaking to Job until Job speaks first. Those not mourning need to take their cues from the mourners and carefully avoid implying that they completely understand what the mourner is experiencing.

Job has also played a very large role in the modern Jewish imagination, most especially in the wake of the Shoah, or Holocaust. There are Jews alive today who have lived Job's story in the sense that they lost their complete families during the Nazi era and later emigrated to Israel, the United States, or other countries, and built new lives, at times remarrying and raising a new family.

Many recent writers (see "Contemporary Reuses of Job" below) and artists have mined images and ideas from Job in the contemporary effort to give voice to individual and communal grief as well as to explore the philosophical and theological issues raised by the Holocaust or what Jews call the Shoah.

Job in Christian Tradition

Job is explicitly mentioned in the New Testament book of James, at 5:11, as a character whose patience is to be imitated, perhaps representing the view that although Job suffered he was in the end restored to God's favor. There are a number of phrases in the book of Job that have become familiar and gained usage within the life of Christians and the church. As in Judaism, Christian tradition also makes use of Job's proclamation that "the LORD gave, and the LORD has taken away; blessed be the name of the LORD" (Job 1:21). Perhaps more familiar to contemporary Christians are the words of Job in 19:25 (KJV): "I know that my redeemer liveth," made especially popular by Handel's *Messiah*. When read in the context of the book of Job, it is clear, as most interpreters agree, that Job is not so much speaking of a spiritual redeemer or hope in an afterlife, but of someone who will eventually, even if after his death, vindicate his case of innocence.

Contemporary Reuses of Job

Job is one of the most widely referenced biblical books in contemporary literature. Thus Archibald MacLeish's *J.B.*, Neil Simon's *God's Favorite*, Chaim Grade's *The Quarrel*, and Elie Wiesel's *The Trial of God* are attempts to bring a retold version of the story to contemporary audiences. The protagonist in Bernard Malamud's *The Fixer* certainly has strong resonances with Job. Perhaps the most powerful update of the problem of theodicy raised within Job is found in Dostoyevsky's *The Brothers Karamazov*, when Ivan challenges his brother Alyosha to explain away innocent suffering by introducing some devastating examples of the suffering of children. Dostoyevsky heightens the interrogation of God found in Job by showing that even in the light of later Western beliefs in heaven and hell, concepts not fully developed when the book of Job was written, it is hard to justify the suffering of the innocent. In short, it is difficult to see how the future heavenly reward of the righteous or the eventual punishment of those who inflicted suffering on the innocent can rectify the inexplicable suffering experienced by too many children in our world.

THE FIVE SCROLLS

SONG OF SONGS

The Song of Songs, or perhaps better, "The Greatest Song" or "Song of all Songs," is one of five short scrolls called the five *megillot*. Within Jewish tradition, each scroll is used on a particular holiday with Song of Songs being read on Passover, perhaps because God's love affair with Israel as a people begins with God's redemption of Israel from Egyptian slavery. The book, a mere eight chapters long, is unique in the Bible in that it contains a series of love poems, some, such as those found in chapter 5, containing rather racy sexual metaphors. In fact, elsewhere in the Hebrew Bible, human love is at times viewed negatively in that it often leads to the loss of self-control as occurs when Shechem rapes Dinah and in Amnon's rape of Tamar (Genesis 34 and 2 Samuel 13) or when Samson is said to love Delilah, a love that leads to his imprisonment and blinding. Here, however, love is celebrated, and it is important to note that Deuteronomy and various prophetic books regularly speak of God's great love for Israel and in turn Israel's obligation to love God with complete devotion. The Hebrew Bible's pervasive use of the trope of divine-human love may explain how even though the Song never directly mentions God, both Jews and Christians have come to read the text as describing the love between God and the respective Jewish and Christian communities, or between God and the individual soul. In fact, the great Rabbi Akiva (martyred in the 130s CE) went so far as to say that the whole world only existed, so to speak, for the day on which the Song of Songs was given to it.

Controversies and Debates

Traditionally the Song is attributed to King Solomon, most likely because his name is explicitly mentioned several times in the text, most prominently in the opening inscription (1:1). Furthermore, according to 1 Kings 11, Solomon had an exceptionally large harem of women suggesting he was a great lover, and 1 Kings 4:32 reports that Solomon composed over one thousand songs. Most scholars would date the book much later, perhaps in the postexilic era when Aramaic was the imperial language of the Persian Empire inasmuch as the Hebrew in the book at times shows evidence of being influenced by Aramaic.

Both the genre and the unity of the book are hotly contested. The often difficult and cryptic language of the Song can and has given rise to many theories. Some turn to Sumerian or Mesopotamian ritual texts and see the book as modeled after a *hieros gamos*, that is, a sacred marriage between deities reenacted by humans, as was done to celebrate the marriage of Dumuzi and Inanna, Sumerian deities. Others accept the connection to wedding imagery, but suggest that the poems in this book may have developed out of a common wedding practice, with distinct poems sung on each of the seven wedding feast days. Yet a third theory proposes that the book was a drama with several acts and three characters: the woman, who is courted by two men, a lowly shepherd and King Solomon. Yet another suggestion seeks to compare the Song to ancient Egyptian love poems and thus sees the Song as a mundane series of love poems, but not necessarily a unified composition that was used in a specific ritual context.

While it not clear that the book forms a tight unity, there are recurring patterns such as the repeated attempt to describe the beauty of the woman's various physical attributes by comparing her eyes, hair, teeth, lips, and other features to various natural, pastoral, and architectural images. This occurs specifically in four places, at 4:1-7; 5:10-16; 6:4-10; 7:1-9. The catalogues of natural images could indicate that the Song was produced by the same circles responsible for wisdom-oriented texts like Job and Proverbs since these texts also show a strong interest in carefully observing and describing elements of the natural and physical world. Furthermore, there is one recurring refrain found in 2:7; 3:5; and 8:4 which suggests the intent to weave the distinct parts of the Song into a larger unity:

I adjure you, O daughters of Jerusalem,
    by the gazelles or the wild does:
do not stir up or awaken love
    until it is ready! (2:7)

Insofar as the ancient rabbis read the Song as a description of the ongoing love affair between God and the people of Israel, they came to understand this verse as warning to the Jewish community against trying to hasten the arrival of the messianic era before its duly appointed time.

201

Isn't Song of Songs Too Racy for the Bible?

The immediate answer to this question is no, because, well, it *is* in the Bible. However, the matter is not quite so simple and in fact there are reasons to believe that Song of Songs appears to have faced some resistance in being recognized as part of the biblical canon, as one can deduce from Rabbi Akiba's hyperbolic defense of its value. Further, as we noted above, for many years the text was primarily read allegorically (that is, as a metaphor for God's love of his people), and in fact reading it as relating to human love was discouraged. The reasons for this controversy become very clear in reading verses like Song 5:4-5:

> My beloved thrust his hand into the opening,
> and my inmost being yearned for him.
> I arose to open to my beloved,
> and my hands dripped with myrrh,
> my fingers with liquid myrrh,
> upon the handles of the bolt.

Though some have suggested that these might simply refer to the lover opening a door for her beloved, these verses seem laden with sexual imagery. Many scholars concur. Without foreclosing on the possibilities for deeper meaning or allegorical readings, many Jewish and Christian readers today recognize that the book also celebrates the wonder and joy of sexual union between a man and a woman.

The Power (and Danger) of Love

Song 8:6 contains a moving description of the power and the danger of love as an emotion. Love is said to be strong like death, and the power of jealousy (an emotion that frequently travels in the company of love) is said to be as harsh or fierce as Sheol, the underworld. The following verse then indicates that what is being described here is the difficulty of extinguishing the passionate emotion of love once it is ignited. As noted above, the Israelites told cautionary tales about the potential dangers of love. However, it also hints at the ability of love to transcend death.

Concluding Reflections

Song of Songs reminds us that sexual attraction, romance, and sexual activity are part of what it means to be human according to the Bible. It also reminds us that these things were as valued by the ancients and the religious elite who compiled the Tanakh as they are to modern culture. That both the Jewish and Christian traditions have read this literature as pertaining to God and his people is perhaps even more radical. Though one might be tempted to think that such allegorical readings attempt to squelch these texts, the opposite could be true. That God could love his people as passionate lovers love each other not only legitimizes sexual passion and activity but also teaches us something about the great passion God is said to have for his people, and the passion expected of God's people for God.

Bernard of Clairvaux, a twelfth-century Christian interpreter who wrote some eighty-six sermons on the book, argued that humans are instructed to, among other things, fear, honor, and love God, yet it is love that is most prized in Scripture. He then goes on to demonstrate why love is the most valued and should most animate the spiritual life: "Of all the feelings and affections of the soul, love is the only one by which the creature, though not on equal terms, is able to respond to the Creator and to repay what it has received from him. . . . For when God loves us he desires nothing but to be loved. He loves for no other reason, indeed, than that he may be loved, knowing that by their love itself those who love him are blessed" (Saint Bernard of Clairvaux, *Cantica Canticorum [Sermons of the Song of Songs]*, in *Bernard of Clairvaux: Selected Works*, trans. Gillian R. Evans [Mahwah, NJ: Paulist Press, 1987], 83:4, pp. 272–73).

RUTH

Introduction and Overview

In a mere four chapters, this book narrates a wonderful tale that touches on a host of themes including: the nature and extent of familial obligations, the meaning of friendship, the treatment of foreigners and those in need, the difference between acting morally and going beyond what the moral minimum requires, and the possibility of starting life anew after a personal tragedy. The story begins in Moab, a country located southeast of Israel, and narrates a series of misfortunes that had befallen a Judean man named Elimelech and his wife, Naomi, who had moved to Moab due to a famine in their homeland Bethlehem. They had two sons who had each married a Moabite woman. When all the males in the story die, Naomi begins her journey home to Bethlehem with her two daughters-in-law in tow. On the journey Naomi tells both daughters-in-law to return to their homes and seek new husbands there. While Orpah returns, Ruth insists on making her new life with Naomi back in Judah. Once back in Bethlehem the story takes a somewhat romantic turn and narrates how Ruth fortuitously comes to glean grain in the field of Boaz, a close relative of Naomi. Boaz quickly comes to the aid of the impoverished Ruth and her mother-in-law Naomi and soon agrees to redeem Elimelech's land and marry the widowed Ruth. Boaz and Ruth have a son, symbolizing a rebirth for Naomi. The story concludes with a genealogical notice that the child will turn out to be King David's grandfather.

Controversies and Debates

There is some debate about when the book of Ruth was written. While set in the time of the Judges, a period lasting from approximately 1200–1000

BCE, it is unlikely to have been written earlier than the time of David, whose birth is acknowledged in the final verse. In truth the evidence suggests it was written quite a bit later. For example, Ruth 4:7 says, "Now this was the custom in former times in Israel . . ," which demonstrates the need to explain a custom that not only was no longer practiced, but a custom totally unknown to the current audience. Although not conclusive, the strongest evidence of an exilic or postexilic date is that the book appears to challenge the prohibition on intermarrying with Moabites. While rooted in a law found in Deuteronomy 23 that many would place in the seventh century BCE, the books of Ezra and Nehemiah, written during the Persian era (538–333 BCE), describe attempts to strictly enforce the ban on intermarriage with Moabites and other foreigners, a ban that the story of Ruth appears to contest.

Women's Voices and Perspectives?

Many contemporary readers have noted the unusual prominence of woman characters in Ruth and the fact that women's thoughts, words, and actions occupy so much of this book. Some even wonder whether Ruth was written by a woman or originated in oral form among women in ancient Israel. Such a hypothesis is speculative, of course, and it is possible for a male to present the plight of females with great sympathy, seen, for example, in Nathaniel Hawthorne's *The Scarlet Letter*. While the story is embraced by some feminists, others critique the fact that in the end Ruth must be saved by Boaz, and Naomi's value in society is contingent on the birth of a male heir to continue her husband's lineage. However, others would highlight that this 2,500 year old story portrays how vulnerable women in a traditional patriarchal culture can become in certain circumstances, possibly providing a subtle critique of this very culture.

"Go and Uncover His Feet"

In reading the book of Ruth, one cannot help but wonder what exactly happened between Ruth and Boaz at night in chapter 3. Boaz had eaten and likely had some wine as well, and had fallen asleep in the threshing area. Ruth, having washed and anointed herself, the equivalent of a woman today preparing for a date by putting on perfume, came in stealthily and "uncovered his feet," and then went to sleep next to Boaz. It is hard to escape the idea that Naomi's instruction to Ruth that she "uncover his feet" contains a sexual innuendo, especially given that "feet" in Hebrew can function as a euphemism for genitalia, and "uncovering" someone can serve as a euphemism for sexual intercourse. However, Boaz's praise of Ruth's integrity in 3:11 (he calls her a "worthy woman,") suggests that while the story has a sexual overtone, Ruth did not actually engage in any sexual behavior. Perhaps part of the story's appeal is the heightened sexual tension developed by the storyteller here, even if no sexual activity has taken place. This is not uncommon in many romantic comedies and sitcoms even today.

Figure 21. An artistic rendering of the story of Ruth. Note that the lower left panel depicts Ruth lifting up Boaz's garment as he sleeps. Frans Basnage. Amsterdam: Linderbergh, 1721. Courtesy Smith College Libraries.

Theological Reflections on Ruth

Naomi's life experience has some resemblance both to the book of Job and to some of the ancestral stories in Genesis. Like Job, Naomi loses everything and finds herself in an impoverished and barren state complaining that God has treated her harshly. Yet by the end of the story, she is beginning life anew as symbolized by the birth of her grandchild. And like Abraham and Sarah, Naomi is driven out of the land due to famine. Furthermore, when she arrives back home she is too old to bear children anymore. While God does not intervene to perform a miraculous conception as he does with Sarah, new life is brought about by very unusual means. First, like Tamar in Genesis, Naomi's husband's lineage is perpetuated through a levirate marriage. To remind the reader, this was a legal procedure by which a kinsman of the dead relative biologically fathers a child with the wife of the deceased, yet the child legally becomes the heir of the deceased man. In this case, not only is there a levirate marriage, but this marriage occurs with a Moabite woman, adding an additional complication because texts like Deuteronomy 23 ban Moabites from joining the Israelite community and thus would seem to prohibit Boaz from marrying Ruth. When one looks at King David's larger family tree, one discovers that two of his ancestors were involved in levirate marriages and each marriage also involved the violation of a legal protocol. While Ruth is of Moabite stock, Tamar was Judah's own daughter-in-law and thus he was prohibited from having intercourse with her. Yet, the Bible seems to be saying that God finds ways, sometimes scandalous, to fulfill promises that in human eyes were certain to fail.

Another important theological theme emphasized in Ruth is that for goodness to flourish one must at times be willing to go above and beyond what is legally required. Within the story both Ruth and Boaz are contrasted with two other perfectly decent people. Ruth's sister-in-law, Orpah, acts in an understandable fashion when she opts to return home to her mother's house in Moab. Similarly, the unnamed relative of Boaz is within his rights when he decides not to redeem the property belonging to Naomi's deceased husband and sons because it may imperil his own inheritance in that any son born to Naomi would not be legally his. However, the story suggests that one should emulate the behavior of Ruth and Boaz, who both acted in self-sacrificing ways. Thus Ruth leaves her home and her people and ties her fate to her impoverished and barren mother-in-law instead of seeking a husband nearer to home who could have more easily provided for her. And Boaz is willing to marry Ruth even though the child she might bear would legally not be his own.

Ruth in Jewish Tradition

Ruth is read in synagogues on Shavuot (the Feast of Weeks), a spring holiday that occurs approximately seven weeks after the start of Passover. In the

Hebrew Bible, Shavuot is a festival celebrating the first produce of the new harvest. The notice in Ruth 1:22 informing us that Naomi and Ruth arrived in Bethlehem at the start of the barley harvest (that is, the earliest yearly harvest) helps explain why the book of Ruth came to be associated with the early harvest festival of Shavuot. While the biblical story of Ruth highlights Ruth's Moabite status throughout, the rabbis saw Ruth as a model convert to Judaism. This may provide yet an additional association between Ruth and Shavuot, a holiday that the rabbis linked to the revelation of the Torah at Mount Sinai. Ruth's proclamation in 1:16 that "your people shall be my people, and your God my God" can be read as suggesting that she was a convert to Judaism who accepted the Torah and its 613 commandments. In some sense every Jew accepts the Torah anew each year at Shavuot when one celebrates God's gift of the Torah. Thus Ruth's commitment to Torah is a model for all Jews.

Ruth in Christian Tradition

Ruth is one of three foreign women who are singled out among a list of mainly men as ancestresses of King David in the Gospel of Matthew. Jesus himself is produced through a very unlikely and even scandalous set of events like those experienced by Tamar and Ruth. Whatever the case, Matthew's inclusion of these "outsider" women in his genealogy seems to be an early hint of his coming vision of Gentile inclusion, culminating in Matthew's concluding "Great Commission" by Jesus to make disciples of the Gentiles.

The early church quite often viewed Ruth as a type, or representative, of the church in that she was an outsider who joined Israel. Origen, an early church father, viewed the manner in which Ruth entered Israel to be a paradigm for the ways in which pagans enter the church. As a continuing sign of this tradition, the book of Ruth today is read within most modern lectionaries in the weeks following Pentecost (the holiday Christians celebrate in lieu of Shavuot), a time when Gentiles began to join the church, as described in the book of Acts.

LAMENTATIONS

Introduction and Overview

The title *Lamentations* is derived from the Latin and Greek translations (*threni* and *threnoi* respectively) of the Hebrew word for poetic laments, *qinot*. The Hebrew title of this book is *ekhah*, which is derived from the opening word, *how*, as in "How lonely sits the city / that once was full of people" (Lamentations 1:1). These ancient laments often begin with the question *how* as a way of highlighting an abrupt fall from a blessed to a now very desolate state. The book contains five poems of lament, each one a chapter long, and chapters 1–4 are alphabetical acrostics. As the reader will recall from our discussion of certain psalms, this means that each verse (or in the case of chapter 3, each group of three verses) starts with a letter of the alphabet proceeding in order from the first letter *aleph* through the entire twenty-two letter Hebrew alphabet to the last letter, *tav*. Acrostics were likely employed to help facilitate memorization inasmuch as ancient Israel was still primarily an oral culture. Interestingly enough, chapter 5 is not an acrostic, but also contains twenty-two verses.

Acrostic Lament

It is impossible for an English Bible translation to capture everything in the original language, something particularly evident when it comes to translating acrostic Hebrew poems. How can a translator possibly preserve the meaning of the poem while producing twenty-two equivalent English words for Hebrew ones? In other words, how can he or she start each new sentence by matching the progression of the Hebrew alphabet but using the English alphabet (A, B, C, and so on)? Some attempts have been made to do just this, and a particularly noteworthy example is the translation of English author, theologian, and priest Ronald Knox (1888–1957), seen below:

> Alone she dwells, the city . . .
> Be sure she weeps; there in the darkness . . .
> Cruel the suffering and the bondage . . .
> Desolate, the streets of Sion . . .
> Exultant, now, her invaders . . . (Lamentations 1:1-5 Knox, abridged)

Controversies and Debates

Hebrew manuscripts place this book among the Writings, something Jewish tradition affirms. The Septuagint, the ancient Greek translation of the books in the Hebrew Bible, however, contains an opening line that attributes Lamentations to Jeremiah and places it right after the book of Jeremiah, in amongst the Prophets (something still followed by most Christian Bibles). Almost all contemporary scholars find this authorship claim unlikely both because it would be difficult to explain why the Hebrew text of Lamentations would have removed the passage attributing authorship to Jeremiah, and because often the language and content of Lamentations does not easily match Jeremiah's outlook. For example, would Jeremiah, who spent his whole life warning the people of Judah to repent, have authored a passage like 2:14, which claims that Israel's prophets failed to declare her sinful ways?

Another area of debate concerns whether the individual chapters in Lamentations were composed by the same person at the same time, and thus how unified the book is. Each chapter of the book is a distinct poetic lament, and the viewpoint varies in different chapters. For example, chapter 3 is much longer and more complex than the others, not only containing three verses for each Hebrew letter (thus having sixty-six verses total as opposed to the more usual twenty-two) but also having a distinct first-person voice that closely resembles the individual laments found in certain psalms (something that possibly gave rise to notion that Jeremiah, who experienced the devastating destruction, penned the larger work).

Understanding Lamentations

One significant difference between society today and ancient Near Eastern society concerns the role ritual plays in relation to emotion. Many today reject set communal rituals as empty because they often do not reflect one's current emotional state. Thus, there is a modern tendency to personalize rituals so that they always reflect what one currently feels and thinks (for instance, when people write their own wedding vows, supplementing or at times totally displacing more classical wedding ritual language). By contrast, in the ancient Near East, as well as in many societies in which ritual plays a much larger role, set rituals were used to help participants feel and understand what a larger society or group *should* be feeling. For example, in ancient Israel there were professional wailers (see Jeremiah 9:17-22). One might think of these performers as the opposite of cheerleaders at our sports events. These mourning facilitators helped set the mood and may have led chanted ritual dirges like the poems we find in Lamentations. Communally reciting these set liturgical texts helped the whole community evoke and work through feelings of grief and experiences of trauma. One place in our societies where we have such rituals is on the anniversaries of societal tragedies such as the ritual of reading aloud the names of everyone who perished at each site on 9/11. The very act of repetition both brings up memories of the horror and provides a therapeutic outlet to come to terms with the loss.

Jerusalem, Zion, and Daughter Zion

Lamentations contains a number of personifications of the nation of Judah and its capital city, and these are used somewhat interchangeably. Thus 1:6 speaks of daughter Zion's loss of glory, while 1:7 describes Jerusalem's sins, and then 1:11-16 has Zion/Jerusalem speak in the first-person about her tragic situation. While Zion may have originally referred to a specific fortress in Jerusalem, in Lamentations it appears to refer to the whole city of Jerusalem or even all of Judah and the larger territory of Israel, as well as to the Israelite inhabitants of these areas. Note how Lamentations 1:17 uses the terms Zion, Jerusalem, and the people descended from Jacob in a manner that suggests they are poetic equivalents:

Zion stretches out her hands,
    but there is no one to comfort her;
the LORD has commanded against Jacob
    that his neighbors should become his foes;
Jerusalem has become
    a filthy thing among them.

By using these terms as synonyms, the author subtly and skillfully draws all of the people together in a communal lament.

211

The Challenging Theology of Lamentations

Lamentations is not simply a book expressing grief by narrating the tragic events that befell those living in Judah at the time of the Babylonian destruction of Jerusalem. Like many psalms of lament, it contains confessions of communal wrongdoing and an acknowledgment that the exile from the land, at its deepest level, stemmed from God's anger at Israel's sins—not the military might of Babylon. Though when taken to extremes such a theology can in effect end up blaming those who are victimized rather than the perpetrators, it is quite common and not completely unhealthy that those who suffer a tragedy might take moral inventory and ask in what ways, if any, they contributed to the disaster and how they might amend their ways in the future. This is similar to the national soul-searching that happens after, say, a school shooting in North America. People understandably ask whether the violence that is so pervasive in our media has played a role, or whether our societies have allowed bullying in schools to go unchecked, or whether gun laws have become too loose. In any case, these confessional texts within Lamentations and elsewhere in the Hebrew Bible are aware that the causes of any event are complex. What is interesting is that while these texts often accept personal and communal wrongdoing they also at times question whether the punishment has exceeded the crime and thus they question God's justice even while affirming it:

> Look, O LORD, and consider! To whom have you done this? Should women eat their offspring, the children they have borne? Should priest and prophet be killed in the sanctuary of the Lord? (Lamentations 2:20)

Furthermore, although the bulk of the book describes God as the one who rightly destroyed Jerusalem for the sins of the people, a number of passages recognize that the Babylonians and those who helped them committed crimes that will eventually also be punished by God (1:21; 3:58-66; 4:21-22). Finally, while those praying regularly acknowledge their sinful past behavior, they also at times mention that their generation received the punishment for the sins of past generations who are now long gone (5:8).

Lamentations in Jewish Tradition

Lamentations is read aloud on the Tisha b'Av (the ninth day of Av), a fast day usually occurring in late July or early August. Tisha b'Av marks the destruction of both temples (586 BCE and 70 CE) and is also linked to other Jewish tragedies including: the date on which God informed the rebellious desert generation that everyone but Joshua and Caleb would die in the wilderness; the date in 136 CE on which the Roman emperor Hadrian established a pagan shrine on the site of the temple; and much later this date was linked to the decree expelling Jews from Spain in 1492. These associations are not primarily an attempt to record history as it occurred but rather to give religious meaning to such tragedies by seeing them as part of a pattern while creating a ritual for the community to express their sorrow over each and all of them. In fact, evidence suggests that the first temple itself was destroyed not on the ninth but either on the seventh or later on the tenth of Av (2 Kings 25:8 and Jeremiah 52:12, respectively).

Lamentations in Christian Tradition

Use of the book of Lamentations is relatively limited in the early and later church. However, it is notable that the popular Christian hymn "Great Is Thy Faithfulness" draws directly from Lamentations 3:21-23, a passage that offers a ray of hope within an otherwise dark poem. More obscure is Lamentations 4:20 and its reference to *christos kyriou* in the Greek Septuagint, words that can be translated as the "Lord's anointed" or the "Lord's messiah." This title is often linked to Jesus of Nazareth by Christian interpreters, the one believed to be the Lord's anointed, or Messiah, within Christianity. The verse in question states:

> The LORD's anointed, the breath of our life,
>   was taken in their pits—
> the one of whom we said, "Under his shadow
>   we shall live among the nations."

This is not to suggest that the author of Lamentations foresaw the first-century Jesus to be the anointed one depicted here. Rather, the early church likely found this verse useful in expressing its understanding of Jesus' theological significance. Not only can the verse be read as expressing a connection between the anointed one and the Holy Spirit ("the breath of our life"), but it also articulates the idea that this messiah suffered in being taken to the "pits" (or in Greek "their destructions").

213

QOHELETH

Introduction and Overview

The book of Qoheleth, titled *Ecclesiastes* in most English Bibles (not to be confused with the apocryphal book Ecclesiasticus), derives both its Hebrew and English name from the title of the speaker in the book. The word *qoheleth* is derived from the Hebrew word for "congregation" or "assembly," and it is often understood to mean something like "the convener of the congregation" or possibly "collector" as in a collector of great sayings. Others have suggested that the title means something like "the preacher" or "the teacher." Whatever the case, it is a title, not a proper name. Within the same opening verse we are informed that Qoheleth is "the son of David, king in Jerusalem." This notice no doubt led to the traditional view that the book was authored by Solomon. But for reasons discussed below, almost all scholars believe the book was written in the postexilic period, at least 500 years after Solomon's time. Further, being called a "Son of David" in the postexilic period may not have been an indication of direct lineage, but a title of honor.

Qoheleth belongs to the same stream of skeptical wisdom found in Job. But, unlike Job, Qoheleth is written from a first-person perspective with some biographical asides, although this might be a literary device employed to test various wisdom ideas rather than provide information about the writer's personal life. The brooding and unflinchingly honest assessment of life with its many difficulties, pleasures, injustices, and contradictions makes Qoheleth not only one of the most unusual books in the Bible, but also a book that seems especially well suited to many people in our own contemporary setting.

214

Controversies and Debates

There is strong evidence that the book was written between the fifth and third centuries BCE, when Judah was under either Persian or (from 333 BCE) Greek control. The text of Qoheleth has a few Persian loan words such as the word *pardes*, meaning "garden," in 2:5. Also, the book's vocabulary shows some Aramaic influence, a language that the Persians eventually came to use for administrative correspondence. One of the major debates surrounding Qoheleth is how much this book is indebted to Greek philosophy and how much the book is simply a natural development of Israelite and larger Near Eastern wisdom ideas. The style of the book and its sometimes radical conclusions have led some scholars to compare it to certain Greek philosophical groups like the Epicureans or the Stoics. Interestingly enough, the book has no actual Greek loan words in it, and scholars have had difficulty finding much if any evidence of direct borrowing. This is not to say that the Greek philosophical tradition may not have influenced the author of this book, but rather that such influence is likely indirect, perhaps reflecting a general intellectual shift in the broader Mediterranean area. Others have looked for parallels in Ancient Egyptian and Mesopotamian texts. Oddly enough, the most striking parallels may be with the Gilgamesh Epic, a vastly more ancient mythic text. For example, in chapter 9, Qoheleth reflects at length on human mortality and gives advice to enjoy life and, more specifically, to "Let your garments always be white; do not let oil be lacking on your head." This passage closely echoes advice that was given to the hero Gilgamesh when he expresses his sorrow over the death of his friend Enkidu, and his fear of his own eventual death.

Vanity of Vanities

The expression often translated "vanity of vanities" occurs near the opening and closing of the book at 1:2 and 12:8. The Hebrew word *hevel*, translated as "vanity," can be found over thirty times within the intervening chapters. Here one must note that this translation is particularly obscure today because most English speakers now understand *vanity* to mean being conceited about one's appearance (or achievements). In older English usage, *vanity* more commonly meant "unprofitable" or "worthless." Even the older meaning of *vanity* (unprofitable or worthless) does not fully capture the meaning of the Hebrew *hevel*, however. The reader should know that this Hebrew word's root meaning is "vapor" or "breath" and implies that an object so named is ephemeral and quickly passing. In fact, *hevel* (or in English, Abel) is the name of Adam and Eve's second born son, a character whose life is cut short. The book of Qoheleth struggles greatly with the fact that not only is human life quite short, but that life itself is cyclical and thus all experiences have an ephemeral quality inasmuch as they quickly fade away. But as some scholars point out, Qoheleth uses the word in a variety of ways and within the book it often means an activity that is incomprehensible or even absurd. Take for example the usage in 8:14:

> *There is a vanity [hevel] that takes place on earth, that there are righteous people who are treated according to the conduct of the wicked, and there are wicked people who are treated according to the conduct of the righteous. I said that this also is vanity [hevel].*

The word *hevel* here is not implying that this problem is ephemeral, but that the situation is difficult to comprehend and makes no sense. Another expression used several times in Qoheleth, "chasing after wind" (e.g., 1:14 or 2:11), conveys both the ephemeral nature of much of human experience as well as the idea of its absurdity.

The Wisdom of Qoheleth

Qoheleth often tests certain sayings of the wise. Thus in 2:14 the speaker quotes a widely accepted axiom of Wisdom literature: "The wise have eyes in their head, / but fools walk in darkness." This saying equates the advantage of being wise over being foolish with being sighted versus being blind. In short, the fool might as well be blind because even though he has eyes, he cannot perceive and thus is functionally blind. In the following verses, Qoheleth notes several problems that make it difficult for him to accept this saying fully. Firstly, the wise person will die just like the fool and in the long run no one will remember either of them (2:16-17). Furthermore, while the wise person acts with prudence and thereby prospers, he must eventually leave the fruits of all his hard work to someone else who not only might act foolishly, but who in any case gets to enjoy the fruits of someone else's labor (2:18-23).

Among biblical books, Qoheleth is unusual for its blunt social criticism. Such a writer may well have had wealth and prestige, but he openly criticizes the often unfair ways in which society is organized. Qoheleth 5:8-9 points out that the efficiencies produced by a royal bureaucracy come at a cost: Such structures create social injustices, and those who are maltreated by the system have little recourse because each official in the system blames societal problems on someone else, usually the one above his pay grade. It is interesting, however, that Qoheleth goes on to highlight the way in which those who are wealthy in society, those who have much, are not necessarily more satisfied in that desires, even when seemingly met, are ultimately unquenchable. "All human toil is for the mouth, yet the appetite is not satisfied" (6:7) or "The lover of money will not be satisfied with money; nor the lover of wealth, with gain. This also is vanity" (5:10).

It is important to understand Qoheleth's relationship to other, more standard biblical wisdom texts like Proverbs. All wisdom texts recognized that injustices occurred. But the sages in Proverbs or the view found among Job's friends tend to see such injustices as both anomalous and short-lived and thus as fitting into a worldview that perceives the world as guided by divine justice. In other words, "You reap what you sow." In 8:12-13 Qoheleth himself even assents to this fundamental wisdom belief: "Though sinners do evil a hundred times and prolong their lives, yet I know that it will be well with those who fear God, because they stand in fear before him, but it will not be well with the wicked, neither will they prolong their days like a shadow, because they do not stand in fear before God." But unlike the more standard wisdom teachers, Qoheleth cannot bring himself to look at the many times God's justice does not prevail as mere exceptions that prove the rule. Thus in 8:14, cited in the previous sidebar, he points out that he has at times witnessed the wicked receive the reward of the righteous, and the righteous receive the punishment of the wicked. Some scholars suggest that the placement of Qoheleth directly after Proverbs in the Christian canon is therefore not coincidental, but meant to provide a realistic counterbalance to the retribution theology so prevalent in Proverbs.

One of the most beautiful and haunting passages in the book is the reflection at the beginning of chapter 12 that uses a series of images and idioms to describe old age, dying, and death. Just as modern Westerners have a tremendous number of idioms to describe death, some of which are rather odd (kicked the bucket, bit the dust, croaked, and so on), here we find several expressions for death including: the silver cord is snapped, the golden bowl is broken, the pitcher is broken at the fountain, and the wheel is broken at the cistern.

The Afterword

Just as the book opens with a notice about the speaker in 1:1, the book also closes with a short biographical notice summarizing Qoheleth's life work and its value. This is followed by words that warn against excessive study and that inform the reader what is really important: keeping God's commandments because this will lead to right judgment. It is hard to escape the feeling that this sits at some odds with the rest of the book:

The end of the matter; all has been heard. Fear God, and keep his command-ments; for that is the whole duty of everyone. For God will bring every deed into judgment, including every secret thing, whether good or evil. (12:13-14)

The most likely explanation is that the book originally ended at 12:8, which would have underlined and driven home the speaker's main point that life is but a vanity of vanities. However, it seems the afterword was added to the text to temper Qoheleth's somewhat radical viewpoint by bringing this book into relationship with the larger viewpoint of the Hebrew Bible.

Qoheleth in Jewish Tradition

While some early rabbis raised concerns that Qoheleth might be unsuit-able for general reading, ultimately it was given a prominent place in the yearly liturgy, being read during Succot, the Festival of Booths. This is an unusual liturgical pairing in that Succot is a harvest festival that is defined by the Hebrew words *zeman simchateinu*, "the time of our joy," but the book of Qoheleth seems rather fatalistic and pessimistic. Clearly, the ancient Jewish sages who made this pairing noted Qoheleth's recurring advice to enjoy food and drink and enjoy life while in this world (5:18; 8:15; 9:7). But they likely had an additional insight: True joy in life comes not from deluding oneself about the fact that our lives are fleeting and often trouble filled, but rather in finding ways to embrace the limited and sometimes difficult lives we live.

Qoheleth in Christian Tradition

It is perhaps not surprising that the book of Qoheleth, or Ecclesiastes, has been interpreted in sharply different ways within Christianity down through the ages. Perhaps most representative of two rather polar viewpoints are the interpretations of the church father Jerome (c. 340–420 CE) and that of German Reformation leader Martin Luther (1483–1546 CE). For Jerome, a devout monk, the book confirmed that life and the things of this world are fleeting, which in turn called for ascetic penance and withdrawal from the world and its illusory pleasures. For Luther, however, the book spoke not to the fleeting nature of life or a deformation of the good world that God cre-ated, but to the wickedness of the human heart and its failure to be content with God's gracious and good gifts. It seems both interpreters found ideas that fit their theological stances in that one embraced the monastic life and the other rejected it altogether.

Qoheleth and Popular Culture

Qoheleth's down-to-earth advice and realistic assessment of life has made it an attractive source to draw upon in our contemporary society. Two rather famous examples include the title of Hemingway's *The Sun Also Rises*, drawn from Qoheleth 1:5 (in the King James Version translation), and the well-known rock music song "Turn, Turn, Turn" by The Byrds, which sets Qoheleth 3:1-8 to music.

ESTHER

Introduction and Overview

The scroll of Esther is read aloud in synagogues on the holiday of Purim. This late winter/early spring holiday celebrates how the Jewish community in ancient Persia averted a potential mortal threat through a series of unusual and often comical twists, as narrated by the book of Esther.

The story begins by relating how Queen Vashti, the wife of Ahasuerus (likely Xerxes), king of Persia, lost her royal standing and how the beautiful and charming Jewish orphan Esther (raised by her cousin Mordecai) eventually became the new queen. After these events, we are introduced to Haman the Agagite, whom the king promotes above all his other servants. While everyone else in the court regularly bows to Haman in acknowledgment of his status, Mordecai the Jew refuses to do so. Haman becomes so angry that he hatches a plan to destroy not only Mordecai but all of Mordecai's people—that is, all the Jews living in Persia. In a powerful scene, Mordecai in turn tells Esther that she must risk her status and even her life by approaching the king and pleading to him on behalf of her own people who are endangered.

The plot then takes a number of tense and often humorous turns and reaches a climax when Haman is hanged on the very gallows he constructed for Mordecai, and the Jews are given royal permission to defend themselves against those who seek to harm them. The holiday of Purim is instituted as an annual celebration of the Jewish people's success in averting this catastrophe. In fact, the word *Purim* refers to the "lots" that Haman cast to determine the day on which he would punish Mordecai's people.

Controversies and Debates

Two interesting recent debates concerning the book of Esther are actually intertwined with each other. The first centers on whether the book should be read as a secular folktale or whether it is in fact deeply theological. Esther is an unusual biblical book in that God's name (or God as a character) never appears in the Hebrew version of the text. Thus the question is, might God's presence be implied? Those who see the book in more secular terms think not. But many argue that God's presence can be strongly glimpsed in at least two ways. First, when Esther is reluctant to go to the king to save her people, Mordecai tells her that if she refuses, help will arise from another place (Esther 4:14). This may indeed be a cryptic hint at God's providential care for his chosen people. More to the point are the tremendous number of amazingly well-timed coincidences and reversals of fortune that pervade the whole narrative and thus suggest that God may be guiding events.

Here a second argument comes into view concerning whether this book might best be viewed as a type of extended wisdom narrative. One of the most common tropes or recurring themes found in wisdom texts is that the wicked are caught up in the very webs they weave and the righteous are ultimately saved by their good deeds and intelligent foresight. Note the following verse from a wisdom oriented psalm: "They make a pit, digging it out, and fall into the hole that they have made. Their mischief returns upon their own heads, and on their own heads their violence descends" (Psalm 7:15-16). Haman appears to be wickedness and folly incarnate and as such he is hoist by his own petard. And Mordecai, as a wise and righteous person, is ultimately protected by his wisdom and virtue. Furthermore, much of Wisdom literature describes a type of natural theology in which wisdom is rewarded and folly punished simply because that is the way the world is set up. It might be said that God often resides in the background in much of Wisdom literature, and this would then explain God's conspicuous absence from Esther. Yet, as appealing as this reading is, many scholars would object to classifying Esther as a narrative wisdom tale because the themes it deals with are so universal. While the triumph of good over evil is emphasized in wisdom texts, it is also found in many other genres of biblical (and other) literature.

Esther as Innerbiblical Midrash

It is important to note that two of the main characters in Esther are linked to a narrative in 1 Samuel. Because of this, some see the book as a form of innerbiblical midrash, or expansion, of an existing biblical story, in which an author imaginatively spun out the stories of later descendants of two earlier characters. The two characters in 1 Samuel are Saul, Israel's first king, and Agag, the king of the Amalekites, a group viewed as Israel's mortal enemy. In 1 Samuel 15, Saul is charged with annihilating all the Amalekites but he fails to execute this charge fully. Thus in Esther 2:5, Mordecai is linked to Saul's lineage when he is described as the son of Kish, a Benjaminite (see 1 Samuel 9:1), while Haman is genealogically connected back to Agag, an Amalekite, in Esther 3:1. The story in Esther is thus seen as an attempt to set history aright by having Mordecai correct Saul's failure and fully destroy the arch-enemy of Israel.

Esther and Diasporic Life

The book of Esther suggests a particular view and approach toward Jewish life in the diaspora, that is, life lived outside of the Holy Land when no Jewish state nor (likely) a Jewish temple existed. Unlike Daniel, for example, which opens with a story about the need for Jews to maintain their distinct identity in a diasporic context, Esther appears a stark contrast. Not only does the Jewish Esther intermarry, but she dines at the king's table with no mention of any special food provisions like those found in Daniel 1. Further, there is no explicit future hope mentioned of a coming messiah or a restoration of the Jews to their national homeland. In fact, God is not even mentioned. It seems, then, that this story intends to tell Jews how to survive in a foreign context and to influence the shape of political affairs. Certainly messianic and apocalyptic trends played an important role in some streams of Second Temple Jewish thinking. But it is worth emphasizing that some Jews had a much more this-worldly outlook and thought that, for at least the foreseeable future, any salvation the Jews would experience was to be obtained by human actions in the here and now, with God working behind the scenes rather than radically intervening in history. The diversity of the Jewish Scriptures' theological viewpoints is thus clearly seen in the preservation of both these rather different streams of thinking about the role of God and ability of humans to shape the future.

Esther in Judaism

Purim, while a late biblical holiday of much less sacred significance than say Passover or Succot, is widely celebrated among contemporary Jews. It is a

The Additions to Esther

Although not preserved in any known Hebrew manuscripts, some Greek manuscripts include additions to the story of Esther, some of which may indeed have been penned originally in Hebrew or Aramaic. These additions were known as early as the first century CE in that Josephus, the Jewish historian, references material found therein. These additions include explicit religious language lacking in the standard Hebrew version of the book. Thus the words *Lord* or *God* occur over fifty times in these additional materials, making the tenor of the story much more God-centered and religiously oriented. Such additions seem to function similar to *midrash*, filling in narrative gaps and explaining divine purposes in various events. Following the practice of the church father Jerome (who translated the Latin Vulgate), these additions are often placed at the end of the book, or in the Apocrypha section of modern Bibles. Although Catholic and Eastern Orthodox Bibles include these additions, they are not included in the Tanakh in Judaism.

festive occasion during which one is indeed commanded (in the Talmud) to become inebriated enough to be unable to fully distinguish between "blessed be Mordecai" and "cursed be Haman." The *megillah* or "scroll" of Esther is read twice—once on the night of Purim and once during the day. The evening service is festive to the point of becoming raucous. During the reading of the megillah, revelers dressed in costumes engage in very loud booing, hissing, and using various types of noise makers to utterly efface every mention of the wicked Haman's name. The whole day has a festive atmosphere in which small gifts of food are exchanged and charity is distributed to those in need.

The significance of Purim has grown over the course of Jewish history due to the many atrocities committed against the Jewish people. Thus, for example, modern Jews often view Hitler as a Haman figure, something understandable given that both wished to annihilate the Jews because of a perception that they did not fully belong to the society in which they currently lived (see Haman's speech in Esther 3:8).

Esther in Christianity

Due in part to its lacking any explicit mention of God but also to its Jewish-centric focus, the book of Esther was not only viewed with suspicion by many Christians through the ages, but some wanted to remove it from the biblical canon altogether. The church largely ignored the book for many centuries (virtually *no* church fathers commented on it) until the time of the Christian Reformation at which time Luther, the Protestant reformer, proclaimed his outright disdain for it, even stating that he wished the book did not exist at all. Thankfully, today the picture is quite different, likely related to the fact that Christians are returning to their Jewish roots, in recognition of the Jewishness of Jesus and the early church. It may also reflect the fact that Christians today increasingly find themselves in a situation a little closer to that described in the book of Esther, one that the Jewish people have experienced for millennia: living as a minority people within a foreign, more dominant culture.

DANIEL

Introduction and Overview

The book of Daniel, which tells the story of Daniel, a Judean in exile in Babylon, can be divided into two halves. Chapters 1–6 narrate several tales involving Daniel and his friends, set in the Babylonian and Persian imperial courts. Chapters 7–12 relate a series of visions that Daniel experiences that scholars classify as an apocalypse. The term *apocalypse* literally means "to uncover" or "unveil." Apocalypses often contain extended conversations between the person who is having the vision and angelic beings. These angelic beings either guide the person through otherworldly realms or give a detailed portrait of the coming new era and often the end of history as we know it. In Daniel 7–12, the focus is on the events and timing leading up to the arrival of God's coming reign on earth. The underlying theological question that helped generate this and much other apocalyptic literature is: When will God finally judge the unjust oppressors?

One of the ways the two halves of the book of Daniel are woven together is that Daniel 2:4b–7:28 is written in imperial Aramaic (the language used in the Persian empire's correspondence), while the beginning and end of the book are written in biblical Hebrew. Thus both halves of the book have some Hebrew and some Aramaic, with the Hebrew acting like a set of bookends that surrounds the Aramaic in the middle of the book. Also, we should note that while we here follow the usual Jewish placement of the book by locating Daniel among the Writings, Christian Bibles follow the Greek ordering and place Daniel immediately after Ezekiel, regarding Daniel to be a major prophet in line with Isaiah, Jeremiah, and Ezekiel.

Controversies and Debates

While some of the stories and visions in Daniel are set in the Babylonian kingdom at the end of the sixth century BCE, the court tales were likely composed in the eastern Jewish diaspora in the fourth or third centuries BCE (that is, among the communities of Judeans who never returned from Babylon). Further, the consensus view is that chapters 7–12 were written during the Maccabean revolt, probably in the 160s BCE in the land of Israel. While both halves of the book report details that sound historical, many of the specific references to times, places, and people appear to be inaccurate. Thus 5:31 speaks of "Darius the Mede" but Darius is a difficult character to pinpoint, and if anything was a Persian who lived after the time in which Daniel's character is presented as being active. In 7:5 the Medes are depicted as a full empire, but there is no record that this actually was the case. Still, some chapters, like Daniel 11, cast as a future prophecy, contain a reasonably accurate account of the interactions between the Syrian Greek (called the Seleucid) and Egyptian Greek (called the Ptolemaic) rulers who each at times controlled the fate of those living in Judea, from the time Alexander the Great died in 323 BCE until the Maccabean revolt in the 160s BCE. Daniel also contains reflections on the Maccabean revolt and the reasons for the abolition of the regular temple service. While the apocryphal books of the Maccabees suggest that parties within the Judean community helped instigate these changes, texts like Daniel portray the Seleucid king Antiochus IV as responsible for these shifts.

The Court Tales: Chapters 1–6

The court tales of Daniel focus less on the non-Jewish empires that came to control much of the world and their fate than on the Jews living in these empires—that is, how Jews living under foreign rule can maintain their traditions even while being loyal to and serving the emperor. In some ways this concern forms the theme of the book. As noted earlier, Daniel 1 discusses the difficulties of attempting to keep Jewish food laws, or keeping kosher, in a diasporic setting. Thus whoever authored the stories in Daniel was more concerned about ritual norms than was the author of Esther, who never mentions any concern about Esther eating impure foods or marrying a Gentile. However, both texts reckon with the problem that Jewish religious distinctness and practices at times seem to attract the attention of Gentiles who are unwilling to tolerate such religious differences. Daniel 3 and 6 contain stories about Gentiles who are enraged at Jewish religious differences or speak negatively about Jewish separation from contemporary Babylonian religious norms because they are jealous of the success of certain Jews (which also occurs in Esther). Interestingly enough, Daniel 3 draws a firm religious line in the sand when its Jewish heroes state not only that they are willing to die rather than violate the biblical injunction against idolatry but also that they believe the God of Israel is truly the only God, whether he intervenes to save them from their impending death or not.

Daniel in the Lion's Den

For many people raised in Western society, the story of Daniel in the Lion's Den is likely as familiar as Noah and the Ark or Jonah and the Great Fish. Readers might be interested to know that in the apocryphal book of Bel and the Dragon (see 31–42) we find a partial explanation of how Daniel survived his time in the den through a miracle of God. In this story, the prophet Habakkuk is told in a vision to feed Daniel, who is in the den. Upon indicating that he does not know where the lion's den is in Babylon, an angel appears who promptly carries Habakkuk by his hair to deliver the meal, which in turn nourishes Daniel and allows him to live.

Figure 22. An angel carries Habakkuk by his hair to deliver food to Daniel, as narrated in Bel and the Dragon 31–42. Courtesy National Library of the Netherlands (Ms KB 76 F 5).

The Apocalyptic Visions: Chapters 7–12

A number of the texts in this second half of the book narrate the unfolding of history up to the point at which the writer is composing this work, and then they articulate (or "foretell") details about a coming era in which God will punish those who are oppressing Israel. The result is that God will restore Israel to her rightful, preeminent status. Thus chapter 7 uses four animals to symbolize the four kingdoms that have ruled over Israel since the exile: The lion (Babylon), the leopard (Persia), the bear (the Medes), and the fourth fearsome beast that had ten horns (a series of Greek rulers). In chapter 8 we have slightly different symbols: The ram with two horns (likely Persia and Media), the goat with one horn (Alexander the Great); the four horns that grew on the goat when the one great horn was broken; (the four generals who took control of Alexander's empire when he died suddenly); and the little horn sprouting from one of the four newer horns (Antiochus Epiphanes IV). Chapter 11 reports a similar sequence of events but casts it as a type of prophetic historical prediction and does not use animal imagery. Using multiple forms of imagery in this way is found in other apocalyptic works like the book of Revelation.

A major aim of these types of apocalyptic texts is to reassure the audience that while they are indeed experiencing unjust oppression at the hand of wicked foreigners, this is only a temporary state of affairs that is quickly drawing to a close. The text reports that even now angelic beings like Michael are fighting various heavenly forces who represent Israel's oppressors (see Daniel 10:21, or the similar role Michael plays in Revelation 12:7-9). In places, these types of apocalyptic texts go further and hazard exact predictions of when the current oppression will end. Clearly such predictions are risky and often prove false as one can see by the way in which the original date given in Daniel 8:14 appears to be adjusted forward two other times in Daniel 12:11 and 12:12.

Innerbiblical Interpretation

Daniel 9 contains a parade example of the way in which later biblical writers were themselves involved in interpreting biblical texts that had already achieved scriptural status. Thus Daniel 9:2 states that Daniel prayed for Israel's restoration on the basis of Jeremiah's prophecy that the exile was to last for only seventy years (see Jeremiah 25:11 or 29:10). Then, in Daniel 9:24, the angel Gabriel gives Daniel a new way to understand why Jeremiah's prophecy of eventual restoration after seventy years was not already fulfilled. Gabriel tells Daniel that the seventy-year period is to be understood as seventy weeks of years, that is, as 490 years. There are a number of interesting features to this interpretive move. To begin, while the temple had indeed been rebuilt in the late sixth century BCE, some Jews came to believe that as long as Judea was ruled by foreigners, Jeremiah's prophecy of Israel's restoration still had not been fulfilled. When Daniel 9 reinterprets Jeremiah's prophecy, the author not only seeks to find a way for Jeremiah's prophecy yet to be fulfilled, but he also finds a way to make Jeremiah speak to much later audiences.

One notices very similar interpretive strategies in certain Dead Sea Scrolls like the *pesher* (or line-by-line commentary) on Habakkuk that seeks to apply this more ancient text to the current difficulties this particular community experienced. Even today one finds certain Jewish and Christian interpreters engaging in similar attempts to use the biblical text to predict the outcomes of contemporary events.

Daniel in Jewish Tradition

Daniel 12:1-3 contains one of the earliest explicit references to a scene of final judgment in which many of the dead are resurrected, with the wicked being punished and the righteous being rewarded with eternal life. One of the central tenets of rabbinic Judaism, the Judaism that flourished after the Second Temple was destroyed in 70 CE and came to represent the dominant form of Judaism to this day, was a belief in the resurrection of the dead and the reward of the righteous. Although Judaism also came to affirm the non-bodily preservation of the soul, in some sense, one was most fully oneself only when one's soul and body were again reunified. While the idea of resurrection only became fully articulated in rather late texts like Daniel 12, it grew out of earlier biblical antecedents that implied that in certain unusual circumstances God had the power to bring life to the dead. This explains how Elijah and Elisha each brought a dead child back to life and it also illuminates why texts like Psalm 30 speak of being healed as being brought back from the realm of death.

Daniel in Christian Tradition

It would be difficult to overstate the importance of Daniel for the authors of the New Testament, especially the Gospels. Although the reader may not find extensive quotations from Daniel in the Gospels themselves, the authors of these texts describe Jesus as someone given "dominion, glory, and a kingdom"

(Daniel 7:14) by God, and see Jesus as playing a role similar to that of Daniel 7's "Son of Man." The title "Son of Man" is regularly used by Jesus for himself and on its own (as indicated elsewhere in the Hebrew Bible) the term holds a meaning not far from "human being." However, when used in the context of Daniel 7 it seems to take on a messianic meaning, indicating someone given a special place in God's workings:

As I watched in the night visions,
　　I saw one like a human being [son of man]
　　　　coming with the clouds of heaven.
And he came to the Ancient One
　　and was presented before him.
To him was given dominion
　　and glory and kingship,
that all peoples, nations, and languages
　　should serve him.
His dominion is an everlasting dominion
　　that shall not pass away,
and his kingship is one
　　that shall never be destroyed. (Daniel 7:13-14)

It is not hard to see obvious parallels between this passage and the Gospels' portrayal of Jesus as the "Son of Man," especially when we look at Mark 13, a passage known as the "little apocalypse." Not only is Jesus understood by the gospel writers to bring about an everlasting Kingdom never to be destroyed, but he is believed to be the one to whom God hands over "dominion and glory and kingship"—that is, power to rule over and judge all humanity, an image made particularly apparent in the book of Revelation.

EZRA–NEHEMIAH

Introduction and Overview

While printed as two books in most English translations, the books of Ezra and Nehemiah were originally thought of as one continuous book. Within the Septuagint, Ezra–Nehemiah is found among the historical books following Kings and Chronicles, while in the standard Hebrew text they are placed toward the end of the Writings immediately before 1–2 Chronicles (the order used in this textbook). Some ancient Jewish sources placed Ezra–Nehemiah at the very end of the Tanakh. The reader should be aware that there are two books in the Apocrypha, 1 and 2 Esdras, which are also associated with the figure of Ezra. In fact, 1 Esdras contains some of the same materials found in Ezra–Nehemiah. And, as with Daniel, part of Ezra is also in Aramaic (4:8–6:18).

The materials in Ezra–Nehemiah can be conveniently divided into three distinct sections dealing with three differing periods. Ezra 1–6 narrates events surrounding the return to Judah of a group of Babylonian exiles and then continues by describing their rebuilding of the Second Temple (538–515 BCE). Ezra 7–10 recounts Ezra's efforts to strengthen the community during the time he spent in Jerusalem (probably beginning in 458 but the dating is debated, as discussed below). The book of Nehemiah, the third section, describes Nehemiah's efforts beginning in 445 BCE to rebuild Jerusalem's walls and to initiate various social and religious reforms.

The reader will notice that these books incorporate a number of documents such as various letters and royal decrees as well as lists of people who returned to Judah and lists of temple implements. The book can at times leave a reader confused because it often groups its material by theme rather than presenting things in sequential, or chronological, order. Further, certain matters get retold, adding to the confusion. As discussed in more detail below, a number of scholars have tried to place the events narrated in Ezra–Nehemiah into an orderly sequence, but no proposal has yet produced a widespread consensus.

Controversies and Debates

Scholars often debate whether the author (or authors) who produced 1–2 Chronicles also authored Ezra–Nehemiah. It is widely recognized that there are many shared similarities in the outlook and vocabulary between these two sets of writings. In fact, Ezra 1 picks up the story where 2 Chronicles ends. Yet, there are some differences in vocabulary and theology, such as how each work refers to the chief priest, that have led some to conclude that Ezra–Nehemiah and Chronicles were each produced by a different author or set of authors.

As mentioned, these two books are highly challenging to read and understand because the narratives are not in chronological sequence. Some even argue that the order of the two books should be reversed and that Ezra in fact arrived in Jerusalem after Nehemiah, not before him. While Ezra 7:1 informs us that Ezra began his journey in the seventh year of King Artaxerxes, we know that there was more than one king by that name. If the king is Artaxerxes I, then Ezra arrived in 458 BCE, or around twelve years before Nehemiah's mission. Those who argue that Artaxerxes II is meant believe Ezra was only active beginning in 398 BCE, and that Nehemiah's story took place a half century earlier. Each scenario solves certain enigmas but raises others. Because our knowledge of Judean history in the Persian period is relatively scant, any attempt to place each section of these books in its correct historical setting is at best a hypothesis subject to revision.

Intermarriage with Foreign Women

Both Ezra 9–10 and Nehemiah 13 record a conflict between each figure and certain Judean returnees who are taken to task for marrying "foreign women." There is a widespread tendency among recent commentators to condemn Ezra and Nehemiah's actions as a type of exclusionary racial prejudice or xenophobia. But some caution is in order here. Even if one accepts that texts like Ruth and Isaiah 56 were produced by groups who were critical of (and sought to challenge) Ezra and Nehemiah's more restrictive views of Israelite identity, these more open views still recognize that most if not all

Israelites are part of a genealogically linked people reaching back to Jacob and ultimately Abraham. In truth, the book of Ruth is about a Moabite woman who utterly renounces her native religious heritage and seeks to find a home among the people of Israel. This is in stark contrast to the situation described in Nehemiah 13:24 where Judean men had married foreign women who at times not only maintained their birth culture but also chose to raise their children to speak a foreign tongue, potentially threatening these children's Judean identity. The point to be grasped is that communities and nations inevitably draw certain boundaries and that the debate is not over whether all boundaries should be eliminated but over where exactly such a boundary should be drawn. Minority cultures, whether they be the Second Temple Jewish community or contemporary groups like Native Americans, often have trouble maintaining their traditions in the face of assimilatory pressures. While encouraging endogamy by frowning upon intermarriage with outsiders is seen as narrow-minded today, it is unclear that a traditional culture could survive without such an impulse, especially when a group faces possible cultural extinction (as in Ezra–Nehemiah).

The Torah as a Foundation Document of the Second Temple Community

It is now widely recognized that many of the books in the Hebrew Bible likely reached their final form during the exilic and postexilic periods. As noted in our chapter "Modern Approaches to the Bible" near the beginning of this book, many believe that one can best understand books like Genesis by reading such texts in relation to the political and religious concerns found in Ezra–Nehemiah. For example, some see a strong correlation between Ezra and Nehemiah, who each set out from the area near the Tigris and Euphrates to return to rebuild Jerusalem, and the life stories of Abraham or his grandson Jacob, who also make similar journeys from the same area to Canaan. Furthermore, both Genesis and Ezra–Nehemiah focus a great deal of attention on not marrying "Canaanite" women and on tensions with the local non-Israelite population (compare Genesis 34 to Ezra 9–10). Other scholars acknowledge that the final text of the Torah might well have spoken to a Persian-era audience, but point out that the diverse and sometimes contradictory viewpoints found within the Torah suggest a drive to preserve a wide array of ideas, many of which are more easily correlated with earlier periods in Israel's history (see discussion of "Ideological and Sociopolitical Criticism" in our chapter "Modern Approaches to the Bible").

233

> ## The First Instance of Biblical Interpretation?
>
> It is worth highlighting that Nehemiah 8 records a scene in which the Torah is read aloud and explained to the large group of returnees who seem unfamiliar with much of the content they are hearing. Whether this was the whole Torah or only some of its legal sections, it seems likely that a group of learned scribes brought together a wide array of narrative and legal texts and that this very act turned Judaism into a religion focused on the interpretation of Scripture. While the process of turning what were likely more fluid traditions into Scripture began at least as early as the seventh century BCE when Deuteronomy was written, it reached new heights in the Persian period. Chapters 9 and 10 of Nehemiah go on to indicate that the laws found in this Torah came to function as a community constitution that the citizens of Jerusalem and Judah swore to uphold. This should not be taken to mean that no one in preexilic times knew any of the Torah or lived by its commandments. Thus, as we note earlier in this book, it is widely believed that much of Deuteronomy already existed in the seventh century BCE. But unifying a vast array of diverse traditions into a single book of the Torah, a collection whose content was often opaque to many laypeople, meant that one now needed skilled scribes to read and interpret God's will as found in this written Torah.

Ezra–Nehemiah in Jewish Tradition

The figure Ezra is so highly regarded in rabbinic Jewish tradition that it is said that "the Torah could have been given through him if Moses had not preceded him" (*Tosefta Sanhedrin* 4.4). In fact, in one Jewish tradition Ezra is (re)given the Torah by God after it was destroyed by fire (see 2 Esdras 14). Whatever the case, the ancient rabbis understandably see Ezra as their progenitor. This is because once the Torah traditions were brought together and promulgated as the law governing Jewish life, one now needed skilled interpreters of Scripture, which is exactly the role rabbis came to play. Thus Ezra's activities are seen as a model by the ancient rabbis who produced a vast array of innovative interpretations of Jewish Scripture.

Ezra–Nehemiah in Christian Tradition

Ezra–Nehemiah is one of only a handful of books in the Hebrew Bible that is not quoted in the New Testament. This should not be taken to imply that the book was unimportant or not part of the church's Scripture during the time of the early church, though this lack of attention does suggest that it did not capture the Christian imagination like others. Origen is usually regarded as the first to have split the books of Ezra–Nehemiah into two, and he is followed by Jerome—though the latter calls them the two books of Ezra and elsewhere mentions their unity in the Hebrew tradition. There are very few early Christian commentaries on Ezra–Nehemiah, though the sixth- to seventh-century English monk Saint Bede (673–735 CE) produced an extensive commentary on them. In modern Christian lectionaries, only a few verses from Nehemiah are read (Nehemiah 8:1-3, 5-6, 8-10) during Epiphany, and these verses are paired with Psalm 19 and Luke 4:14-21. When read together, one can see an effort to highlight not only that Scripture is important but also that the reading of Scripture with an interpretation is understood to be part of normative worship in the life of the church.

1–2 CHRONICLES

Introduction and Overview

The books that we call Chronicles are referred to as *divrei hayamim* in Hebrew, meaning "Events of the Days" or "Words of the Days." This originally unified book that is now printed as two books generally narrates the same sweep of Israelite history as found in 2 Samuel and 1–2 Kings and draws heavily on these earlier books. However, in addition to (or perhaps as a result of) its unique emphases, discussed below, 1–2 Chronicles is both much more detailed about some events that are reported more tersely in the Deuteronomistic History and at other times it omits episodes found in 2 Samuel–2 Kings. For example, the events of King Asa's reign are narrated in less than one chapter in 1 Kings 15:9-24, but within Chronicles one finds a much fuller account taking up all of 2 Chronicles 14–16. On the other hand, David's adultery with Bathsheba, his order to allow Uriah her husband to be killed, the rape of David's daughter Tamar, and the whole episode of Absalom's rebellion that occupy 2 Samuel 11–19 are completely omitted. Perhaps as a result of the discontinuity between Chronicles and the other biblical histories, the books came to be called "those things left out" (*Paralipomenon*) in the Greek Septuagint.

First and 2 Chronicles can be divided rather neatly as follows: 1 Chronicles 1–9 contains an elaborate set of genealogies beginning with Adam; 1 Chronicles 10 reports Saul's demise; 1 Chronicles 11–29 narrates David's reign; 2 Chronicles 1–9 relates the events of Solomon's time on the throne; finally, 2 Chronicles 10–36 tells the history of Israel and Judah from the split of the two kingdoms through the Babylonian exile, ending with the announcement of Cyrus that he intends to fund the rebuilding of the Second Temple. Because the history ends here, where Ezra–Nehemiah begins, previous interpreters have at times viewed these two collections as constituting a single unified work by Ezra called the "Chronicler's History," a view that more recently has been questioned.

Controversies and Debates

In addition to debate about whether Ezra–Nehemiah was originally part of Chronicles, scholars have long questioned the historical reliability of additional details or whole new stories that one finds in Chronicles but are not narrated in Samuel and Kings. For many decades it had been assumed that the writer of Chronicles expanded upon or adapted the materials in the Deuteronomistic History when he wished to make a particular theological or ideological point, and that these extra details or changes found within Chronicles had little if any historical value. More recently, however, various scholars have argued that Chronicles may have drawn some of these details from actual ancient documents even while they acknowledge that such details are deployed to make particular theological points. Just as the religious viewpoint of the Deuteronomistic History does not totally negate its historical value, so too may Chronicles indeed be of more historical value than once believed.

Comparing Chronicles to Samuel

A quick comparison of passages in 1–2 Chronicles and 2 Samuel or 1–2 Kings reveals some rather interesting differences in how a story is told. A well-known example is seen when comparing 2 Samuel 24:1 and 1 Chronicles 21:1, both of which begin a story in which David takes a census of Israel:

Again **the anger of the** L*ORD* *was kindled against Israel, and he* **incited David** *against them, saying, "Go, count the people of Israel and Judah." (2 Samuel 24:1, emphasis added)*

Satan *stood up against Israel, and* **incited David** *to count the people of Israel. (1 Chronicles 21:1, emphasis added)*

Whether in the Bible or in a modern day history book on World War II, history is told from a particular point of view and *for a particular purpose*, a purpose that will often shape or minimally affect which details are given, how they are given, and why they are significant. Historiographers today would say that there is no such thing as "disinterested history" and the histories found in the Bible are no different. In this case history is retold in Chronicles in a way that shifts the blame from God to Satan for inciting David to take a census, a census that led to Israel being punished. In what follows we attempt to highlight a few key theological elements that distinguish the theology of 1–2 Chronicles.

The Importance of the Temple in Chronicles

The construction of the temple (1 Chronicles 28–29; 2 Chronicles 2–7), the designation of its personnel (1 Chronicles 23–26), and various sacrificial rituals conducted by Levites and priests (2 Chronicles 29–31; 35) occupy a substantial portion of Chronicles. It is worth noting that temples in antiquity were not simply places people went once a week. Temples in fact were hubs not only of ongoing ritual or "religious" activity but of social, political, and economic activity as well, especially when large crowds of travelers arrived for various festivals. Here it is important to keep in mind that ancient cultures did not separate religion from social and political (or other) activities, as we do in the Western world today. In Chronicles, not only is much space devoted to its construction and related activities but also the Jerusalem temple is given particular significance and emphasis, a temple that was built under a united monarchy and thus had the potential to unify a diverse people in exile.

Theological Currents in Chronicles

While Chronicles seems to draw a good deal of the history it tells from 2 Samuel and 1–2 Kings, it sometimes explicitly rejects certain theological assumptions that play an important role in the Deuteronomistic History. One of the most obvious examples is the distinct ways that 2 Kings and 2 Chronicles each explain why, even after Josiah's reforms, Judah was destroyed. Second Kings 21–22 links the exile to the earlier Judean monarch Manasseh's sinful actions and in doing so suggests that a later generation of Judeans ultimately suffered exile for the sins of an earlier generation. In this scenario Josiah's righteousness only delayed the inevitable coming punishment. But while 2 Chronicles 33 acknowledges Manasseh's sinful ways, it presents him as someone who repented later in life, thus explaining his very long reign. Furthermore, although 2 Chronicles 36 contains a passage arguing that the exile occurred because generations of Judeans had not acted correctly, it makes an explicit point of highlighting the corrupt behavior of Judah's *last* king, Zedekiah, as well of the leading priests and citizens who lived during Zedekiah's reign, thus linking the exile directly to the actions of the generation that experienced it. The author of Chronicles wants to reject the notion that a relatively innocent exilic generation suffered for the sins of Manasseh and his generation who lived at an earlier time. In short, the author of Chronicles appears less comfortable with the idea that people can be punished for the sins of an earlier generation, a view also found in prophetic texts like Ezekiel 18.

The way that Chronicles treats a number of battle scenes points to another noticeable theological shift. Thus in 2 Chronicles 20, for example, the Israelites' primary role in warfare involves an elaborate prayer ritual rather than military action. The people are told that God—not they—will fight this battle, which is precisely what occurs. One can see this elsewhere in Chronicles such as in the following brief excerpt, especially in the final sentence that we have italicized:

> Zerah the Ethiopian came out against them [the people of Judah]. . . . Asa [Judah's king] went out to meet him, and they drew up their lines of battle in the valley of Zephathah at Mareshah. Asa cried to the LORD his God, "O LORD, there is no difference for you between helping the mighty and the weak. Help us, O LORD our God, for we rely on you, and in your name we have come against this multitude. O LORD, you are our God; let no mortal prevail against you." *So the LORD defeated the Ethiopians before Asa and before Judah, and the Ethiopians fled.* (2 Chronicles 14:9-12, emphasis added)

The tendency to retell past stories of Israel's warfare in a manner that portrays Israel as prayerfully waiting for God's victory while attributing the violent actions to God may reflect Chronicles' acceptance of Persian imperial authority or, at the very least, a recognition that in this Persian context one had to rely on God to defeat one's enemies.

David and His Dynasty in Chronicles

The book of Chronicles takes a special interest in both David and Solomon, the most famous kings in Israel's history who ruled over a united kingdom (that is, over both Judah and Israel before it split into Northern and Southern Kingdoms). It may be that the Chronicler's immediate audience, a people who remained geographically dispersed even after some had returned to rebuild Jerusalem, could find commonality in David, as well as in (as already mentioned) the Jerusalem temple his son built. The author's tendency to speak of "all Israel" and "all the people" likewise seems to hint at a concern to unify the people as one. David's dynasty, and Judah more generally (the tribe from which David came), thus comes to take on a new sense of importance in Chronicles. In fact, some have argued that Chronicles is especially sympathetic to David in that the Davidic covenant is given special emphasis, it presents a less flawed picture of the king, and the succession of Solomon to the throne is much smoother here than in 2 Samuel. In any case, this postive portrayal of Judah and David is affirmed by later "Judaism" and plays a role in the development of Second Temple (including Christian) messianism, a movement that awaited the arrival of a new, ideal "son of David" who would rescue Israel.

Chronicles in Jewish Tradition

Chronicles is probably one of the most if not *the* most neglected biblical book within postbiblical Jewish tradition. It is notable that only a single fragment of this book has thus far been identified among the Dead Sea Scrolls. Further, the few medieval Jewish scholars who commentated upon Chronicles make mention of the fact that so little had been written about it previously, and Rashi, the great eleventh-century Jewish Bible commentator, wrote commentaries on every book in the Tanakh except Chronicles. Even so, the manner in which Chronicles retells earlier biblical stories in a fuller form, often adding new theological twists, became a model for various retellings of the Bible found in parabiblical books like Jubilees as well as in more developed, later midrashic collections. Expanding upon the Bible's story was not seen as a violation of Scripture but rather a necessity if one hoped to make Scripture speak to new generations in new historical circumstances.

Chronicles in Christian Tradition

It seems clear that writers of the New Testament were aware of and used Chronicles because we know that Luke 11:50-51 and Matthew 23:35 refer to the murder of Zechariah, a detail that only appears in 2 Chronicles 24:20-22. The reader will also notice that the Gospel of Matthew contains a genealogy similar in format to the one found in the opening chapters of 1 Chronicles, a genealogy that also traces a line to David. Perhaps equally important, however, is that a doxology (a short hymn of praise) found in 1 Chronicles 29:11 seems to have had particular significance for the early church:

> Yours, O LORD, are the greatness, the power, the glory, the victory, and the majesty; for all that is in the heavens and on the earth is yours; yours is the kingdom, O LORD, and you are exalted as head above all. (1 Chronicles 29:11)

Christian readers may recognize part of this passage in that a portion of it became attached to an originally shorter form of the prayer Jesus taught his disciples, a prayer known as the Lord's Prayer, or the Pater Noster ("Our Father"). We also know from ancient documents that this doxology was used in other early Christian settings as well (for example, it appears in the *Didache*, an early Christian document). However, apart from these details, a commentary or two by a church father (for example, Theodoret of Cyrus), and a popular book in the early 2000s based on two verses found in 1 Chronicles (*The Prayer of Jabez*), Chronicles has not received much attention in Christian reflection, similar to the situation in postbiblical Judaism.

* * *

Bridging the Gap:
The Apocrypha between Two Testaments

The reader has now been given an overview of the entire Tanakh, or what Christians call the Old Testament. Before turning to the New Testament, we first provide a brief overview of the Apocrypha, a collection of other books produced by various Jewish communities in Israel and abroad during the Persian and Hellenistic periods, mostly before the time of Jesus (between approximately 300 BCE–70 CE). These books were preserved by certain Christian communities, communities that still use them as Scripture to this day. They also shed tremendous light not only on Jewish life in the land of Israel and abroad during this period, but also demonstrate how the narratives, laws, wise sayings, and other materials in the Tanakh are taken up and pushed in new directions by later generations who had already begun to view these materials as sacred Scripture.

THE APOCRYPHA

THE APOCRYPHA

As noted in our introductory material earlier in this book, the word *apocrypha* literally means "hidden" and possibly was given to these books because they are less well known. Others suggest that the name came about because their origin (or author) was unknown, or even that they contained hidden meanings (an idea suggested by the apocryphal book 2 Esdras 14:44-47). The fourth- and fifth-century church father Jerome appears to have coined the term. The now common use of the term *apocryphal* to refer to something being false, made-up, or dubious is a later usage that came into existence due to post-sixteenth-century Protestant biases against these books. The consensus of the Reformers themselves, however, was that these books were profitable and written by godly people, even if not they did not consider them to be part of the main biblical canon.

Catholics, who make liturgical use of excerpts from these books, often refer to this collection as "deuterocanonical" books. In some Christian Bibles that include the Apocrypha today, these books are often placed between the Old and New Testaments. Other Christian Bibles, however, including some Catholic and Greek Orthodox Bibles, integrate the books into the Old Testament, following the practice of the Septuagint. Until the mid-seventeenth century, most English Bibles, including the landmark translation called the King James Version, included the Apocrypha as part of its books, even if in a separate section. Only later did the English Puritans and others who followed the Westminster Confession of Faith decide that these books should be excluded from printed versions of the Bible.

The Apocrypha section of most study Bibles contain books such as Baruch, Bel and the Dragon, 1–2 Esdras, 1–4 Maccabees, Judith, the Prayer of Manasseh, Sirach, Susanna, Tobit, and Wisdom of Solomon among others. While these books are not part of the Jewish Scriptures, most if not all of them were penned by Jewish writers during and shortly after the Second

Temple period (around 530 BCE to 70 CE). One finds many different genres within the Apocrypha including the short story or novella (Tobit and Judith), historical books (1–4 Maccabees), Wisdom literature (Sirach), and prayer (Psalm 151). While books such as Sirach were written in Hebrew, others like 4 Maccabees were written in Greek.

Since most students in an introductory Bible course are not likely to be assigned all of the Apocrypha, we will concentrate our attention on a few select books. The reader can access basic introductory information about other books in the Apocrypha in most study Bibles.

Tobit

Tobit contains a wonderful Jewish version of classic folk motifs known as the "Grateful Dead" and the "Monster in the Bridal Chamber." In folk stories containing the Grateful Dead motif, the protagonist goes out of his way to bury a corpse, sometimes at great cost or personal risk, and is later helped out by someone who we eventually learn is the dead person. In the case of Tobit, a devout Israelite living in Nineveh, his burial of exposed corpses first endangers his life and then results in his becoming blind. And while he is not exactly helped by one of the corpses he buries, his son and he are assisted later by the angel Raphael (an angel whose name means "God heals"). All of this occurs because of Tobit's great ethic of charity. In fact, a central theme of Tobit is that charitable acts on earth create something of a bank account in heaven from which one can draw when in need. Furthermore, not only can charity at times save one from death but also it is an excellent way to make an offering to God (an idea affirmed in Sirach 4:9-11 and Acts 10:4).

The folk motif of the Monster in the Bridal Chamber narrates how a hero on a quest must save the endangered princess and banish the monster who kills each of her previous suitors. Thus the second major thread in this story concerns the young woman relative named Sarah, whom Tobit's son Tobias ends up marrying, a bride who had previously married seven other men each of whom Asmodeus, the demon in love with her, had killed on their respective wedding nights. The two plot lines converge when the angel Raphael explains to Tobias how to solve the bride's (Sarah's) problem with the murderous demon as well as how to cure Tobit's blindness. Both happen by means of medicines made from a fish that Raphael instructs Tobias to bring ashore after the fish had locked its mouth around Tobias' foot.

Controversies and Debates

There had been a long-running debate about whether the Greek version in the Septuagint was the original language of the book or if the Greek was translated from an older Hebrew or Aramaic original. However, when one Hebrew and a number of Aramaic partial manuscripts of Tobit were found among the Dead Sea Scrolls, a consensus quickly formed that the author wrote in a Semitic language—though it remains unclear if the original text was written in Hebrew or Aramaic.

Another interesting feature of Tobit is that it explicitly mentions Ahikar, a character whose story we know from an Aramaic copy of the *Story of Ahikar*, a text found at a Jewish colony in southern Egypt dating from around the fifth century BCE. The character in the Aramaic story is not in fact Jewish, but here in Tobit he is described as Tobit's relative.

Judith

Judith relates the story of how a modest and pious Jewish widow from the town of Bethulia saved the whole Jewish people through a seductive ruse by which she beheaded Holofernes, the general in charge of an invading Assyrian army. In some sense Judith is a later expansive retelling of Judges 4–5 in which Jael beheads the enemy general Sisera, except Jael is not an Israelite while Judith is. One important thing to note is that this story is quite fanciful and likely would have been perceived as fanciful by an ancient audience. It wildly conflates various historical details such as having Nebuchadnezzar, a later Babylonian king, described as the King of Assyria who ruled from Nineveh, or having him capture parts of Persia that rose after Nebuchadnezzar's time. This would be equivalent to a storyteller today blending details of Napoleon's wars with say World War II.

Judith, like many other documents from this period, wrestles with how to maintain one's religion when one is ruled by those who worship idols or threaten one's religious fidelity. Judith in particular puts forward a model of Jewish women's piety. Of note is that an Ammonite character named Achior warns Holofernes of the power of the Jewish God to protect his people as long as they remain faithful. Holofernes banishes Achior to Bethulia for speaking so insolently. At the end of the story, Achior, upon seeing Holofernes' severed head, converts to Judaism. The idea of Judaism as a distinct set of beliefs to which one could convert arose fairly late in the biblical era, which is unsurprising when one remembers Israelite identity was originally conceived in

246

primarily tribal and ethnic ways. This likely explains why Ruth, even after marrying Boaz, is still called a Moabitess.

While readers today are sometimes troubled by Judith's gory beheading of Holofernes, the ancient audience, and audiences for centuries afterward, viewed her as a pious and courageous woman whose actions are worthy of emulation. In fact, Judith's beheading Holofernes is a popular biblical image found on cathedral walls and in museums around the world.

Figure 23. Artemisia Gentileschi, *Judith Slaying Holofernes.* **1614–20. Galleria degli Uffizi, Florence. Courtesy Wikimedia Commons.**

Sirach

Sirach (also called Ben Sira, or the Wisdom of Jesus Ben Sira, or Ecclesiasticus) is perhaps the most important deuterocanonical book both because of its length (at fifty-one chapters it is the longest book in the Apocrypha) and because of the vast amount of religious, social, and historical information it gives to the reader. Unlike most biblical and apocryphal books, which are either penned anonymously or include large amounts of material that likely were never spoken or written by the person named in the title of the book, Ben Sira, the name of the author of the Book of Sirach, clearly identifies himself as the author of this book in 50:27. Furthermore, historically we have a good sense of when he lived because his grandson translated the Hebrew original into Greek and wrote a preface to the work in 132 BCE. Since the book lacks any reference to the upheaval of the Maccabean revolt in the 160s BCE, it is believed to have been written between 190–180 BCE.

Sirach's outlook is in many ways akin to the outlook found in classic wisdom books like Proverbs. In fact, much of the book contains pithy proverbs, often grouped together on selected topics. But the author also touches on many topics not found in earlier wisdom books, such as probing the idea of friendship or discussing physicians and their work.

Controversies and Debates

For centuries we only possessed the text in Greek. When Hebrew pages of Sirach were discovered in the Cairo genizah (a *genizah* is a place where Jews place worn out books containing sacred literature that must, for religious reasons, be buried or stored and not destroyed), a heated debate arose about whether they were authentic or were simply an attempt to render the existing Greek text back into Hebrew. Eventually, an almost complete Hebrew copy of the book turned up at Masada, Herod's massive fortress in Southern Judea where the last holdouts from the Jewish war of 66–70 CE made their final stand. This ancient text from Masada proved that the Cairo pages were indeed authentic Hebrew texts, not late forgeries.

Highlights of Sirach

One of the most important passages in Sirach is found in chapter 24, where Wisdom is depicted as finding its home among the people of Israel and within the sacred precincts of Jerusalem. Sirach here builds upon the idea of Wisdom as an attribute of God first expressed in Proverbs 1–9 and goes further by equating Wisdom to the Law, or Torah, of Moses in 24:23. While some have seen this as a regressive move in which the scope of universal wisdom is now narrowed to include only Torah, the opposite may well be true. In such a reading, Sirach would be seen as universalizing Torah by saying that the Wisdom found anywhere in the world is an expression of God's universal teaching, or Torah, even while the Torah in its fullest form is found among the Jews who possess the revelation God gave to Israel at Mount Sinai.

Sirach is particularly interesting for the important information it provides about the development of the Jewish canon. While it seems certain that the canon is not yet fully complete, the tripartite shape of the Jewish Bible is clearly alluded to in its pages when the translator mentions difficulties in translating from Hebrew to Greek: "Not only this book, but even the Law itself, the Prophecies, and the rest of the books differ not a little when read in the original" (from the prologue to Sirach). The mention of the Law, Prophecies, and other scrolls neatly corresponds to the three major sections of the Tanakh. Later the author refers to Isaiah, Jeremiah, and Ezekiel, as well as "the bones of the Twelve Prophets," testifying that these fifteen books had already come to be viewed as sacred Scripture (Sirach 48:23–49:10).

Finally, as we highlighted in our discussion on Ezra–Nehemiah above, once these books came to be recognized as sacred Scripture, there arose a need for professional interpreters of these texts. In chapters 38–39, Ben Sira gives us a window into his own life and work when he contrasts a number of other vocations involving physical labor (a farmer, an artisan, a blacksmith, or a potter) with his own nonphysical labors as a sage and a scribe:

> How different the one who devotes himself to the study of the law of the Most High! He seeks out the wisdom of all the ancients, and is concerned with prophecies; he preserves the sayings of the famous and penetrates the subtleties of parables; he seeks out the hidden meanings of proverbs and is at home with the obscurities of parables. (Sirach 38:34b–39:3)

Sirach in Jewish Tradition

While Sirach did not, in the end, become part of the Jewish canon, it is in fact the most cited noncanonical ancient book in rabbinic sources. Incidentally, Sirach's views are much closer to those expressed in Proverbs than the much more controversial book of Qoheleth, raising the intriguing question of why Qoheleth ultimately came to be included in the Jewish canon of sacred literature but Sirach did not. While one can only speculate, one possibility is that Qoheleth obscures his exact identity and the book implies that the author is Solomon, an important figure who was believed to have penned other texts that were part of sacred Scripture. Ben Sira, on the other hand, tells us who he is and one can clearly see that he wrote at a rather late date. Inasmuch as the rabbis may have felt that sources written late in the Second Temple period were no longer divinely inspired, this may have impeded the book of Sirach from being viewed as Scripture.

Wisdom of Solomon

The rather unusual book which we call the Wisdom of Solomon employs Greco-Roman rhetorical techniques to demonstrate how Judaism is in fact the primary bearer of philosophical truth. Some have suggested that it was written in Alexandria, Egypt, because of its strong mockery of Egyptian religious practices, possibly around 30–50 CE, during a time when the Egyptian Jewish community suffered some persecution.

The book can be neatly divided as follows: 1:1–6:11 is the so-called Book of Eschatology, which asserts that the righteous who suffered an early death actually have obtained a postmortem immortality. The section 6:12–9:18 contains a number of wisdom exhortations and abstract theological reflections on wisdom. Wisdom of Solomon 10:1–19:22 is a lengthy review of Israelite history. While no characters are actually named, it is obvious which biblical stories are being described. The greatest amount of attention is focused on the exodus story and the evil Egyptians who oppressed the people of Israel.

Controversies and Debates

While most scholars agree that the Wisdom of Solomon is a Jewish composition, some parts of the book sound strikingly similar to claims made by the early Christian community, a group with views increasingly divergent with the Judaism from which it eventually separated. For instance, chapter 2 describes how a group of wicked people oppresses and ultimately kills a righteous person, arguing that if this man was actually as close to God as he claims, then God should protect him. It goes on to assert that while the wicked assume that this person has died, they are mistaken in that the person is in fact immortal. That this narrative line closely resembles the Passion Story in the New Testament Gospels (see Wisdom 2:13 and 2:16, in particular) may explain why the so-called Muratorian canon fragment has Wisdom of Solomon listed among the books of the New Testament.

Highlights of Wisdom of Solomon

Wisdom of Solomon invokes a number of important Platonic and Neo-Platonic ideas. Thus the author speaks of a soul that preexists the body and sees the body as weighing the soul down (Wisdom 8:19-20 and 9:15). Additionally, chapter 7 contains a long abstract hymn to Wisdom containing a litany of terms drawn from Greek philosophy. The idea of the immortality of the soul that is affirmed in this book represents a new development in how biblical authors explain injustice in this world. The books of Job, Psalms, and Proverbs assume that God will set things right and reward the just while they are alive. But in Wisdom 2:21–3:8, those righteous ones who suffered unjustly during their lives are clearly envisioned as receiving their rewards after death. This of course provides a precedent for the model of postmortem rewards and punishments that is seen in the New Testament.

Another fascinating aspect of this book is its attempt to probe the origins of idolatry and to propose a number of possible explanations, including: Perhaps a parent once lost a young child and subsequently made an image of the child in order to express grief, something which over time grew into a fuller form of idol worship. Alternatively, perhaps a monarch who lived at a distance from his subjects set up images of himself so these subjects could pay homage to him, which again, over time, eventually led to the use of idolatrous images in worship.

Concluding Reflections

This very brief overview of the Apocrypha demonstrates that the literature that ended up in the Bible was part of a much larger body of texts. It also shows how various stories found in the Tanakh continued to generate ever-new interpretations, something that continued with both rabbinic Judaism and early Christianity. In the Apocrypha this is seen especially in the way Wisdom of Solomon reinterprets the exodus, but also in the way stories are built upon biblical precedents such as one discovers in Judith. Readers today often think of the Bible as a museum piece saved from the ruins of a now lost time. But the material in the Bible is part of a vibrant, living, and evolving tradition, a tradition that continues to this day. It is this fact that explains how a sectarian group of Jews in the first century came to see God's promises to Israel, those that pervade both the Tanakh and the Apocrypha, being fulfilled in new ways in the life, death, and resurrection of a figure named Jesus. It is to this story that we turn next.

THE NEW TESTAMENT

THE NEW TESTAMENT: A FEW BASICS

The New Testament did not drop out of heaven. It was written by people who were inspired by what they had experienced by meeting Jesus in person or in the life of the church. Because these authors were rooted in particular cultures with attitudes and concerns different from ours, it is worth thinking about the particular contexts in which each New Testament book was written.

Hellenism and the Covenant People

The Old Testament portrays Israel as God's first love, a covenant people who are to be God's special possession and different from all other peoples (Exodus 19:4-6). With Alexander's conquest of the Mediterranean world beginning in 333 BCE, however, a cultural shift toward Greek ways began, which presented a challenge to Israel's distinct identity (see timeline on pages 48–49). Greek language and culture, including the ideological foundations of this culture, spread throughout the world. Israel, a people now known primarily as Jews, had encountered Greek culture long before Alexander, but it was really his conquest and the subsequent occupation of various lands by Greek rulers that brought about the most urgent challenges to non-Greek peoples in the Mediterranean world. The Roman Republic made its peace with the Greeks by copying and adapting their art, translating their philosophies into Roman-friendly formats, and educating their gifted youth at such intellectual centers as Athens. For Torah-observant Jews whose very identity was predicated on being separate or holy to God, the spread of Hellenism was clearly more threatening. The challenges were probably not unlike a democracy today coming to be occupied by a foreign power attempting to impose a dictatorship on it.

The fact that the New Testament documents were written in Greek poses difficulties for the modern interpreter who must account for the conflict between the Jewish context of this "good news" (or "gospel") and its intended audience, which ultimately turns out to be all peoples, Jews and non-Jews alike. Reading the New Testament thus confronts readers with the question: Does the *Jewish* or *Greek* context more fully illuminate a given passage? "In the beginning was the logos," the Gospel of John begins (AT). Is this "logos" the reason or divine imprint that the Greek philosophy of Stoicism sees as ruling the world? Or does the logos represent something more along the lines of the life-giving word of God, perhaps reflecting a development of the wisdom tradition of Proverbs 1–9, discussed earlier? These concerns should always be kept in mind when reading the New Testament.

Roman Principate

The New Testament was mostly written during the first century of the Roman Empire. The early period of the Roman Empire is called the Principate, a word that derives from a term that the first emperor used for himself, *princeps*—"first one." In one inscription from the time of the New Testament, it seems that the birth of the emperor Augustus and its significance are referred to as the "gospels." Although we often read past the word, the New Testament's use of the term *gospel* may be a challenge to the Roman Empire's "gospels" of domination.

Other connections to the Roman Empire in the New Testament are more obvious, such as where we see Roman soldiers executing Jesus in the Gospels or a city located on seven hills (calling to mind Rome) in Revelation. But the Roman presence also influenced how the authors of the New Testament wrote their stories. As we discuss in greater detail later, this Roman context may help explain why one of the Synoptic Gospels presents the Roman governor Pilate very favorably, seeking to remove all responsibility for Jesus' death from him, or why the book of Acts tends to portray Roman soldiers as the "good guys."

This can lead to certain surreal moments in reading the New Testament. For example, were the Romans really the good guys when we recall that they executed and humiliated Jesus, as well as killed Peter and a number of other early Christians? When Paul—frequently imprisoned by the Romans and, according to tradition, beheaded by them—says that governments are instituted by God and actually are ministers of God for good, is he saying this in an absolute sense or simply being politically cautious when he speaks to a church in the capital of the Empire (Romans 13:1-7)? The New Testament is thus as politically conditioned as any newscast or broadcast of the Olympics we might view on television today. This means that we need to read it in light of its varied political biases. While Romans are depicted as rescuing Paul and his colleagues in the book of Acts, we need to remember that Jews and other people were almost certainly also helping him out of other tight spots not narrated by Acts. And in contrast to Acts, Revelation is extremely negative toward Rome's imperial agenda.

Gentile Composition of Early Christianity

For some reason, the early church gained a stronger foothold among non-Jews, people often called "Gentiles," than it did among Jews. This happened even though Jesus and his apostles were by all accounts Torah-observant Jews who directed their message to Jews. The New Testament includes footage of events that seem to be part of the departure of the followers of Jesus from Judaism into a religion of their own, an event (or series of events) that some scholars call "the parting of the ways." Remembering this and that most of the New Testament was written in a social context in which Gentiles outnumbered Jews among the Jesus-followers, will help the reader better understand much of its content. Thus, in Romans, though Paul spends significant space asking what God is doing with the Jewish people, he is mostly addressing Gentiles, explicitly telling them not to think they are better than Jews who do not follow Jesus. His statements against keeping the "works of the law"—or the Mosaic covenant's law code, especially food laws and circumcision—always seem to be directed at Gentile followers of Jesus. The New Testament uses Israel's Scriptures as a cultural matrix that offers Jesus followers a story to inhabit and a collective memory from which to forge their identity. But it is not clear that it envisions Jewish followers of Jesus ceasing to observe the commandments of the Torah.

Genres of New Testament Literature

The New Testament is a heterogeneous group of materials—a literary hodge-podge, if you will—all canonized as Scripture. It contains four quasi biographies that are labeled "gospel," a genre with no exact analogues outside of Christian writings. This is followed by a history-like narrative that is less biographical than the Gospels, which we call Acts. Immediately thereafter we have twenty-one letters, or epistles, which are followed by an apocalypse called Revelation that concludes the New Testament. It is definitely not a collection that literature professors or religious leaders today would choose for a religion's foundational Scriptures. But these are the documents the church came to recognize, along with the Old Testament, as its sacred texts.

The Gospel Genre

Scholars do not agree on what the Gospels are supposed to be. Are they biographies? They are too selective to be called biographies in an unqualified way, since they narrate only a fraction of Jesus' lifespan. Are they epitomes of Jesus' life and teachings, such as was made for some philosophers? They certainly include some of Jesus' life and teachings, but they also intend to make an impact on the reader in ways that ancient biographical works like Diogenes Laertius' *Lives of the Philosophers* do not. Are they apologetic or theological arguments, showing how Jesus' life and teachings somehow actualize hopes found in the Old Testament? Perhaps, but they are primarily narratives rather than explicit arguments. Most will agree that they are unique, not a genre that is clearly exemplified in other literature from this period.

If we consider their status as narratives and ask what aspects of these stories seem most significant, we are led to focus on their depictions of Jesus' last days, crucifixion, and resurrection. It is in these sections of the Gospels where we find the most random details—for example, the streaker in Mark 14:52—sections in which narrated time seems to be moving most slowly, and where issues raised earlier in each gospel reach some form of resolution. Mark especially has been described as the gospel written backwards, originally a description of Jesus' death to which the first twelve or so chapters were then added at the beginning. But the other three gospels also invest significant space and attention to detail in their depiction of Jesus' last days, crucifixion, and resurrection. It is thus useful to say that the genre of the New Testament's gospels is that of an end-of-life biography, a biography that is especially focused on the main character Jesus' last days on earth.

Acts

"Acts" represents another sort of narrative genre in the New Testament. Although only one example of this type is found in the New Testament, the genre is well attested in other noncanonical early Christian literature, such as the Acts of Paul, the Acts of Paul and Thekla, and the Acts of Peter. The Acts genre is not a biography in the sense that the gospels are, though it does focus on the deeds of the characters for whom it is named. Thus, in the New Testament's Acts of the Apostles, there are two characters, Peter and Paul, whose ministry careers get the spotlight. The narrative of Acts presents a particular view of how the Jesus followers evolved from being a Jewish sect in Jerusalem to a religion with many Gentiles, with a foothold in the capital of the world, Rome. Most examples of this specific genre, whether in the New Testament or elsewhere, provide a biographical introduction to a collection of other writings associated with its main character. In the New Testament, Acts provides a literary bridge between the Gospels and Paul's letters, which immediately follow it in the canon.

Occasional Letters

Paul's letters are all occasional letters, that is, they arise out of specific situations—or occasions—in Paul's life, and are addressed to quite specific situations in the lives of their addressees. As such, Paul's letters are not textbook chapters on various topics such as "What is the church?" or "What should we believe about Christ?" Rather, they are letters calling readers to live out their faith in the circumstances in which they find themselves. Just as letters sent to particular audiences today can quickly become outdated, we would expect that the occasional letters in the New Testament would have quickly lost their appeal. This did not happen, however, since Christians saw how the letters could be read with benefit and applied in new situations.

General Letters

The general (or what scholars call "catholic") letters do not seem addressed to occasions as specific as Paul's letters, or Hebrews for that matter, since there are very few references to specific situations or particular addressees in them. These letters extend from James through Jude and seem to have been written as circular letters that any Christian community could read with benefit. This explains why they, unlike Paul's letters, are all named with their authors' names rather than that of the addressees. To continue our analogy, if occasional letters are like letters sent to a specific addressee about a specific situation, these general letters are more like articles in a handbook or manual that are intended for a variety of audiences to use.

Apocalyptic Literature

The book of Revelation is the one book in the New Testament that represents apocalyptic literature. Its analogues in the Old Testament include Isaiah 24–27 and Daniel 7–12. We should mention that there are sections of the Synoptic Gospels that are also considered apocalyptic, such as when Jesus describes what lies ahead for the city of Jerusalem (see Matthew 24–25; Mark 13; and Luke 21).

Apocalyptic literature tends to be produced by authors in oppressed situations who are convinced that God will intervene to save God's people from their oppressors, usually a foreign government. As such, the genre provides a religious context for unjust and unexplainable situations in a world believed to be ruled by a just and good God.

The apocalyptic genre typically includes the following elements: a morally dualistic view of the universe, a deterministic view of the course of history, tours of heaven, animal and number symbolism, and visions. The book of Revelation is best read alongside other Jewish and Christian apocalyptic texts like Daniel, 4 Ezra, and Mark 13 in order to have a glossary of the images and ideas that are regularly recycled within these types of texts.

Canonization of the New Testament

When we fully appreciate the variety of materials in the New Testament, the question inevitably arises as to how this particular assortment of texts came to be assembled and designated as Scripture. In the introductory material to this volume, we discussed the order in which the New Testament documents became canonized. We also noted the relatively long time it took for the New Testament canon to become fixed. This turned out to be a good delay, since it allowed the church time to sift through and live with the many Christian texts being produced and arrive at those it deemed inspired and most functional for its growing movement. In what follows we will talk a bit more about the factors that appear to have influenced the process of canonization, criteria that help us understand why certain books were included and others excluded from the canon of the New Testament.

Several criteria seem to have been underlying the long process in which early Christians came to recognize the books that would constitute their Sacred Scriptures, a process of collecting, sharing, and using texts in churches throughout the Mediterranean world over several centuries. At first their only Scriptures were the Jewish Scriptures—what Christians call the Old Testament, probably in Greek translation—and the sayings of Jesus, which seem to have been known and repeated by his early followers. After these two sets of texts, however, what seems to have been most important to the early church was the question of apostolic origin. So, we might say that the first criterion is that of "apostolicity": Was this text written by an apostle or someone closely associated with an apostle? The second issue is that of universal relevance: Is this text relevant for people in different places and times? Does it have a "catholicity," by which we mean a universality? The third criterion involved the text's conformity to the rule of faith (a set of creedal beliefs), and a shared sense for orthodox teaching: Does this text teach correct doctrine? These three criteria are summarized by the following terms: Apostolicity, Catholicity, and Orthodoxy. A fourth and final consideration is the reception of the text. Has a particular book or writing been used and recognized as trustworthy over a period of time by different churches? This is different from the other criteria, since it considers people's response to the text, not the text's own qualities.

From a secular viewpoint, the criteria used for determining which texts would become part of the New Testament canon and the lengthy historical process of canonization suggest that the New Testament arose through a merely human process of trial and error and occasional historical accident. But for Christians who consider these twenty-seven texts to be Scripture, the process of canonization is part and parcel of what makes these writings inspired and "required reading" for them.

Tips for Reading the New Testament

The first tip in reading the New Testament is to be alert to the genre of the literature you are reading. A gospel is written in a different framework than an occasional letter. And both of these are written very differently from an apocalypse. To understand the imagery of blood and water coming out of Jesus' side when he was crucified, we need to read the rest of the book in which it occurs. Thus blood and water in the Gospel of John are employed to indicate that blood literally flowed out of Jesus' side, as it would out of any human body that was punctured by a spear (John 19:34). But now consider the description of hail and fire mixed with blood falling on the earth in Revelation 8:7. Since we find this within the genre of apocalyptic, we need to understand that images of the moon turning to blood or blood falling from the sky in other apocalyptic texts tend to signify times of distress for God's people.

A second tip that will enrich your reading and help you see more of what is going on in the text is to read it as if you are an anthropologist attempting to understand an alien culture. In reality, the twenty-seven books of the New Testament were not written for us, but for mostly illiterate Jews and non-Jews who were trying to worship one God in a polytheistic world, while also recognizing that the Jew named Jesus was somehow this God's son. Early audiences heard these texts read to them, since most could not read for themselves. They were trying to make sense of their short and often difficult lives on earth, as we often try to do. Many of them were convinced that their lives were affected by spiritual powers beyond them, and sought protection in their worship of the God of Israel and the Jew they acclaimed as his son. They were a minority in that they did not believe in the many gods so clearly evident to most of the Mediterranean world. Many of them refused to recognize the Roman Empire as the ultimate benefactor for their lives, as the Romans insisted and most non-Romans readily accepted. For example, this meant refusing to acknowledge that "Caesar is Lord," instead reserving that status for Jesus, and many were persecuted and martyred as a result. As you read, therefore, try to imagine how this collection of texts—four gospels, a narrative of "Acts," twenty-one letters and one apocalypse—would sound, and what it would mean, to someone hearing it for the first time in the first or second century.

INTRODUCTION TO THE GOSPELS

Many gospels were written about Jesus. Only four, considered to be among the oldest gospels, became part of the Christian Scriptures. This likely occurred because they had the most extensive record of being used by Jesus' followers, and because these four were viewed as offering an orthodox and authentic portrait of Jesus.

Differences among the Gospels

The first three gospels are called the Synoptic Gospels, or simply "Synoptics." They have this title because they share a similar perspective in their portraits: Luke and Matthew beginning respectively just before or with Jesus' birth, Mark with Jesus' baptism. They all narrate a number of Jesus' miracles, describe how he cleansed the temple just before he was arrested, and record his institution of the Eucharist (or "Lord's Supper") at a Passover meal on the night of his arrest. The fourth gospel, John, is considered to be different and thus not "synoptic." It begins from eternity past with its opening line, "In the beginning was the word . . ." and in general shows a less human, more knowing Jesus. Seven key miracles called "signs" are narrated in this gospel. Jesus' teachings are situated within long discourses, and the material is significantly different from the Synoptics' records of his teaching. The temple cleansing is described as occurring early on in a three-year ministry of Jesus as opposed to within the last week of his life, as portrayed in the Synoptics. Unlike the Synoptics, his last meal with his disciples is not a Passover meal, and no Eucharist is described at that meal.

We hope you come to see the differences among the Gospels that led to the variety within the New Testament. In a sense it is as if each gospel has a camera at a different spot in the stadium, each of which came to be valued by the church. Matthew's camera is positioned among the Jewish fans, focused on Jesus' Jewish identity. Mark's camera is low, right on the ground, focused in on the suffering that Jesus experiences and predicts for his followers. Luke's camera is up in the press box, where he can provide a more panoramic vision that includes Israel and the nations and where he can check for inconsistencies or loose ends that he has seen in the way Matthew and Mark have filmed Jesus. John's camera is in the blimp flying over the stadium; he wants to show the grand, divine nature of Jesus' participation in human life.

Tips for Reading the Gospels

It is useful to be alert to the way in which each gospel seeks to establish continuity with the Jewish Scriptures. For instance, the way Matthew's Gospel describes Jesus fulfilling Old Testament prophecies is quite different from the way John draws on various Old Testament images and symbols in his descriptions of the theological significance of Jesus. In Matthew, Jesus' family's trip to Egypt and later move to Nazareth in Galilee are said to "fulfill" details of Israel's past—forming a reprise of Israel's history, even though many such details are not offered as messianic predictions in the Old Testament. Alternatively, in John, Jesus' actions and words actualize or finally deliver the main idea or divine quality celebrated at a given Jewish festival. Jesus' claim, "I am the light of the world—whoever follows me will never walk in darkness," is set at the end of his time in Jerusalem for the feast of tabernacles, perhaps to show that Jesus is a better guide than the pillar of fire that led the Israelites in the wilderness (John 8:12). And his claim to be God's son and "in the Father" in the context of the Hanukkah festival, which celebrates the rededication of the temple, may be narrated by John to fit with his idea that Jesus replaces the temple (John 10:22, 35-38).

This leads us to ask what sort of portrait each gospel is offering in its depiction of Jesus. It is easy to get sidetracked by the little differences among the Gospels. Why does Matthew describe Jesus casting a legion of demons out of two men, while Mark and Luke describe him doing so out of only one? Why, when Peter denies knowing Christ, does the cock crow twice in Mark but only once in the other gospels? Comparing things in this way can distract the reader. Instead, we encourage you to begin by reading each gospel as its own story. The best reading strategy for any of the four gospels is to read it in its entirety, preferably in one sitting, seeking to understand its distinct portrait of Jesus. It is only after one has a sense of each gospel's whole portrait of Jesus that useful comparisons can be made between them.

"The Gospel of the Lord"

At a traditional Catholic Mass, only an ordained deacon or priest may read aloud from the Gospels. He will hold the gospel book high as he walks to the lectern, or into the midst of the people who stand for the reading. After announcing which of the four gospels will be read, the reader and the congregation make a sign of the cross on forehead, lips, and heart. This expresses that they will keep the words in their minds, speech, and hearts. The reader concludes by proclaiming, "The gospel of the Lord," to which the people respond with words of praise.

Christian emphasis on the sacredness of the Gospels has brought about not only the above reverences in worship settings but many ornate illuminated gospel manuscripts like that below.

Figure 24. Page from the Lindisfarne Gospels. © British Library Board. All Rights Reserved 10/10/2013, 13 Cotton Nero D.IV, f.3.

MATTHEW

Introduction and Overview

Matthew's opening genealogy and this gospel's division of Jesus' teachings into five discourses reminds us of the Pentateuch. The five long speeches in Matthew's Gospel are: the Sermon on the Mount (chapters 5–7), the Mission Discourse (chapter 10); Kingdom parables (chapter 13); Life in God's Kingdom (chapter 18); and the Olivet Discourse or Predictions of Jerusalem's Future (chapters 24–25). When we come to see that the first discourse portrays Jesus as teaching on a mountain about the continuing significance of Mosaic law, it is clear that this gospel, like the beginning of the Prophets and the beginning of the Writings, contains a link back to the Torah. Matthew is attempting to show that his story of Jesus fits integrally inside Israel's story.

Controversies and Debates

One of the most heated debates in New Testament studies is the question of the relationship between the three Synoptic Gospels, sometimes called the "Synoptic Problem." Most scholars suggest that Mark, the shortest gospel, is the oldest gospel. Many also think that Luke and Matthew used Mark as well as another source containing sayings of Jesus, often called Q (from the German word *Quelle*, meaning "source"). Those who disagree with this view usually follow the tradition that Matthew is the oldest gospel.

Another controversy is over how Jewish Matthew's Gospel really is. On the one hand, the surface phenomena noted in the preceding section provide a Jewish façade at the front door of this text. The opening genealogy and the Sermon on the Mount are certainly philo-Judaic, that is, quite favorably disposed to the Judaism its author knew. But is the whole house made of the same material? An early saying from the second century states that Matthew wrote his gospel first in the Hebrew language, and that it was later translated into Greek. This saying might lead us to believe that the whole gospel is very Jewish in nature. On the other hand, as we near the Passion Narrative of the text, there are some editorial moves unique to this gospel that seem anti-Jewish in nature. Readers have to decide for themselves as they read the whole gospel how Jewish it really is.

The Birth and Baptism of Jesus

The first chapter of Matthew makes strong connections back to the Scriptures of the earliest church, or what Christians know as the Old Testament. Note that Jesus is introduced as "son of David, son of Abraham" (1:1). With this introduction, Matthew is setting us up for his claims that Jesus is the ultimate descendant of David and the ultimate descendant of Abraham. Both these characters were promised descendants in the covenants that they received (2 Samuel 7:12-13, 16; Genesis 12:2). The genealogy here in Matthew 1 emphasizes the kingship of David by using the word "king" only of David even though many other descendants of David listed here, like Solomon and Josiah, were in fact also kings. The organization of the genealogy into three blocks of fourteen generations may also be an allusion to David, since the numerical value of David's name is 14.

The Importance of "Gematria"

Before the use of Arabic numbers we use today (1, 2, 3, and so on) became standard, it was common practice in languages like Hebrew to use the letters of the alphabet to count, in addition to spelling words. Thus each Hebrew letter and in turn each word in the Hebrew Bible has a numeric value (*aleph* is 1, *bet* is 2, and so on). The practice of coding numbers into certain words or deriving numbers from various words is called numerology, or in Hebrew *gematria*. The New Testament begins and ends with important numerically valued names: Here at its beginning we need to know that the numerical value of David's name is fourteen to understand the genealogy, and as we will see in Revelation, we need to know the numerical value of a name to understand the number of the beast (Revelation 13:18).

Another key strategy in reading the genre of genealogy in the Bible is to look for unexpected variations in a pattern. Though not a surprise, the genealogy is monotonously male, except for the fact that five women are unexpectedly mentioned, including the final name before Jesus' birth. Also unexpected is the precise character of the women mentioned, in that the first three seem to be *Gentile*, not Jewish (Tamar, Rahab, and Ruth), and the fourth's status as the wife of a Gentile is emphasized in the genealogy (Bathsheba, the wife of Uriah the Hittite). Scholars disagree on exactly why these first four women are mentioned. All were respected in later Judaism. Three of the four—Tamar, Ruth, and Bathsheba—are all identified in the Hebrew Bible as ancestors of the royal family of Judah, the Davidic line. In view of the context here in Matthew, perhaps these Gentile women are named to highlight the international horizons of the covenants God made with Abraham and David and possibly hint at Matthew's eventual message that Gentiles should join God's people. This would in turn help explain why Matthew emphasizes that Jesus was worshiped by foreign kings (Matthew 2:1-12) and concludes his gospel with a call for his followers to make disciples of all the nations (Matthew 28:19). The Davidic lineage as summarized in this genealogy is moved forward by several sexually unusual liaisons, as signaled by these women's names, perhaps preparing the reader for the idea that God is working through Mary, a woman who is pregnant but not by her husband, Joseph.

The birth narrative in Matthew's Gospel is distinctive in the many links it makes to Hebrew Bible prophecies and in its focus on Mary's husband, Joseph, whom the angel calls "son of David" (Matthew 1:20). Only Matthew and Luke provide birth narratives of Jesus in the New Testament. Matthew's version is told from Joseph's perspective; Luke's version is told from Mary's. Here in Matthew we get the unique information of the dreams that Joseph received (1:20; 2:13, 19-20, 22), his initial plan to end his engagement to Mary in a discreet manner (1:19), and his fear of living in Judea under Archelaus (2:22). Since Jesus obtains his lineage to David and Abraham through Joseph, perhaps it is no surprise that this Jewish-oriented gospel focuses on Joseph.

The baptism and temptation of Jesus as described in Matthew show Jesus as a human who gets baptized and is then tempted by the devil, two scenes that fit with many readers' understanding of their own religious experience. Christians consider baptism to be an initiatory rite for all who wish to join them, and their moral universe includes an evil force, personified as the devil or Satan, who can tempt them. In these regards, Jesus is shown here in Matthew as providing an example for those who seek to follow him as Christians. In these scenes Matthew shows Jesus' human identity (something also evident in Mark and Luke), unlike John, who while emphasizing Jesus' divinity downplays the baptism of Jesus and does not mention the temptation. Matthew alone provides the dialogue between John the Baptist and Jesus possibly to address the theological difficulty that Jesus, the very son of God, undergoes a baptism for repentance from sins (3:14-15).

The Sermon on the Mount

If David and Abraham are the two main characters from Israel's past that Matthew wants to place in Jesus' ancestry in chapter 1, the rest of this gospel would also like us to be conscious of Moses as a model in whose steps Jesus follows. Just as Moses ascended a mountain to receive the Torah from the God of Israel (Exodus 19:20), so Jesus ascends a mountain in this gospel, where he teaches his followers a gospel that completely affirms and indeed intensifies the Torah. This first block of teaching in the Gospel of Matthew, and thus the first block of teaching in the whole New Testament, is known as the Sermon on the Mount. Though some of the material is duplicated elsewhere in the New Testament—most prominently in a similar passage in Luke that is commonly called the Sermon on the Plain (Luke 6:17-49)—Matthew's Sermon on the Mount is unique among the Gospels for its high estimation of Torah observance.

This is a good place to return to the variety we find within the New Testament. While all of the New Testament has a positive view of Jesus and is convinced that Jesus came in fulfillment of Israel's Scriptures, the New Testament's authors differ among themselves in regard to the manner in which Jesus fulfills these Scriptures. Thus as Matthew sets Jesus in the Sermon on the Mount, he presents a Jesus who advocates complete observance of Mosaic law for his Jewish listeners. The warning that whoever breaks one of the least of the Torah's commandments will be called least in the kingdom of heaven has even been interpreted by some as a criticism of the Apostle Paul. As the reader will learn, Paul questions the value of keeping Israel's laws after Jesus' resurrection. Whether Matthew 5:19 and the Sermon on the Mount as a whole is intended as a criticism of Paul and correction of his teachings or not, the fact remains that Matthew contains pro-Torah material that Paul would likely not include in his preaching to the Gentiles. One can summarize the basic thrust of the first gospel in the New Testament as follows: Matthew, the most Jewish of the Synoptic Gospels, presents Jesus as the descendant of David and Abraham, who reinterprets the Torah of Moses and expects his Jewish hearers to keep his commandments fully.

But how does Jesus reinterpret the Torah, or what does Jesus add to his contemporaries' understanding of their relationship with God, already secure in the covenants that God promised to their ancestors? Any response to this question must include the idea of the "kingdom of heaven," a phrase that Matthew often uses for "kingdom of God" in order to avoid taking God's name in vain (using God's name casually in everyday conversation risked breaking the third of the Ten Commandments). In Matthew's perspective,

Jesus sent his apostles first to Jewish people only (see 10:5-6; compare Luke 17:11-21). His message to them, that the "kingdom of heaven" had drawn near, meant that God's rule in the land was about to become fully effective. In Matthew's perspective, Jesus' followers are to live, as any observant Jew in the first century would, in anticipation of a judgment in which one's deeds directly affect one's eternal destiny.

Anti-Judaic Polemics in Matthew

Despite Matthew's positive view of the Mosaic law and his sensitivity to Jews who must keep it, this gospel shows signs of what we might call "anti-Judaism," anti-Jewish thinking that some forms of early Christianity adopted in their quest for legitimacy. Thus, unlike the other Synoptic Gospels, Matthew records Jesus as telling his hearers that the kingdom of God will be taken from the Jews and given to a people who produce the expected results that God seeks (21:43; contrast Mark 12:1-12). And in the trial scene near the end of the gospel, it is only in Matthew's Gospel that some Jews in the crowd near the Roman official Pilate shout out, "His blood be on us and on our children" (27:25), likely included to exonerate the Roman Empire. Readers might be confused by these passages, given that Matthew seems to be the most Jewish of the Gospels, going to great lengths to show Jesus' Jewish lineage as well as respect for the Torah. Here it is important to remember that we are reading "inner-Jewish polemics," that is, one Jewish group (Matthew and his followers) is writing against another (those Jews who rejected Jesus). This may not excuse such words but it does help explain them. But the problem is that these passages have been used and replayed throughout church history, most often by Gentiles no longer aware that these heated words were originally exchanged between two groups of Jews, with disastrous and unchristian behavior toward the Jewish community, Jesus' own people. Many Christians today, especially in the shadow of the Holocaust, have confronted their own deep biases against Jews and the Jewish religion, choosing to repent of past sins.

Not Only Jesus Was Resurrected

Another unique feature of this gospel's conclusion includes the description of graves being opened and a number of deceased people entering Jerusalem (27:52-53). This comes in between two other episodes that are found here as well as in the other Synoptics: the tearing of the temple curtain and the centurion's positive description of Jesus (27:51, 54; Mark 15:38-39; Luke 23:45, 47). Matthew no doubt records this small-scale resurrection because he sees it as a confirmation that Jesus' time on earth indeed inaugurated God's rule in the land, which in Israel's Scriptures includes the hope of a resurrection for God's people while under a Davidic ruler (Ezekiel 37:1-14).

Concluding Reflections

This gospel closes with Jesus' parting words, in contrast to those in the Mission Discourse earlier, that his followers are now to make disciples of all the nations, not just the people of Israel (compare 28:18-20 with 10:5-6). The gospel that begins with a genealogy of a "son of David, son of Abraham" now ends with a call for those who follow Jesus to make disciples and teach people from all nations to follow all that Jesus commanded. Matthew, the most Jewish of the Synoptic Gospels, presents Jesus as the descendant of David and Abraham, who reinterprets the Torah of Moses. His hope is that his Jewish hearers might now teach all people to look for the arrival of God's rule as they follow Jesus' teachings.

MARK

Introduction and Overview

The Gospel of Mark is considered by most New Testament scholars to be the first gospel written. Compared to the other gospels it seems to have "rough spots," for example, where Jesus says he does not know something (Mark 13:32) or where there is an unfulfilled promise (Mark 16:7). Scholars usually view these as indicators that this is a first attempt at a gospel.

This gospel, the shortest of the four, provides the basic structure for the other Synoptic Gospels. It begins with the preaching of John the Baptist, the baptism of Jesus, and proceeds to narrate Jesus' miracle-working and teaching, including his three predictions of his death and resurrection, then devotes a significant amount of detail and narrative space to the last week of Jesus before his death, and concludes with a brief account of his resurrection.

Mark has been called a gospel of action. While Matthew and John have lengthy speeches by Jesus, Mark tends rather to build his narrative on terse descriptions of Jesus' actions, often beginning with the word "immediately." At the places where Matthew and Luke include events that Mark narrates, they tend to follow the order in which Mark has arranged the events. Interestingly, these particular stories are usually more detailed in Mark than in Matthew and Luke. Another way to express the last point is that when Matthew and Luke "borrow" narrative material from Mark, they tend to tell the same stories more efficiently, as if to say "see Mark for the longer version."

Controversies and Debates

The second-century author Papias is quoted in the third book of Eusebius' *Ecclesiastical History* as saying that Mark wrote his gospel "not in order"

(3.39.15). This statement makes sense in that Mark frequently shifts the focus of his narrative in abrupt transitions. But does it also mean that Mark does not care about the sequence of narrated events? This question has been answered differently. In the past few centuries, some suggested that Mark's picture is something of a scrapbook that tells the story of Jesus' life on earth with little interest in sequence or literary coherence. Literary scholars today, however, argue that there are understandable reasons behind the arrangement of the gospel, many suggesting that it creates a sense of mystery around Jesus and builds to a climax, where his identity as God's son is only fully revealed at his crucifixion.

As mentioned in the section called "From Scroll to Codex" at the beginning of this textbook, the ending of Mark remains a controversy. The earliest manuscripts end the gospel with Mark 16:8—"And they departed, fleeing from the tomb, for fear and shock gripped them, and they told nothing to anyone, for they were afraid." This is a rather odd and troubling ending. Later manuscripts offer shorter (two sentences added after 16:8 in some manuscripts) and longer (16:9-20) endings, the latter of which seems to be constructed from the other gospels and the book of Acts. A basic—though speculative—explanation for the abrupt, "for they were afraid" ending in the early manuscripts is that the final page of an early codex copy of Mark was lost. Scribes who copied the gospel then added more satisfactory endings, endings readers today must decide to accept or to ignore. Others have suggested that being the first gospel written it did not contain a set of resurrection stories, something that was added later by others, after this type of closing was established as fundamental to the gospels genre.

The Frame of Mark's Gospel

The Gospel of Mark begins with a description of John the Baptist preaching in the wilderness. The first key scene is a short narrative of this character baptizing Jesus—immersing him in water as a sign of repentance for sin. Mark's description of this baptism and his selection of what to put next in the narrative show that he views Jesus as a divine being who is let loose on earth and engaged in power struggles with others who are challenging him. Mark 1:10 says that the heavens were "ripped" or "split" open when God's Spirit came on Jesus. In Mark 1:12 we read that "immediately the Spirit drove him into the desert." The clear sense here is that God's Spirit has come on Jesus in a powerful way. This is confirmed by Mark's portraits of Jesus as healer and exorcist, someone who banishes malevolent powers.

"I Am Legion"

Mark's description of Jesus casting the "Legion" of demons into a herd of pigs and then into the sea (chapter 5) is thought by some to critique Rome's military domination, inasmuch as Legion I and Legion X had a boar on some of their standards, the military banners they carried. In fact, Legion X is known to have spent time in the area identified in this story, Gerasa, and it occupied Jerusalem after the Romans conquered the city and burned the temple in 70 CE.

Figure 25. In the first century CE, a typical Roman army unit called a legion numbered around 5,000 men. The stamp above, from a roof tile, likely dates from the tenth legion's occupation of Jerusalem in 67–75 CE, during and immediately after the siege that resulted in the destruction of the Second Temple. Two symbols of the tenth legion, a Roman galley ship at the top and a boar at the bottom, accompany an inscription that mentions Legion X by name. Courtesy Zev Radovan.

Near the end of Mark, we learn that the temple curtain is "ripped" from top to bottom at the time of Jesus' death. The torn temple curtain is found in the other Synoptic Gospel accounts as well, but we consider it here because only Mark seems to make a verbal link between the "ripped" heavens at Jesus' baptism and the "ripped" temple curtain at Jesus' death. Some readers understand the significance of this "ripped" temple curtain, which separated the holiest section of the temple from areas of the temple where priests could enter on a more routine basis, to be that the temple is no longer necessary after Jesus' death. As the "ripped" heavens signify the immediate presence of God's Spirit in the scene of Jesus' baptism (1:10), so the "ripped" temple curtain points to God's presence on earth in a way that renders unnecessary the temple's twofold function of protecting and making accessible the divine presence.

Scholars such as Jack Dean Kingsbury have noticed that soon after the opening scene of Jesus' baptism, two themes begin to drive the Gospel of Mark: the mistaken identity of Jesus and Jesus' conflict with authorities. In the two sections that follow below, we will briefly summarize how these themes energize Mark's narrative and reach resolution at Jesus' crucifixion.

Confusion over Jesus' Identity

The first theme that runs through this whole gospel could be stated as a question: Who is Jesus? As readers we may come to this gospel with preconceived notions about Jesus as a messiah, and even if not we immediately come to understand who Jesus is from the narrative of his baptism, when God's voice tells him that he is God's (beloved) son in Mark 1:11. However, these things are not known by the other human characters in the gospel itself. Even the disciples often misunderstand who Jesus is. When Jesus casts out demons, these demons immediately understand who Jesus is, but Mark tells his story as if none of the humans present at Jesus' exorcisms hear what these demons are saying. While we the readers are privy to this information, other people in Mark's Gospel keep asking who Jesus could be, given the powerful acts he regularly performs. In Mark 6:14-16, we learn that some have drawn incorrect conclusions regarding Jesus' identity—he is a prophet who has come back to life, or, as the ruler Herod Antipas thinks, Jesus is John the Baptist come back to life. These wrong conclusions add suspense to the narrative, since we the readers are left wondering when people will fully understand who Jesus is.

Jesus himself contributes to the confusion. He regularly tells the "unclean spirits," not to announce who he is. He also tells people not to announce that he has healed them. This repeated silencing is sometimes called the "messianic secret," and contributes to the apocalyptic nature of this gospel. Other features of this gospel that seem apocalyptic are the parable of a Seed That Grows Secretly (4:26-29), found only in Mark, and Mark's description of Jesus' words about the last days of Jerusalem (chapter 13), where Jesus reveals details about the future to certain disciples in private. We describe Mark as "apocalyptic" because this gospel claims to reveal secrets, especially the kingdom of God, which is "near" but beset by opposing forces.

In the second half of this gospel, Mark shows people gradually coming to understand who Jesus is. Peter correctly identifies Jesus as the Messiah. A blind man calls Jesus by a nickname for the Messiah, "the son of David." As Mark describes Jesus entering Jerusalem, in what has come to be called his Palm Sunday entry or triumphal entry (Mark 11), we hear the crowd cheering Jesus while they use language from the book of Psalms to affirm that Jesus is a ruler in the line of King David. A key moment in this gospel's chronicle of the quest for Jesus' identity is at his trial, when, before the high priest, Jesus quotes a passage from the Old Testament book of Daniel that depicts a human/divine "son of man" who receives authority to rule the earth from God. In Mark's narrative, the high priest immediately realizes that Jesus' answer amounts to a messianic claim that he, as a religious authority, deems blasphemous. In the rest of the trial and crucifixion narrative, Jesus' identity is presented ironically. The Roman soldiers mock Jesus as a fake king, clothing him in purple and putting a crown of thorns on his head. When he is on the cross, with the sign that reads—Jesus of Nazareth, King of the Jews—the authorities are sure that Jesus is not king of the Jews. But they use the opportunity for fun, sarcastically calling Jesus a king while he is in front of them on the cross. However, in an ironic twist for the reader who accepts Mark's opening words and the early narrative of Jesus' baptism where Jesus is called the Messiah and God's son, these taunts by bystanders finally correctly identify Jesus. It is only when Jesus is on the cross that his messianic identity is fully revealed. For Mark, Jesus is a messiah who cannot be known and followed until one witnesses his suffering on the cross. Though not always recognized, it seems that Mark's idea is that the Messiah Jesus was meant to suffer and die, and that those who follow this Jesus will also experience opposition or suffering because they identify with Jesus. The opposition or suffering they experience is a way of participating in Christ's death and hence in his eventual resurrection.

Jesus' Conflict with Authorities

While Jesus is presented as God's Son "let loose" on the world in this gospel, he is not depicted as having an easy romp. The narrator makes a comparison between Jesus and the "scribes" in 1:22 that portrays Jesus as more authoritative. Jesus' repeated announcement that the kingdom of God has come near, beginning in Mark 1:15, seems to be a controversial idea in Mark's narrative world. Especially significant is how early in the gospel we read that Jesus is put on the authorities' "hit list" (Mark 3:6). This makes it appear as if for almost Jesus' entire public ministry the authorities were preparing to put him to death. This is quite different from what is found in the other Synoptic Gospels and in John, where significant opposition to Jesus builds, or even seems to come only in the last week before Jesus' crucifixion.

In the narratives that follow, the authorities oppose Jesus indirectly at first. But finally near the end of the first half of this gospel, in Mark 8:11-13, we see a direct confrontation that deals with Jesus' identity and mission on earth. By the time Jesus reaches the temple in Jerusalem during the last week of his earthly life, we see him involved in a deep controversy with those in power over the question of his own authority (11:27–12:34). And throughout the narrative, the kingdom of God, the rule of God on earth, is what Jesus seems most invested in. In fact, his last words in this gospel's depiction of the Last Supper are a look ahead to the kingdom of God: "Truly I tell you, I will never again drink of the fruit of the vine until that day when I drink it new in the kingdom of God" (14:25).

An additional irony in the scene on the cross occurs when the leaders mock Jesus. Since he healed and helped so many others, but now is dying on the cross, the leaders think Jesus surely does not have God's authority to teach. They conclude that he is an imposter because he cannot come down from the cross. The readers, however, have already been told by Mark's narrative that it is God's will that Jesus is destined to die in this violent manner. For the readers, therefore, the scene is one of irony. The authorities seem to have won the conflict, but the readers understand that this person on the cross, and the kingdom he has announced, will prevail in the end.

Jesus' Conflict with Authorities Brings Persecution

Related to this conflict is an emphasis on Jesus' death sentence by crucifixion. Despite being the shortest of the Gospels, Mark's Gospel spends proportionally more space on the final days before the crucifixion than the others. While all four of the Gospels in the New Testament portray persecution as something Jesus predicted for his followers, in the specific saying in which Jesus tells his disciples that if they give up family or possessions they will receive much, only Mark has Jesus add that they will also receive persecutions (Mark 10:30). It is possible that Mark's emphasis on persecution is because this gospel was written in Rome during a time when the government was arresting and at times executing Christians.

The High-Definition Gospel

Mark's Gospel makes for great reading precisely because it focuses in on details that are otherwise ignored in the other gospels. For example, while all four gospels narrate Jesus feeding the five thousand, only Mark tells us that the people sat down on *green* grass, in groups of *one hundred or fifty people* (Mark 6:39-40). In the narrative of Jesus' trial that all four gospels record, it is only Mark who captures the rather unusual detail of the man running away naked (Mark 14:51-52). Mark does not explain the significance of these details; their enigmatic presence therefore adds to the mysterious nature of this gospel. These enigmatic details, along with the rather abrupt original ending of this gospel (discussed earlier), further enhance the theme of the "messianic secret."

As mentioned, the details of this gospel often underline Jesus' humanity. This gospel in particular emphasizes that Jesus was unable to perform many miracles in his hometown because of the unbelief encountered there (Mark 6:5-6). Similarly, this gospel doesn't seem to be bothered by quoting Jesus' confession that he does not know when he will return (Mark 13:32).

Concluding Reflections

For its intensity in describing Jesus' actions and conflicts with others, this gospel that portrays Jesus as "God's Son on the loose" has challenged readers to follow Jesus even through persecution and suffering, since it is finally only at the cross where Mark makes clear what sort of messiah Jesus is. While it seems to lack the literary polish of Luke or the symbolic depth of John, the Gospel of Mark proves to be the favorite gospel of many readers, since its intensity and action-filled portraits of Jesus offer a vantage point that seems nearer to the lives of Jesus and his first followers than the other gospels.

LUKE

Introduction and Overview

Luke's Gospel begins with a prologue that explains his purpose for writing (1:1-4). The very last word in this prologue is a Greek word perhaps best translated as "certainty." Luke's goal is to help people be certain of the background and details of Jesus' life, death, and resurrection.

To help achieve this goal of certainty, Luke reaches further back to tell Jesus' story than either Matthew or Mark. Luke begins with the announcement of John the Baptist's birth, followed by the announcement of Jesus' birth to Mary, and then the narration of Jewish rituals surrounding Jesus' birth and childhood that emphasize Jesus' connection to the Jerusalem temple. If it were not for Luke, many of these prebirth, birth, and childhood stories of Jesus would be unknown to us.

Chapter 3 introduces John the Baptist at work, as well as Jesus' genealogy. Then, from the beginning of chapter 4 through 9:50, we have an account of Jesus' teaching and miracles that is similar to those found in Matthew and Mark, though some of the material is arranged differently. Between 9:51 and 19:28, we find a section unique in Luke's Gospel—what scholars call the travel narrative. In this section, Jesus is traveling to Jerusalem, and Luke uses this framework of the journey to narrate sayings and events that Luke has found in his sources. The section is marked off by Luke with the use of words "being taken up" and "going up" in its first and last verses. From 19:29 through to the end of the book, we have the narrative of Jesus' final week in Jerusalem, trial before Pilate and Herod, crucifixion, resurrection, appearances to disciples, and ascension to heaven. This final section is bracketed by temple scenes: Jesus' triumphal entry into Jerusalem and cleansing of the temple is narrated in the last half of chapter 19, and in the final scene of the gospel, Luke portrays the

278

disciples praising God in the temple. For Luke, who seems to have a special affinity for the Jerusalem temple, this is a fitting ending not simply for the section that begins with the temple cleansing, but for the gospel as a whole, since the first narrative scene of the gospel is a time of prayer at the temple.

Controversies and Debates

Luke is the only canonical gospel that has a sequel, the book of Acts, which is written by the same author. This very fact has produced heated debates about whether the books are best read as forming a single, coherent literary unity or as two distinct books on different topics by the same author. If one opts for an integrated reading of these two books, one will be more apt to see correspondences between Jesus and Paul (the central character in Acts) than if one simply reads them as separate narratives written by the same author.

The four gospels of the New Testament come to us as anonymous works. Early on in the process of transmitting manuscripts they were given titles using the names Matthew, Mark, Luke and John, but the texts themselves nowhere mention who authored them. In the case of the gospel we call Luke, the authorship question is sharpened, since Luke is elsewhere called a physician (Colossians 4:14). This specific description of Luke has prompted some readers of this gospel to ascribe its distinctive features to a physician's powers of observation. But there is little evidence that a physician composed this gospel. The gospel nowhere presents this as a characteristic that will help us understand it, and there are places where the potential significance of Luke's distinctive wording can be lost by the dismissive explanation, "He wrote it this way because he was a physician."

A final controversy worth noting is that although most contemporary Christmas plays and crèche scenes combine the details of Matthew and Luke's distinct birth and infancy scenes (for example, the Magi in Matthew and shepherds in Luke), a careful reading reveals that the two stories are different. In Luke, Jesus' parents reside in Galilee but go to Bethlehem because of a mandated census and end up in a manger because the local inn had no space. In Matthew, however, all we learn is that at about two years of age, Jesus is in a house in Bethlehem with his parents. They then flee to Egypt and only later end up in Galilee. It is likely that both stories are as guided by the unique theological concerns of each author as they are by actual historical considerations. In fact, though distinct in their descriptions of a virgin birth, both narratives of Jesus' birth and childhood are clearly modeled on certain miraculous birth stories found in the Hebrew Bible, such as those describing the births of Isaac, Samuel, and Samson, who are all born to women who had been unable to conceive a child for many years. For example, notice that Sarah, who bears Isaac, and Samson's unnamed mother only conceive after God or an angel informs these women that, contrary to what seems possible, each will soon bear a son. So too it is with Mary. The birth stories found in Luke and Matthew also may be influenced by what Greeks and Romans expected regarding the birth and early years of great figures.

Songs and Stories of Birth and Childhood

If we were to compare the descriptions that Matthew and Luke provide of Jesus' birth, we might say that Matthew is written as a documentary and Luke is written as a musical. While Matthew narrates Jesus' supernatural birth in a straightforward manner with connections to the Jewish Scriptures explicitly documented, Luke narrates the birth with poetic responses or songs provided by Mary the mother of Jesus, Zechariah the father of John the Baptist, the angelic choir on the night of Jesus' birth, and Simeon—the old man who guided by God's Spirit blesses the infant Jesus in the temple. These songs, which we will discuss below, are known to many today by the first word or phrase of each song as they are found in the Vulgate or Latin translation.

Mary's response of praise after being greeted by her cousin, Elizabeth, who is pregnant with John the Baptist, is often called the *Magnificat*. This song is very similar to Hannah's response of praise when her son Samuel was presented to the Lord. Both songs highlight God's ability to raise the poor into favor and to bring low the powerful. Among observant Catholics and some Protestant groups the *Magnificat* is prayed daily at evening prayer. Zechariah's response to the miraculous birth of his son, John the Baptist, is often called the *Benedictus*. It highlights how God keeps his promises, especially the covenants he made with Abraham and David, and predicts that John the Baptist will be a prophet who will prepare the way for the Lord. The *Benedictus* is prayed daily at morning prayer.

Simeon's response to Jesus, set in the poignant scene of Jesus' presentation in the temple upon the day of Mary's ritual purification after the birth (Luke 2:29-32), is called the *Nunc Dimittis*. The last phrases of this song, based on the series of four Servant Songs found in Isaiah 40–55, call Jesus "a light for the nations' revelation" and "glory of your people Israel." These ideas nicely encapsulate how Luke and Acts present Jesus. Though the other three gospels do not contradict these emphases, none of them choose to use such phrasing, and their portraits are less grand than Luke's "big picture" optimism of a poor baby destined to contribute to Israel's splendor. The *Nunc Dimittis* is prayed daily at night prayer.

These early chapters of Luke describe Jesus' birth in a manger, the angelic choir singing at his birth, and the visit of the shepherds—all unique to Luke's Gospel. Descriptions of Jesus' growth are phrased in words used for the boy Samuel's growth. Unlike the Gospel of John, where Jesus has heated and dangerous confrontations in the temple, Luke wants to show that Jesus, like Samuel long ago, is perfectly at home in God's house. It is only Luke who narrates the circumcision of the infant Jesus and the presentation in the temple (see image below). Also unique to Luke is the three days the twelve-year-old Jesus spends in the temple, culminating in his description of Jesus being occupied with "my father's matters" (2:41-49). Luke has a very positive view of the Jerusalem temple, and this contributes to its modeling of Jesus' boyhood after the priest Samuel, who was raised in God's house.

The genealogy of Jesus as found in Luke 3:23-38 differs significantly from the one found in Matthew 1:1-17. In general, Jesus is presented here in Luke as the quintessential human, "son of Adam, son of God," unlike Matthew's presentation of Jesus as the quintessential Jew, "son of David, son of Abraham." But as we have seen above, Luke juxtaposes his idea that Jesus came for all humanity with his idea that Jesus is uniquely the splendor of Israel. Given Luke's positive portraits of the temple, it is likely that his reference to Jesus as

Figure 26. Interestingly, only Luke, considered to be written by a Gentile, describes Joseph and Mary following Jewish rituals for the infancy and boyhood of Jesus. Unknown artist, *The Circumcision of Christ*, 1470. Carved walnut. Courtesy Smith College Museum of Art, Northampton, Massachusetts (SC 1955:68).

"about 30 years old" is motivated by a desire to show that Jesus' public ministry began when he had reached the age that priests typically began their work in the temple (Luke 3:23, drawing on Numbers 4).

Jesus in Galilee

Luke 4 places Jesus' sermon in his home synagogue as the inaugural announcement of Jesus' ministry. Only Luke provides a direct quotation of Jesus' sermon, with explicit references to Elijah and Elisha and their interactions with Gentiles. In what follows, Luke portrays Jesus performing miracles that remind the reader of famous miracles performed by these earlier prophets. Jesus heals the Roman centurion's servant, a miracle that illustrates the concluding point of Jesus' first sermon. The point here is that, contrary to expectations, God sometimes sends his prophets to the Gentiles instead of the Jews. The following miracle is unique to Luke. Jesus' raising of the widow's son shows him to be a prophet like Elisha, who raised the Shunammite's son (4:24-27; 7:1-10; compare 2 Kings 4:18-37). This is underlined by the location Luke specifies, Nain, which is near the site of Shunem where Elisha performed his miracle. Luke's narration of these miracles clearly attempts to establish Jesus' place among Israel's prophets.

The other significant sermon that Luke provides in this section is Jesus' Sermon on the Plain in Galilee (Luke 6:17-49). Luke's Sermon on the Plain represents an abridged and edited form of Matthew's Sermon on the Mount. One important difference between the sermons is that where Jesus says "Blessed are the poor in spirit" in Matthew, Luke presents Jesus as addressing those with any kind of poverty: "Blessed are you poor" (Matthew 5:3; Luke 6:20).

Marginalized People

The difference between Matthew's "poor in spirit" and Luke's "poor" indicates Luke's eye for marginalized people. One aspect of the *certain* and *complete* perspective of this gospel is its inclusion of people not included in other gospels. Luke in particular highlights marginalized people, bringing them into his story in ways that the other gospel writers do not. He mentions the poor, Samaritans, children, and the shepherds, all of whom would have been ignored in most people's portraits of first-century life in Israel. Along these lines, Luke describes a number of women not mentioned in any other gospel, such as Joanna and Susanna.

But Luke is not content merely to mention these marginalized people. This gospel portrays Jesus eating with many people, including those that other leaders would shun. This portrait of Jesus as the friend of the marginalized fits with the idealized portraits of Jesus as the one who fulfills the good things God has promised to Israel, including raising up the lowly (Luke 1:52).

The Travel Narrative

In Luke's Gospel and its sequel, Acts, we find the journey used as a narrative framework. Here in his gospel, after portraying Jesus' ministry in Galilee, Luke provides a travel narrative that builds suspense for readers awaiting his arrival in Jerusalem. In both books, the "journey" is a literary device that organizes the narratives and holds readers' attention. Luke places a number of Jesus' parables in the travel narrative section (9:51–19:28).

Repentance

A favorite theme of Luke is repentance, so it is not surprising that he portrays people, whom we do not see in other gospels, repenting. In the parable of the Lost, or "Prodigal," Son, this wayward child repents when in dire straits. This parable must be read in light of the two parables that precede it, all showing how much God values the repentant sinner. Later in the second of two parables on prayer, Jesus shows how it is the repentant sinner whom God hears and justifies, rather than the proud, self-righteous man in Luke 18:9-14. In the story of Zaccheus, this tax collector repents of the ways he has gained money (Luke 19:1-10). In the crucifixion story, even one of the thieves who is being crucified alongside Jesus repents. All of these stories are unique to Luke, emphasizing this special theme.

Jesus' Trial, Crucifixion, and Resurrection Appearances

Luke's narrative of Jesus' trial is unique among the Gospels for the favorable light in which he portrays Pilate and his soldiers. Only in this gospel do we hear Pilate asserting Jesus' innocence three times; and only in this gospel do we find Herod's soldiers, perhaps Jewish, probably not Roman, mocking Jesus. The favorable light in which the Romans are presented here is related to Luke's presentation of Jesus as a "light to the nations" on the stage of the

Roman Empire (Luke 2:32; 3:1; see Isaiah 49:6). It may also be an attempt to exonerate the Romans and shift the blame on to the Jews, since this gospel was written and valued when Christians sought favor from the Romans.

The resurrection appearances Luke narrates are significant for the explicit connections he makes between Jesus' death and the earlier Hebrew Scriptures. In Luke 24:25-27, we hear Jesus telling two of his followers that it was necessary for him to suffer. We also hear Luke's claim that Jesus explained what Moses and *all* the prophets said about him. Then in verse 44 of the same chapter, we get an additional description that emphasizes how everything written in the Law of Moses, the Prophets, and the psalms had to be fulfilled. This statement is early evidence for the division of the Jewish Scriptures into Law, Prophets, and Writings (what Jews call the Tanakh). Since the following verse describes Jesus opening his listeners' minds to understand the unique way Christians would come to read the Jewish Scriptures, it is clear that a straightforward reading of the Hebrew Bible does not overtly point to the necessity of the Messiah's death. Such a reading is only evident to those standing within the very faith tradition the gospel advocates.

Concluding Reflections

The emphasis on the necessity of Jesus' death and the need for the Hebrew Scriptures to be fulfilled in Jesus' life is a way that Luke provides certainty to readers. This certainty, based on the assurance that things are proceeding according to God's plan, leads to joy among its witnesses. Luke shows us this joy throughout his gospel and—alone among the Gospels—he concludes with a portrait of the disciples returning to Jerusalem with great joy, worshiping and blessing God in the temple.

This gospel begins its story before the other Synoptic Gospels, with its depiction of the announcement to Zecharias of John the Baptist's birth. It ends after the other gospels, with a more detailed description of the ascension of Jesus to heaven and a report of what the disciples did after the resurrection. This broader frame allows for it to appear more complete than the other gospels, a feature that also contributes to the certainty its author seeks to evoke in readers.

JOHN

Introduction and Overview

John is very different from the Synoptic Gospels. It begins in eternity past, with Jesus, the *logos* (the divine word) active in the creation of the world. Indeed, the way that this gospel begins seems to be an intentional allusion to the creation narrative we encounter at the beginning of the Bible: "In the beginning, God created the heavens and the earth" (Genesis 1:1 NIV). The light/darkness, sight/blindness, and up/down polarities found throughout this gospel can all be related to the Genesis 1 creation narrative on which its prologue is dependent. But this gospel adds the idea that the incarnation of Jesus and his role in explaining God to humanity is in the same category of significance as God's creation of the heavens and earth. Both for the signs John narrates and for the presentation of Jesus as heir and intermediary of God's glory, this gospel presents meanings below the surface of the actions and discourses of Jesus. Perhaps this is what Gregory the Great had in mind when he said that John's Gospel is shallow enough for a child to wade in but deep enough for an elephant to swim in.

Controversies and Debates

In a way that is different from Luke, authorship has figured in controversies about John. First, there is the historical question arising from the oblique references to an author behind the text, identified most often as "the beloved disciple" (see for example 13:23 as well as the crucifixion image near the end of this chapter). Who is this gospel's author? Then there is a second historical question: Did Jesus really give the long and theologically heavy discourses that we find in John, marked with such metaphors as "I am the bread of life" or "I am the door" (6:48; 10:9)? These seem quite different from the shorter, more direct sayings of Jesus narrated in the Synoptics.

In addition there is the theological controversy over this gospel's anti-Judaism. While deeply valuing Judaism's institutions and Scriptures, the Gospel of John often identifies those who do not believe that Jesus speaks for God, or those who are hostile to Jesus, as "the Jews" (*Ioudaioi*). From beginning to end, it is clear that the author includes "Jews" among unbelievers who threaten and evoke fear among the Jesus followers. But there is debate over exactly how anti-Judaic this gospel is. Why would this gospel's author, most likely a Jew, repeatedly refer to Jesus' opponents pejoratively as "the Jews" or quote Jesus telling Jewish religious leaders that their father is the devil? Clearly, some difficulty that this author has experienced with Jews who did not regard Jesus as he did has affected his narrative. Some readers are probably now thinking, "If Jesus criticized religious leaders of his day, why is this a problem?" The difficulty is that after this gospel came to be the Scripture of a predominately Gentile church, it was used in anti-Judaic ways, with later Christians imagining that Jesus and his disciples were in fact Christians who rejected a retrograde Jewish religion, rather than Jews who came to believe in Jesus as the Son of God. These ideas influenced Martin Luther to call for all synagogues to be destroyed and likely provided cover for later Christians who failed to act when ethnic Jews were persecuted and murdered by the German state in the last century.

The Book of Signs

John's Gospel calls the miracles that Jesus does "signs." The first eleven chapters of this gospel are often called "the book of signs." It seems plausible that John wrote this gospel to have seven signs, even though all seven are not numbered. The traditional identification of the signs is as follows: Jesus, at his mother's prompting, turns water into wine (2:1-11); Jesus heals the ruler's son (4:46-54); Jesus heals the lame man (5:2-47); Jesus feeds the five thousand (6:1-15); Jesus walks on the storm-tossed Sea of Galilee and brings the disciples' boat promptly to its destination (6:16-21); Jesus heals the man born blind (9:1-41); and Jesus raises Lazarus from the dead (11:1-53). Four of the signs that are narrated in this gospel are placed within discourses—long monologues in which Jesus explains the meaning of the sign. And this points to a key feature of John's narrative about Jesus' miracles. John treats the very limited number of miracles he narrates as much more than supernatural acts.

These actions of Jesus are signs that tell readers something about Jesus or about humanity's place in the world.

All four of the Gospels describe Jesus' feeding of the five thousand. But only John provides a long speech after this sign, in which Jesus says that those who follow him must eat his flesh and drink his blood. The speech is conspicuous in John, since John contains no narrative of the Last Supper. It seems as if John has placed his ideas regarding the Eucharist into this "bread of life discourse," in which Jesus emphasizes that his flesh must be eaten and his blood must be drunk in order to have life, a difficult saying that the author refuses to rationalize or soften (6:26-65). Interestingly, John narrates Jesus' final night with his disciples not as a Passover meal that turns into the Eucharist as the Synoptics do, but rather as a preparation for the Passover (13:1). The day of Jesus' death is the day of preparation, on which Jews observing Passover will slaughter their lambs (18:28; 19:14, 31). Here Jesus explicitly becomes the Passover lamb.

When one reads John chapter 9 about how Jesus healed the man born blind, you can see that the sign and the discourse that follows is telling us who Jesus is. But it is also prompting us to think about who is really blind and what sight means. John is more explicitly theological than the Synoptic Gospels in his narratives of Jesus' miraculous deeds.

Faith Leads to Life

"Faith" in the Gospel of John is sometimes shown as inadequate or weak faith (2:23-25 or 20:24-29) and other times as strong faith (4:39-50; 20:29). In general, believing in Jesus just because he has done a supernatural sign is not considered adequate or strong faith in this gospel. It is rather those who have believed in Jesus based on his word, whether or not they have seen any miracles, who are considered to have adequate and strong faith. Faith in John's Gospel is supposed to lead to life, as the emphatic, first ending of the gospel tells us (20:31).

This life is usually described in John's Gospel as "eternal life." Many Christians would define "eternal life" as life that begins after a believer dies, a life that consists in living with God in heaven forever. But this is not how John uses the term. The Gospel of John treats "eternal life" as a present possession of those who know God and his son, Jesus (6:47; 17:3). For John, "eternal life" is more about a spiritual quality of life rather than the temporal extent of life or a life hereafter.

Jesus' Crucifixion

John 12–20 is often called "the book of glory." This section emphasizes Jesus' glory both for his explicit description of receiving glory from God and for his calm spirit and sense of control when approaching death. Jesus' "hour" finally arrives, in which he will die a death that will somehow show the world God's glory. Contrary to the Synoptics, Jesus does not pray that God will remove the "cup" of his tragic death; instead he prays that God would glorify himself (compare John 12:27-28 with Matthew 26:38-39). It seems ironic to us that the death of a criminal would be a glorious event, but this is how Jesus

describes it in John. Even the crucifixion, a cheap and messy way that the Romans used to execute those who broke their ordered society, is for John's Jesus a glorious death. Notice that Jesus on the cross seems to announce his thirst only in order to fulfill Scripture and does not die a gruesome death, but simply hands over his spirit (19:28-30).

While on the cross, Jesus speaks to his mother and to the beloved disciple, making statements that are only found in John's account of the crucifixion. These statements further illustrate how John depicts the crucifixion as a glorious event.

Figure 27. A seventeenth-century depiction of the crucifixion of Jesus. Christian iconography frequently pictures Christ's blood falling on Adam's skull and femur bones (seen at the base of Jesus' cross), to illustrate the New Testament's portrait of Christ as a second Adam, one who sets right what went wrong in Adam (Romans 5:14-15 and 1 Corinthians 15:20-22). Crispijn I de Passe, *Crucifixion*, undated. Engraving on paper. Courtesy Smith College Museum of Art, Northampton, Massachusetts (SC 1951:215).

Here Jesus, very much in control of what is happening, makes provision that his mother now take the beloved disciple as her son, and that this beloved disciple take Mary to be his own mother. The words gave rise to the early Christian tradition that John the apostle cared for Mary until her life on earth ended. On another level, many Christians understand this exchange to be Jesus' way of inviting all followers of Jesus to consider Mary to be their own mother. However one reads John's allusive references to Mary, one can see that he is emphasizing her significance not as virgin mother as in Matthew and Luke, but as companion and guide for those following Jesus (see for example 2:1-5; 19:25-27).

Jesus as Culmination of Judaism

John's Gospel is known for narrating John the Baptist's description of Jesus in the following way: "Behold, the lamb of God, who takes away the sin of the world" (1:29). In this gospel, Jesus is shown in Jerusalem for three Passovers, and then his crucifixion is presented as the death of a Passover lamb in two ways: (1) John correlates the time of Jesus' dying with the day when Jews ritually slaughtered their Passover lambs; and (2) John draws on language from the ritual instructions for preparing Passover lambs when describing Jesus' condition on the cross (19:32-36; Exodus 12:10, 46). The "Behold, the lamb of God, . . ." saying, often used in Christian liturgy, is really the tip of a theological iceberg in that language from other aspects of Judaism is applied to Jesus throughout the Gospel of John. The verb for setting up the tabernacle is applied to Jesus' life on earth (1:14), followed up by a description of the glory evident in Jesus' life. Steadfast love and faithfulness, the two qualities repeatedly ascribed to the God of Israel in the Jewish Scriptures, are linked to Jesus in a way that assigns more value to Jesus than to the law of Moses (1:17). Also, in the middle of John's Gospel, Jesus is described as participating in Judaism's festivals in Jerusalem. In addition to the Passover, Jesus is also present in Jerusalem for the feast of booths (Succot; 7:2-39) and at Hanukkah (10:22-30).

Icebergs are dangerous. Many Christians have shipwrecked on John's theme of Jesus as the culmination of Judaism, something that can quickly descend to the blasphemy that God has abandoned his first love, the covenant people, the Jews. It is difficult to find a singular position on the status of Jews in the New Testament. There are places that seem to equate Christless Jews with Christless Gentiles as equally outside of salvation (John 3:18; Acts 4:12). But there are other places that seem to bend over backwards to say that

God's love for his people Israel does not falter and he will indeed save all Jews (e.g., Romans 11). Indeed, when Paul considers this question he argues that those who say God has abandoned the Jews are trivializing God's covenant relationship with the patriarchs and libeling God's character as undependable (Romans 11:28-29). Readers of John who choose to follow the Jesus this gospel portrays must therefore remember the unfortunate family division that this gospel reflects, and keep in mind that it also portrays Jesus in a respectful relationship with the skeptical Pharisee, Nicodemus (3:1-13).

First and Second Endings

John seems to have two endings, with John 20:30-31 functioning as a first conclusion to the gospel. This ending is preceded by stories that depict Jesus breathing the Holy Spirit on his apostles, authorizing them to forgive sins, and it brings the reader into the circle of those who are challenged to believe in the resurrected Jesus. The author, whom tradition identifies as John, the youngest of the twelve apostles, tells us that he has selected a limited amount of material to communicate that Jesus is the Messiah, the Son of God. His conclusion makes clear that he did not communicate this simply to record history, but to motivate readers to believe in Jesus, so that readers would gain life by identifying with this Son of God.

The second ending, chapter 21, seems to rehabilitate Peter's image, give us a picture of Peter's martyrdom, and legitimize the beloved disciple who was not martyred, perhaps in order to inspire readers to follow Jesus wherever he calls them.

Chapter 21 resolves the paragraph of John 13:36-38 in which Peter insists he will be loyal to Jesus as far as giving up his life for Jesus. In John 18, Peter denies Jesus three times. This is considered a shameful act, in light of Peter's promise to "lay down [his] life for [Jesus]" (13:37). Here in the second ending, Jesus asks Peter three times if Peter loves him. Each time Peter answers affirmatively. It is as if Jesus is asking Peter if he loves him three times to allow Peter a chance to undo or hit the reset button for each of his three earlier denials.

Interestingly, there is a little bit of a game being played here, because Jesus asks Peter if he loves him with an *agapē* (God-inspired, self-giving) love the first two times. Peter responds with a different verb, that he loves Jesus with a more common, brotherly love. The third time, Jesus asks Peter if he loves him with this more common, brotherly love, and Peter is sad that Jesus asks this. The sense could be that Peter is sad that Jesus is questioning even if he loves him with brotherly love. So Peter responds by saying, "Lord, you know all things; you know that I love you with brotherly love" (John 21:17 AT). This "game" in which Jesus seems to be asking for a love that Peter cannot claim to have seems to be showing Jesus testing Peter's honesty. Peter is allowed to undo his three denials by confessing his love three times, but in response to Jesus' questions Peter is admitting the human limitations of his love for Jesus.

Following this comes a prediction of Peter's martyrdom. The readers of John's Gospel would have known the early church tradition that Peter was crucified in Rome, during the persecution started by emperor Nero around the year 64 (see Tacitus, *Annals* 15.44). In that sense, Peter's prediction that he would lay down his life does come true. In the conclusion of this gospel, Peter then asks Jesus about the other person present, the beloved disciple, "What about him?" Jesus' answer, "If I want him to remain until I come, what is that to you? You follow me!" is then explained as the source of a false rumor that the beloved disciple would not die (21:21-23 AT). The beloved disciple is then identified as the gospel's author, whose witness is true. Both the first ending at the end of chapter 20 and this second ending at the end of chapter 21 thus call readers living after the apostles have died to follow Jesus.

Concluding Reflections

It is clear from its narratives of Jesus' signs, the discourses that accompany them, and the narratives describing Jesus' knowledge and actions all leading to his glorious death that John is theologically deep. Whether one agrees with its claims about Jesus or not, one can see that the Gospel of John presents Jesus' actions and words as holding significance beyond what is initially seen or heard. Perhaps it is fitting that this theologically rich gospel concludes the four and highlights the distinct perspectives of the preceding Synoptic Gospels.

ACTS

Introduction and Overview

The book we call "Acts," or "Acts of the Apostles," is a bridge between the Gospels and Paul's letters. It provides a narrative framework in which to read those letters and functions as a foundational story explaining the beginnings of the early church.

Acts develops the theme of the Holy Spirit, already seen in Luke, now highlighting how the Spirit empowers the followers of Jesus. The Jewish holiday on which the Holy Spirit comes, Pentecost, is an agricultural festival observed fifty days after Passover. Jewish tradition celebrates Pentecost as the anniversary of Israel's reception of the Torah on Mount Sinai, as well as the anniversary of the death of David, a significant idea in Peter's Pentecost sermon and in a later sermon in Acts by Paul. For our author, the timing of the coming of the Spirit certainly fits with Paul's idea that Gentile Christians should not take the Torah—Mosaic law—upon themselves but should rather "walk by the Spirit." On the anniversary of God's gift of divine instruction to Israel (Torah), God now sends the Spirit on Jesus-followers as their new guide for life, which Acts describes as the fulfillment of the prophecy found in the prophet Joel.

The first twelve chapters of Acts center on what happens in and around Jerusalem. Then from chapter 13 to the end of the book, Acts follows Paul in his travels outside of Jerusalem and the Holy Land, among the Gentiles. In some sense the two halves are bound together in that already within the first half of Acts we read of a major turning point in the life of a traditional Jewish adherent, later identified as a Pharisee, named Saul (Acts 9:1-29). This person who set out to persecute believers in Jesus has a conversion experience and changes his name to Paul, the main character in the second half of the book. The same Paul is traditionally credited with writing the thirteen letters that follow Acts. The conversion and commission of Saul narrated three times in Acts (9:1-29; 22:3-21; 26:9-20) is a significant moment in the life of the church, since this person becomes the apostle (or Christ's ambassador) to the nations (Gentiles). Included in his commission is a call to suffer for Jesus (9:16).

Controversies and Debates

One major debate regarding Acts is whether its author was actually familiar with Paul personally, or tells his story based on reports. There are three sections of Acts that use "we" to narrate the unfolding story, as if the person writing those narratives was personally accompanying Paul on the specific travels narrated in these sections (16:10-17; 20:5–21:18; 27:1–28:16). Readers can't help but wonder, did the author actually join Paul for some of his travels, or did he merely switch into the first-person plural to make his narrative look like the type of history he was trying to write, hoping to draw his audience into the story?

Acts makes no mention of or quotation from Paul's letters. If the author of Acts had not read Paul's letters, it could suggest that he was not an eyewitness to Paul's mission work. Some scholars find enough verbal connections to lead them to claim that the author is familiar with Paul's letters. Of course, the author of Acts may well have known these letters but opted to shape his narrative apart from them.

Yet another area of controversy in Acts concerns the repeated pattern of Jewish unbelief, Gentile responsiveness, Jewish opposition, and eventual rescue of Paul and others by Roman authorities. This leads many to think the author biased his history toward the victors, that is, Gentiles living in the imperial Roman world. Has the author's anti-Judaism penetrated the text? How far has the author's vision of a unified Christianity caused him to bend the historical record? These are some of the questions scholars and others debate.

Looking at Acts in Detail

The words of Jesus to the apostles in Acts 1:8 are roughly programmatic for the rest of the book: "But you will receive power when the Holy Spirit has come upon you; and you will be my witnesses in Jerusalem, in all Judea and Samaria, and to the ends of the earth." Acts narrates how once the power of the Holy Spirit comes upon the apostles (2:1-13), they witness to Jesus in

Jerusalem (chapters 2:13–7:60), Judea, Samaria (8:4-25), and to the ends of the earth (8:26–28:31).

The narrative of Acts begins in Jerusalem and ends in Rome. This is a geographical sign for what the author shows in the book—those followers of Jesus whom the book portrays as the predecessors of the "Christians" are first a sect of Judaism. By the end of the narrative, the next generation of this group are Gentiles living throughout the Mediterranean world, including Rome, the capital of that world. So Acts in this sense is a "tale of two cities."

But along the way, Acts locates significant developments in Antioch, a bustling metropolis in antiquity whose ruins are found today in Antakya, Turkey. Here followers of Jesus are first called Christians, from here Paul begins mission trips, and here the question of whether Gentile Jesus-followers need to keep Mosaic law arises. Thus Acts is more than a "tale of two cities," since Antioch represents an intermediate step in Acts' portrait of transition from Jewish sect to an independent religion, distinct from Judaism.

Peter Says "Repent!" to the Jews (Acts 1–12)

Peter, a prominent disciple in the Gospels and friend of Jesus, takes center stage in the early stories of Acts. One of his sermons is found in the Pentecost narrative (2:14-40), and after he and the Apostle John heal a lame man we find another. The chapters that follow show Peter as a powerful leader and miracle worker. His third, final sermon within Acts 10 is interrupted by the descent of the Holy Spirit on the household of a God-fearing Gentile named Cornelius.

Calls to repent come in 2:38 and 3:19. This is a favorite idea for the author of Luke and Acts, but it is a generalization when applied to Peter's sermons, since Peter also encourages belief in Christ in his sermons. As mentioned, the opening twelve chapters of Acts describe the Holy Spirit coming upon Jesus' followers at Pentecost (what Jews call *Shavuot* or "Weeks"). They describe the crowd at this scene as including Jewish pilgrims from various parts of the world and proselytes, Gentile converts to Judaism (2:5-10). Here mention is made of how early followers of Jesus included "Hellenistic" (Greek-speaking) residents in Jerusalem as well as "Hebrews" (6:1).

While these early chapters in Acts are focused on Jerusalem and the land of Israel, they depict Peter as spreading the news of Jesus to non-Jewish peoples. In Acts 8, Peter and John go to Samaria and help the converts there to receive the Holy Spirit. And in Acts 10–11, Peter travels to a Roman centurion's home, announces Christ to the household, and baptizes the household after the Holy Spirit comes upon them. This is significant, since in Galatians it seems like *Paul* is the Gentile-friendly missionary for the early church, while Peter (also called "Cephas") is the conservative who wants to guard the Jewish character of the Jesus movement (Galatians 2:11-16). Acts wants to show that the first steps in extending the membership of this movement to non-Jews came through Peter, thus giving credibility to Paul's mission to non-Jews as well. Of course, the very different portrayal of Peter in Paul's own letters suggests that Acts may be an attempt to imagine the early Jesus movement as more unified and less fractious than was actually the case. If so, one might draw an analogy to the way that the portrait of Israel's unified conquest of Canaan as found in Joshua tends to smooth over the fractious picture in Judges. When biblical narratives report historical events, they are often less interested in the hard facts than in the deeper theological meaning these events hold for those who accept these texts as Scripture.

Paul Says "Believe!" to the Gentiles (Acts 13–28)

In the second half of Acts, we see Paul going to Diaspora Jews (Jews living outside the promised land). His mission is to offer them the good news about Jesus. Some accept this news; others reject it. When the rejection is such that Paul cannot teach the Jewish community in a given town, he then redirects his message to the Gentiles. The notion that Paul only turned to a Gentile audience after each Jewish audience rejected his message stands in some tension with places in Paul's letters that indicate he was to preach to Gentiles while Peter and others would preach to Jews. Acts is likely shaping its narrative for theological purposes, and in this instance may be attempting to illustrate the meaning of Paul's expression "to the Jew first, then the Greek" found in Romans (1:16; 2:10).

Paul's mission trips are interrupted by what scholars call the Jerusalem Council narrative in Acts 15. Here, a council of Jewish followers of Jesus debate whether or not Gentiles who want to follow Jesus as their messiah and worship the God of Israel are required to observe the Mosaic law. As we might expect from earlier narratives in this book, Peter speaks up at this council to endorse Paul's decision not to require Gentiles to keep Mosaic law. James speaks last in the council's deliberation and he reappears in a later visit of Paul to Jerusalem. James is the leader of the Jesus followers in Jerusalem, someone known for observing Torah. The council ends in consensus: Gentiles who follow Jesus need not keep all of Mosaic law, but they need to follow a simplified set of laws that include abstaining from food offered to idols, meat from strangled animals that still contains blood, and sexual immorality. The council's decision is an affirmation of Paul's mission, since it shows the guardians of the Jewish roots of the Jesus movement endorsing Paul's "Torah-free" gospel for Gentiles. In Acts' portrait of these early years of the Jesus movement, its author wants to show that Jesus followers were not separating those who observed Torah from those who did not. Both were to live together in harmony. The decision that the council reaches is never cited in Paul's letters, again suggesting that Acts 15 presents an idealized portrait of a unified church in support of Paul's mission rather than a strict recording of history.

By the end of Acts, Paul is at Rome announcing the kingdom of God there and teaching freely about Jesus. This is an effective segue into his letters, which begin with his letter to the churches of Rome, the letter we call "Romans"—the next book in the New Testament.

Conclusion

Paul's letters give evidence of conflict among those announcing Jesus to others, most especially over whether Gentiles must observe Torah laws like circumcision and abstaining from certain foods. By contrast, Acts presents a picture of a harmonious network of Jesus followers who endorse Paul's view that the Gentiles can join the Jesus movement without having to obey the Torah in its entirety. Regardless of how historically accurate Acts is, the book influences how people read Paul's letters. It prompts readers to consider Paul and his churches as significant first steps in the growing Jesus movement while recognizing the Jewish roots of Paul's gospel.

Introduction to the Letters of Paul

The Significance of Paul's Letters

In comparison to the narratives in the Gospels or the book of Acts, the genre of letters, or what scholars sometimes call "epistles," allows a more straightforward explanation for how later generations are to live out the Christian message. And, once Paul's letters are linked to Acts' narrative about Paul, they seem especially fitted for giving advice to the church and its members.

When readers take Paul's letters seriously, they can evoke existential connections between Paul the author and readers, or between readers and Christ. The letters also raise philosophical as well as theological questions on issues still affecting readers: the nature of human freedom in relation to sin, law, and God; and the nature of a person's identity as an individual and as a member of a culturally defined group.

How Many Letters Did Paul Write?

There are thirteen letters in which Paul is listed as the author, occurring consecutively in the canon from Romans to Philemon. In the eighteenth century, when people began to study the Bible as one studies other literature, the authorship of some of these thirteen letters came into question. Many scholars now think Paul wrote fewer than the thirteen letters attributed to him, so it is necessary to qualify what we mean when we say "Paul's letters." Scholars are in general agreement that seven letters (the "uncontested letters") were written by Paul: Romans, 1–2 Corinthians, Galatians, Philippians, 1 Thessalonians, and Philemon. The remaining letters—Ephesians, Colossians,

2 Thessalonians, 1–2 Timothy, and Titus—are often called deuteropauline. This means that they are regarded as coming from Paul in a secondary sense, perhaps written by a disciple (or disciples) of Paul.

When Did Paul Write His Letters?

None of the letters that bear Paul's name are dated. At times letters in the ancient Mediterranean world conclude with notation of the day, month, and year of the Roman emperor or other local ruler. It is possible that Paul's avoidance of mentioning such royal dates functions as an implicit critique of the allegiance that Rome demanded. Or, perhaps omission of this information was intended to signal that a letter's message was not time-conditioned. Whatever the case, instead of dating the letter to a human ruler's reign, Paul usually invokes glory to God forever or refers to Christ's return.

Paul's letters are not ordered according to the date of their composition or the events of Paul's life, but are instead ordered according to length, from longest to shortest. Determining the chronology of Paul's life must therefore come from elsewhere. Though many scholars do not trust the narrative of Acts to provide a completely reliable chronology of Paul's ministry, most end up using Acts to some degree, in the absence of other more verifiable sources. The chronology of Paul's letters is set in relation to two events: his visit to Galatia and his appearance in a tribunal in Corinth before the Roman proconsul Gallio (Acts 18:12-17). However, these are not sufficient to provide a chronology on which all agree. With this caveat and an acknowledgment that some of these letters may have been written after Paul died in mind, we will provide the reader with a possible reconstruction of the sequence of Paul's letters.

Chronology of Paul's Life and Letters

early to mid-30s CE	Paul joins the Jesus followers
late 40s to early 50s CE	1 Thessalonians; 2 Thessalonians (if Pauline)
53 CE	1 Corinthians
53–56 CE	Galatians; letters grouped together as 2 Corinthians
56–57 CE	Romans

60–62 CE or Ephesians and Colossians after 64 CE	Ephesians (if Pauline); Philippians; Colossians (if Pauline); Philemon; Paul possibly dies in his first imprisonment in Rome
63 or after 64 CE	1 Timothy (if Pauline); Titus (if Pauline)
64 CE or later	2 Timothy (if Pauline)
64 CE	Paul dies as a martyr in Rome

Table 4.

Conclusion

As readers, it is easy to focus on specific issues or questions that arise when reading Paul's letters. But the main things to keep in mind are that we are reading someone else's mail, preserved because it addresses issues that still concern people today. As we read Paul's letters—whether we read these letters very skeptically or as Scripture—it is helpful to keep in mind that they were written to people in settings very different from ours, though they address many issues we still encounter today.

ROMANS

Introduction and Overview

Many consider Romans to be Paul's most complete letter, in the sense that it covers more theological topics than his others. In Romans, Paul introduces himself to churches in Rome that he did not start, in order to gain support from these churches for an upcoming trip to Spain (15:23-24). To accomplish these goals, he seeks to explain his gospel, challenge the propaganda of the Roman Empire, and clarify misunderstandings people had about him or his gospel.

After a greeting and explanation of the basis of the letter (1:1-17), Paul launches into a description of the righteousness or justice of God, which he presents against a backdrop of human sinfulness (1:18–3:31). After using a passage from Genesis to bolster his case, Paul describes the benefits brought by righteousness based on the faithfulness of Christ: freedom from death (chapter 5), freedom from sin (chapter 6), freedom from a counterproductive relationship between human beings and the law (chapter 7), and union with Christ and the gift of the Holy Spirit (chapter 8). Then, in Romans 9–11, Paul explores whether God will remain faithful to Israel, even if Israel does not always remain faithful to God, a question first raised in chapter 3. Having reasserted God's faithfulness to Israel, Paul then deals with life in society (12:1–13:13), a specific problem in the Roman churches (14:1–15:6), and concludes the letter with a summary and blessing (15:7-13). At the end of the letter, Paul indicates his travel plans and gives final greetings to specific people in the Roman churches (15:14–16:27).

Controversies and Debates

One important controversy surrounding Romans concerns how one should read it. Is it a textbook-like "compendium of Christian doctrine" as

Martin Luther's collaborator, Philipp Melanchthon, called it? Or is it a letter focused on specific circumstances in Rome, arising out of Paul's particular life situation with no generalizations about Paul's gospel or *the gospel* to be made from it? If one follows the former option, the interpreter usually tries to read the letter as making one, coherent theological argument. If the latter option is followed, the stops and starts in the organization of the letter are noted, as well as the differences in Paul's treatment of the Mosaic law here in comparison to his letter to the Galatians. In this option, the letter is read as historically conditioned, not a general textbook.

A second controversy related to Romans concerns the centrality of ethnic Israel within it. This controversy arises out of a tension in the letter, one that seeks to balance the idea that God first communicated with Jewish people and gave them a wonderful heritage with the idea that God is impartial and judges all people according to his divine will. The latter side of this tension—God's impartiality toward all—combined with recurrent anti-Semitism, led many previous commentators to emphasize God's judgment on ethnic Israel and to view chapters 9–11 as a parentheses or tangent in the letter. Here again, one feels the effects of the Holocaust and the ways that Christian anti-Judaism enabled it. Recently, quite a few Christian thinkers have begun to acknowledge the centrality of ethnic Israel throughout Romans and notice that chapters 9–11 end with Paul's statement that God will save all Israel. The controversy has not entirely abated, however, for Paul's statements in 9:6-9 are read by some as indicating that Paul is using "Israel" to refer to the church, not the physical descendants of Abraham. These interpreters read Paul's redefinition of Israel in 9:6-9 as trumping the possibility that the salvation of "Israel" (in 11:25-27) refers to God's gracious reception of ethnic Israel, that is, the Jewish people. For reasons we discuss later, this reading is tenuous, especially because Israel is there referred to as enemies "as regards the gospel" (11:28), hardly a description Paul would use of the church.

Righteousness or Justice

In Romans, Paul is attempting to describe how people are made just or righteous, using the Greek term *dikaiosynē*, often translated as "righteousness." This idea of *righteousness* has an ethical dimension and it could just as easily be translated as *justice*, even in the theoretical explanations Paul gives in the first half of Romans. A helpful strategy in reading Romans is to substitute the word *justice* for *righteousness*. This allows readers to see the social dimensions of Paul's letters, and helps to tie together the doctrine of chapters 3–4 of Romans with the social teachings in chapters 12–15.

Greek Matters: Faith *in* Christ or Faith(fullness) *of* Christ?

It is commonly stated that Paul teaches justification by faith. But whose faith does Paul have in mind? Paul uses an ambiguous phrase twice in the section where he defines God's righteousness: Paul writes that it comes by "the faith of Jesus Christ" (3:22) and that God is just and the justifier of the one who is from "the faith of Jesus" (3:26). An early printing of the King James Version translated 3:22 in this somewhat awkward (but accurate) way, but the dominant pattern in English translations is to translate the phrase as "faith *in* Jesus Christ." This is possible, though the word "in" is not actually present in the Greek. The noun phrases "Jesus Christ" and "Jesus" in these verses stand in the genitive (or possessive) case, which means they can relate to the noun "faith" that it accompanies in different ways.

One possibility is that "faith of Jesus Christ" in 3:22 does actually mean "faith *in* Jesus Christ," suggesting that Jesus Christ is the object of the believer's faith. But "faith of Jesus Christ" here can legitimately be translated "Jesus Christ's faith," potentially describing the faithful obedience that Jesus displayed throughout his life on earth. The difference plays out in how one describes the agency involved in receiving God's righteousness. Does someone receive God's righteousness primarily because this person places his or her faith in Jesus Christ? Or does someone receive God's righteousness primarily because Christ had faith, displayed in his obedience to God? Perhaps this need not be an either/or question. Some in fact argue that the phrase means both—it refers to Christ's faithfulness, to which humans respond in faith.

How Universal Is Christ's Salvation?

Unlike Paul's first letter to the Corinthians that follows, Romans often looks past its immediate audience and seems to make statements regarding all humanity. In the last half of chapter 5, Paul offers some expansive horizons for his readers. Here Paul considers what it was like for people on earth before God gave the law to Moses. He considers why people suffered death before there was a Mosaic law whose violation was said to lead to death (like asking how people can go to jail when there is no law against what they did). He also explains how Christ's death addresses the general problem of human sinfulness (5:12-21).

In Romans 5:18-19, Paul uses the words "all" and "many" to describe those whom God will save by Christ's act of obedience. However, there is debate about whether Paul's use of "all" means all of humanity—in the distributive sense of "all"—or whether the word "all" is used in a more focused way.

Does the statement, "Terry coaches all the students at the school," mean that Terry coaches every single student in the school, or does it mean that if any student is on the school's athletic teams, Terry will be that student's coach? The way one responds to this question can be affected by how one reads the parallel construction regarding how all have become sinners. So when you read Romans 5:13-21 ask yourself if Paul is saying that Christ will save all in a distributive sense, that is, every single human being, or whether what he says implies a more focused sense, meaning that Christ will save all who get saved. What is clear is that Paul sees Christ as a new Adam, as though Christ is starting a new pattern for the human race.

The Divided Person in Romans 7

Romans is known for its monologue in which Paul says "I do not do the good that I wish, but rather I do this evil that I do not wish" (7:19; see 7:7-25). There are many situations in discourse in which the pronoun "I" has a special sense that deserves precise definition. For example, in Helen Reddy's celebrated song, "I Am Woman," who is the "I"? Is Helen Reddy claiming that she herself is "strong . . . invincible," someone who "can do anything"? Or is she claiming that every woman, in a distributive sense, has these characteristics? Close reading, including her "watch me grow" stanza of the song, may help readers hone in on what she meant. We must do the same close reading of Paul's monologue.

Interpreters of Romans read this section closely and debate whether the "I" who is speaking in Romans 7 represents Paul before he became a Christian, after he became a Christian, or whether it represents someone besides the individual, such as the nation of Israel or a generic human person. The question is sharpened for readers who consider this letter to be Scripture, an authoritative text that describes what it is like to follow Christ. If the "I" refers to someone in their *pre*-Christian mode of existence, then one gains the impression that Paul does not expect Christians to be consistently sinning in their daily lives. But if the "I" refers to someone who *is* a Christian, then one may get the impression that Paul allows that Christians might sin against their better judgment or wishes.

Romans as Paul's Damage Control

Besides explaining his gospel in this letter, Paul seeks to dispel rumors that have been circulating about him. These rumors may explain why he is so concerned for his life as he anticipates travelling to Jerusalem before his planned trip to Rome (15:25-32). The rumors may be summarized as follows.

First, Paul wants to make clear that he does not teach that people who have identified with Christ or believed in Jesus can now live however they want. Since he actually mentions that people are slandering him in this way, it is clear that he is writing to silence this rumor (3:8). He seems particularly bothered by this rumor, since he returns to the question again in 6:1, "Shall we persist in sin that grace may abound?" His immediate answer in the next verse is "Of course not!" and he spends the rest of chapter 6 explaining why and how Christians must live holy lives.

Second, it is probable that Paul seeks to silence a rumor that he has abandoned his Jewish heritage, that he doesn't like Jews, or that he thinks God has abandoned Israel. Paul points out that he is Jewish (11:1) and he likely surprises his skeptical readers with a very positive answer on the advantage of Jews in 3:1-2. He later continues the list of advantages that this group of people has in 9:4-5. Even after spending about three chapters discussing Israel's unbelief in Messiah Jesus, he still affirms that in the future, "all Israel will be saved," since "the gifts and call of God are irrevocable" (11:26, 29). As mentioned, some Christians have tried to redefine "Israel" here to mean the church, but the immediate context of 11:26 requires that we understand Paul to mean ethnic Israel. Paul looks forward to a time when God will save the Jewish people despite their currently being enemies "as regards the gospel." Paul's urge to silence the rumor that he doesn't like or value his fellow Jews also accounts for his fairly frequent description of Jews as his "kin" or "relatives" in this letter.

The Strong and the Weak

As sometimes happens in churches today, the churches in Rome that Paul is addressing seemed to disagree on what food and drink people should or should not consume and on whether or not Christians should observe a Sabbath day (14:1-5). Paul's response in 14:1–15:6 is surprising. He asks the "strong," those with the more robust, carefree consciences, to respect the "weak," their fellow believers who are more conscientious and sensitive in regard to abstaining from certain foods (14:14-16). In so doing, Paul says that those with "strong" faith or consciences will be following the example of Christ, who modeled giving up his rights for others (15:1-3).

Figure 28. Letters in antiquity were typically penned by a secretary (or amanuensis). Romans 16:22 names "Tertius" as Paul's amanuensis. The next verse mentions "Erastus, the city treasurer," likely at Corinth, where scholars believe Paul composed Romans. This inscription from ancient Corinth credits possibly the same Erastus with paving the marketplace at his own expense. Courtesy of Michael J. Towle.

Concluding Reflections

Overall, this letter, written by Paul at a precarious moment in his life, continues to raise big questions about human existence, the role of law in human experience, and the place of a chosen people among all other peoples and groups. For those readers who accept this letter as Scripture, the letter has much to say, whether they read it as a "compendium of Christian doctrine" or as an inspired letter that Paul wrote for a specific occasion. The letter will challenge both sorts of readers to live holy lives in ongoing worship to God and to remember that the family reunion they hope to attend may include some unexpected relatives.

1 CORINTHIANS

Introduction and Overview

In 1 Corinthians, Paul deals with problems and questions posed to him by the church that he founded in the city of Corinth. The first four chapters seek to bring unity to the church, which was divided into at least four groups. Then Paul goes on to provide instruction on sexual relations (5–6), married life and singleness (7), eating food offered to idols (8–10), proper conduct in church meetings (11–14), and the coming resurrection (15). The final chapter of the letter includes instruction on taking up a collection for those in need in Jerusalem, after which Paul concludes the letter with final greetings.

As we will see, the letter is a fascinating slice of how Paul the Diaspora Jew deals with behaviors that are culturally acceptable to Greeks in Corinth, but unacceptable to him. From his "Jews seek signs and Greeks seek wisdom" section in the opening chapter through to the end of the book, we see the culturally agile Paul attempting to steer his church from behavior allowed in Hellenistic culture toward behavior of a holy and unified church.

Controversies and Debates

One controversy related to this book concerns the Corinthian church members' *eschatology*, that is, ideas about the end of the world and times leading up to it. Because Paul has to deal with flagrant immorality (for example, incest in chapter 5 and consorting with prostitutes in chapter 6), and because he writes a long chapter arguing that there really is a resurrection of the dead and thus Christians are to live moral lives now (15:30-34), scholars debate whether ideas about living in the end times were prompting these distinctive behaviors among the Corinthians. Some assume that church members in

Corinth held to "realized eschatology," a view that the end times had already arrived and thus "all things [were] lawful" for them (6:12; 10:23). This would explain why Paul writes that, to the contrary, the resurrection of believers' bodies is yet to come and therefore they have to be careful in how they live today (15:30-34, 58). Other scholars argue that the Corinthians' immoral behavior shows that they *lacked* an eschatology; that is, they didn't think enough about the end times and the destiny to which their identity in Christ called them.

First Corinthians 14:34-36 often causes modern readers to bristle with its apparent direction that women are to be silent in the church. This seems to contradict what Paul has already written in 11:5, 13, where he seems to assume women will pray and prophesy during church services. Various explanations are offered for Paul's command that appears to silence women. One is that a later author inserted this command, though there is no direct manuscript evidence that this is a late addition to the text. Another explanation is that 1 Corinthians 11:5 and 13 refer to women praying and prophesying in private, so 14:34-36 should be understood to mean that Paul really didn't allow women to speak in public church assemblies.

Paul's Two Goals in 1 Corinthians

Beginnings are always significant, and the beginning of 1 Corinthians gives us a significant clue as to Paul's goals in this letter. In 1 Corinthians 1:2, Paul says he is writing "to the church of God that is in Corinth, to you who have been sanctified in Christ Jesus, called to be holy, with all those everywhere who call upon the name of our Lord Jesus Christ." In this verse we can see that Paul twice assigns the idea of holiness to this church ("sanctified . . . called to be holy"). As is evident from reading the letter, there were people in the church who were not living a holy lifestyle, but Paul is calling them to such a lifestyle since their identity as Christ followers depended on following Christ who is believers' "sanctification" (1:30).

A second goal in the quotation from 1:2 above is that Paul is calling this church to unity. He will be asking them to be unified among themselves in the first several chapters of the book. Later he asks them to contribute money to a collection for poor believers back in Jerusalem (16:1-4). This will build unity between the Gentile believers in the Greek city of Corinth and the Jewish believers in Jerusalem.

Love Trumps Knowledge

For Paul, the way to holiness and unity is through love. Some of the people from this church whose conduct Paul criticizes appear to have considered their behavior to be justified by a special knowledge that they had. In response to such claims of special knowledge, Paul takes pains to show that love matters more than knowledge, both love of God and love of neighbor (8:1-3; 13:8-13).

In 1 Corinthians 8:1–11:1, Paul is asking those whose apparent knowledge allows them to eat food offered to idols to be more aware of others' sensitive consciences. He actually asks those who are ready to eat anything to give up their own right to eat food offered to idols, out of respect for those with sensitive consciences and to promote harmony in the church. While Paul's response is thus similar to what we saw in Romans 14:1–15:6, here we see Paul giving a different example for this behavior—his own pattern of taking no payment from churches he is serving (9:1-27). Paul's point is that if he can give up his right to take payment for his ministry, then those with special knowledge can give up their supposed right to eat food offered to idols.

Paul's most famous tribute to love, 1 Corinthians 13 (often recited at Christian weddings today), occurs in the context of Paul's advice regarding some chaotic worship services. It seems that some Corinthians took pride in speaking in tongues, which here appears to refer to a prayer language that most people could not understand. Paul makes clear that love is the most important quality to seek after, more than speaking in tongues or any prophetic ability or knowledge. Paul counsels that church meetings always be conducted in an orderly way. Here we see a strong emphasis on creating peace and unity among community members.

To Marry or Not to Marry

In chapter 7, where he talks about how married couples should regularly continue marital relations (7:1-5), Paul appears to be responding to questions the church gave him about whether husbands and wives should abstain from sexual relations. Here, as he has already done in 6:12, Paul quotes something people were saying in Corinth and then corrects it. At the beginning of chapter 7, quoting others he states that "It is good for a man not to touch a woman" (7:1). The following verbs in his response, including "fulfill his duty," "do not deprive each other" and "return to one another" (AT) all emphasize that, to the contrary, sexual relations are to be a regular part of marriage. Later in this chapter he counsels single people against marriage, counsel motivated by the circumstances of his day (see 7:25-26, 29). The phrase "present distress" in 7:26, as well as "the time is running out" in 7:29 seem to indicate that Paul thought that difficult circumstances in Corinth, perhaps some kind of crisis or a food shortage, made it advisable not to marry.

Concluding Reflections

This letter, which deals with a number of problems that the church in Corinth experienced, offers a window onto how the Corinthians were affected by their surrounding culture. Without directly appealing to the Torah, Paul attempts to unify and call his church back to what he perceives to be moral lifestyles. In doing so the people will be unified, made holy, and made ready for the resurrection.

2 CORINTHIANS

Introduction and Overview

Despite Paul's hope for a unified and peaceful church in Corinth, his second (known) letter to the Corinthians emerges out of a strained relationship between him and the people there. Paul explains his own hurt, expresses forgiveness to a person who offended him, and argues for his legitimacy over rivals who have countered his authority in Corinth (chapters 1–2; 10–13). Along the way, Paul relates his life and its struggles to God's purposes and in chapter 12 he describes a mystical experience he had.

Controversies and Debates

At first reading, 2 Corinthians appears to be one letter. However, many think it represents excerpts from as many as five letters. To understand why people view this letter as a composite, try reading 2 Corinthians 6:13 and then skipping to 7:2. The logical flow between these verses serves as strong evidence that 2 Corinthians 6:14–7:1 may have been an insertion from another letter. Since 1 Corinthians 5:9 indicates that Paul sent a letter before 1 Corinthians, directing believers to avoid certain people, some suggest that 2 Corinthians 6:14–7:1 comes from that prior letter Paul wrote to Corinth. According to the five-letter composite theory, 2 Corinthians 1:1–6:13 and 7:2-16 are from a letter Paul sent to explain why he did not visit when planned, a letter seeking reconciliation with the Corinthian church. Second Corinthians 6:14–7:1 is a piece from an earlier letter he had sent to Corinth, warning the Corinthians against intermarriage with unbelievers. Chapters 8 and 9 represent material from two fundraising letters that Paul sent out for the collection he was gathering for the poor believers in Jerusalem. Finally, chapters 10–13 come from an emotionally charged "tearful letter" in which Paul pleads with his church in Corinth to follow him, rather than some rival teachers whom he calls the "super-apostles."

Other scholars view the letter as written by Paul, just as we find it. They suggest that the letter as it is makes sense as a multilayered plea for reconciliation between Paul and the church of Corinth. There may be something to this; relationships between church founders and their churches are complex. We must allow Paul the freedom to have included pleas for reconciliation, encouragement to contribute to his collection, and a defense of his apostolic leadership within the same letter. Even if we accept the idea that its parts come from different letters that Paul wrote, the editor who put the letter together did so in a way that did not generate any of these source critical hypotheses until the eighteenth century.

Forgiveness and Reconciliation

In 2 Corinthians 2:5-11, we can see Paul openly forgiving the church member who insulted him, and asking the rest of the church to forgive this person as well. We also see Paul's transparency in describing his own difficulties and the despair he felt because of them (1:8-9; 7:5). Throughout the letter, we see Paul giving a theological perspective on the mutually strained relationship he has with this church. The reconciliation that Paul seeks with the Corinthian church mirrors the reconciliation that God has offered in Christ, which could lead to a stronger relationship between Paul and this church. And he notes that the difficulties he has experienced have proven to be opportunities to experience God's comfort (1:8-11; 7:5-7).

Letter and Spirit

In 2 Corinthians 3:4-18, in the wake of describing himself as a servant of the new covenant, Paul makes some startling claims about his ability to read Scripture, claims that still haunt attempts by Christians and Jews to read Scripture together today. Aside from Paul's account of the Eucharistic liturgy in 1 Corinthians 11, this is the only place where the term "new covenant" from Jeremiah 31:31 appears in Paul's letters. Building on the new covenant idea, Paul implies that his ministry is inaugurating a new covenantal era based on the Spirit, not like the original Mosaic covenant based on the "letter" of the law. He goes on to describe the Ten Commandments carved on stone tablets as part of a ministry of death. Paul then says that his ministry of the Spirit will be more glorious than the giving of the Ten Commandments. The first difficulty here is that Paul implies that the Mosaic law brings death, which disregards how this law is presented in the Old Testament as well as the positive descriptions Paul gives of Mosaic law in Romans. Paul goes on to claim that Jews who do not follow Jesus have a veil over their eyes as they read their Scriptures. To take this at face value today ignores the learning, devotion, and careful work that Jews have exerted for millennia in preserving and studying Torah, work that has benefitted Christians. Paul seems to be using rhetorically charged language to pull his audience away from the rival teachers and back to himself and his Torah-free gospel for Gentiles.

"When I Am Weak, Then I Am Strong"

The letter of 2 Corinthians is the most emphatic example of Paul's theology of weakness. In addition to the difficulties and despair mentioned above, in this letter Paul also describes himself as physically carrying the death of Jesus and afflicted by a "thorn in the flesh" or "messenger from Satan," likely a physical ailment that God will not heal (4:10; 12:7-8). Paul finds God's power working where he (Paul) is most weak or vulnerable, just as God raised Christ in power after he was crucified as a weak victim. We see this theology of weakness in some of the Gospels' accounts of Jesus' life and death on earth as well as in depictions of martyrs in Revelation. But Paul is the one who articulates the idea most explicitly: Dimensions of human existence characterized by death or weakness cause Paul to sense that God is energizing him and using him for a special purpose.

Concluding Reflections

Second Corinthians is significant for its windows onto Paul's strained relationship with an important church, and the way he finds theological orientation in the chaotic and troubling experiences of his itinerant and marginalized existence. As such, it includes Paul's own actualization of the idea of incarnation, how God's presence is at work in the messy and mundane details of life.

GALATIANS

Introduction and Overview

Galatians is known as Paul's angry letter. This is probably because it includes two curses and no thanksgiving or good wishes in the greeting (1:8-9), the frustrated question, "O stupid Galatians! Who has bewitched you?" (3:1 AT), and Paul's wish that those meddling with the Galatians' understanding of the gospel would castrate themselves (5:12). Clearly Paul is not happy.

The letter's greeting is focused on calling attention to the Galatians' departure from what Paul originally taught them (1:1-9). There follows a section where Paul makes it clear that he received the message—"gospel"—that he taught the Galatians directly "through a revelation of Jesus Christ" (1:12), and that he has always been true to this gospel and never allowed it to be changed by what other people might do or say (1:10–2:21). Galatians 3:1–4:11 is a comparison of the Abrahamic and Mosaic covenants, used by Paul to claim that his gospel follows the pattern of the earlier of these covenants, the Abrahamic covenant.

After a short appeal to the Galatians to remember the good relationship they once enjoyed with Paul (4:12-20), he again attempts to use the Jewish Scriptures to make a point. In Galatians 4:21-31, Paul tells the story of Hagar and her son Ishmael in relation to Sarah and her son Isaac. Paul uses this Genesis story as an allegory, in which the slave woman and her son represent Mount Sinai—the Mosaic covenant given there, and the Jerusalem of Paul's day—while the free woman Sarah and her son Isaac represent children of the promise and the heavenly Jerusalem. From 5:1 to 6:10, Paul reflects on the freedom to which Christ followers are called, and what this freedom means. He has been insistent so far in the letter that his Gentile audience not attempt to follow Mosaic law, but now he offers some positive ethical guidelines, which include living in accord with God's Spirit and displaying virtues he calls the "fruit of the Spirit" (5:16, 22-23). In the final section of the letter, Paul indicates that he had personally penned (in large Greek letters) a greeting and makes an appeal against trying to keep Mosaic law to avoid being persecuted as a Christian (6:11-18).

Controversies and Debates

One major controversy regarding this letter is exactly in what ways Paul is negative toward good works or virtuous actions performed by humans. The text of Galatians seems to be discouraging its addressees from relying on "works of the law," indicating some type of performance of the Mosaic law, as a necessary part of what it means to follow Christ (Galatians 2:16; 3:5, 10). From the time of Martin Luther on, many Christians have read these statements that negatively portray "works of the law" as meaning that Christians should not consider virtuous actions as in any way contributing toward their salvation.

Recently scholarship has demonstrated both that first-century Judaism included an emphasis on God's grace and that Paul's own letters say a lot about virtuous living. In turn, there has been a growing recognition that Paul's repeated endorsement of faith over works of the law in Galatians does not preclude an emphasis on moral living, as is clear from Galatians 5. This realization leads some to explain that Paul's repeated call to abandon "works of the law" in Galatians refers specifically to the Jewish "identity badges" of circumcision, food laws, and Sabbath—specific observances or "works" that distinguished Jews from non-Jews in the Diaspora. In this reconstruction, Paul is concerned that Gentiles not take on these distinct Jewish identity markers but that they still obey certain moral laws of the Torah laws such as worshiping God alone, telling the truth, and refraining from murder, adultery, stealing, and coveting.

Stigmata

At the conclusion of the letter, Paul says he bears on his body the "marks of Jesus." Paul's word for "the *marks* of Jesus" in Galatians 6:17 is *stigmata*. Though these marks were probably scars on his back from repeated lashings or whippings he received for announcing the good news about Jesus, Galatians 6:17 is the biblical basis for the idea that certain people, including St. Francis of Assisi, so closely identify with Jesus that they mystically and unintentionally receive the *stigmata*—scars or bleeding wounds in the places that Jesus received them: the hands, side, and feet.

The Apocalyptic Orientation of Galatians

Galatians contains language that presents the world as plagued by evil powers from which Christ has rescued Christians (1:4). The difficulty for Jews and Christians is that Paul's argumentative rhetoric goes even further than 2 Corinthians 3 by speaking about the Mosaic law as one of the "elemental powers" that has enslaved humanity (4:9). Christ is presented in the beginning of Galatians 4 primarily as someone who rescued all of humanity from the law, a strange thing to argue when the Torah was never given to Gentiles in the first place. Paul views Gentile observance of "the works of the law" as equivalent to returning to previous servitude.

Instead of circumcising all males and keeping the other Mosaic commandments, Paul tells these Gentiles to love their neighbor as themselves and "live by the Spirit," letting the Holy Spirit guide them (5:14, 16). In Paul's apocalyptic perspective, humanity that was bound under elemental powers is rescued by Christ, and the Holy Spirit gives humanity an alternate power that protects them from returning to servitude under the elemental powers.

Galatians as Window on Social Relations in Diaspora

In Galatians 2:11-14, Paul describes how he confronted Cephas (whom we know as the Apostle Peter) in Antioch, for his inconsistent behavior around Gentiles. Paul writes that he saw Cephas eating with Gentiles regularly, but that after "some men from James" came, Cephas withdrew from eating with them, since he was afraid of "the circumcision" (that is, Jews who promoted circumcision as essential). Paul tells the story to the Galatians to explain that he has a clear understanding that, in Christ, Jews can eat with Gentiles, and Gentiles do not need to convert to Judaism to sit at the same table with Jews. After all, Paul claims that he has a direct commission from Christ himself, and he is not under the authority of the Jerusalem apostles.

From this story, it is evident that Jews associated with James in Jerusalem sought to preserve the holiness of the Jewish people by keeping themselves separate from Gentiles who might have been considered ritually unclean according to Mosaic law. Paul's letter to the Galatians is thus motivated by his quest to unify the church, composed of both Jews and Gentiles.

315

> ## Was the First Pope Infallible? The Story of Peter and Paul
>
> The fourth- and fifth-century church father Jerome questioned how it could be that Paul confronted Cephas (Peter) publicly and seemed to have won the confrontation. Jerome concluded that this confrontation was only staged as a teaching moment for the Jews and Gentiles attending the church in Antioch. By contrast, Augustine, writing around the same time, insisted that Cephas, though the leader of the early Christians, was actually wrong for his actions of first eating with the Gentiles but then withdrawing when purity-conscious Jews arrived. This debate between Jerome and Augustine poses questions to believers reading their Scriptures. To what degree are those whose stories are told in Scripture examples for readers? If the text is inspired and true, are the characters' actions in this text always inspired and trustworthy? How prone to error are the leaders of a religion, including those who figure significantly in a religion's Scriptures, in this case Peter, the first pope according to Catholic tradition?

Galatians and Judaism

Circumcision was regarded as essential by the Judaizing teachers in Galatia, those who sought to impose observance of the law on Gentile believers. The fact that the discourse of Galatians keeps mentioning circumcision suggests that it is a trope, or controlling theme, implying that whoever gets circumcised is also bringing his entire family under the obligations of the whole Mosaic law.

As mentioned, Paul's argument against requiring God-fearing Gentiles to keep the Mosaic law involves a comparison of the Abrahamic and Mosaic covenants in Galatians 3. Paul notes that the Abrahamic covenant is the earlier and more foundational covenant of the two. Since this covenant was activated by Abraham's faith and not by keeping the laws of the Mosaic covenant, not yet given in Abraham's era, it is enough, Paul suggests, that these Gentiles connect with God by faith as Abraham did (3:5-7). Paul argues that the "seed" Abraham was promised is Christ, and since these Gentiles are identifying with Christ, they do not need and should not be required to keep all the Torah's laws (3:16).

There are at least two puzzles in Paul's argument. First, it is difficult within Judaism and many forms of Christianity to separate faith from actions, as the rhetoric of Paul's argument could suggest here. In fact, he seems to recognize that one's actions are necessary for salvation later in the letter (Galatians 5:13–6:10). Second, although Paul presents it as such, the Abrahamic covenant as found in the rich tapestry of the Genesis narratives was not limited to faith. It also included the specific command for circumcision, the very action Paul demands his audience avoid. Paul attempts to correct this final weakness of his argument when he repeats it later in Romans (written after Galatians but placed before it in our New Testament). There Paul argues that since Abram was declared righteous in Genesis chapter 15, before receiving the command in Genesis 17 to circumcise himself and all his other males, righteousness before God is really based on faith, and commands such as circumcision are incidental to attaining righteousness before God.

The allegory that compares these two covenants in Galatians 4:21-31 is also troubling for the way in which it equates the Mosaic covenant with slavery, despite the witness of the books of Exodus and Deuteronomy that this covenant liberated the Israelites from slavery. Paul's allegorical move here is on the same wavelength of argumentation that calls those who advocated observance of Mosaic law "dogs" or expresses the wish that those advocating Gentile circumcision would castrate themselves (Galatians 4:25; 5:12; Philippians 3:2-3). When we read Galatians in light of other texts such as Romans, it becomes obvious that Paul's vehement tone here was a desperate attempt to keep his church members from converting to Judaism, not a systematic statement on how Christians should regard Judaism. It is unfortunate that this letter was so cherished by Martin Luther, a founder of Protestant Christianity. His view has canonized the outrageous language of the letter as though it applies in all situations or can be applied against any form of Christianity and various forms of Judaism that one chooses to equate with Paul's opponents in Galatians. Instead, Christians should carefully note Paul's rhetorical situation in Galatians. He is focused on keeping his church members following Christ, since he thinks that if they convert to Judaism they will lose this focus.

Concluding Reflections

Galatians sizzles with Paul's appeal that his church members in Galatia not convert to Judaism, but rather continue to view faith as sufficient for a life-giving relationship with the God of Israel. Its heated rhetoric shows how convinced Paul was that the faith of Christ is what brings salvation to Gentiles. Near the end of the letter, where Paul talks about behavior, it is clear that he views moral actions as included in the responsibilities of these Gentile believers. Paul expects his church members to be animated by the Holy Spirit, who actualizes moral actions in their lives. This letter, like the entire collection of Paul's letters, is passionately concerned with a question Paul has inherited from his Scriptures: How are God's people to live in relation to this world's cultures and institutions? Despite the challenges of reading this letter as Scripture, it shows us the intensity and complications that accompanied Paul's church planting efforts.

EPHESIANS, COLOSSIANS, AND PHILEMON

Introduction and Overview: Ephesians and Colossians

Ephesians

Ephesians is thought to have been a circular letter that was sent to a number of churches in western Asia Minor, the first-century name for the Roman province on the west side of the country we now call Turkey. The phrase "in Ephesus" in Ephesians 1:1 is missing in some of the earliest manuscripts, so some scholars think it was added later as a way to connect this letter to one of the churches that Paul started.

Ephesians begins with a thanksgiving prayer for the way that God has blessed believers in Christ (1:3-14). There follows a long section on how God has brought Gentile Jesus followers from being dead in sins to being favored by God's merciful love, now experiencing unity with God's people the Jews (2:1-22). After reflecting on his own place in God's mysterious plan to unite Gentiles with Jews, Paul offers a prayer for his audience and blessing toward God (3:1-21). The last three chapters contain generalized, practical instruction for how believers should live their lives. Within these chapters we find one of the most famous household codes of the New Testament, which gives instructions on how husbands and wives, children and parents, slaves and masters are to relate to each other (5:21-6:9). Later in the final, sixth chapter, Paul tells his audience to put on the full "armor of God," using the imagery of the God of Israel as a divine warrior pictured in the book of Isaiah (compare Isaiah 59:15-19).

Figure 29. The ruins at Laodicea, a city mentioned four times in Colossians and in the book of Revelation as well. At the end of Colossians, Paul instructs the people at Colossae to read his letter to the people there and to read the letter he sent to that church. The city was approximately ten miles from Colossae. Courtesy Rjdeadly, Wikimedia Commons. This work is liscensed under the Creative Commons Attribution-Share Alike 3.0 Unported (www.creativecommons.org/licenses/by-sa/3.01/).

Colossians

The city of Colossae is located about a hundred miles east of Ephesus. If Ephesians was a circular letter meant to reach Ephesus and other nearby locations, this might explain the many similarities we will note between Ephesians and Colossians, the letter sent to Colossae.

After a greeting and thanksgiving, Colossians includes what many consider to be a hymn of praise to Christ as firstborn of all creation and head of the church (1:15-20). In chapter 2, Paul asks his readers to "walk" or live in Christ, warning them to beware of "philosophy and vain deceit" (2:6-8). After an apocalyptic description of Christ destroying powers and authorities by his death (2:13-15), Paul tells his readers not to let others judge them in regard to what they eat or drink, or in regard to what religious days they observe, including Sabbaths (2:16). The material that follows indicates that the Colossians liked some form of religion that included the worship of angels, along with the observance of dietary and other ritual laws (2:16-23). The warnings Paul gives here suggest that there were some questionable teachings circulating in Colossae, which scholars today refer to as "the

Colossian heresy." Chapter 3 opens with a call for readers to live a holy life followed by a notice that Christ followers no longer are distinguished as "Greek and Jew, circumcised and uncircumcised, barbarian, Scythian, slave, free," a description that reminds us of what Paul wrote in Galatians 3:28. The household code found in Ephesians is given in abbreviated form in Colossians 3:18–4:1. The final, fourth chapter of Colossians contains greetings from those traveling with Paul. The instructions to exchange letters with the church in Laodicea so that Paul's letters to each of them may be read in the other church shows us that Paul expected, at least in this case, that his letters be exchanged and read beyond the churches to which he originally addressed them (see image on previous page).

Controversies and Debates

Though both letters begin with greetings from Paul, Paul's authorship of these letters is contested. Ephesians in particular uses expressions that do not occur in other letters attributed to Paul. Also, there are long and somewhat unusual strings of words, such as "the wealth of the glory of his inheritance in the saints" (1:18), or "in order that he might display in ages to come the surpassing wealth of his grace in kindness in us in Christ Jesus" (2:7) that are not found in other Pauline Letters.

Though Paul does quote positively from the Ten Commandments when he tells children to obey their parents in Ephesians, there is also a negative caricature of the Mosaic law in chapter 2 that seems to be at odds with the positive descriptions of Mosaic law Paul offers in Romans 7. Some readers suggest that a follower of Paul interpreted Paul's Torah-free gospel in a direction that led to such a negative caricature. This, combined with the differences in style mentioned above, lead some to question the Pauline authorship of Ephesians.

Colossians 2:16 seems to associate Sabbath observance with the "powers and authorities" over which Christ triumphed. While this association is similar to Galatians 4, it appears inconsistent with Paul's positive appraisal of Mosaic law in Romans, as well as with the respect he asks to be shown toward those who observe one day above others (Romans 14:5-6). Colossians is thus also questioned as genuinely Pauline. However, it certainly fits his general style and the basic emphases of his undisputed letters, which leaves readers with mixed signals regarding Mosaic law. Perhaps the questionable teaching in Colossae required Gentiles to observe Mosaic law, a proposition Paul did not accept (Galatians 3).

Comparing Household Codes and Other Parallels

The practical teaching that Paul offers in Ephesians 4:1–6:9 seems to be duplicated in Colossians 3:12–4:1. Notice how these sections of practical teaching cover the same topics, in the same order: married couples, parents and children, masters and slaves. It is easy to think that Paul is merely passing on what the Jewish or Greek cultures dictated regarding the submission of wives to husbands, children to parents, and slaves to masters. But when one reads the guidelines closely, such ideas as husbands loving their wives as they love their own bodies, parents not provoking their children to anger, and the counsel that slave owners have a master in heaven all seem to be deconstructing the rationale for the dominant social hierarchies by reminding readers of higher levels of authority than their own. Because Christ loves the church and because God is the owner of everyone, the relationships of husbands and wives, parents and children, and masters over slaves are all transformed in the light of these higher realities.

These letters share other similar ideas and phrases, as the chart below shows.

Major Parallels in Colossians and Ephesians

Colossians	Ephesians	Content of Parallel Texts
1:14, 20	1:7	Redemption through Christ's blood
1:4, 9	1:15-16	Paul prays constantly for the church since he has heard of her faith
2:13; 3:6	2:1-5	Gentile believers were dead in sins before Christ
3:15-17	5:15-20	Be thankful; sing praises
3:18–4:1	5:21–6:9	Marital, filial, owner-slave relationships
4:7-9	6:21-22	Commendation of Tychicus

Table 5.

Mystery

Both of these letters are often noted for their use of the term *mystery*. Paul uses *mystery* to designate a truth that has been hidden in the past but is now revealed. In these letters *mystery* can refer to different ideas. In Ephesians 1:9, it seems to refer to God's specific purpose to sum up everything in Christ. In Ephesians 3:3-4, the "mystery" seems to be the full participation that the non-Jewish "nations," or "Gentiles," have in the good news of Christ Jesus. Later in Ephesians, Paul will say that the relationship of husbands and wives is a mystery that points to Christ's relationship to the church (Ephesians 5:31-32).

Paul the Prisoner

Ephesians and Colossians are part of a group of Pauline works sometimes called his "captivity epistles." Most people think that Paul was imprisoned in Rome or Ephesus when he wrote these letters, as well as Philemon and Philippians. Notice his perspective in Ephesians 3:1 and 4:1. Though imprisoned by some earthly power, probably Rome, Paul calls himself a "prisoner of Christ Jesus" (Ephesians 3:1) or "prisoner in the Lord" (Ephesians 4:1). The same idea is repeated later in Philemon verses 1 and 9. What is significant is that Paul views his imprisonments as being primarily for Jesus Christ. He does not call himself a prisoner of Rome. This attitude leads him to write letters and praise God while in prison (see also 1 Corinthians 4:9-13; 2 Corinthians 11:23). Though it may be difficult to see from our cultural vantage point, experiencing imprisonment or being prosecuted by civil authorities was a common experience in the New Testament and was foundational to the identity of the first Christians.

Introduction and Overview: Philemon

Philemon is linked with Colossians because some of the people mentioned at the end of Colossians are also greeted in Philemon and the letter itself is addressed to Philemon, a wealthy person who likely lived in Colossae. Further, there are parallels in that the book of Philemon is also considered a prison letter. Perhaps more than the other letters in the New Testament, however, including Ephesians and Colossians, the short book of Philemon is deeply linked to a singular pressing issue that Paul is eager to address. The scenario behind Philemon seems to be that Paul has befriended a runaway slave named

Onesimus. Though he wants to keep Onesimus with him to help in his ministry (Philemon 13-14), Paul is compelled to send him back, and the letter is largely a plea to Onesimus' rightful slave owner, Philemon, to be reconciled to him as a fellow Christian brother.

Controversies and Debates

The main controversies surrounding this very specific letter center around what historical situation it reflects and how this letter of Christian Scripture should be read by later readers. The slave whom Paul seems to be recommending in this letter is named Onesimus, a name commonly given to slaves that means "useful." Paul says that he is sending Onesimus back "no longer as a slave, but rather as more than a slave [literally "hyper-slave"], a beloved brother" (16). The situation that is commonly reconstructed for this letter, as touched upon above, is that Onesimus was a slave to Philemon in the town of Colossae. After some rupture in their relationship that involved theft or vandalism, Onesimus ran away. He crossed paths with the imprisoned Paul, perhaps in Rome. Onesimus became a Jesus follower, and Paul is now sending him back to Philemon, his owner.

In the world in front of the text, this letter has been used to prove that the Bible supports slavery and that slaves should not consider running away from their masters. More recently, however, on the basis of Galatians 3:28, which says that in Christ there is no longer slave nor free, many read the letter as opposing slavery in general. In this reading of Philemon, Paul's statement in verse 16 that the slave is now a brother is prioritized over his statement in verse 14 that seems to recognize that the slave Onesimus is someone else's property.

Paul's Request

In verses 10-14, Paul has made it clear how dear and useful Onesimus is to him, and that he wanted to keep Onesimus, but that he didn't want to do anything without Philemon's permission. In verse 21 of Philemon, Paul says that he is convinced of Philemon's obedience, and that he knows that the recipient will do more than he is asking. These expressions lead many readers to infer that Paul is asking for something between the lines of this letter: that the owner of Onesimus will release him to join Paul.

Because of the signals within the text that Paul is asking for more than he explicitly says, the debates continue in regard to what happened after Paul sent this letter. We do not know for certain what happened to Onesimus, but in a letter dated to the year 110 a bishop of the church of Ephesus named Onesimus is mentioned (Ignatius to the Ephesians 1:3; 2:1). While the time-line makes it unlikely, some suggest that Philemon indeed did free his young, runaway slave and that about fifty years later, this former slave was the bishop of Ephesus. Though it is difficult to be sure of the specific outcomes of this letter, it is likely that some or all of Paul's requests in this letter were followed. If the letter's original recipient had not followed the requests it contains, he would have had strong incentive to destroy the letter, so as to leave no evidence of his decision to ignore the requests of the apostle to whom he was indebted (Philemon 19).

Concluding Reflections

The three letters considered in this chapter vary in their specific focus. Philemon is most specific, addressed to one person about a particular situation. Colossians seems more generalized but does contain specific instructions to avoid a marginal—some would say heretical—form of teaching and behavior (Colossians 2:16-23). Ephesians seems the most general. This has led some to say it was a circular letter from the beginning, sent to a group of churches in western Turkey, the area called Asia Minor in the first century. All of the letters portray a hopeful, imprisoned Paul, ready to convey God's grace and peace to those who read them.

PHILIPPIANS

Introduction and Overview

Philippians is quite unlike letters such as Galatians and 1 Corinthians in which Paul spends much ink addressing various problems he wishes to correct in these communities. In Philippians, the imprisoned Paul maintains an upbeat attitude since he continues his "crime" of announcing the Roman criminal Jesus as Savior and Son of God, while asking his audience to stay unified, to live according to God's peace, and to accept his thanks.

Controversies and Debates

While Paul addressed this letter to the church in the Roman colony of Philippi, there is disagreement as to whether Paul penned this letter while imprisoned in Caesarea Philippi, Ephesus, or Rome. Reference within the letter of Philippians to the household of Caesar makes Rome a likely location (4:22). This debate draws attention to the fact that scholars tend to accept Paul's authorship of Philippians. However, some think that its form in our Bibles represents a composite of two letters Paul wrote. In any case, this controversy does not affect our understanding of the major themes of the letter to which we now turn.

The Prisoner Paul Affirms Christ

Philippians shows that Paul's allegiance to Christ, the Son of God, was proclaimed in an environment where many thought of the Roman emperor as the son of God. The Christ hymn of Philippians 2:6-11 describes

326

Christ as being in essence God, then emptying himself and becoming a slave. While human he humbled himself, obeying God all the way to the point of death. Because of this, God gave Jesus a name above every name, so that everyone should kneel and confess that Jesus Christ is Lord to the glory of God (2:6-11). Not only does there seem to be a play on the name used of Israel's God ("LORD") here, but so too was the emperor routinely called "lord," and he was the one person to whom all in the Western world should bow. Since Jesus was crucified as a criminal by the Romans, Paul's inclusion of this poetic description of Christ is a direct insistence that Jesus—and not the emperor—is God's true son, whom all creation will acknowledge as Lord.

This Christ-centered worship in the face of Roman dominance is seen again in Philippians 3:19-20. There Paul describes enemies of the cross of Christ, and then says that Christians' citizenship is not on earth but in heaven from where they await a savior, the Lord Jesus. Roman emperors were called "savior" (for example, the Priene Inscription from 9 BCE acclaims Augustus as savior), continuing the precedent set when the dictator Julius Caesar was so acclaimed. Paul's words on God's peace may also be a reminder that God's peace is the only real peace, as opposed to the counterfeit Roman peace (4:6-9). Paul, likely writing from a Roman prison to the church in the Roman colony of Philippi, is rather rebellious. He refuses to shift his loyalty from Christ to the emperor, even while imprisoned by the Roman authorities.

A Call to Unity and a Thank-You Note

In Philippians 4:2-3, we find a more focused echo of what Paul wrote in Philippians 1:27–2:5. There, near the beginning of the letter, Paul called the church to a unity built on humility in personal relationships. Here in Philippians 4:2-3, Paul actually addresses two church members by name and asks them to be unified in their thinking. He also asks Clement and other church members to help bring unity. In Philippians 4:10-19, Paul offers an extended thank-you for the gift that the Philippian church sent to him. It is unclear what this gift was, but it was not uncommon in antiquity for prisoners to need the support of others to survive. In this thank-you, Paul says that he has learned to live at a very low standard of living, even while at other times he has lived with plenty (4:12).

Concluding Reflections

Philippians highlights the ideological conflict between a Jew following Jesus as Son of God and the Romans who called their emperors sons of God. Christians continue to draw inspiration from this letter, one that shows Paul radically following Jesus as the "true" son of God whom the Romans ignored and then executed. This letter reveals a countercultural and revolutionary strain in the early Jesus movement that time and again has helped Christian believers challenge and change the dominant status quo.

1 Thessalonians

Introduction and Overview

First Thessalonians is regarded by many scholars to be the earliest of Paul's letters, possibly written in the late 40s CE. The letter shows that Paul's gospel was never simply proclaiming justification by faith, since 1 Thessalonians describes plenty of behavioral changes Paul expects of members in his church. The letter gives the impression that Paul has recently announced his message regarding Jesus in Thessalonica, and that after leaving he is concerned to encourage those who responded to his message to keep following Jesus. This is confirmed by his statement that the Thessalonians "turned to God from idols, to serve a living and true God, and to wait for his Son from heaven, whom he raised from the dead—Jesus who rescues us from the wrath that is coming" (1:9-10).

The letter gives us evidence of how Paul instructed new Christians early in the life of the church. Paul's expectations for these believers include worshiping the true God, waiting for his Son to return (1:9-10), and living in ways that "are worthy of the God who calls you into his kingdom and glory" (2:12). These ways include living sexually chaste lives (4:3-8), showing love to others (4:9-12), never seeking revenge (5:15), praying and giving thanks (5:16-18), and avoiding all forms of evil (5:22).

Controversies and Debates

A major minefield in this letter is its description of "the Jews" in 2:15-16: ". . . who killed both the Lord Jesus and the prophets, and drove us out; they displease God and oppose everyone by hindering us from speaking to the Gentiles so that they may be saved. Thus they have constantly been filling up the measure of their sins; but God's wrath has overtaken them at last." Paul seems to leave an opening for what would become standard fare in later periods of church history: the idea that since the Jews crucified Christ and persecuted Christians, they experience God's wrath. It is possible that Paul is writing out of heated disagreements or events he had just experienced (Acts 17:1-10). We need to remember that when he deals directly with the special place the Jews occupy within God's plan in Romans 9–11, he is much more favorable than he is in 1 Thessalonians 2:14-16. This has led some to suggest that a later, likely non-Jewish, author inserted these words, though there is no clear manuscript evidence for this. Others note that even if Paul did pen them, in his later more mature writings like Romans he speaks in a more loving way about his own people, the Jews.

The Rapture

First Thessalonians is famous for its "rapture" paragraph. Our word "rapture" comes from a word that means "caught up" in 1 Thessalonians 4:17. It is the same word that Paul uses in 2 Corinthians 12 while describing "someone" who was "caught up to the third heaven." This paragraph uses words for "coming" (*parousia*), "appearance" (*epiphaneia*), and "meeting" (*apantēsis*) that were used for official visits that emperors and other leaders made to Mediterranean cities. These words from the standard protocol for political visits indicate that Paul was not describing a scene in which people are raptured up and disappear. Rather, just as a city's citizens would come out of their cities to meet a visiting dignitary and accompany him back into their city, Paul is predicting believers will ascend to meet Christ and then accompany Christ down to earth, where Christ will hold court as judge and king. The purpose of 4:13-18 is to give hope to believers who are grieving over their loved ones who have died. Unlike popular portrayals today, it is not attempting to communicate exactly when Christ will return, or precisely what that event will look like.

Christ vs. Roman Emperor

Early in 1 Thessalonians 5, Paul uses the slogan "peace and security," a phrase used by Roman propaganda to package Rome's rule over conquered peoples. First Thessalonians 5:3 is a clear prediction of judgment on those who put their hope in the Roman Empire. It may be that Paul is speaking words of judgment against the temple that was built in Thessalonica during the reign of Augustus for the imperial household. The persecution mentioned in 2:14 may have come from church members' reluctance to worship the Roman emperor in this structure. The final blessing that invokes the "God of peace" to preserve people at the coming of Jesus is also an insistent statement that Christians' loyalty belongs to Christ and not to the Roman Empire and the peace, or *pax Romana*, it claimed its emperor bestowed (5:23).

Concluding Reflections

First Thessalonians provides basic instructions to new believers in Jesus, probably Gentiles who were formerly polytheistic and ready to worship the Roman emperor when asked. The letter challenges them to take on an entirely different worldview, worshiping the God of Israel and waiting for Jesus, his Son, to return and set things right on earth.

2 THESSALONIANS

Introduction and Overview

Though its authorship is disputed, if authentic, this letter seems to have been written just a month or two after Paul wrote 1 Thessalonians, in order to correct a misunderstanding about "the day of the Lord," a term found in that earlier letter concerning Jesus' return.

Controversies and Debates

Many scholars believe that this letter is pseudonymous, that is, forged in Paul's name by someone else. It is similar in style to, and overlaps in content with, 1 Thessalonians; and it is easy to imagine someone writing this letter to clear up a misunderstanding. But arguments against Paul's authorship are not conclusive for this letter. While its similarities to 1 Thessalonians could reveal an attempt to imitate that letter, and thus suggest it is a forgery, it seems likely that if we only possessed the second letter without the first, few would question whether Paul wrote it.

Day of the Lord

Paul's paragraph in his first letter to the Thessalonians on Jesus' coming (4:13-18) apparently sparked misunderstanding, just as there is still speculation and disagreement among Christians today on the timing of Jesus' return. Second Thessalonians 2:1-12 attempts to dispel a rumor that the "day of the Lord" has already occurred. The phrase "day of the Lord" is a term Paul or one of his associates is adapting from the Old Testament and applying to

Jesus' return to earth as judge. He says that this day will not happen until an "apostasy" occurs and the "lawless one" publicly appears (2 Thessalonians 2:3). He then explains that after this Christ will come to judge this lawless leader (2:8). If there will be a period of tribulation, such as a popular book and movie series called Left Behind envisions, then it seems it will precede Christ's coming. In such thinking, believers will have to live through a period of testing and trial on earth, as the book of Revelation describes.

Work within Community

Second Thessalonians also returns to an issue 1 Thessalonians only briefly touches upon, the responsibility of all church members to work. In 1 Thessalonians 4:11-12, Paul instructed church members to work so that they did not need others to support them. Paul had shown them this by his own example, as he took pains to describe in 1 Thessalonians 2:9. Paul probably worked as a tentmaker, so that he did not have to ask for money from the Thessalonians when he was staying in their town and planting a church there. So now in 2 Thessalonians 3:7-12, the author reminds the readers again of this example and then tells them that if anyone in the church does not want to work, that person should not be given a share of the community's food. It is possible that some church members mistakenly thought that Christ was going to come back very soon, so soon that they thought they did not need to work. The author thus also corrects this misunderstanding and challenges them to work, to do their share in providing for what they themselves need for daily life. Yes, Christians are to share with others, but they are also asked to carry their weight, as Paul wrote years later to the Galatians (Galatians 6:2-5).

Concluding Reflections

Second Thessalonians opens a window onto how Paul's letters could be misunderstood. Its attempt to correct a misunderstanding of 1 Thessalonians has been valued by Christian readers as a clarification regarding the return of Christ and clear teaching regarding life within Christian communities.

1 TIMOTHY, 2 TIMOTHY, AND TITUS

Introduction and Overview

First Timothy, 2 Timothy, and Titus are together called the "Pastoral Epistles" or "Pastoral Letters" because in them Paul writes to individuals who are pastors (Timothy and Titus), leaders of Christian people, about how to fulfill the role of pastor in a church. First Timothy identifies Timothy, its addressee, as the pastor of the church in Ephesus, and the letter of Titus identifies its addressee, Titus, as the pastor on the island of Crete. Both of these letters provide descriptions of specific offices in a local church: bishop (or overseer); deacon (a word that means "servant"); presbyter (or elder); and widow. All three of the Pastoral Letters contain certain sayings that seem to be benchmarks or creeds that the pastors are to teach to their congregations. The letters present themselves as the last compositions of Paul before his martyrdom.

Controversies and Debates

Some scholars have raised serious questions about whether Paul himself wrote these letters, because they seem to reflect a later time when churches were more organized. Thus the Pastoral Letters say a lot about church "offices," or specific positions of leadership or service within the church, while the undisputed letters of Paul, like Galatians or 1 Corinthians, say nothing about these offices and seem to reflect a less organized church structure.

A second controversy concerns the prohibition on women teaching or exercising authority over men (1 Timothy 2:11-15). Those who think that Paul did not write 1 Timothy regard this viewpoint as coming from a later period

334

when someone sought to consolidate church leadership in the position of one male overseer or bishop. We will discuss this passage in the context of Paul's other writings below.

Trustworthy Sayings and Creeds

The Pastorals are known for the repeated phrase "This saying is trustworthy," one that either introduces or concludes certain policies or benchmark ideas. This phrase and the policies or ideas that accompany it are found in 1 Timothy 1:15; 3:1; 4:7-10; 2 Timothy 2:11-13; and Titus 3:3-8. The last of these seems to be a statement said at baptism, since it describes that rite. This baptismal saying also applies words routinely used for the Roman emperor to God: "When the kindness and generosity of God our savior appeared . . ." The quoted phrase could just as easily be found in a description of the Roman emperor, since the emperor was more openly regarded as "God our savior" in the Mediterranean world of the first century than was the God of Israel. Perhaps this language was an attempt to heap praise on God by using words normally reserved for the emperor, or perhaps the author was delivering a subtle jab at Roman imperial pretensions.

As noted above, the Pastoral Letters introduce guidelines regarding qualifications for church offices. The offices are those of bishops or overseers in 1 Timothy 3:1-7 and Titus 1:7-9, deacons in 1 Timothy 3:8-13, widows in 1 Timothy 5:3-16, and elders in 1 Timothy 5:17-20 and Titus 1:5-6. Many of the qualifications are the same for bishops and deacons. The difference between bishops and deacons seems to be primarily that bishops are supposed to be competent teachers and this qualification is not listed for deacons.

Misogyny or Respect for Innate Differences?

In a way that seems consistent with the discourse on husbands and wives in Ephesians, the author of 1 Timothy says that he does not permit a woman to teach or exercise authority over a man (2:11-15). Because the same Greek word can mean "man" or "husband" and another single Greek word can mean "woman" or "wife," it is possible that the author is talking about a relationship between husband and wife here. The fact that this passage invokes Adam and Eve seems to reinforce this possibility. The author's argument that the husband is in charge because "Adam was formed first, then Eve" (1 Timothy 2:13) is also similar to Paul's argument in 1 Corinthians 11:8—"For man did not come from woman, but woman from man"—that also functions as an argument for a hierarchy in which the husband is understood as being in authority over the wife.

Statements like these are very difficult for many in our culture to accept. But we need to remember that in this same collection of writings—the Pauline Letters—we also have some extraordinarily egalitarian statements as well. For example, shortly after the hierarchical language in 1 Corinthians 11:3-10 in which Paul asks the women in Corinth to respect the surrounding culture and wear a head covering when in church meetings, to show that they are under their husbands' authority, he writes: "Woman is not independent of man or man of woman in the Lord. For just as woman came from man, so man is born of woman; but all things are from God" (1 Corinthians 11:11-12). Here in 1 Timothy, the same author who writes what may sound like a chauvinistic statement to our ears, also asks that any true, older widow be honored, supported by the church if her family cannot support her, and given the independence—and the authority that comes with it—of not being expected to remarry (1 Timothy 5:3-14). And of course Paul is known for his radically egalitarian statement, with respect to ethnicity, class, and gender: "there is neither Jew nor Greek, there is neither slave nor free person, there is not male and female; for you are all one in Christ Jesus" (Galatians 3:28).

In the end, it is best to acknowledge that the New Testament authors have different sensibilities than ours, while recognizing that it is unrealistic to expect perfect consistency. The truth is, most individuals and societies live with many inconsistencies. Thus the Declaration of Independence proclaimed that "all men are created equal" but slavery remained legal for nearly another century in the United States. At a basic level, Paul asks readers to love their neighbors as themselves, and to promote the unity of the church. These central ideas can serve as a foundational guide as readers try to sort out what Paul is saying to their faith communities today.

Persecution

Second Timothy 3 contains the idea that following Christ will inevitably bring suffering—"All who want to live religiously in Christ Jesus will be persecuted" (2 Timothy 3:12). In the context of the many Christians who have been martyred over the course of Western history, this text rings true. The ending of 2 Timothy makes it sound like the author, presumed to be Paul, realizes that he is about to be martyred soon. Later in this textbook we will examine how the experience of suffering imprisonment or death because of one's identification with Jesus is considered and evaluated, in particular when we look at 1 Peter and Revelation, books preoccupied with this aspect of religious identity.

Concluding Reflections

The Pastoral Epistles give us a portrait of an imprisoned Paul, near the end of his life, giving advice to two pastors, Timothy and Titus. If we accept these books as written by Paul, they represent the last letters he wrote. In our New Testaments, however, the letter of Philemon is placed after the Pastorals, probably because it is the shortest of Paul's letters within a collection that is arranged from longest to shortest. We have already studied Philemon alongside the letter that was sent with it, Colossians.

So this is our farewell to the Apostle Paul and the books associated with him. Tradition tells us that Paul was beheaded along the Ostian Way outside the ancient city of Rome at about the same time that Peter was martyred (Eusebius, *Ecclesiastical History* 2.25.7-8). One extrabiblical account says that when the Roman soldier's sword severed Paul's head, milk spurted out of his beheaded body on to the executioner (*Acts of Paul* 11:5). Though probably not true, this is congruent with the Christian idea that Paul's teachings provide both milk and solid food to those readers who take and read his letters seriously (1 Corinthians 3:2).

HEBREWS

Introduction and Overview

Hebrews reads like a sermon designed to motivate its audience to hold on to Jesus as the final and foremost representative of the God of Israel. Jesus is thus shown to be greater than the angels (1:3–2:18), greater than Moses (3:1-6), and a better priest than priests from the line of Aaron who ministered in the tabernacle and later in the Jerusalem temple (4:14–5:10; 9:11–10:18). He is a better priest because he is God's Son who entered God's very presence with his own blood as a sacrificial offering, allowing him to inaugurate a new and better covenant than the Mosaic covenant (8:1-13). Jesus is applauded as the architect and chief example of faith, showing what it means to be faithfully obedient to God the Father (12:1-3). Overall, the letter encourages its readers, who have undergone some persecution, to follow Jesus and keep meeting with other followers of Jesus, rather than returning to a Christ-less observance of Mosaic law.

Interestingly, Hebrews is written in polished, literary Greek, which in many ways stands out from the more common, everyday Greek used in most of the New Testament. Its opening sentence includes alliteration on the letter π as found also in the opening sentence of Homer's *Odyssey*. Clearly, it is attempting to be an ambitious, epic sermon.

Controversies and Debates

For centuries the letter of Hebrews was included within the collection of Paul's letters. The astute reader of the New Testament will notice that it still follows the Pauline collection in most Bibles. Beginning in the sixteenth century, both Catholic and Protestant students of the New Testament began to view the letter as not written by Paul. The reasons for this are: it nowhere claims to be written by Paul, unlike the letters of Romans through Philemon in our New Testament; its literary style is clearly different from Paul's; and in Hebrews 2:3, the author locates himself (or herself—some have suggested that Priscilla was its author) a generation after the apostles. It would be very uncharacteristic for Paul not to sign his name and, as someone who insists that he is an apostle who saw the risen Jesus and received a commission directly from him, to write that the gospel was "confirmed to us by those who heard," as we find in Hebrews 2:3. Earlier in this book, we discussed that a criterion for New Testament canonicity was *apostolicity*, that is, being written by an apostle or someone closely associated to one. Many believe that attaching Hebrews to Paul's letters was important for just this reason. A significant and understandable motive behind some people's continued insistence that this letter is indeed written by Paul is the desire to keep the letter central or authoritative, something potentially at risk if the author is unknown.

Can Salvation Be Forfeited?

Hebrews 6:4-8 seems to indicate that previously baptized Christians who fall away from their faith can lose their salvation. This paragraph says that it is impossible for these people to come once more to repentance, a view that seems to be in accord with what Paul suggests in 1 Corinthians 9:24-27. Modern Christian ideas that a person cannot fall away from faith, often referred to as "eternal security" or "perseverance of the saints," are sometimes linked to Augustine but in fact are really a newer development brought about by Protestant Reformers like Calvin. Though Augustine taught that the elect would persevere and be saved, he taught a much more modest form of this idea and allowed for the possibility that those whom God had justified might not reach salvation. The "once saved, always saved" idea prevalent in some circles of North American Christianity is largely derived from Calvin's recharacterizing of salvation as an unconditional gift which could not be lost. Hebrews 6:4-8 thus poses a significant challenge to those who say that they are certain they will attain salvation.

Supersessionism

One of the major themes of Hebrews is its many explicit statements that Christianity has superseded and thus displaced previous forms of Judaism. In its desire to show Jesus to be a better priest than the priests from the line of Aaron, Hebrews says that Jesus ministers a new covenant, better than the covenant Moses transmitted to Israel at Mount Sinai. This leads to the author's radical claims that the Mosaic covenant is old and about to disappear (8:13) and that, contrary to what the Torah teaches, it never effectively dealt with sin (10:1-4). The argument typically moves in the following way: Jesus is greater than various persons from Israel's past; if those who disobeyed Moses or sacrificed in the temple in Jerusalem got punished for their sins, those who disobey Jesus, who is a higher messenger of God who effected atonement for sins in the true temple in heaven, will get punished much more. These claims and the repeated argument must be read, as we saw with Galatians, in light of their rhetorical moment. This letter is trying to keep people from converting or reverting to a Torah observant form of Judaism, and thus uses hyperbole to denigrate Judaism (Hebrews 12:18-29). This type of supersessionism is interesting in that it shows how early Christians use Old Testament themes and ideas to highlight the special status of Jesus, but by doing so they often suggest that the Old Testament has now served its purpose and its laws and rituals are now irrelevant.

The Great Cloud of Witnesses

Chapter 11 contains a lengthy recital of various well-known Old Testament characters. However, this chapter is not a "hall of fame of faith," as some Bibles' headings suggest. In fact, some of those it lists as examples of faith are depicted in the Old Testament as displaying questionable behaviors and even lacking what we understand as faith. For example, Hebrews makes mention of Sarah as a great figure from the past, but Genesis 18 depicts her as receiving a rebuke from God for openly doubting God's ability to overcome her infertility very late in life. Similarly, Moses is described in Hebrews as leaving Egypt while not fearing the wrath of the Egyptian king, but Exodus 2 reports that he first left Egypt precisely because of this. Isaac is depicted as intentionally blessing Jacob over Esau in an act of faith, when Genesis is clear that he was tricked. Gideon and Samson are likewise highlighted as heroes of faith, characters who are hardly exemplary in the narratives about them in Judges. We see that Hebrews 11 contains a list of people who are sometimes heroic but sometimes doubting, all of whom God helped. These less-than-perfect characters remind us therefore that God will help people despite their shortcomings. Also, equally important is that the author of Hebrews views faith as something more than mere intellectual assent, believing in God, or maintaining perfect behavior. Though the people listed in chapter 11 differ among themselves in the degree to which they can be called faithful, what is clear is that at the climactic end of this list, Jesus is singled out as the ultimate example of faithful living (12:1-11).

Concluding Reflections

"Those from Italy greet you," we read near the very end of this letter. This epic sermon, which is often analyzed in light of its Old Testament quotations to be exclusively Jewish in background, is also responding to the Roman world in which it was written. In the last chapter as well we read "Here we have no lasting city, but we seek a city that is to come" (13:14). The phrase would have undoubtedly caught the notice of its first-century readers, since Rome was the eternal, or lasting city, according to the *Aeneid* and other Roman propaganda. This leads us to observe that three traits of Jesus that are specially emphasized in Hebrews are also traits of Aeneas as portrayed by the famous Roman poet Virgil: Both Jesus and Aeneas are obedient sons, both function as priests for their people, and both lead their followers to a divinely founded city. This implicit critique of Roman propaganda provides some context for the supersessionism of Hebrews. Yes, Hebrews is out to rewrite the master story of Judaism—to tell the story of a messiah who eclipses the priests in Jerusalem and serves in a greater temple in heaven, rather than on earth. But at the same time, the author's account of Jesus represents a supersessionist rereading of Rome's master story. The true hero is Jesus, not Aeneas, according to this author.

As a polished sermon focused on what Jesus has done for humanity, this letter has been valued by Christians for two millennia. The letter challenges its readers to relate the narratives by which they orient their lives—whether the Jewish Scriptures or the master story of Rome—to Jesus, faithful son of God.

INTRODUCTION TO THE GENERAL LETTERS

The seven letters from James through Jude have traditionally been called the catholic or general letters. The adjective *catholic* (with a small *c*) here means "universal" or "general," in that these letters seem to have been addressed to a universal audience, rather than to a single church as most of Paul's letters were. Yet this title for all seven general letters is not entirely unproblematic, for the letters 2 and 3 John seem to have been addressed to specific churches.

The title for these letters comes from a time when Hebrews was regarded by many as written by Paul. It therefore offered a shorthand way for New Testament readers to identify the two letter collections included in the New Testament: Paul's letters (including Hebrews, once considered Pauline) and the general letters, written by different authors, to Christians throughout the Mediterranean or at least throughout Asia Minor (for example, see James 1:1 and 1 Peter 1:1).

Since most of them are not addressed to single churches or persons as Paul's letters are, these are named for their authors, rather than their addressees. The addressees of James and 1 Peter are described in these letters' opening greetings as being the twelve tribes scattered abroad in the diaspora. These letters seem to use this diasporic greeting to refer to Jesus followers living throughout the Mediterranean world who are temporarily exiled from life in heaven while in this world, rather than referring to those actually exiled from the land of Israel.

Greeting the followers of Jesus throughout the Mediterranean world, whatever ethnicity they happen to be, as "the twelve tribes" or "exiles of the diaspora" is not incidental. It is a surface indicator of a deeper change from the way Jews read their Scriptures. These books read the Jewish Scriptures as though they are directed to Gentile Christians (1 Peter 2:9-10) and they use Israel's stories as though they are these Gentiles' family history (James 2:21-25; 2 Peter 2:6-8). Such reading is amply attested in Paul's letters but the general letters take for granted what Paul self-consciously explains: Israel's story is the church's story.

While James and 1 Peter might have been composed by the early 60s, just after Paul's letters, the other general letters may have been written a decade or two later. As a whole, this collection shows that its authors are concerned about three main challenges to Christian communities: false teachers, persecution by governmental authorities, and the delay of Jesus' *parousia*, or return. Since these concerns are also addressed in the book of Revelation, these general letters provide a useful introduction both to the problems churches faced in the latter third of the first century and to the New Testament's final book.

JAMES

Introduction and Overview

The Letter of James has a strongly positive view of Mosaic law and good works. For those who have grown up reading Paul's letters as suggesting that the Torah's laws are now obsolete, or doing good works does not matter at all for Christians, James may be jarring. As the New Testament book that is the closest to Wisdom literature, James is difficult to outline and summarize in the same way that Proverbs is. Its themes of seeking God for heavenly wisdom, being very careful in one's speech, and being humble before God are all reminiscent of (and congruent with) the wisdom tradition of the Old Testament.

Tradition identifies the author of this letter as James the "brother" or relative of Jesus, respected for his Torah observance and prayerfulness, who died tragically in Jerusalem in the mid-60s. This James is perhaps also the one who has the last word in the Jerusalem council described in Acts 15.

Controversies and Debates

The most controversial aspects of James are its teaching on the Torah and its insistence on works as a necessary part of following God. Both of these aspects contribute to a controversy regarding the extent to which this letter challenges, contradicts, or merely supplements Paul's teaching that Gentiles are justified by faith, apart from works of the law. In what follows, we explore some of the issues related to this debate.

James 2:8 calls the Mosaic law the "royal law." James 2:12 calls it the "law of freedom." In this sense James seems much closer to the traditional Jewish view that the law is a life-promoting set of instructions, mediating a fulfilling relationship with God. These portraits of the Torah in James are very different from the problematic Torah of Romans 7, one that cannot help a person to live well. As we shall see, James differs from Paul on the Torah in other ways as well.

James quotes Genesis 15:6, an Old Testament verse that the Apostle Paul repeatedly quotes, but he uses it quite differently than Paul (compare Romans 4:1-24 and Galatians 3:6-14 with James 2:14-26). James uses the passage in conjunction with the story of Abraham's life to argue that the belief Abraham placed in God clearly showed itself in Abraham's *obedience* to God's commands, rather than faith alone. Paul's rather negative view of "works of the law" may stem from the fact that he was trying to convince a Gentile audience that they need not observe the full array of the Torah's laws, especially those related to Sabbath, food, and circumcision, to be right with God. By contrast, James seems to have a more positive appreciation of "works" and even of the more controversial idea of "works of the law." One key difference between Paul and James is that James is much more explicit about Abraham's active obedience in his willingness to sacrifice Isaac (James 2:21-23).

Using the Phrase "God Willing"

James 4:13-16 seems to explain Proverbs 27:1, which warns of boasting about future outcomes. In doing so, it seeks to teach readers how to talk about the future in ways that please God. The "God willing" one hears some Christians say when they talk about the future may well come from this section of James, although traditional Jews and Muslims speak similarly, suggesting that this practice may be a general religious habit.

The Sermon on Mount Packaged as Wisdom Literature

As Wisdom literature, James does not have a running argument that continues through the whole letter. Rather, it involves short maxims, sayings, or short paragraphs that cover wise living. Though James only mentions Jesus by name twice (1:1 and 2:1), the author's wisdom orientation has quietly adopted much from Jesus' Sermon on the Mount in Matthew chapters 5–7. Rejoicing in trials (Matthew 5:10-12; James 1:2), doing and not merely hearing God's word (Matthew 7:24-27; James 1:22), and the necessity of showing mercy (Matthew 5:7; James 2:13) are just a few of the many places where James seems to track with or directly draw upon the Sermon on the Mount.

Despite lacking a running argument, finding and gaining wisdom clearly stands at the heart of the book. Notice how wisdom is offered as freely available to those who seek it from God at the very beginning of the book (1:5-7). At the end of chapter 3, James emphasizes the value of wisdom from above in contrast to the wisdom from below that readers should avoid. Here, as in the Wisdom literature of the Old Testament, there is a moral dimension to wisdom that is sometimes missing in how the word is used today.

James 3:1-12 is a meditation on the significance of speech and the power of the tongue. This is a standard and crucial topic within Wisdom literature. James 4:11-12 counsels people not to speak evil of their "brother" or neighbor. James 5:12 again returns to speech, this time telling people not to take oaths, but to be so honest that there is no need to swear by something else. The prohibition against oath-taking may come from this letter's dependence on the Sermon on the Mount or an earlier version of that sermon (see Matthew 5:33-37). But it also fits with the emphasis in Wisdom literature inasmuch as Ecclesiastes 5 expresses a similar concern over rash oaths.

Anointing the Sick

Many Catholics and Protestants anoint sick people with oil when praying for God to heal them, a practice mentioned in James 5:14-15. Those who have observed little vials of oil in front of a Protestant church, or those who have been to a traditional Christian "Blessing of the Oils" service that are then used for the anointing of the sick, are witnesses to the importance of this passage in the life of the church.

Concluding Reflections

Though not a running argument as we saw in the book of Hebrews, James offers much food for thought and many guidelines for living in accord with God's will. The letter indicates that if readers follow its teachings, they will imitate "Christ Jesus, who became for us wisdom from God" (1 Corinthians 1:30).

1 PETER

Introduction and Overview

This letter encourages Christians to remain faithful when they find themselves in trouble with or persecuted by a government for following Jesus. It is said to be written by Peter, likely from Rome and is addressed to believers called "the chosen sojourners of the dispersion," literally "diaspora," here referring to Christians scattered throughout the Roman provinces in what is today modern day Turkey.

The greeting in this letter is unique in its call to believers for "obedience and sprinkling of the blood of Jesus Christ," probably indicating that the author wants his audience to stay obedient to Jesus even when the government that killed Jesus—the Roman Empire—is threatening them (1:2 AT). After a blessing, the author immediately turns to the "testing of your faith, more valuable than gold that is tested by fire" (1:7). In every chapter of this letter, reference is made to actual suffering that Christians are experiencing. The author repeatedly returns to the idea of being faithful while suffering with Christ. The term "obedience" that we noted above seems to be key for the whole letter. Besides obedience to the truth that leads to loving others (1:22), this letter asks its audience to obey government (2:13-17), slaves to obey their masters (2:18-25), and wives to obey their husbands (3:1-6). Chapters 4 and 5 continue to remind readers that since Christ remained obedient to God even through suffering, they should keep following God by imitating Christ.

Controversies and Debates

The most controversial idea in this letter is that those who are following Jesus are somehow a continuation of Israel. Thus, the term *diaspora* regularly used of Jews living outside Israel is here applied to the letter's Christian audience, as are special descriptions of the Israelites (see 2:9-10; compare with Exodus 19:4-6 and Hosea 1:10; 2:23). However, the anti-Judaic rhetoric of the Gospel of John is missing here. And based on the repeated concern with obeying God in a stressful time of persecution, it is likely that the move in 1 Peter to link the early church to the people of Israel is motivated more by a need to ground its vulnerable Christian audience in a common story than it is to displace or exclude Jews.

The Fiery Trial in Rome

The phrases "tested by fire" and "fiery trial" in this letter are noteworthy, especially since Christians were blamed for a major fire in Rome in 64 CE (1:7; 4:12). The Roman historian Tacitus tells us that Nero tried to shift the blame for the fire off himself and onto the Christians. Though Tacitus is clear that Christians didn't start the fire, he still regards them as following a depraved superstition and doesn't seem too bothered when describing the creative and gruesome ways by which Nero apparently put them to death. Since there is no compelling reason to date 1 Peter much after 64, it is best to view this letter as composed shortly after Nero began executing Christians around that time. It is also possible that the image of the roaring lion in this letter would have evoked the scenario in which Christians were executed by being thrown to the wild animals in public spectacles held in locations such as the Coliseum in Rome (5:8).

Obedience to Government

First Peter 2:13-17 contains the most straightforward call for obedience to government that we find in the New Testament. First Peter as a whole calls Christians to obey God by following Christ, even to death. This passage on obeying government is therefore not a call for readers to abandon or hide their Christian identity when the government asks them to do so. Rather it serves as an encouragement to be upstanding citizens even though public opinion might be against them.

Wives and Husbands

As with Paul's letters, it may be difficult for readers today to accept that wives are to submit to their husbands as 1 Peter 3:1 suggests. When compared to Jewish or Greek cultures, Roman culture allowed women more independence. The author of 1 Peter thinks that in the case of wives whose husbands are not believers, these wives should live quietly and chastely in their homes, since this will move their husbands toward the faith. The counsel on adornment and hairstyles seems to be culturally linked to the practices of those in the Roman Empire at the time. Coins from around this period show Nero's second wife, Poppaea Sabina, with a single braid in her hair. Our author, likely wanting Christian wives to be more modest than Roman women like Poppaea, prohibits the braid as a result (3:3).

Figure 30. Like the hairstyles and clothing of First Ladies today, the hairstyles of emperors and their wives were closely watched by those living throughout the Roman Empire. The obverse side (right image above) of this coin from 63/4 CE Syrian Antioch, pictures Poppaea Sabina with braided hair. Courtesy Roma Numismatics Limited. www.RomaNumismatics.com.

The "Harrowing of Hell"

First Peter 3:18-20 and 4:6 are the source of our understanding of the so-called harrowing of hell. After his crucifixion, Jesus visited the dead and proclaimed his victory over sin and death to them. This notion is not only affirmed in the Apostles' Creed, but is widely found in the many artistic depictions of Christ storming hell or leading people out of Hades. In the imagery from an illuminated manuscript on the next page, one can see Christ, triumphant over the demons and rescuing people from the devil's mouth.

Suffering with Christ

When Christians are persecuted or executed for their faith, as some around the world still in fact experience, they might be said to "suffer *for* Christ." But 1 Peter takes special care to point out that Christ had to suffer here on

Figure 31. The harrowing of hell was a popular theme for religious art and drama in the middle ages. In the painting depicted above, the artist relies on language found in Psalm 69:14-15 to depict Christ rescuing people out of the devil's mouth. Courtesy The Walters Art Museum.

earth; and when Christians suffer, they are seen to be suffering *with* him, or in the pattern that he has provided (1 Peter 2:21; 3:17-18). This may be Peter's variation on Paul's description of Christian existence as "carrying in the body" the dying of Christ (see 2 Corinthians 4:8-10).

Conclusion

For its repeated calls to expect opposition and persecution, 1 Peter is the New Testament letter most focused on faithfulness to Christ through suffering. For some Christian readers in the West, the social situation behind this letter seems very distant. Yet all can relate to the difficulty of being true to one's religious convictions in the face of opposition or contrary expectations from a government or wider secular culture. First Peter repeatedly calls believers to follow Christ through trials on earth into a life with Christ that continues beyond death.

2 PETER AND JUDE

Introduction and Overview

Because they share some of the same material and 2 Peter seems to be literarily dependent on Jude, we consider these two books together in this chapter. Second Peter opens with a testament in which the author, said to be the Apostle Peter and near death, reminds his audience of the reliability of what he has taught them. The second chapter is a warning against false teachers and is probably adapted from the Letter of Jude. Second Peter closes with a response to those who no longer looked for Jesus to return.

Controversies and Debates

From very early on some church fathers questioned whether 2 Peter was really written by Peter. Thus its passage into the canon proceeded by fits and starts rather than by unanimous consensus. This is not entirely typical of New Testament letters; and so these early discussions on its authenticity are quite important and interesting. In the end, however, the letter was accepted by a critical mass of church fathers as being authored by Peter and so was included in the canon. Most scholars today regard it to be a pseudonymous work, that is, written by someone else after Peter's death but in his name, because the author protests too much that he really is Peter (1:16-18). Furthermore, the reference to Paul's letters at the end of 2 Peter likely indicates composition well after the 60s, when Peter and Paul were martyred.

A second controversy concerns the precise relationship between 2 Peter and Jude. Similar expressions are used for the false teachers in both texts and the author (or authors) uses the same illustrations to make his points,

352

drawn from the Hebrew Bible or corporate memory (evil angels, Sodom and Gomorrah, Balaam). The controversy around these things relates to who is dependent on whom (or whether they both drew from a common source). Since in general literary works tend to grow rather than shrink over time, it is probable that the author of 2 Peter used Jude as part of a longer composition and cleaned it up by removing two extrabiblical references and clarifying Jude's quotation of an angel's rebuke to Satan.

A Testament: 2 Peter 1

The author begins by testifying that as long as he is in his physical body, which he knows he will leave soon, he will continue to remind his audience about God's call to Christians to live upright lives. In 1:16-21, there is a clear reference to Peter's experience on the Mount of Transfiguration (see "Christian Use of Exodus" for more on this scene), followed by an affirmation that "the prophetic message" as well as scriptural prophecies he brings are reliable since they come from God's Spirit. Overall, 2 Peter is concerned to present the tradition it is passing on as reliable as opposed to the example and teaching of the unreliable false teachers, who state that Jesus will not return (chapters 2–3).

Warnings against False Teachers: 2 Peter 2 and Jude

Both 2 Peter 2 and Jude target "false prophets/teachers" or "intruders"; mention evil angels, Sodom and Gomorrah, Balaam; and describe sensual sins. To put this in the language of 2 Peter, these are people "who follow the flesh with its depraved desire" (2 Peter 2:10). But Jude is unique in comparison with 2 Peter and the rest of the New Testament for its quotations from extrabiblical literature. Jude 9 summarizes a story of Michael the archangel arguing with the devil over the body of Moses, a story that likely comes from a book called *The Assumption of Moses*. Jude also includes a quotation from the book of *1 Enoch*. While this latter book is part of the Old Testament in the Coptic Church, it is not included in Western Christianity's Scripture in either its Catholic or Protestant canons. Enoch's prophecy of judgment is quoted here to support Jude's message that the "godless sinners" will be judged and do not deserve a hearing. These types of references demonstrate that certain books no longer found in our Bible today were at one time treated as sacred Scripture.

Greek Matters: The Delay of the *Parousia*: 2 Peter 3

The final chapter of 2 Peter adds a discussion about the delay of Christ's return, or what is sometimes called the *parousia*, a Greek word meaning "physical presence" or "arrival." The sense is that the false teachers have said that the *parousia* of Christ will not happen, since there has been such a delay. The text counters this by saying that God's timetable is different from ours—"with the Lord one day is like a thousand years and a thousand years like one day" (2 Peter 3:8). Readers are therefore challenged to remain ready for Christ's return, living holy lives (2 Peter 3:11). Note that here, as in James and 1 Thessalonians, the return of Christ is pictured as a day of judgment (2 Peter 3:10), unlike many Christians' assumptions that it will be pure joy.

Paul's Collected Letters

Second Peter 3:14-16 is the only place in the New Testament where the letters of Paul are recognized as a collection known to readers. The phrase "all his letters" in reference to Paul shows that this was written by someone who could assume that his audience had a collection or at least knowledge of Paul's letters and that these writings were authoritative. Yet, it is fascinating to see that Paul's letters are described as difficult and the object of distortion. One could say that the later compositions of the New Testament—such as Hebrews, James, and 1–2 Peter—seek to help guide their audiences in how to read Paul's letters.

The Jude Doxology

The final blessing in Jude, or what some call the Jude doxology, contains a widely cited description of God and his sustaining power. The references to God as "savior" and the ascription to God of "glory, majesty, power, and authority from ages past, now, and for ages to come" stands in contrast to typical discourse of the time that dated letters based on the year of an emperor's reign. This deep and rich hymn continues to be used in Christian liturgy and worship services today.

Concluding Reflections

Both 2 Peter and Jude are concerned with false teachers, a common concern among the later books of the New Testament, evident in the letters of John and Revelation as well. In addition, 2 Peter is concerned to provide its audience with a sense of the reliability of the stream of tradition in which its author stands, and to explain the delay of Jesus' return. These matters were especially relevant to the church as it grew and came of age.

THE LETTERS OF JOHN

Introduction and Overview

The short letters of 1–3 John call readers into a community marked by a distinct ideology and lifestyle. The community is composed of people who will declare that Jesus is Son of God and that he actually became human. The lifestyle consists in confessing one's sins while trying to avoid sinning again, loving one's neighbor, and maintaining a separation between the community and the outside world. The following terms are used metaphorically in these letters: life, death, brothers, antichrists, light, darkness, and world. These metaphors allow readers to locate themselves meaningfully within a symbolic universe. Notice that the first six terms may be read as pairs of antonyms or polarities that draw a boundary between the community of believers and those perceived to be outside of it.

Controversies and Debates

The traditional view is that these letters were written by the apostle named John who also wrote the gospel by that name. Scholars influenced by modernity's quest to identify authorship based on internal textual criteria—with no voice given to tradition—suggest that these letters were written by someone other than the author of the gospel, based on minor stylistic differences. With the meager evidence we have, it is difficult to firmly prove either the traditional or the modern critical view.

The Human Nature of Christ

First John shows similarities with the Gospel of John. This letter begins with "What was from the beginning . . ." a clear allusion to "in the beginning

356

was the Word" of John 1:1. While the *gospel* emphasizes first the transcendence of Christ the Word in his existence from eternity past and involvement in creating the world (John 1:1-3), this first *letter* of John emphasizes Christ's immanence with the phrases "what we have heard, what we have seen with our eyes, what we looked upon . . . that was with the Father and was made visible to us—what we have seen and heard we proclaim now to you, . . . " (1 John 1:1-3 AT). This idea of Christ's immanence figures strongly later in this letter, where the confession that Jesus has "come in the flesh," that is, become fully human, is a sign of the Spirit of God's presence in a person (4:2-3; 2 John 7). The author seems to be aware of those early Christians who stated that Jesus was not actually human but only appeared to be so. For the author of these letters, this view, later branded as a heresy, was as grave an error as it would be to say that Jesus is not God's Son.

Tests of Faith

The letter of 1 John is most significant for its tests regarding whether one is truly following Christ. These tests include: walking (= living) in the light; admitting and confessing our sins; loving one's brother or sister; avoiding a lifestyle of sin, but doing righteousness instead; keeping Christ's commandments by loving one another; acknowledging that Jesus was fully human; and believing in the testimony of God about the Son.

A Command Both Old and New

First and 2 John are significant for the way they play off "old" and "new" in describing the love commandment (see especially 1 John 2:7-8 and 2 John 4-6). The strategy of labeling ideas and behaviors as "old" or "new" and playing them against one another is something the New Testament has inherited from the prophets of the Jewish Scriptures. This old vs. new strategy helps Christian readers make sense of their two-part canon by highlighting the continuities that the teachings of Jesus have with the story of Israel as found in the Jewish Scriptures as well as by pointing to the new developments of these teachings within the New Testament.

Guard the Community

First John 2:18-19 and 2 John 7-8 indicate that some people, whom this letter calls "antichrists," have left the community in question. John addresses those who have remained to encourage them to stay in the community by walking in the truth. The letters suggest that leaving the community means leaving Christ. These letters thus offer a scenario different from the individual Antichrist—a term most translations capitalize—the character who comes into view in texts such as Revelation 13. First John 2:18 is emphatic that there are a number of antichrists, and 2 John continues this emphasis. Here the antichrists are in the world, which in 1–3 John is diametrically opposed to the believing community. In this very polarized view, a person can either live in the believing community or in the world, but not in both. In this regard, 1 John is similar to the book of Revelation, which sets Babylon against the followers of the lamb, with nothing in between (1 John 5:19; Revelation 18:4-10). In the metaphors of 1 John, the community is the place of light, while the rest of the world is in darkness.

Unsurprisingly, 2 John is thus especially concerned with maintaining the community's boundaries. It is addressed to "the chosen Lady and her children," a family metaphor that surely fosters the community's cohesion. Besides the warning against antichrists already mentioned, this letter prohibits extending a communal welcome to anyone who does not truly believe that Christ came as a human being.

Third John, similar in length to 2 John (that is, short), further develops the idea of showing love toward others featured earlier in 1 John 3:17-18. The letter insists that its addressees show hospitality to traveling Christian workers, an idea that we find in other early Christian literature (Hebrews 13:2; *Didache* 11:3–13:7).

Concluding Reflections

These three letters' emphasis on living in a community of distinct ideology and lifestyle presuppose the necessity for community in order to live out the New Testament's call to imitate Christ. The world may be against those in the community, but they are called to love one another and faithfully follow Christ, who lived as a fellow human, then died and rose for the world.

REVELATION

Introduction and Overview

The opening verses of the book state that it is a revelation of Jesus Christ as well as a prophecy concerning events that will occur soon. The book of Revelation (there is no "s" on the end of the title as many assume) is an apocalypse, a book arising out of a stressful state of affairs in which the writer's situation seems hopeless from a human perspective. Apocalyptic literature usually contains some of the following characteristics: rewritten history, a deterministic view of the world, strong moral dualism, predictions of supernatural intervention, guided tours of heaven, and divine deliverance after the shaking of the earth's foundations.

The context of the book is the persecution that its author and other Christians throughout the Mediterranean world were experiencing. John, the author of the book, is exiled on an island called Patmos, likely as a result of his religious activities. Based on what we read in two of the seven "letters" in the first vision of the book (2:10, 13), his description of martyrs asking for God to avenge their deaths (6:9-11), and his pictures of those who reach heavenly bliss (19:6-8; 20:4-6), it is clear that the implied audience of this text is also facing persecution for their worship of Jesus instead of revering an earthly governmental authority. The thesis of the book is that Jesus, the Word of God, will ultimately vindicate all who consistently witness that he is above all human authorities.

There are four visions presented in this book, introduced by the phrase "I was in the Spirit" accompanied by verbs for seeing and hearing. Vision one contains the first portrait of Jesus, followed by letters to seven churches (1:10–3:22). Vision two describes the church both in heavenly bliss and in the throes of a struggle against a malicious government on earth (4:1–16:20).

359

Vision three describes Christ as a warrior called the Word of God who defeats the malicious government (17:1–20:15). Vision four describes a final rest in a new Jerusalem located on a new earth (21:1–22:17).

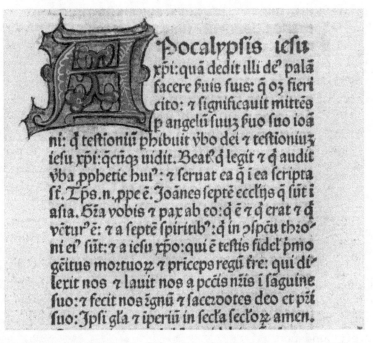

Figure 32. Ornate text of the beginning of Revelation. *Biblia latina.* **Venice: Jenson, 1476. Courtesy Smith College Libraries.**

Controversies and Debates

A central controversy surrounding this book turns on how to read it. There are three main possibilities. Should we read it as (1) a prediction of events still in our future; (2) as a warning of what could happen to followers of Jesus in the late first and second centuries if the Roman Empire continues its course of aggressive domination; or (3) as a meditation on what the Jewish Scriptures have to say for Christians who are oppressed by a pagan government? We will see that since aspects of the book include all three of these functions, it is best to keep all of these reading strategies in mind.

The authorship of Revelation is also debated. Many scholars doubt that the "John" who wrote this is the apostle associated with the Fourth Gospel. Some suggest that it is another John, or perhaps someone writing in his name. But there are no significant data to confirm or falsify such hypotheses.

The Seven Churches

The first vision, found in 1:10 through 3:22, is the message of Christ to the seven churches. The vision begins with a picture of Christ as a warrior, drawn from Old Testament imagery in Daniel and Isaiah. This vision emphasizes Christ's passage through death and back to life, leading to his power over death and Hades and his authority over the seven churches to whom he will give messages. It is noteworthy that the first vision begins with a picture of Christ, helping the reader see that the opening words of the whole book, "The revelation of Jesus Christ," indicate first that the book seeks to provide significant portraits of Jesus, rather than simply provide pictures of "what must soon take place" (1:1). These seven churches are located in seven prominent cities in the first century Mediterranean world, likely placed in the order of a common travel route of the day.

Lamb, Martyrs, Beast

The second vision begins with scenes of heaven, where Jesus is pictured as a slain lamb (5:6, 9, 12). Both the picture of Christ as the divine and powerful "son of man" from Daniel 7:13 that we find in the first vision (1:13-16) and now the picture of Christ as the slain lamb in the second vision are meant to encourage readers to stay true to Christ no matter the penalty that governments might impose upon them. And later in this vision, if one links "the slain lamb" with the immediately following phrase "from the foundation of the world," there is the sense that Christ's death was in God's plan from eternity past (13:8). The picture of Christ as ideal and vindicated martyr encourages the reader to view his or her sufferings for Christ as also part of a plan from long ago, thus motivating the Christ-follower to persevere.

The question "how long" posed in Revelation 6 to God by those who have been martyred drives this part of the book. This question builds on a long tradition reaching back to various lament psalms and the book of Job. The answer, that they must wait for more deaths, might trouble many today. Another answer to their question comes in the description of God's rewards for the elect in heaven (7:9-17). Because the destiny of those who remain faithful to God is ultimately to live with God in heaven and be present in a place where God wipes away every tear (an image drawn from Isaiah 25), those who are being persecuted can and will endure.

In a way that shows how the world is shaken during the time when an evil government rules the whole earth, Revelation uses vivid pictures. Like many Old Testament prophetic texts, one should not read the scenes in each vision in linear fashion, as though they are in consecutive order. Indeed, many scholars think that the description of the trumpets that angels blow in chapters 8–11 are a heaven-centered vision of the same phenomena described in chapter 16 as the seven bowls, now from the perspective of earth.

At the end of the seventh trumpet, there is a description of God's temple in heaven being opened and the ark of God's covenant being visible in the heavenly temple (11:19). There follows a description of a woman who is pregnant with a son "destined to rule all the nations with an iron rod" (12:5). It seems probable that this ruler is Jesus the anointed one, and therefore his mother must be Mary. This, therefore, is the scriptural foundation for the Catholic description of Mary as queen of heaven (12:1).

The Number of the Beast

Revelation chapter 13 is famous for its description of "the beast." Since the first beast is a ruler who has been fatally wounded and yet lives, most scholars think this alludes to Nero, whom some expected to come back from the dead. The beast's number provided in 13:18 is clearly meant to be interpreted, since the verse indicates that one with wisdom can calculate its number. As we learned when considering the number 14 at the end of Jesus' genealogy in Matthew 1, before the introduction of Arabic numerals, Greek and Hebrew languages used their letters also to signify numbers. Scholars of Revelation observe that when the name "Nerōn Caesar" is spelled with Hebrew letters, it totals 666 and thus this beast probably refers to Nero. For the first readers, who did their math with letters, Revelation 13:18 would therefore be read as follows: "Let whoever has wisdom [Let whoever can figure the numerical values of letters] calculate the number of the beast, for it is the number of a man [find a person's name with the numerical value of . . .]"An alternative manuscript of the New Testament reports that the number of the beast is 616, either working with the spelling "Nero Caesar" or else identifying emperor Caligula as the beast, since the numeric value of his name totals 616. It seems highly likely that the "beast" therefore refers to a Roman emperor like Nero, who persecuted Christians, or one like Caligula, who regarded himself as divine.

Revelation processes what is happening on earth by means of the imagery and language of earlier Scriptures. This second vision in particular uses the Old Testament to communicate that times will be more difficult for believers throughout the earth than they were for Israel in the past. It does this by intensifying Old Testament apocalyptic imagery. Thus the little book that John eats is bitter in his stomach and concerns the whole earth, unlike the little scroll that Ezekiel eats which concerns Israel alone (10:8-11; compare Ezekiel 2:8–3:3). And the beast that comes out of the sea is a combination of the four beasts from the sea that Daniel saw, as if the one government threatening God's people in Revelation is a combination of four mighty kingdoms that troubled the earth before (13:1-2; compare Daniel 7:1-7).

The Prostitute and the Warrior

The third vision that begins in chapter 17 equates Babylon with the first-century Roman Empire by subtle allusions such as mentioning that this city is built on seven hills and that it rules the kings of the earth. The prostitute named "Babylon" is described in these chapters as dressed in very expensive fashion, foreshadowing the critique of Rome's economic imperialism in chapter 18. In the tradition of Old Testament prophetic texts like Hosea and Ezekiel, both intercourse with a prostitute and prostituting one's own body are linked to idolatry, since selling one's self for material gain or temporary pleasure means one is worshiping someone besides the God of Israel and thus committing idolatry.

In chapter 19, Christ returns as a warrior to judge the evil kingdoms of the earth. The sword that comes out of his mouth is a biblical image for the power that God's word carries. This scene of Christ's return as a warrior who judges evil rulers on earth begins to answer the martyrs' question posed in Revelation 6:10. When the beast and false prophet are thrown into the sulfur lake, we know that the driving question of unchecked, evil governments on earth is finally being addressed by God. The result is a peaceful time on the earth that lasts for one thousand years, likely a symbolic number indicating a long period of time, the description of which provides the basis for the "thousand year reign of Christ" or "millennium" (one thousand years) affirmed by some Christians.

New Jerusalem, Renewed Eden

The fourth vision spotlights the New Jerusalem, God's answer to the oppressive and evil city of Babylon. Babylon has fallen; its economy has collapsed, and it has been judged by Christ. Now the author signals to us that a new vision is beginning (21:2; "I also saw"). This vision is of a new heaven and new earth. Notice that there is no longer any ocean, or region of chaos, on earth. The city represents a place where God lives with people. The city's twelve gates are named for Israel's tribes; the city's twelve foundations are named for the twelve apostles. The twelve tribes imagery here and elsewhere underlines a central axiom of the New Testament: God's covenant with the Jewish people is the starting point for any discourse about how God relates to Gentiles. Here we again find images of the "old" and "new," such as we saw in 1 John, but now they are used in an apocalyptic description of the community's identity. Now that God is present with his people, there is no longer need for a temple on earth (21:22). Notice also how the imagery of Eden signals that the curse is gone and that there is no chance for humanity to become corrupted again by the knowledge of good and bad, since this tree is not mentioned here. Instead, the tree of life is found on both sides of the river that flows from God's presence. Even for those who think that most of Revelation refers to imperial Rome of the first and second centuries, the material in this fourth vision is to be fulfilled in the future. This last vision is also clearly inspired by Isaiah's picture of Jerusalem as the highest city in the last days, to which all the nations of the world will come when God makes a new heaven and new earth and by the Eden-like images of the future Jerusalem found in Ezekiel 47.

Concluding Reflections

Revelation is an Old Testament–based meditation on the persecution early Christians experienced under the early Roman Empire. Those who read the book as if the beast and its actions refer to a future time often attempt to correlate various world events with the apocalyptic imagery of Revelation. Unfortunately, this type of reading misses the fact that once we recognize that Revelation's immediate concern is Rome, the book actually becomes more, not less, relevant to readers today. The enduring message of Revelation is that God will reward those who remain loyal through persecution, and that in the end God will live with humanity on a renewed earth.

EPILOGUE

As the reader has now gleaned, the New Testament, like the Hebrew Bible, contains contrasting viewpoints and internal tensions. The Gospels offer a variety of portraits of Jesus. The Letter of James appears to correct one of Paul's letters; part of 2 Peter seems to improve upon Jude. But this variety within the New Testament, necessary as it is to acknowledge, is less significant than the question of how the New Testament relates to the Jewish Scriptures or Christian Old Testament.

A Shared Question:
The Hebrew Bible and the New Testament

The New Testament inherits a question from the Hebrew Scriptures: How should God's people live within this world? While the Sermon on the Mount in the Gospel of Matthew and the Letter of James seem very positive toward motivating readers to keep Mosaic law as a way of life, Paul's letters discourage those Gentile readers who would want to keep Torah, though at times Paul quotes from Torah as though he regards its principles as relevant for Gentiles. Though difference in audience is part of the explanation, it is clear that different authors regard Torah in different ways.

In regard to this same question of how God's people are to live in the world, the New Testament continues to affirm what the Old Testament affirms, that God cares deeply about the actions of people and will judge them according to how they live and treat others. The Gospels, with their lengthy expositions of the life and teachings of Christ, as well as the many letters and the final apocalypse of the New Testament, all speak in response to this question. But the question itself, and the parameters for answering it, come from the Jewish Scriptures.

Shared Covenants

The New Testament accepts without question the significance of the covenants first described in the Jewish Scriptures. All its authors assume that there is nothing better than to be in covenant relationship with God. All are positive about the Abrahamic, Mosaic, and Davidic covenants, whether or not they think that all of them apply equally to Gentiles as to Jews. While the New Testament preserves evidence of early Christians' uncertainty regarding Mosaic law, even Paul's letters that seem most ready to dispense with this law refer to it for moral guidance. Sinai remains the one mountain that faith cannot move.

In seeking consistency with the Jewish Scriptures' emphasis on covenants while also accounting for the significance of the Christ event, some of the New Testament texts prioritize the "new covenant" idea of Jeremiah to a degree not seen in the Old Testament. These New Testament texts make a connection not fully articulated in the Old Testament, that the Davidic Messiah, whom Christians identify as Jesus of Nazareth, helps bring that long-awaited new covenant. In doing so the New Testament thus attempts to integrate what happened in the life and death of Jesus into the covenant theology its authors continue to value.

Here, as in the Jewish Scriptures, the reader faces the question of encountering and living in relationship with the transcendent God who is beyond human understanding. While the covenants of these prior Scriptures are now complicated by the life, death, and resurrection of Jesus, the quest for living as God's people remains a quest integrally bound up with understanding and participating in the covenants God first made with the Jewish people.

Thus, while Jews recognize only the Tanakh as Scripture, and Christians have a two-testament Bible, both groups are shaped by ideas that pervade the Jewish and Christian Scriptures even while at times both read these central ideas in disparate ways. Yet matters are even more complicated than this. Even within each tradition many Jewish and many Christian communities disagree about how to live one's life in accord with God's wishes as they are expressed in the Jewish and Christian Bibles. Of course, as we hope the reader now recognizes, such disagreements occur within Scripture itself and are in fact what makes the biblical tradition—and these communities—so vibrant, enabling generations of new readers to interpret the biblical text in innovative ways while still calling on the LORD, the God of Israel.

CPSIA information can be obtained
at www.ICGtesting.com
Printed in the USA
LVHW050029070619
620438LV00002B/5/P

9 781426 751073